THE COMPANY STATE

Also available:

ACTION FOR A CHANGE: *A Student's Guide to Public Interest Organizing* (revised, 1972), by Ralph Nader and Donald Ross

THE CHEMICAL FEAST: *Ralph Nader's Study Group Report on the Food and Drug Administration,* by James S. Turner

THE CLOSED ENTERPRISE SYSTEM: *Ralph Nader's Study Group Report on Antitrust Enforcement,* by Mark J. Green with Beverly C. Moore, Jr., and Bruce Wasserstein

THE INTERSTATE COMMERCE OMISSION: *Ralph Nader's Study Group Report on the Interstate Commerce Commission and Transportation,* by Robert C. Fellmeth

OLD AGE: THE LAST SEGREGATION: *Ralph Nader's Study Group Report on Nursing Homes,* Claire Townsend, Project Director

POLITICS OF LAND: *Ralph Nader's Study Group Report on Land Use in California,* Robert C. Fellmeth, Project Director

SMALL—ON SAFETY: *The Designed-in Dangers of the Volkswagen,* by The Center for Auto Safety

SOWING THE WIND: *A Report for Ralph Nader's Center for Study of Responsive Law on Food Safety and the Chemical Harvest,* by Harrison Wellford

UNSAFE AT ANY SPEED: *The Designed-in Dangers of the American Automobile* (expanded and updated 1972) by Ralph Nader

VANISHING AIR: *Ralph Nader's Study Group Report on Air Pollution,* by John C. Esposito

THE WATER LORDS: *Ralph Nader's Study Group Report on Industry and Environmental Crisis in Savannah, Georgia,* by James M. Fallows

WATER WASTELAND: *Ralph Nader's Study Group Report on Water Pollution,* by David Zwick with Marcy Benstock

WHAT TO DO WITH YOUR BAD CAR: *An Action Manual for Lemon Owners,* by Ralph Nader, Lowell Dodge, and Ralf Hotchkiss

WHISTLE BLOWING: *The Report on the Conference on Professional Responsibility,* edited by Ralph Nader, Peter Petkas, and Kate Blackwell

THE WORKERS: *Portraits of Nine American Jobholders,* by Kenneth Lasson

YOU AND YOUR PENSION: *Why You May Never Get a Penny—What Should Be Done About It,* by Ralph Nader and Kate Blackwell

*Ralph Nader's Study Group Report on DuPont in Delaware*

# THE COMPANY STATE

*by James Phelan & Robert Pozen*

*Grossman Publishers* NEW YORK 1973

First published in 1973 by Grossman Publishers
625 Madison Avenue, New York, N.Y. 10022
Published simultaneously in Canada by
Fitzhenry and Whiteside, Ltd.
SBN 670-23357-9
Library of Congress Catalogue Card Number: 70-184474
Printed in the U.S.A.
All royalties from the sale of this book will be given to the Center for Study of Responsive Law, the organization established by Ralph Nader to conduct research into abuses of the public interest by business and governmental groups. Contributions to further this work are tax deductible and may be sent to the Center at P.O.B. 19367, Washington, D.C. 20036.

# The Delaware Study Group

James L. Phelan, *Project Codirector*
University of Texas at El Paso, B.B.A. 1968
Yale Law School, third-year student
Robert C. Pozen, *Project Codirector*
Harvard College, B.A. 1968
Yale Law School, third-year student
Alan M. Katz, *Associate Project Director*
Duke University, B.A. 1970
James W. Olson, *Associate Project Director*
University of California at Berkeley, A.B. 1969
Yale Law School, third-year student
Deanna Nash, *Senior Editorial Assistant*
San Jose State College, B.A. 1963
University of North Carolina at Chapel Hill, Ph.D. 1970
Ellen Harrison, *Associate Editorial Assistant*
University of Pennsylvania, B.S. 1970
Tufts Medical School, first-year student
Terry Fischgrund, *Researcher*
Smith College, B.A. 1968
Ralph Gingles, *Researcher*
University of North Carolina at Chapel Hill, B.S. in Bus. Adm. 1968
University of Virginia Law School, J.D. 1971
Member, North Carolina Bar
Charles Lee Horstman, *Researcher*
Rice University, B.A. 1970
Daniel Amory, *Associated Group Member*
Harvard College, B.A. 1967
Yale Law School, third-year student

EDITORIAL ASSISTANTS
Barbara Brown
Sasha Harmon
Kendra Heymann

James Owens
Allan Winkler

PRODUCTION
Connie Jo Smith
Pauline Postotnik
Dee Moore
Jeanine Rickert
Sue Fagin
Ruth Fort

SPECIAL PROJECTS IN DELAWARE
David Clough
Debbi Cundiff
Gerald P. Doherty
Ellie C. Eichbaum
Jim Fuqua
Janet Hickman
Nancy Jewett
Ed O'Donnell, Jr.
Patricia Petro

The Delaware Study Group would like to thank the many public officials in the Wilmington, New Castle County, Seaford, and Delaware state governments who aided our research. We appreciate the general policy of cooperation followed by these people. We extend a special thanks to the DuPont employees and the numerous other private citizens in Delaware, both named and unnamed in the book, who provided us with information and enthusiasm, and for whom this book was written. We also wish to express our appreciation to E. I. du Pont de Nemours & Company, Inc., at least for the limited cooperation extended to our persistent requests for information. (See Chapter 2.) Finally, we thank our classmates, professors, and associates who took time to read various parts of the manuscript; their comments were most helpful. But the Delaware Study Group takes full responsibility for what appears in the book.

# Introduction by Ralph Nader

E. I. du Pont de Nemours & Company began in Delaware in 1802 with a little gunpowder plant on the Brandywine River and spread, after many corporate acquisitions, throughout the United States and many foreign countries. It is now the world's largest chemical company. But its headquarters and its "political economy" remain rooted in Delaware.

DuPont dominates Delaware as does no single company in any other state. The scope and mechanisms of its influence are studied and assessed in this report. Virtually every major aspect of Delaware life—industry, commerce, finance, government, politics, education, health, transportation, media, charitable institutions, environment, land, recreation, public works, community improvement groups, and taxation—is pervasively and decisively affected by the DuPont Company, the DuPont family, or their agents.

The wealth and power of this family dynasty have not escaped wide public notice, but they have escaped detailed public study. This report is concerned only with DuPont in Delaware, not with DuPont outside Delaware or with DuPont's consumer products. There were a number of cogent reasons for selecting DuPont and for concentrating the efforts of the study group in Delaware.

First, DuPont is a mammoth enterprise and has many of its activities in a compact geographical area. These characteristics permitted a gathering of facts that would not have been possible with a more dispersed, less visible company.

Second, DuPont was no stranger to many issues now enveloped in the concept of "corporate responsibility." Largely because it has substantially controlled Delaware for decades and because it received a sustained public relations setback in the thirties because of congressional investigations into its munitions sales and profiteering during World War I, DuPont has probably thought more about its role in the community, its public image, and its relations with other institutions than most giant corporations. Consequently, the study group could observe a historical process in ascertaining what standards of performance could be applied to DuPont policies and practices as they affect Delaware.

Third, DuPont's techniques in using its power are, by and large, not as crude or roughshod as is so often the case in textile, paper, or coal company towns. DuPont's deployment of direct and derivative power in the state is complex, subtle, far-reaching. It is festooned with the symbols of respectability, stolidity, charity, and recognition. But, like bad medicine that goes down sweetly, the effects of the company on the community too often include damage across a score of areas, as detailed in the following pages.

Fourth, there is little hesitation or doubt in DuPont's corporate view about community involvement. A decade ago, the company plunged into community activities directly and through a variety of official and charitable institutions. Its employees, liberally released for part-time or full-time civic duties, proliferate throughout the state's institutional structure. The family's ownership of the two major daily newspapers is not concealed, nor are the obvious consequences. The same can be said of the DuPont complex's legal control over two of the state's largest banks; and the list goes on, as the report details. With such a high intensity of involvement, the idea that DuPont is to be judged solely on the basis of its profit (and it is a very profitable company) or the wages it pays is rejected by a long line of company executives, including Lammot du Pont Copeland, recently retired as DuPont's board chairman, who said:

> Business is a means to an end for society and not an end in itself, and therefore business must act in concert with a broad public interest and serve the objectives of mankind and society or it will not survive.

This attitude explains in part DuPont's intense interest, as distinguished from concern, in this report. For even if DuPont Company executives and family members have convinced themselves of the rightness of their paternalism and charitable giving toward the community, there still remains the nagging realization that something is wrong in the state of DuPont. That something includes poverty, racism, urban dislocation, discriminatory highway monuments to DuPont's corporate needs, gross underpayment of income and property taxes by the DuPonts and the other rich, manipulated legislators and public officials, a business-coddling judiciary, a disgraceful state of health and education for all but the well-to-do, and the brooding inhibitions on dissent and diversity of community initiatives which sometimes come from the omnipresent DuPont complex.*

The relatively small city of Wilmington (pop. 80,000) displays great contrasts between the businessmen, who profit by day and scurry to the suburbs by night, and the poor and blue-collar people, who suffer a deteriorating city whose principal forms of renewal are malls near DuPont buildings and highways to get the suburbanites in and out quickly. The company and the extended DuPont family structure loom so large in the wealth of Delaware that they bring up the averages to levels which belie the plight of many Delawareans. The per capita income in Delaware for 1970 was $4,324, compared with the national average of $3,921. Given these conditions, and many others analyzed in this study, it must have occurred to some of the more thoughtful DuPonters that much more can be done to make a big company do better by a small state. For a giant corporation, owned by one of the world's wealthiest families, consistently profitable, and with substantial operations in a small state like Delaware (pop. 550,000), the potential of becoming a relatively model corporate citizen is very real.

For such a process to emerge, the DuPonts will have to be challenged before they respond. Their pattern of response will itself make a revealing chapter in the growing chronicle of corporate behavior in this country. Will they realize that they can give more to the community by relinquishing some of their power instead of accruing more? Will they recognize that by fully paying their fair share

* Typical of the far-reaching penumbra of DuPont's deterrence is a clause in its pension plan that provides for cancelation of a retired employee's rights to receive benefits if he has involved himself in "any activity harmful to the interest of the company."

of state income, property, and estate taxes, they would be contributing far more to the state than by their charitable contributions in both dollars and achievement? These are only two of many questions that are considered in this report. But the most important immediate impact, one hopes, will be to generate a greater and more detailed awareness in Delawareans of how, when, and where DuPont power works and to encourage a greater examination by DuPont leaders of the company role and the family role in the future of the state.

One of the first steps in such a self-examination by the DuPont Company is for management to ponder why it must conceal so much that should be public information. The study group came up against this systematic secrecy right from the beginning. There were roadblocks at every turn. The company tried to prohibit interviews with employees on their own time. Procedures for interviewing employees at work required the presence of a company lawyer, a public relations man, and a tape recorder. The lawyer decided what questions should not be answered. The employee could hardly help being affected by such conditions. True to its concern for appearances, the company offered cooperation in theory but withheld it in practice. Questions submitted in writing about matters not remotely connected with trade secrets were frequently unanswered or labeled "confidential" when the information would be at all significant. Tours of some company plants were allowed, but workers could not be spoken with, even in the lunchroom. Because of such restrictions on freedom of speech, many employees and residents spoke with the study group anonymously.

This is not to say that DuPont responded harshly, petulantly, or with totally closed doors. But more openness might have been expected of a company whose written claims about its public pride and civic responsiveness are so grandiose. In addition, DuPont officials apparently prejudged this report from the beginning. But the researchers who produced this report were as fascinated by the prospect of finding models of progressive change within and around the DuPont complex as they were concerned that the contrary might often be the case. They conducted approximately 500 interviews with Delawareans in all walks of life, including company employees and directors, DuPont family members, lawyers, leaders of the black community, representatives of white ethnic groups, physicians, city and state politicians, bankers, real estate agents, educators, clergymen, newspaper reporters, architects, scientists, engineers, blue-collar workers, union officials, and social workers. They read countless newspaper files, reports, studies, and public relations releases. They lived in the city of Wilmington but traveled throughout the state, from chateau country to Dover to Seaford. Two members of the group even found themselves invited to the sanctum of sanctums—the Wilmington Club. And they thought long about the issues and the problems surrounding the DuPont Company and the DuPont family.

But the corporate impact on ever-widening communities is by no means restricted to situations similar to DuPont and Delaware. The spread of corporate power into control of public government and allocation of public resources; the growth of hazards to people and environments from the uncontrolled effects of widening technologies; the increasingly determined management of larger social systems by giant, multinational corporations—these and many other problems created by the corporate Leviathan demand intensive citizen scrutiny. This report will contribute toward an understanding of such problems.

Washington, D.C.
November, 1971

# Contents

CHAPTER 1

# *Welcome to the Company State*

"Welcome to Delaware—the State that Started a Nation" proclaims a freeway billboard greeting visitors to the home of E. I. du Pont de Nemours & Company, Incorporated, the company that started an industry. In Delaware, DuPont * employs about 25,000 men and women, 11% of the state's work force, and generates 20% of the state's gross product.

Down Delaware Avenue in Wilmington, the "Chemical Capital of the World," your view is dominated by DuPont's new Brandywine Building and its towering neighbors, the DuPont and Nemours buildings. This is the heart of Wilmington—the financial center of Delaware and DuPont's international headquarters. Most of the state's banks are centered here, as are its major law firms, three DuPont family brokerage houses, and the offices of charitable foundations and businesses connected with the DuPonts.

* This book uses the spelling "DuPont," rather than "du Pont," to refer to the company and the family as a whole. When an individual family member is named, the spelling is "du Pont." We have adopted this system for several reasons. The title "DuPont Company" or "DuPont" is a convenient shorthand for the company's full name. Using a capital "D" for the DuPont family makes clear that the reference is to the whole family and not to an individual. Family members differ on putting a space between "du" and "Pont." We have decided to leave a space, for consistency and to avoid confusion in lists of family members.

The DuPont Building contains the modest two-room office of Christiana Securities Company, the DuPont family holding company that owns controlling interest in the DuPont Company and fully owns the two major daily newspapers in Delaware. One wing of the DuPont Building houses the Hotel DuPont, Wilmington's best. The Playhouse, Wilmington's only legitimate theater, is also in the DuPont Building, and is owned by the DuPont Company. An enclosed walkway high above Tenth Street connects the DuPont Building with the offices of Delaware's largest bank, the Wilmington Trust Company, controlled by the DuPonts.

Across the square from the DuPont Building stands the city-county office building, holding the chambers of the county executive, a former DuPont Company lawyer, and Wilmington's mayor, whose father was a prominent DuPont executive.* Here also is Delaware's chancery court, where businesses from all parts of the country come to take advantage of the state's lenient corporation laws.

At noon small clusters of well-dressed men walk from the DuPont headquarters to the exclusive Wilmington Club for lunch with bank presidents, corporate directors, judges, and DuPont family members. A few blocks away is the Valley, Wilmington's major black and Puerto Rican slum.

You must travel far from the Valley to reach the homes of the DuPont family. Some live in a quiet neighborhood off Pennsylvania Avenue near city limits, in what once was the city's most fashionable area, near the Alexis I. du Pont Middle School, the Eugene du Pont Convalescent Hospital, and Tower Hill, one of several elite private schools in Delaware.

Beyond lies Kennett Pike to Greenville, the center of DuPont "chateau country." This area contains the Wilmington, Greenville, and Bidermann country clubs, all boasting many DuPonts as members. Bordering the Wilmington Country Club is the grandest DuPont showpiece, Winterthur Museum—a 150-room mansion on the $10 million estate of the late Henry F. du Pont. Toward the banks of the Brandywine River, where the DuPont Com-

* Most of the research for this book was done in the summer of 1971, and facts are the latest available as of that time.

pany began, are signs conjuring up feudal France—Louviers and Bois des Fosses. On a hill overlooking the river, pastures, gardens, winding paths, cornfields, and cottages is majestic Granogue, home of Irenee du Pont, Jr.

Coming back toward Wilmington on Montchanin Road, you pass the DuPont Company Country Club, with two golf courses, a clubhouse, and an elegant main building. The putting greens give way to barbed wire fences guarding the DuPont Experimental Station, DuPont's largest research facility, a group of campuslike buildings with shaded lawns. The country club and the Experimental Station, together with parks and undeveloped private land, cordon off the DuPont estates from the suburban developments of middle-level DuPont employees. As you leave chateau country, neon signs flash on the highways through the middle-class neighborhoods. Sprinkled through these districts are many DuPont facilities—Chestnut Run, Haskell, and Stine laboratories, the Glasgow and Edgemoor plants, the Centre Road office building, the Louviers engineering facility, and the Newport pigments plant.

Only one major road leads to the southern counties of Delaware—the DuPont Highway, named after T. Coleman du Pont, who planned and built it, then gave it to the state. Following the DuPont Highway, you cross over the Chesapeake and Delaware Canal, which literally and symbolically divides Delaware in two. Below the canal agriculture predominates, and the prevailing mores are Southern and rural. DuPont's nylon plant in Seaford is one of the few industries in the two southern counties. The major city downstate is Dover, the state capital. From this sleepy town of 20,000, Governor Russell W. Peterson, a former DuPont executive, administers the affairs of Delaware.

The Delaware Study Group, a team of seven researchers, began to investigate DuPont's impact on Delaware in June, 1970. Delaware is an apt state for a study of corporate responsibility. Since the state is so small and DuPont is so large, the impact of the corporation and its owners on the surrounding community is fairly evident. In states with many companies, it might be impossible to distinguish the effects of one company from the others. In addition, Du-

Pont was an appropriate choice for this study because it has a national reputation as a liberal, progressive firm; the company's public relations materials picture DuPont as being active in community affairs. If we looked at a thoroughly corrupt or blatantly irresponsible corporation, we might confuse greed and fraud with the inherently difficult structural relations between a corporation and a community.

From studying this clear-cut example of corporate behavior in Delaware, we hope to provide a framework for assessing the community policies of large firms throughout the country. There are numerous company towns in America and many more places in which several large businesses present a united front in public affairs.

While mammoth corporations are usually evaluated as national entities, important issues of corporate responsibility are related to the location of their factories and offices in specific cities and states. The dilemmas faced by DuPont in Delaware are similar to, although more pronounced than, the community problems confronted by every major corporation in America today. Businessmen throughout the country must respond to the urban crisis, environmental protests, and stockholder challenges to company social policy. Public officials and private citizens are faced with increasing power in the corporate sector. Yet there are currently no clear guidelines as to what corporate responsibility should mean in the United States. On the one hand, Milton Friedman, noted economics professor at the University of Chicago, wrote recently, "There is one and only one single responsibility of business—to use its resources and engage in activities designed to increase its profits." [1] On the other hand, Frederick Kappel, former chairman of American Telephone and Telegraph, said, "Businessmen themselves must take a direct hand in helping solve the nation's social problems." [2]

To evolve a coherent set of guidelines for corporate responsibility, we must begin by piercing the veil of business rhetoric and focusing on certain empirical questions. Corporate social commitment is a series of concrete managerial decisions either to participate in or stay out of certain types of community activities; it is the systematic consideration by corporate officials of the implicit social effects of business activities on community problems. The courts have made clear that a corporation can undertake any program that benefits it in the long run by making its community a better place in which to live.[3] However, local residents cannot go to court to make a firm donate money to a particular project or refrain from becoming involved in some community activity. Corporate responsibility is not a question of whether America should permit or abolish corporations, nor is it a stark choice between corporate neglect or domination. Corporate responsibility is the problem of structuring public laws, other institutions, and corporations themselves to channel business toward democratic processes and public goals. It is the selection of an intermediate ground of corporate contributions without creating community dependence.

A corporation is a legal fiction; it has neither a body nor a soul. Governments create corporations through broad enabling laws and endow them with certain organizational characteristics. In America, states first allowed firms to incorporate only for specific purposes—manufacturing one product or holding land in a certain county. In the mid-nineteenth century, states began to permit incorporation for any type of activity within their boundaries. Though corporations could be sued for acting beyond the powers granted in their corporate charters, soon even this limit on corporate power was swept away as corporations were chartered "to do business" or "to make money." Incorporation is now a simple process of filing papers, and corporate power is an accepted fact of American life.

The state provides a corporation with a broad range of privileges. It may pay special income tax rates, raise capital by issuing stock, centralize management of large business ventures, insulate stockholders from personal liability for business debts, and survive perpetually unless dissolved by its investors.

In return, corporations have obligations to the government. The corporation must abide by democratic processes of policy formation, and it must contribute taxes to the state. It must obey the law.

This definition of a corporation implies a conception of

corporate responsibility. As a legal fiction, the corporation has no independent justification for existing or operating; it is only a tool to attain public goals as well as private gain. If the corporation dominates the citizenry or drains government resources for its own use, then it has made itself a master instead of a servant. Behind this conception of corporate responsibility are two main premises: All citizens should have a significant voice in decisions that seriously affect them, and all should have equal opportunity to enjoy the material benefits of American life.

To judge the utility of the corporate fiction to Delaware, two main questions must be answered. The first concerns the *process* of decision making: Who makes the crucial public and private decisions in Delaware? Consumers are one kind of decision maker. If they can choose among many products, they can decide what goods are manufactured by threatening not to purchase certain ones. But if one corporation has a monopoly over an important area, *it* will decide what goods and services are offered, because consumers have no choice. A second decision maker, then, is the company's board of directors. If community groups are represented on corporate boards, they can influence company decisions. But if the board contains no public representatives, community groups may not even know that decisions are being made. Finally, the public decision-making process takes place in legislatures and administrative bodies. If citizens elect officials who publicly debate major policy issues, then citizens can hold government accountable. But if special interests formulate policy behind closed doors, citizens cannot vote them out of office.

The second main question regarding corporate responsibility concerns the *outcome* of decision making: Whose interests are served by important private and public decisions? Corporations may undertake civic projects, but they may be oriented toward improving the firm's public image, not meeting the public's needs. Or the state may carry out projects to serve the interests of the rich despite an ostensible commitment to equal opportunity. In Delaware, one can distinguish at least six major groups which might benefit or suffer as a result of a particular policy: corporate executives, the upper class (revolving around the DuPonts), middle-class professionals and scientists, blue-collar workers and small businessmen, the white poor (mainly rural), and the black poor (predominantly urban).

If corporate responsibility is thus defined in terms of the *process* and *outcome* of important policies, corporations will be judged from the public viewpoint, the only viewpoint that squares with the fact that corporations are chartered by the public. In contrast, the two major alternative definitions of corporate responsibility—business statesmanship and profit maximization—are based on the firm's perspective: the decisive criterion is the company's return on investment, not the promotion of democracy or the increase of living standards in the surrounding communities.

Many DuPont executives currently follow the business statesman theory. According to this theory, corporations work to increase long-term return on investment. Managers have power because they have the foresight and expertise to carry out long-range plans. While managers are guided partly by supply and demand, they are also aware that a bad public image will in the long run hurt productivity and sales. To build up an attractive image, corporations advertise, distribute public relations material, and make charitable contributions. They play a large role in local and national affairs, since cultivating an amicable government is in their long-run interest. Executives may join government boards, employees are encouraged to work in civic organizations, and the firm often takes stands on important community issues.

The crucial assumption behind business statesman theory, as DuPont's president made clear in an interview, is that corporate pursuit of long-term profit will necessarily serve the needs of the community over the years. Or to paraphrase General Motors' Charles Wilson, "What is best for DuPont is best for Delaware." The problem is that the community may disagree, and DuPont can always extract consent by threatening to leave or not to expand, since it is mobile and the community stable. Donald Carpenter, while head of the company's operations for manufacturing film, showed the stick that accompanies the DuPont carrot:

> Just so soon as a community commences to impose unreasonable and unjust burdens upon an industry, it follows as the night the day that the industry will begin to decline, its products can no longer compete in the market place, its volume drops off, its employment asset in a community becomes a liability.[4]

Of course, DuPont judges what community conditions are "unreasonable" or "unjust." Since there is no clear-cut answer as to what is rightful corporate action, there may often be conflicts between a community and DuPont. Because DuPont management has the final say, the company's conception of rightfulness will usually win out in the long run.

Like the business statesman theory of corporate responsibility, profit theory is inadequate to judge DuPont's role in Delaware.* According to profit theory, a firm manifests corporate responsibility merely by maximizing its profit each year. Under this approach, corporate managers do not join civic groups or undertake community projects to generate good will for the business in the future. If a firm has high earnings each year, then it will serve the community by issuing dividends to stockholders, making products for consumers, and paying wages to employees. Profit theory was espoused by Irenee du Pont, Jr., in an interview about the company's role in Delaware:

> While [the citizen] may not be the man who actually pays for a DuPont product, or actually receives a DuPont dividend, or receives a paycheck from the DuPont payclerk, he's everybody in the community [who] is somehow related, somehow, some way related to one of those three functions even though he may just swat a fly with a polyethylene flyswatter that came out of a Dupont extruder sometime in its history.

But du Pont's argument is not convincing. For most Delaware citizens who are DuPont stockholders, an increase in dividends would be insignificant relative to the

* This critique of profit theory is directed at its definition of corporate responsibility; it is not an attempt to deal with all the complex problems of profit theory as a model for the whole economy, problems which have been dealt with at length by many economists.

impact of the company's local policies. DuPont expansion in the Wilmington area might bring a few dollars more in dividends, but the stockholder might have to pay higher land prices caused by an influx of corporate employees. While Irenee du Pont may consider flyswatters important to the citizens of the state, few Delaware consumers do. A consumer may pay less for teflon products since the company does not install proper air pollution control equipment, but he pays more in health and cleaning bills because of pollution. In regard to employees, 89% of the Delaware work force does not receive wages from the DuPont Company. Moreover, increases in profits are not necessarily passed on to DuPont's laborers.

Thus neither long-run returns nor annual corporate profits are good measures of DuPont's impact on Delaware. To assess corporate responsibility in the state, we must examine the *process* and *outcome* of important decisions made in Delaware. These decisions are of three main types: those made in the private sphere—the inner sanctums of the DuPont Company and family; semiprivate or quasi-public decisions made in the meeting places of corporate agents closely tied to the DuPonts; and public decisions—those made in the offices of local and state government.

An analysis of decision-making in Delaware must begin with the formal relations between major groups and individuals in the state, though such an analysis must ultimately focus on who actually wields power and what interests are really served by certain policies.

In Delaware, the DuPont Company, the family, and other influential groups have so many institutional ties that together they form a *corporate establishment.* The boards of these institutions are so meshed that their leadership forms a *corporate elite.*

The DuPont Company and the DuPont family are linked through the Christiana Securities Company, the family holding company with controlling interest in the corporation. Nine of the 10 Christiana Securities directors are DuPont family members. Through Christiana, the family also controls the Wilmington Trust Company, the largest bank in Delaware. Twelve of the bank's 24 directors are directors of the DuPont Company, DuPont family members, or both, and 3 more directors work for DuPont either directly or through law firms (see Table 1-1). Christiana Securities also owns 100% of the News-Journal Company, which operates Wilmington's only daily newspapers. Seven of the 9 directors in the News-Journal Company are board members for DuPont, Christiana, or the bank.*

These three firms, and the family, are linked with other Delaware businesses through capital investment and personal ties. The family owns almost 100% of the Delaware Trust Company. Personal ties establish DuPont influence in the Bank of Delaware and Farmers Bank of the State of Delaware. A top DuPont executive is on the board of the state's two major utilities—Diamond State Telephone and Delmarva Power and Light. The four most prominent law firms in the state, many of whose lawyers serve on the boards of businesses related to DuPont, represent the DuPont Company or family. DuPont executives and family members serve as directors of Laird, Bissell, and Meeds and two other brokerage houses. DuPont family members own Altantic Aviation (world leader in sales of noncommercial aircraft), Summit Aviation, a computer service company, and many real estate companies and engineering firms in Delaware. Moreover, through several holding companies, the DuPont family controls large amounts of land and owns stock in other corporations.

The DuPont Company and family, important throughout the Delaware business community, also serve as directors in nonprofit agencies. DuPont executives and family members serve as directors of at least 100 agencies (see Appendix 1). The Greater Wilmington Development Council, formed by the corporate community in 1960, is the most powerful community redevelopment agency in Delaware; GWDC's two chairmen since 1963 have been DuPont family members with high positions in the company. United Fund and Council of Delaware (UFC) finances an ever-widening range of social services. In 1969 four of the six officers of the United Fund were DuPont Company or family members; the campaign chairman, one of the vice-

* In April, 1972, DuPont and Christiana Securities announced formation of a committee to study possible merger of the two corporations.

**TABLE 1-1.**
*The Delaware Triumvirate*

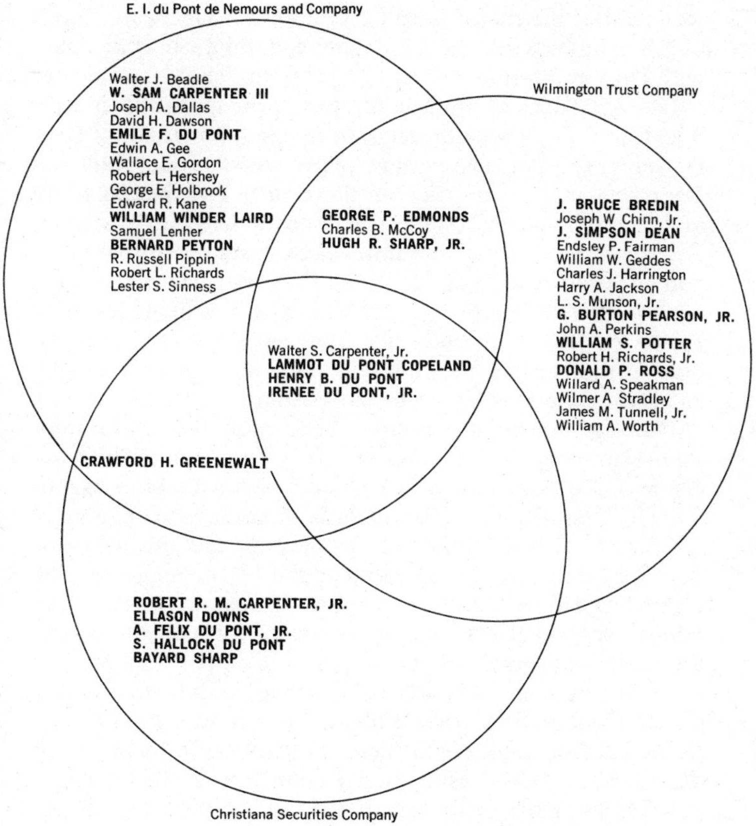
E. I. du Pont de Nemours and Company
Walter J. Beadle
W. SAM CARPENTER III
Joseph A. Dallas
David H. Dawson
EMILE F. DU PONT
Edwin A. Gee
Wallace E. Gordon
Robert L. Hershey
George E. Holbrook
Edward R. Kane
WILLIAM WINDER LAIRD
Samuel Lenher
BERNARD PEYTON
R. Russell Pippin
Robert L. Richards
Lester S. Sinness
Wilmington Trust Company
GEORGE P. EDMONDS
Charles B. McCoy
HUGH R. SHARP, JR.
J. BRUCE BREDIN
Joseph W Chinn, Jr.
J. SIMPSON DEAN
Endsley P. Fairman
William W. Geddes
Charles J. Harrington
Harry A. Jackson
L. S. Munson, Jr.
G. BURTON PEARSON, JR.
John A. Perkins
WILLIAM S. POTTER
Robert H. Richards, Jr.
DONALD P. ROSS
Willard A. Speakman
Wilmer A Stradley
James M. Tunnell, Jr.
William A. Worth
Walter S. Carpenter, Jr.
LAMMOT DU PONT COPELAND
HENRY B. DU PONT
IRENEE DU PONT, JR.
CRAWFORD H. GREENEWALT
ROBERT R. M. CARPENTER, JR.
ELLASON DOWNS
A. FELIX DU PONT, JR.
S. HALLOCK DU PONT
BAYARD SHARP
Christiana Securities Company

DuPont family members indicated by boldface type.

chairmen, and the heads of the majority of United Fund committees were also personally tied to some DuPont group. DuPont Company directors and family members occupy 9 of the 20 self-perpetuating seats on the 28-man board of trustees of the University of Delaware, the only university in the state. Similarly, in the Wilmington Medical Center, the major hospital in northern Delaware, 9 out of 12 members of the executive committee are affiliated with DuPont groups.

Not only does DuPont control the private institutions influential in public-sector decision making, but DuPont family members hold numerous public offices. Reynolds du Pont is a major financier of the state's Republican party and majority leader of the state senate. W. Laird Stabler, Jr., was a state legislator until elected state attorney general in 1970. Pierre S. du Pont IV was a state legislator until his 1970 election to Delaware's only seat in the U.S. House of Representatives. C. Douglass Buck, Jr., is president of the New Castle county council. G. Burton Pearson, Jr., is a member of the state Bank Advisory Board.

DuPont Company employees are even more prevalent than family members in Delaware government. The governor of Delaware, Russell Peterson, was a DuPont executive. In 1969–71, 2 of the 19 state senators were company employees, while 7 company employees and the wives of 2 retired employees were among the 39 members of the Delaware House. DuPont employees chair important administrative agencies—the state board of education and the state transportation commission. Company employees are also members of at least 6 other commissions. New Castle County Executive William Conner was an attorney in the DuPont legal department. Four of the 6 members of the 1969–71 New Castle county council were DuPont employees, as is the chairman of the county planning board. The mayor of Wilmington is the son of a former DuPont Company director and 2 members of the city council are employees. The mayors of Bethany Beach and Farmington are company employees. DuPont employees are on the town councils of 7 other Delaware towns.

Since business executives and family members are so tied to other Delaware institutions, DuPont cannot claim to be an ordinary firm maximizing profits among numerous competitors. And as this book will show, the normative assumptions of the business statesman theory are fallacious. DuPont's long-run interests are not necessarily identical with those of Delaware.

# Part I

# The DuPont Company

CHAPTER 2

# Power and Its Abuse in Corporate Government

In 1802 the DuPont Company began with a gunpowder business along the Brandywine River near Wilmington, with the encouragement of President Thomas Jefferson, who sent the company its first order. The Barbary War, the War of 1812, and the Civil War were great boons to the DuPonts, who used their wartime profits to build larger factories in Delaware. Since then, company growth has been based on close government ties, wartime profits, and monopolistic mergers.

The rapid development of the California gunpowder industry after the Civil War threatened DuPont. To meet the threat Henry du Pont organized seven powder companies into the Gunpowder Trade Association (the Powder Trust). The trust divided the United States into sales districts, set minimum prices, specified production quotas, and waged price wars against other firms. Beginning in the 1870s, DuPont bought up competitors. By 1881 DuPont was producing 61% of all American gunpowder. Between 1902 and 1911 the company swallowed up 64 powder manufacturers. As the names of more and more members of the Powder Trust changed to DuPont, the company outgrew the association and dissolved it in 1904.

The dissolution of the Powder Trust did not undo the monopoly in the industry. In 1907 the government sued the company for suppressing competition; it then produced 64% to 74% of American output in five types of explosives and 100% of the privately produced smokeless powder. DuPont lost the suit, and the Court said:

> It is a significant fact that the Trade Association was not dissolved until June 30, 1904. It had been utilized until that date by Thomas Coleman du Pont, Pierre S. du Pont and Alfred I. du Pont in suppressing competition and thereby building up a monopoly. Between February, 1902, and June, 1904, the combination had been so completely transmuted into a corporate form that the Trade Association was no longer necessary.
>
> Consequently, the Trade Association was dissolved and the process of dissolving the corporations whose capital stocks had been acquired, and concentrating the assets in one great corporation, was begun. . . . The proofs satisfy us that the present form of combination is no less obnoxious to the law than was the combination under the Trade Association agreement.[1]

After discussions with President William Howard Taft and Attorney General George W. Wickersham, an ex-DuPont lawyer, DuPont was allowed to divide itself. At the same time, with help from some military men, corporate executives convinced the government to let DuPont's smokeless powder monopoly continue. DuPont remained the largest American explosives manufacturer. Moreover, the new firms spun off from DuPont—Hercules and Atlas—were in the hands of DuPont family members until the threat of another suit forced them to sell most of their stock in these companies 39 years later.

With a near monopoly of the munitions market, DuPont made such whopping profits during World War I that it earned the nickname "Merchants of Death" in Senator Gerald P. Nye's committee hearings during the 1930s. In that war the company supplied over 40% of the explosives used by the Allies, who subsidized construction of new

DuPont facilities and paid an inflated price for powder. DuPont's profits during the war years were $237 million. Its capital increased from a prewar figure of $83 million to $308 million; employment jumped from 5,500 to 85,000.

With these tremendous profits, DuPont bought controlling interest in General Motors. Pierre S. du Pont, who served first as president of the DuPont Company and later as president of General Motors, explained:

> DuPont had lost the military business, or knew it would be lost very shortly, and in the interim between the earnings of the military business and what might come after that, we needed something to support the dividends of the DuPont Company.[2]

The GM stock did the job. Throughout the 1920s and 1930s, DuPont bought out companies in markets where it had a prewar foothold: plastics, paints, textiles, and dyes. DuPont became a major producer of many of these, and in some areas, like dyes, became the nation's leading producer. At the same time, DuPont expanded into new product lines. It bought out foreign and domestic manufacturers of films, acids, synthetic ammonia, and firearms. The company acquired exclusive North American rights to produce two new French products, rayon and cellophane. In its own labs, DuPont created new, big-selling products: neoprene synthetic rubber (1931), Lucite acrylic resin (1937), nylon (1938), teflon (1943), Orlon (1948), Dacron (1950), and mylar polyester film (1958).

The corporate juggling and shuffling characteristic of this period can be seen in the pigment and dye industry. In 1928 DuPont bought the Grasselli Chemical Company, a huge operation with 23 factories. Before Grasselli was merged into DuPont, its pigment and dye division was separated from the rest of the company. In 1931 the pigment and dye divisions of Grasselli, the Krebs Pigment and Chemical Company, and the titanium pigment business of Commercial Pigments Corporation were merged to form the Krebs Pigment and Color Corporation. DuPont owned 70% of the new firm; the remaining 30% was given to the former owners of Commercial Pigments. Three years later,

DuPont bought this 30%. In 1942 the Krebs Pigment and Color Corporation was made part of the rapidly expanding DuPont Company.

With World War II, DuPont again rapidly increased its production of explosives, arms, and other supplies for the armed forces. While it did much work for the government, DuPont was careful to avoid flagrant profiteering like that of World War I. The company built the Hanford Engineering Works and Clinton Engineering Works for the Manhattan Project for only $2 in paper profits. But the projects gave the company ample returns in the form of technical know-how and new facilities. And DuPont got federal contracts worth three times as much as its World War I explosives contracts. In addition, DuPont built factories at federal expense and sold $900 million worth of goods produced at these government-owned installations.

Between 1939 and 1964, DuPont fought 19 antitrust suits. In the most important, filed under the Clayton Act in 1949, DuPont, Christiana Securities, and numerous family members were accused of acquiring stock in General Motors with the effect of limiting competition or creating a monopoly. In 1957 the Supreme Court convicted the defendants, saying:

> The wisdom of [General Motors' widespread use of DuPont products] cannot obscure the fact, plainly revealed by the record, that DuPont purposely employed its stock to pry open the General Motors market to entrench itself as the primary supplier of General Motors' requirements for automotive finishes and fabrics.[3]

DuPont had to divest itself of all its GM stock, which over the years had yielded the company more than $2 billion.

E. I. du Pont de Nemours & Company, Incorporated, is now the largest chemical firm in the world. In 1969 the DuPont Company's gross sales were $3.6 billion. (Delaware tax revenues were less than $300 million.) The company paid $288 million in salaries to employees *within Delaware alone,* roughly equal to the state budget that year. Innumerable Delaware companies rely on DuPont as a supplier, contractor, or customer. According to a study done for the Delaware Study Group by two Delaware economists, DuPont generates 20.8% of the gross state product.*

Because Delaware is DuPont's headquarters, the company has tremendous influence over state citizens. So vast and pervasive is DuPont's influence that it is very important to Delaware citizens how DuPont makes corporate decisions and whose interests these decisions serve.

### *Corporate Decision Making*

The formal structure of decision making in the DuPont Company is shown in Table 2-1. The table shows stockholders at the top and below them the board of directors, elected annually by the stockholders. The board is broken down into four committees; under them are the industrial, treasurer's, secretary's, and staff departments. Industrial departments are organized according to their products. The staff departments are for nonproduction specialties, such as law and advertising, that assist the industrial departments.

DuPont is proud that, as the *DuPont Facts Book* emphasizes, stockholders "are found in every state of the union, the District of Columbia, most territories and possessions, and in many foreign countries." Each stockholder can come to annual stockholders' meetings in Wilmington to express his opinion on corporate policies. But opinion and influence are radically different things.

To the extent that any stockholders influence the corporation's decisions, that power is limited to the DuPont family. While 92% of DuPont's more than 250,000 stockholders are individuals, individual stockholders hold only 28% of the stock. Of this 28%, DuPont family members individually own about one-quarter, or 7% overall. Institutions, including banks, charitable organizations, and insurance companies, control the other 72%; one institution alone—Christiana Securities, a holding company for the DuPont family—owns 28.5% of the company's stock.

* The gross state product is the market value of goods and services produced by a state's economy before deduction of intermediate products used by businesses in that same accounting period.

TABLE 2-1.
*DuPont Company Organization (as of March 1, 1970)*

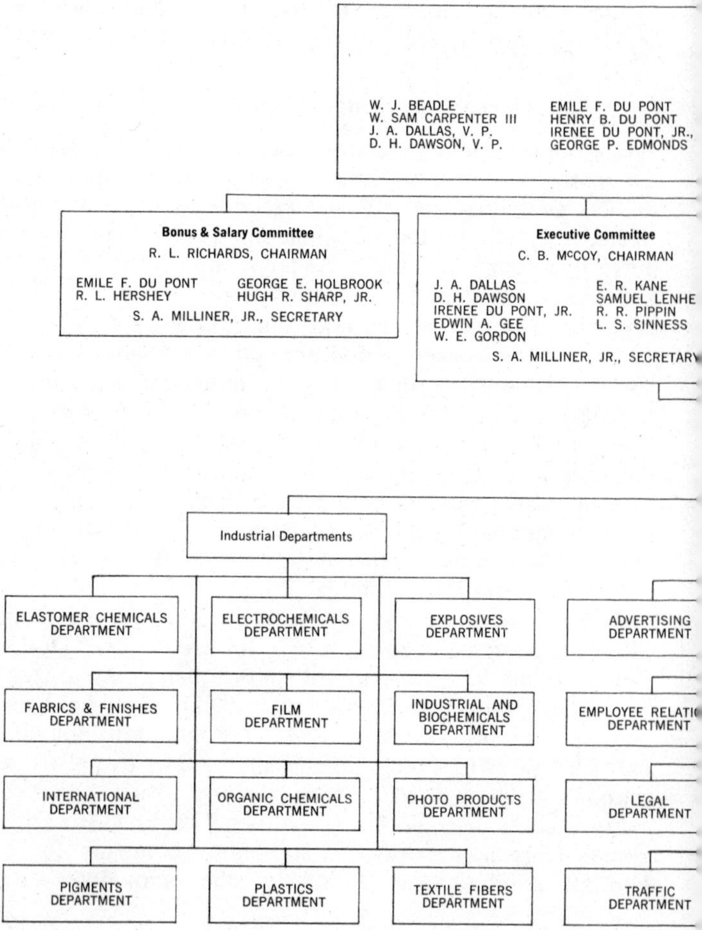
W. J. BEADLE
W. SAM CARPENTER III
J. A. DALLAS, V. P.
D. H. DAWSON, V. P.
EMILE F. DU PONT
HENRY B. DU PONT
IRENEE DU PONT, JR.,
GEORGE P. EDMONDS
Bonus & Salary Committee
R. L. RICHARDS, CHAIRMAN
EMILE F. DU PONT
R. L. HERSHEY
GEORGE E. HOLBROOK
HUGH R. SHARP, JR.
S. A. MILLINER, JR., SECRETARY
Executive Committee
C. B. McCOY, CHAIRMAN
J. A. DALLAS
D. H. DAWSON
IRENEE DU PONT, JR.
EDWIN A. GEE
W. E. GORDON
E. R. KANE
SAMUEL LENHE
R. R. PIPPIN
L. S. SINNESS
S. A. MILLINER, JR., SECRETARY
Industrial Departments
ELASTOMER CHEMICALS DEPARTMENT
ELECTROCHEMICALS DEPARTMENT
EXPLOSIVES DEPARTMENT
FABRICS & FINISHES DEPARTMENT
FILM DEPARTMENT
INDUSTRIAL AND BIOCHEMICALS DEPARTMENT
INTERNATIONAL DEPARTMENT
ORGANIC CHEMICALS DEPARTMENT
PHOTO PRODUCTS DEPARTMENT
PIGMENTS DEPARTMENT
PLASTICS DEPARTMENT
TEXTILE FIBERS DEPARTMENT
ADVERTISING DEPARTMENT
EMPLOYEE RELATI
DEPARTMENT
LEGAL DEPARTMENT
TRAFFIC DEPARTMENT

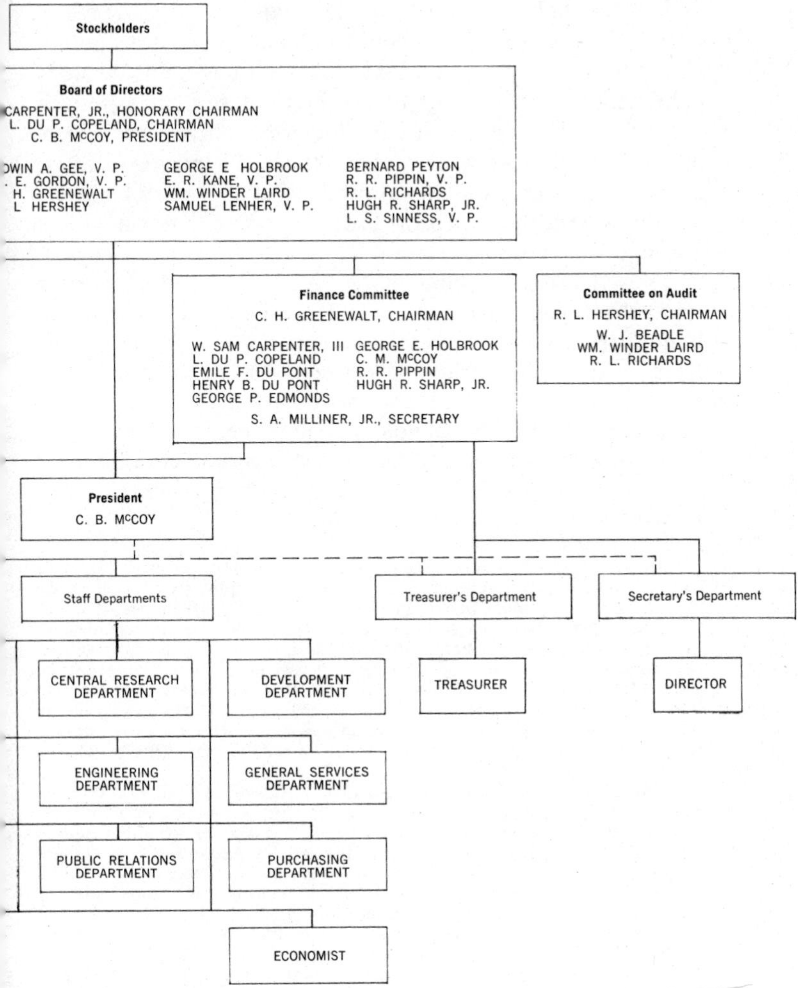
Stockholders
Board of Directors
CARPENTER, JR., HONORARY CHAIRMAN
L. DU P. COPELAND, CHAIRMAN
C. B. McCOY, PRESIDENT
WIN A. GEE, V. P.
. E. GORDON, V. P.
H. GREENEWALT
L HERSHEY
GEORGE E HOLBROOK
E. R. KANE, V. P.
WM. WINDER LAIRD
SAMUEL LENHER, V. P.
BERNARD PEYTON
R. R. PIPPIN, V. P.
R. L. RICHARDS
HUGH R. SHARP, JR.
L. S. SINNESS, V. P.
Finance Committee
C. H. GREENEWALT, CHAIRMAN
W. SAM CARPENTER, III
L. DU P. COPELAND
EMILE F. DU PONT
HENRY B. DU PONT
GEORGE P. EDMONDS
GEORGE E. HOLBROOK
C. M. McCOY
R. R. PIPPIN
HUGH R. SHARP, JR.
S. A. MILLINER, JR., SECRETARY
Committee on Audit
R. L. HERSHEY, CHAIRMAN
W. J. BEADLE
WM. WINDER LAIRD
R. L. RICHARDS
President
C. B. McCOY
Staff Departments
Treasurer's Department
Secretary's Department
CENTRAL RESEARCH DEPARTMENT
DEVELOPMENT DEPARTMENT
TREASURER
DIRECTOR
ENGINEERING DEPARTMENT
GENERAL SERVICES DEPARTMENT
PUBLIC RELATIONS DEPARTMENT
PURCHASING DEPARTMENT
ECONOMIST

With over 35% of the stock, the DuPont family has always been the controlling stockholder.*

Through control of company stock, the DuPont family and the board of directors dominate stockholders' meetings and proxy fights, eliminating the major means by which citizens and stockholders could influence corporate policy. No shareholder proposal has a chance of winning a proxy fight without the support of the DuPont family, especially since the company's board of directors solicits the proxies of all stockholders who cannot attend the meeting. Large institutional stockholders almost invariably vote their proxies along with the board of directors, which has yet to lose a stockholder vote.

Thus decision making in DuPont is far different from what the formal structure would indicate. Power is in the hands of family members and corporate managers, who have traditionally held all the seats on the board of directors (see Table 2-2).** The board does not reflect a broad spectrum of stockholder, employee, or public interests, nor even a cross section of the business community.† And it is virtually self-perpetuating. It renominates and reelects itself each year at the stockholders' meeting domi-

* Moreover, the DuPonts perpetuate their control by transferring stock only within company and family circles. For example, shortly before he died in December, 1963, Irenee du Pont, Sr., held 575,000 shares of Christiana and 12,000 shares of DuPont stock. Almost all of them remained in the family. Two months before Irenee's death, his guardians transferred 160,000 shares of Christiana stock to eight trusts for his children. When he died, 119,312 shares of Christiana and all the DuPont stock went into eight trusts established for his eight heirs; another 160,000 shares went in trust to his son, Irenee, Jr., to be administered as a charitable foundation. In a private sale only for DuPont family members, the heirs purchased 96,000 more shares of Christiana.

** Family members have also used their positions as DuPont Company directors to extract personal favors from the company. Crawford H. Greenewalt had the DuPont tax department devise ways to save taxes on the estate of his father-in-law, Irenee du Pont, Sr. According to a DuPont employee, Greenewalt's book on hummingbirds was "polished" by the company's public relations department. Lammot du Pont Copeland, Sr., persuaded the PR department to check out a potential purchaser of the family's News-Journal Company. H. B. du Pont's Atlantic Aviation Company sold DuPont at least 10 airplanes; and, according to a former DuPont executive, H.B. used the company's maintenance facilities to repair his yacht.

† In 1971, the DuPont Company added to its board of directors Dr. Caryl Parker Haskins, president of the Carnegie Institute from 1956 to 1971. Dr. Haskins, a geneticist, was well known at DuPont and in the chemical industry as a whole before joining the DuPont board.

nated by DuPont family members and corporate managers holding stock proxies.

The executive and finance committees of the board have the most important roles in setting corporate policy. The company president and vice presidents comprise the executive committee, which meets at least once weekly. It has two main functions, advising and evaluating industrial departments by their return on investment, and deciding important firmwide issues, like a decision to buy a new subsidiary or set corporate policy toward environmental laws.

The DuPont family at one time dominated the executive committee; now the key to its influence in DuPont is the finance committee, which meets biweekly. Six of the nine members of this committee are family members. Its most significant functions are to approve all capital outlays of any significance made by the industrial departments, review reports from the company's secretary and treasury departments, and supervise the company's cash flow. By supervising cash flow and capital outlays, the DuPont family can keep a close check on corporate policy without becoming too involved in administrative detail.

Within the last few years, the board of directors has developed a community affairs committee. According to its chairman, Irenee du Pont, Jr., the prime responsibility of this committee is to keep the board informed of significant events in those localities with DuPont facilities. The other main function of the committee is to coordinate the community relations activities of plant managers. Although Chairman du Pont says the committee is a key method for communities to influence corporate policy, it contains no neighborhood leaders from Wilmington or any other city—only DuPont executives. So far, the committee has mainly commissioned surveys. In a survey on housing, education, and minority employment in the Wilmington area, the committee contacted only individuals *within* the DuPont Company. The head of the study, John Oliver, said that he had not even spoken with a DuPont employee who had been active on the educational committee of the Greater Wilmington Development Council. In a second survey, the community affairs committee sought information from other corporations about community relations policies. Du-

TABLE 2-2.
*Directors of E. I. du Pont de Nemours, Incorporated*
*(as of October, 1970)*

| *Name* | *Director since* | *Retired or Active DuPont Employee* | *Membership on Executive Committee* | *DuPont Family Member* |
|---|---|---|---|---|
| Walter J. Beadle | 1946 | yes | retired | no |
| Walter S. Carpenter, Jr. | 1919 | yes | retired | no |
| W. Sam Carpenter III | 1967 | yes | no | yes |
| Lammot du Pont Copeland | 1942 | yes | retired | yes |
| Joseph A. Dallas | 1968 | yes | active | no |
| David H. Dawson | 1955 | yes | active | no |
| Emile F. du Pont | 1944 | yes | no | yes |
| Irenee du Pont, Jr. | 1959 | yes | active | yes |
| George P. Edmonds | 1966 | no | no | yes |

| | | | | |
|---|---|---|---|---|
| Edwin A. Gee | 1969 | yes | active | no |
| Wallace E. Gordon | 1965 | yes | active | no |
| Crawford H. Greenewalt | 1942 | yes | retired | yes |
| Robert L. Hershey | 1958 | yes | retired | no |
| George E. Holbrook | 1958 | yes | retired | no |
| Edward R. Kane | 1969 | yes | active | no |
| William Winder Laird | 1965 | yes | no | yes |
| Samuel Lenher | 1955 | yes | retired | no |
| Charles B. McCoy | 1961 | yes | active | no |
| Bernard Peyton | 1955 | no | no | yes |
| R. Russell Pippin | 1964 | yes | retired | no |
| Robert L. Richards | 1954 | yes | retired | no |
| Irving S. Shapiro | 1970 | yes | active | no |
| Hugh R. Sharp, Jr. | 1952 | yes | no | yes |
| Lester S. Sinness | 1963 | yes | retired | no |

Pont will not let neighborhood residents read this information.

A 1971 stockholder proposal designed to provide some input into corporate policy making by representatives of stockholders, employees, customers, and the public was resoundingly defeated. The proposed advisory committee would have been appointed by members of the board of directors who would also have been represented on the committee. Although the DuPont board includes only one person who is not a company executive or family member, DuPont says a broadly based committee would be wasteful "because existing management overview of social concerns would be duplicated." Because the DuPont board controls the stockholders' meetings, the eventual defeat of the resolution was inevitable.

Few important corporate decisions are put to a stockholder vote. The 1970 proxy statement listed only five issues. The most important was the election of the board of directors, which had renominated itself. There were also votes to ratify the use of independent public accountants, a vote on the bonus plan (which must be presented to the stockholders every five years), an amendment to the certificate of incorporation to ensure that the bonus plan be continued, and an amendment to the pension and retirement plan. The 1971 proxy statement listed nine proposals; only the one proposed by management and the reelection of the board passed.

### THE CORPORATION AND THE PUBLIC

Since Delaware citizens who are not DuPont executives or family members do not have an effective voice inside the structure of corporate policy making, the question arises whether they can participate in corporate decision making outside the structure. According to company vice president Irenee du Pont, Jr., the public has an important effect on corporate policy making through the balance sheet. That is, the community's view on corporate policy will affect company profits. A DuPont executive put it this way:

> In establishing the free market and modeling it on our political system, we have applied to the commercial scene that fine system of checks and balances that keeps our govern-

> ment in a state of equilibrium. Here on the one hand we have the zeal and the drive of the salesman, full of commendable ardor for his product and eager for the sale. Here on the other hand, we have the cool and objective appraisal of the buyer, skilled in defining value, impersonal in identifying overstatement.[4]

DuPont's vision of the free market place can hardly apply to itself. First, DuPont, like many large companies, is a heavy advertiser, and several studies have shown that such advertising creates artificially high demand for products by impairing the consumer's ability to make a free choice.[5] Second, any economics textbook shows that consumer "checks and balances" can work only in a market of many small, vigorously competing producers. The Justice Department has sued DuPont many times because of its near monopoly in some product lines; in others, DuPont's only rivals are a few other giant corporations. Third, DuPont sells few products directly to the consumer; 95% of all DuPont sales go to other business firms for industrial use. To exert pressure on the company through the market, Delaware consumers would have to trace DuPont products through to retail goods, where the DuPont contribution to a final product might only be a small fraction of its value. In 1960 DuPont reported, for example, that a $25 nylon dress used less than $2 worth of nylon. Fourth, DuPont sells throughout the world, rendering consumers in any locale—especially a relatively small one like Delaware—incapable of effective economic pressure through a boycott. In 1969 DuPont sales totaled $3.6 billion; consumers in Delaware could not even dent the company's sales.

Since a consumer boycott is not a viable community strategy, do employees refuse to work for a company they think has not hired enough blacks? Do stores refuse to sell office supplies to DuPont because the company does not hire enough women in supervisory positions? A well-developed economic literature shows that the balance sheet does not reflect external effects of firms on the community.[6] A company that pollutes, for example, has no economic incentive to install control devices because they yield no profit. While theoretically all those harmed by pollution could join to force the company to install controls, in practice the organization of the harmed families into an effective counterforce to the corporation is virtually impossible.

Nor is DuPont management willing to give the public a formal role in corporate decision making. Top executives steadfastly refuse to open decision making to those groups in the community seriously affected by DuPont policies. Corporation president C. B. McCoy said he opposed Campaign GM's proposal to have stockholders elect three directors to represent the public. Irenee du Pont was unwilling to have the community formally represented in key places of authority. He opposes having an advocate of consumer interests on the board; he is unwilling to tolerate representatives on the board from regions of the country in which DuPont has facilities. Although du Pont felt plant managers should consult with community leaders on certain corporate policies, he denies the desirability of any formal structure including community representatives. Both McCoy and du Pont oppose any method of public election for officers of giant corporations like DuPont.

### CORPORATE SECRECY AND PUBLIC ACCESS

One way to gauge the public's role in corporate decision making is to examine its access to information. If it cannot get information on DuPont policies toward the community, it will never be able to influence DuPont decision making.

The company has a legitimate right to protect its competitive position by guarding genuine trade secrets. But the suppression of information about community issues unrelated to trade secrets is a widespread company policy. President McCoy told the Delaware Study Group that information would be confidential if it could be "harmful to the corporation." Under this vague standard, the company can easily withhold information of great interest to the public even though it does not concern trade secrets—as it does with information on minority employment. DuPont was so reluctant to give out statistics on minority employment that corporate officials denied possession of information which DuPont was required by law to compile. On July 14, 1970, the study group asked for "the number and position of minority employees by department and state." DuPont replied on July 22 that such information was not available. Later, in response to an interrogatory, DuPont stated that the corporation did not have information available concerning DuPont minority employment in Delaware but could give us total minority employment in Greater Wilmington. However, members of the study group had learned that the Employer Information Report EEO-1 of the Equal Employment Opportunity Commission, mandatory for any firm with more than 100 employees, required a breakdown of employees into nine occupational categories and four minority groups. As of 1970, this information had to be filed plant by plant. Moreover, a black employee informed us that once or twice a year each department of DuPont submitted a report to the executive committee listing the number of blacks in various job levels. Finally, a plant manager unaware of the company's official denial referred to a report containing the Edgemoor plant's exact percentage and numbers of minority employees, by job classification and race.

DuPont has distributed glossy public relations material extolling the corporation's antipollution efforts but refuses to share its data on effluent discharges and stack emissions. Some DuPont officials rationalize their refusal by saying that numbers are too easily misunderstood and misused. Under this theory, people should not know anything about pollution because they do not know everything about it. DuPont also argues that citizens can get the information from the government. Company officials know that Delaware has no law requiring government agencies to disclose data to local citizens. Moreover, DuPont often has more information about its own plants than do state governments. For instance, when the Delaware Study Group sought emissions information about DuPont's nylon plant in Seaford, the state air resources unit did not have the data. But the state people said the DuPont Company, having more monitoring stations than the state, had complete information on its own pollution.

If DuPont is doing such a fine job of curbing its own pollution, why is it unwilling to make the specific figures public? Even citizens without scientific expertise could make valid judgments about DuPont's performance by comparing the applicable figures with health standards, federal and state air quality and emission standards, and amounts of pollution from other sources. At the very least, the public could see DuPont's progress. In its numerous publications on pollution, the company fills pages with executive committee resolutions, glossy pictures of new plants, and, over and over, the amount of money spent by DuPont on pollution control. But the company never tells how much environmental damage DuPont is causing; how much *net* expenditure after tax write-offs are made for pollution control; what control technology is available but not installed; or how the amount spent compares to the amount *needed* to control DuPont pollution.

The corporation also denies the public access to information necessary to evaluate DuPont's relation to governmental bodies. The company has a formal policy statement of guidelines for employees who are elected to political offices and a memorandum on implementation procedures; DuPont refuses to make them public. Trade associations, which provide companies with a way to bypass federal laws against corporate political contributions, also serve as legislative lobbies for business.[7] When asked by the study group to list its ties with trade associations, DuPont said the task was too burdensome.

DuPont is especially secretive with information about the company's impact on individual communities. When the Delaware Study Group inquired about DuPont's total assets in Delaware, management said such figures were not kept on a state-by-state basis, but Samuel Lenher, a DuPont board member, announced in a public speech that DuPont has a $600-million investment in Delaware. The study group asked: "What plans does the company have for expansion in Delaware in terms of facilities, land acquisition, and new employees through 1980? Is a new office building planned for Wilmington?" DuPont replied: "This request is declined on the ground that the information is confidential." The company will not disclose the capitalized value of its facilities in Delaware. Without the company's own estimate of book or capitalized value—something very difficult for a citizen to estimate—there is no way citizens can check the propriety of DuPont real estate assessments. Such information is not available to the public through property assessment offices because they do not list capitalized values.

Despite DuPont's record of nondisclosure of information, DuPont vice president Irving Shapiro, official liaison with the Delaware Study Group, said in a 1971 speech that the DuPont Company is willing to share hard facts with critics:

> When someone challenges our stance, we are in a strong position if we say, "Here's our data; where's yours?" That helps stop some of the rhetoric that clouds the air.[8]

Shapiro indicated further that DuPont was probably willing to "declassify" a good deal of information about its various programs. Lest anyone think the DuPont Company has had a major policy shift since hiding so much information from the study group, as suggested in an *Evening Journal* editorial two days after Shapiro's speech,[9] here is how a DuPont spokesman substituted rhetoric for facts about water pollution at the Chambers Works plant:

> In some instances we're not in compliance with the allocation, and until we get certification, we don't think it would be proper to disclose what we discharge. We think the figures could be misleading.[10]

### CORPORATE CHARITY AND COMMUNITY INTEREST

Another way to examine community input into corporate decisions is to look at a company's charitable giving program. Under federal law, a corporation can receive a tax deduction for charitable gifts amounting to 5% of its taxable income. Delaware state law gives corporations direct tax credits up to $50,000 on their state income tax bills for donations to community improvement organizations that qualify under the state's Neighborhood Assistance Act. DuPont's charitable gifts in 1969 totaled $4.9 million, allocated by several top management committees. Nearly half supported science programs in colleges, universities, and secondary schools nationwide. Other gifts went to business schools, public charities like the Red Cross, and special programs in Delaware. No private foundations received DuPont money directly. DuPont could have claimed tax deductions for $30 million more in gifts, and turned down many requests for money.

Committee decisions directly affect three groups that do not share in making the decisions: stockholders, employees, and the community-at-large. Stockholders are affected because dividends are reduced and because they may live where donations are made. Employees live in communities near company facilities, which often receive gift money, and, presumably, might have received higher salaries but for the donations. The community has a direct interest because the donations go to it. Since these three groups are not represented in the decision-making process, reconciliation of any competing interests is made by management alone, with little accountability to the affected groups.* As long as gifts are made to groups qualifying as public charities under the federal tax laws, and as long as management is acting in the "long-term interest" of the corporation, there is no statutory constraint on management's decisions.

The charitable donation is thus an extension of the firm's economic power. As the authors of a major text on corporations wrote:

> the concentration of a large proportion of the wealth of [the] community in the hands of business corporations has made corporate gifts essential if charities are to be privately financed.[11]

Because a big corporation has a big share of the community's resources, this power can be enormous. And DuPont has far greater resources than any other corporation, private group, or public body in Delaware; the company can exercise a great amount of power by giving or not giving within the state.

There are overall effects from corporate giving that are inherent in a company state like Delaware, where a single economic institution dominates the resources available for charity in the state. DuPont's public image is, of course, greatly enhanced in the minds of citizens. But public groups

* DuPont's gifts are made on an ad hoc basis, according to Harlan Wendell, assistant director of the public relations department and a member of one of the contributions committees. In an interview with the study group, Wendell indicated that only vague notions of company interest and community need are used by the committees to allocate the company's donations.

come to depend on DuPont to support numerous charitable causes, so that the company is viewed in a similar way as the public government—as a prime source of public benefit. But corporate citizens do not have the opportunity to subject corporate power to the same democratic concepts of accountability as they do the public government. Moreover, donations are not necessarily based on community priorities, and community groups cannot make rational long-range plans when dependent on DuPont ad hoc donations.

DuPont's donations in Delaware—several hundred thousand dollars in 1969—show both the positive and negative impacts of corporate gifts on the community. The company helped an Upward Bound program—a small-scale project for educating high school dropouts (about 20 people participated)—at the University of Delaware and made gifts to upgrade teaching in inner city schools. These gifts were valuable social improvement capital that might otherwise have been unavailable. On the other hand, the company's charitable giving has sometimes been detrimental. As detailed in Chapter 14, the DuPont Company has aggravated the inequality of educational opportunity between the DuPont-run University of Delaware and the predominantly black Delaware State College. Sixty thousand dollars went to the Greater Wilmington Development Council, an organization run by DuPont executives, who guided redevelopment in Wilmington according to their own ideas and notions of the best interest of the community—ideas which, as Chapter 8 will show, have often been detrimental to the community. There has been no widespread community participation in the council's programs.

The donation of DuPont employees at company expense to public groups shows how community groups without sufficient funds of their own are sometimes excluded from DuPont's charity, while the requests of other groups, with DuPont management interest, were granted. According to company officials, donations of employees' time have been in great demand. At least two major community-based groups serving low-income residents of Wilmington requested the aid of DuPont employees for accounting and administrative help. DuPont turned them down. The only requests granted went to Downtown Wilmington, Inc., the

Governor's Economy Study, and the National Alliance of Businessmen. All are solidly connected with the corporate establishment. Downtown Wilmington was put together by the Greater Wilmington Development Council. The Governor's Economy Study was organized by several corporate executives at the request of Governor Russell Peterson, a former DuPont executive. The National Alliance of Businessmen is an attempt by large corporations to promote minority employment voluntarily—a program notable for its lack of success during the last two years in Wilmington under the guidance of a DuPont employee.

There is much to be said for corporations' charitable gifts. When community resources are divided unequally, the dispersal of corporate resources via charitable donations can be a mark of responsible behavior. But the goal of developing a viable form of corporate and community democracy requires that affected interests be represented in the process of allocating corporate charity—particularly in a company state, where the proper functioning of democracy itself is affected by corporate actions. DuPont's charitable gifts in Delaware often have been made to worthwhile institutions and endeavors. But because management alone now exercises the power implicit in the concentration of community resources within the corporation, at times the company has used donations to serve its own unarticulated purposes, to the detriment of other community groups.

### THE UNITED FUND AND COUNCIL OF DELAWARE

The most revealing illustration of the decision-making bias in corporate giving is the relation of DuPont to the United Fund and Council of Delaware (UFC). The United Fund in Delaware was started by Francis V. du Pont in 1946 to sort out requests to the corporate elite for money. Within the last decade, much of the money has come from DuPont employee contributions. UFC is the only charity officially advocated by DuPont to its employees. Management sets contribution goals per employee, department, and facility. During the annual fund-raising drive, a chart in the lobby of the DuPont Building compares the progress of the departments toward their goals. Representatives of UFC rally enthusiasm by speaking at DuPont installations. Managers, knowing the amount contributed by each individual subordinate, may pressure an employee to make a donation. Consider this letter:

> Central Research Department
> Experimental Station
>
> Date Oct. 3, 1968
>
> TO: [name withheld]
> FROM: D. S. Donalson
>
> I note that you have not made a contribution to the United Fund during the present campaign. This is your privilege and all contributions, to this and other worthwhile efforts, must be considered voluntary. However, the need is great. Our campaign does not end until Friday. I hope you will change your mind and find it possible to make a contribution no matter how modest.

Despite the UFC's dependence on employee contributions, the DuPont business empire monopolizes UFC policy making. Nineteen sixty-nine was the first year that a representative of organized labor served on the UFC Board. Of the 85 directors on the 1969–70 UFC Board, 28 were DuPont Company executives or DuPont family members, as are 12 of the 31 members of the board's executive committee. The presidents of UFC since 1965 have been Pierre S. du Pont III, Joseph Chinn, Jr., of Wilmington Trust Company, and now Samuel Lenher, a member of the DuPont board of directors and former member of the DuPont executive committee. The campaign chairman for 1970 was Werner C. Brown of Hercules, Inc., while the 1969 campaign chairman was David Dawson, vice president and director of DuPont.

Community groups have no influence on how the United Fund distributes its tax-exempt monies. At one time, a Community Services Council linked loosely with the fund tried to ascertain community desires and attempted to channel money to meet them. But the corporate elite running the United Fund disapproved of this committee's consumer orientation. Led by a DuPont Company vice president, the United Fund transformed the Community Services Council into an inside planning council, headed by two DuPont executives. Shortly afterwards, the DuPont executives forced the director of the planning council to leave. He explained, "UF was telling the agencies what to do instead of trying to meet the needs they perceived."

Recently, the UFC began to review the activities of recipient agencies to establish guidelines for UFC support. None of these studies involved the consumers of agency services; yet as a result of a pilot analysis of three recipient agencies, UFC told one to change about 90% of its program, phased out funding of a second, and greatly increased support of the third to assume responsibilities previously met by the state government. A bulletin says, "The UFC is yours, and your neighbors', it belongs to and is run by the citizens of Delaware." But in effect, the evaluation process is a mechanism by which corporate managers tell community agencies and their clientele how to use the donations.

Moreover, the corporate elite has recently used the UFC to extend its influence into southern Delaware. In 1969 UFC moved virtually to control the United Fund of Central Delaware and the Bi-County Fund. These red-feather organizations will retain their independence only as legal entities; the DuPont-dominated United Fund will assume all responsibility for administration and fiscal affairs.

In sum, the DuPont-related groups have created an alternative government in Delaware. United Fund's annual expenditures total $4.4 million per year, almost as much as New Castle, Delaware's most populous county, spends on public safety, judiciary, health and welfare, and recreation, as well as on legislative, executive, and staff agencies. The United Fund has its own taxing system and election procedures; the major difference is that the UFC is beholden only to corporate executives. When the United Fund and Council of Delaware cuts off funding, there is no vote, no recourse to the court, and no alternative source of funding unconnected to the DuPonts. If the UFC did not play such a large role in Delaware, state government, which is theoretically accountable to the whole community, would have to allocate tax revenues to support the programs.

## *Corporate Impact: Minorities and Pollution*

Although Delaware citizens clearly have very little voice in corporate decision making, DuPont spokesmen insist that there is a harmony of interests between the company and the community and that corporate executives will implicitly make decisions that serve all citizens. This argument is undercut by DuPont's practices even in the two areas where the company claims to be one of the nation's most progressive firms—minority advancement and pollution control.

In the late 1950s, company facilities in Delaware still had separate bathrooms for whites and blacks, and company publications like the *Management Newsletter* rarely mentioned minority groups. Blacks were excluded from supervisory positions of any kind. In 1959 Governor Russell W. Peterson, then a DuPont executive, drew up a plan to integrate Chestnut Run, a company facility in the Wilmington area. Peterson's plan called for the promotion of only four blacks to low-level jobs as stenographer, truck driver, chemist's helper, and clerk. The plan was considered too radical. According to current political associates of Peterson, his DuPont career was temporarily stalled because of his proposal. Peterson himself says the plan "was not too well received by an intermediate point between me and the top." Less than a year later, when President Eisenhower asked Crawford Greenewalt, then president of DuPont, to support racial integration in industry, the company put the plan into effect.

DuPont now claims to be firmly committed to racial integration and social mobility for minority groups. The house publications extol the company's efforts to hire more blacks. A recent report called *Equal Opportunity* shows many pictures of blacks together with photos of DuPont recruiters. While the report gives statistics on the problems faced by black people in America, it has only one statement on the number of minority employees at DuPont—a claim that black employees increased by 1000 in DuPont facilities across the country during 1968. But the report does not reveal what percentage of white-collar jobs are held by minority group members.

Data on minority employment undercut the company's self-image. While overt discrimination seems to have disappeared, vestiges of racism remain. Although DuPont refused to give the study group figures on the racial breakdown of white-collar employees, approximations can be made from reports for the chemical industry in Delaware. DuPont employs over three-quarters of the chemical industry in Delaware, and blacks comprise about 15% of the state's population. Yet according to the 1969 Report #1 of the Equal Employment Opportunity Commission (EEOC), Delaware's chemical industry is below the national average; there are no black sales workers, and blacks make up only .9% of total white-collar employees: .4% of professionals, .4% of officers and managers, 1.5% of office and clerical helpers, and 1.2% of technicians. In the chemical industry nationwide, 1.1% of white-collar employees are black compared to .9% for Delaware's chemical firms, despite the state's relatively high black population. The chemical industry also compares unfavorably with other state industries in terms of minority employment.

Such statistics put DuPont's rejection of the nationwide church-sponsored Project Equality in a clearer light. Church members have persuaded over 15,000 firms to undergo a compliance review on their minority employment programs. In the Delaware area, over 400 companies, including the large banks, Delmarva Power and Light, and Sun Oil Company, have agreed to work with Project Equality. If a firm does not pass the compliance review, which analyzes community racial composition and company personnel policies, church members work with executives to formulate ways to increase minority jobs. DuPont made a policy decision not to participate in Project Equality if approached by the Delaware group, claiming that Project Equality would have entailed high costs and duplication of efforts.

In contrast, DuPont supported Plans for Progress, a similar program to Project Equality except run by businessmen. DuPont even loaned a top executive to head the program. Plans for Progress, however, has not been very successful. Firms are not required to establish an affirmative action plan that is periodically reviewed, many companies in Plans for Progress have not met their hiring pledges, and firms like DuPont still have less than 1% blacks in white-collar positions.

One of the most poignant examples of DuPont's racial policies is in Seaford, where the company makes nylon in what executives call a "model plant." When DuPont first built the Seaford plant in the 1930s, the company had free reign. No other large firms were in the area. Despite a local population that was 10–20% black, DuPont hired minority residents only for a few menial jobs. It now has only 10 to 15 blacks in supervisory positions out of an employment force of about 4000, according to a DuPont foreman in Seaford. Black workers complain that the company union does not process their grievances effectively. DuPont abolished segregated facilities at Seaford around 1960. In 1969 DuPont ran a very successful program for about 25 hard-core unemployed, including many blacks. The program has now been discontinued.

The company's policy of racial segregation has been implemented outside the plant as well. DuPont built a large employees' country club in Seaford, which was off-bounds for blacks. While the club has officially been opened to blacks since the early 1960s, no blacks are members yet. A few years ago, before the official desegregation, a prominent black politician from Seaford tried to attend a University of Delaware reunion at the DuPont country club but was turned down on racial grounds. Since blacks are not members of the country club, no black organization can rent the clubhouse for meetings.

DuPont also claims to be making great efforts in developing new minority-owned businesses. The company has a wealth of experience in finding new products and discovering new ways to manufacture old ones. In addition, DuPont has a large customer service department, which deals with an extremely broad range of industrial activity—adopting and converting DuPont products to the needs of other firms. Despite the company's development skills and its constant need for office and plant supplies, which could make DuPont a regular customer for minority enterprises, DuPont has not yet found one attractive opportunity for establishing a new minority-owned business. Several years ago, the company assigned Monroe Sadler, head of the development department, to formulate a minority business proposal. Sadler came up with only one idea—manufacturing wooden pallets, the platforms used to transport goods in a warehouse; according to several sources, including a warehouseman at DuPont's Edgemoor plant, wooden pallets are rapidly being replaced by aluminum pallets and plastic containers.

DuPont also claims to be a leader in pollution control efforts. In 1938 DuPont's executive committee resolved that pollution abatement was a subject "of major importance and one which should receive study of the same type as is applied to safety work and fire prevention." [12] The resolution even recognized that pollution control must be considered part of the normal cost of doing business. This policy, as interpreted by President C. B. McCoy, means that "no new plant may be built, no new process approved unless the plans include workable methods of waste disposal or treatment. The methods must meet or exceed all legal requirements." Old plants and processes are to be brought in line with the same policy. The board of directors formed an air and water resources committee in 1946 and an environmental quality committee several years later. These committees formulate policy and coordinate environmental activities.

Yet DuPont has spoken out against the 1965 Federal Water Quality Act, the 1967 Air Quality Act, the 1970 Water Quality Act, and the various standards developed pursuant to these federal laws as "new, arbitrary demands that are being imposed throughout the country." [13] DuPont has successfully weakened state antipollution laws through its lobbyists and technical experts (see Chapter 13). Under the guise of technical infeasibility, DuPont has argued for time to study pollution. DuPont has been studying the problem for over 30 years.

The company seldom stops polluting until forced to do so by government. DuPont's production of a mercurial fungicide, trademarked as "Ceresan," is a case in point. As early as 1958, scientists documented cases of birds dying from mercury poisoning after eating mercury-treated seed grains, and in 1963 scientists found dangerously high mercury levels in seed grains treated with mercurial fungicides.[14] Levels ranged from 23 to 34 parts per million (ppm), while natural concentrations are below .08 ppm.[15] One group of scientists later observed that

> such dressed grain would thus be particularly hazardous if it ever found its way directly into human food sources or if eaten by wild animal populations after planting.[16]

Various studies in 1965, 1968, and 1969 indicated high levels of mercury in numerous foods. And, most important, one study reported that the mercury content of certain food products in Sweden *dropped when the use of mercurial seed disinfectants was discontinued.*[17] Despite such early documentation of possible dangers, DuPont failed to take its mercurial seed disinfectant off the market until 1970, only after learning that the Department of Agriculture was about to withdraw permission for the company to sell the product.

DuPont's production of tetraethyl lead (TEL), used in gasoline, is a clear example of the preeminence of profits over public health. TEL is a major source of lead in the atmosphere, and substantial amounts of lead in the air can be very harmful. As William Megonnell, assistant commissioner of the National Air Pollution Control Administration, said:

> Lead is not tolerable. Sixteen per cent of the particulates in the District of Columbia are from automobiles and ninety per cent of that is from lead.[18]

A recent report from the Environmental Protection Agency stated:

> Lead accumulates in humans with prolonged or repeated exposure to high environmental lead levels. . . . There is evidence that non-occupational exposures to elevated ambient air lead concentrations may increase the body burden of lead, though this evidence has not been confirmed in all studies.[19]

The report also stated: "The magnitude of the problem hardly justifies a 'wait and see' attitude, for acute poisoning is associated with a high percentage of irreversible central nervous damage in children, and repeated exposure to high environmental levels of lead greatly increases the risk of irreversible damage."

Yet DuPont president C. B. McCoy argued in an interview with the study group:

> We have no evidence that TEL per se is a serious health problem. A great deal of work has been done to try to prove if it does do any harm, and nothing has been produced yet. We have no reason to take it off [the market].

DuPont's policy is to wait for the conclusions of exhaustive public testing before taking a possibly harmful product off the market. The company, as perpetrator, shifts the burden of proof to the community, as victim, to prove a product injures human beings.

By a massive propaganda campaign and the massing of research, not manufacturing, facilities in Delaware, DuPont has built an image as a fairly clean company in its headquarters state. However, DuPont's two major industrial plants in the Wilmington area—Edgemoor and Chambers Works—have only a mixed record in pollution control. The processes at DuPont's Edgemoor pigment plant generate hydrochloric and sulfuric acid and sulfur dioxide waste. Until 1968 the sulfuric acid, only minimally diluted by a single ponding, was dumped into the Delaware River. Now DuPont puts most of the waste into a barge and dumps it into the Atlantic Ocean. This is fine for the Delaware, but less pleasant for the ocean. It is only a short-term solution. Already environmentalists are voicing alarm over ocean pollution, and one of the danger areas they cite is off the east coast of the United States. Furthermore, the Edgemoor plant still discharges 262,500 pounds of scantily treated acid wastes into the Delaware River every day, the largest discharge of any Delaware industry, along with 28,500 pounds of iron, 25 pounds of lead, 25 of zinc, and 20 of nickel per day.[20] The Biochemical Oxygen Demand (BOD) * of the waste is 53,400 pounds.

* Biochemical Oxygen Demand measures the amount of dissolved oxygen needed to decompose organic wastes in the river. One pound of BOD will leach one pound of oxygen from the water, impairing water quality and, if the BOD is great enough, making the water unfit for fish life.

Chambers Works, too, has been dumping thousands of pounds of acid waste with only primary treatment into the Delaware River for years. DuPont did not begin to develop secondary treatment until the Delaware River Basin Commission (DRBC), acting pursuant to the Federal Water Quality Act, set a timetable requiring DuPont to develop full secondary treatment of wastes by 1974. In conjunction with this move, DuPont donated land at the Chambers Works site plus $375,000 for a pilot project to test the feasibility of regional secondary treatment for industries and municipalities in southern New Jersey. The effect has been to delay waste treatment. While waiting for the verdict on the feasibility of joint treatment, the corporation still dumps wastes after only primary treatment. According to newspaper accounts, the 100 million gallons discharged daily from Chambers Works into the Delaware River have a BOD of 81,000 pounds.[21]

The DRBC has proposed quantitative water quality standards for the Delaware River to be reached by the mid-1970s. The DRBC allocated 21,000 pounds of BOD load to Chambers Works, a 75% reduction. The new standards would allow no visible oil, no debris, scum, or floating materials, and only 20 ppm ammonia and nitrogen to be released from a single source. In public hearings on the proposed standards in 1971, DuPont condemned them as being too stringent and unnecessary,[22] even though 21,000 pounds of BOD is equivalent to the raw sewage of over 125,000 people.

Both Edgemoor and Chambers Works have also caused air pollution problems in Delaware. According to local residents and the plant manager, Chambers Works released pollutants into the air primarily at night until a few years ago—deceiving the citizenry. The sulfuric acid mist from Edgemoor stacks used to be so bad that garages had to be built to protect employees' cars from corrosion. New Castle County air monitoring station data show that steam from the Edgemoor plant still contains some 100–125 pounds of acid mist per day. When New Jersey passed a law limiting the sulfur content of fuel oil and coal for industrial use, DuPont sued the state, contending that air quality standards should vary according to regional concentration of industry. Such regional standards would have allowed DuPont to release more pollutants from its massive Chambers Works plant in southern New Jersey than plants could release in northern parts of the state. In its lawsuit, DuPont alleged that just partial compliance with the New Jersey law would cost the company close to $1 million a year. When the state seemed likely to prove its case, DuPont withdrew the suit and shifted to low-sulfur fuels. But by obtaining a court injunction while the suit was pending, the company saved close to $2 million and blocked the enforcement of sulfur fuel content standards throughout the entire state for two years.

Faced with strict pollution control regulations from New Jersey and the DRBC, DuPont has chosen to pull out rather than clean up. In September, 1971, the company announced plans to move a significant part of its dye-making operation from Chambers Works to Puerto Rico, primarily * because of the costs to bring the plant into compliance with state and regional environmental standards.[23] Several thousand residents of New Jersey and Delaware will lose their jobs as a result.

DuPont indirectly contributes to pollution by subcontracting its dirtiest processes to small companies outside the public limelight. These subcontractors cut costs in part by inadequate pollution control. One of these plants is the Galaxie Chemical Company, built by two ex-DuPont employees in 1961 near the Delaware border in Maryland. Galaxie purifies chemical wastes from DuPont and other corporations. Inspectors from the Maryland Division of Air Quality Control have found carbon tetrachloride, benzene, tetrachloro-ethane, methyl ketone, and methylene chloride in the air of the valley where the plant is located. Tetrachloro-ethane, the most toxic of all chlorinated hydrocarbons, according to the U.S. Public Health Service, is deadly to humans at concentrations above 5 ppm for any period of time. The Maryland inspectors recorded ambient air levels of 5–9 ppm near the Galaxie plant. The Mary-

* Another important reason for the move to Puerto Rico is New Jersey's new 5% sales tax on purchases of business equipment and the commonwealth's offer to suspend corporate income taxes for 15 years for plants employing Puerto Ricans.

land Health Department brought a nuisance complaint against Galaxie; evidence brought out in the 1970 trial indicated that 8 to 10 persons living near the plant suffered from pancreatis, a rare disease that can be caused by various chemicals. The plant was shut down.

DuPont simply contracts out the dirty work and washes its corporate hands. It has failed to ensure that the work being done by Galaxie and other subcontractors is not inimical to the health of people living near the various plants. This negligence directly contradicts DuPont's policy of requiring purchasers of its products to handle them with the same safety precautions as DuPont requires of its own employees. According to Dr. C. A. D'Alonzo of the DuPont Medical Department, DuPont will either stop selling a product to a customer if he is unable to handle it safely or will delay sale of a product until proper precautions are taken.[24]

Since 1938, when DuPont declared that pollution abatement was "of major importance," the company has invested, according to its figures, $146 million (through 1969) for pollution control in all of its plants in the United States. This figure includes expenditures for pollution abatement devices, in-plant process changes, and recovery of waste materials. In Delaware, DuPont capital investment to control pollution totaled $9 million: $500,000 for solid wastes, $3.7 million for air pollution, and $4.8 million for water pollution. DuPont's investment in pollution control equipment is 1.5% of the total capital investment of $600 million in Delaware. To operate all of its pollution control devices around the country in 1969, DuPont said it spent $30 million. For a company with gross sales of $3.6 billion in 1969 and net profits of $371 million, the amount spent for pollution control is minuscule.

CHAPTER 3

# Working on the Ladder: DuPont Employees

A key theme of American labor law is industrial democracy. The National Labor Relations Act, the Landrum-Griffin Act, and other federal statutes on employer-employee relations are aimed in large part at providing workers with a voice over important decisions in the industrial arena. As the 1902 report of the United States Industrial Commission pointed out in words equally applicable today, industrial democracy is necessary to the proper functioning of political democracy:

> Only experience with democratic forms and methods can develop the good that is in democracy; but so far as employers take a long look ahead, and act in the interest of the ultimate welfare of society, it is believed that they will encourage rather than repress the growth of democratic government in their industries. . . . If they adopt a repressive policy they may perhaps succeed in it; but so long as the tradition of freedom is strong in the minds of the working people they cannot destroy the aspiration for a measure of self-government in respect to the most important part of life.[1]

The lack of industrial democracy at DuPont is particularly important in a company state like Delaware, where DuPont employees make up 11% of the work force.

## *Making Employment Policy*

As in most American corporations, management makes employment policy for DuPont. The board of directors sets employment policy for the whole company. Each member of the board's executive committee works as a liaison with a few industrial and staff departments; in this capacity, he can recommend that employment policies be instituted, vetoed, or presented to the board for revision. The employee relations department, responsible to the directors, advises the industrial departments about interpretations of the board's policies. General managers in each department control the day-to-day implementation of employment policy.

Next on the employee ladder are several levels of supervisors. Supervisors are supposed to inform employees of corporation policies and to keep top executives aware of employees' feelings. There is an inherent conflict between a supervisor's duty to those below him and his duty to those above. The problem is that advancement depends upon satisfying those above. Middle-level administrators thus identify upward with the interests of corporate directors. DuPont employees have no way to assure that supervisors will pass on correct information or fight for their grievances.

Nor do employees have any direct input into policy making. Work rules are set by the managers. For example, employees should definitely have a role in assuring plant safety. Although DuPont has a relatively good safety record in Delaware, some dangerous practices do exist. The company has tried to make a good safety record appear phenomenal by questionable tactics. According to many employees, injured workers are often transported from their sickbeds to work so that a statistician can report that no workdays have been lost due to accidents or injuries; blue-collar workers have also been singled out and severely reprimanded for minor injuries. This harassment has made employees reluctant to report minor injuries. Nonmanagerial employees on plant safety committees would presumably stop such practices, which victimize their peers for the sake of company image; but in negotiations with its Niagara Falls, New York, union, DuPont has refused even to bargain over union membership on safety committees. Even at the Newport, Delaware, plant, where administrative policies state that a union officer or representative should be included on accident investigation teams, no union member has participated in any of the several recent accident investigations, according to current union leaders.

Similarly, DuPont employees have no role in determining such personally important aspects of production as the work shift system. At Seaford the system is physically unhealthy and socially disruptive. A typical four-week schedule involves five shift changes. A worker begins the midnight shift on Friday and works the same shift until the next Friday, when he is off from 8 AM until he goes on the morning shift on Monday and Tuesday. He then has Wednesday and Thursday off, and on Friday he is back on the midnight shift. After a week of night work, he gets his weekend plus Monday and Tuesday off, works the 4 PM to midnight shift on Wednesday and Thursday, and on Friday returns to the night shift for another week. According to Richard Emory, president of the Seaford Independent Union, if employees were allowed to formulate the shift system with the help of independent medical advice, they would push for a system which kept each worker on the same schedule for at least a month at a time and would do away with the seven-day work week.

DuPont even refuses to provide employees with a copy of the rules implementing its union contract. The day-to-day working rules are made by top executives who leave interpretations to supervisors. During the 1970 contract negotiations, the Niagara Falls union asked management to provide every employee with a booklet explaining the work contract, so every employee could familiarize himself with procedures unhindered by discretionary or arbitrary interpretations by low-level managers. Their request was denied by the plant manager, who claimed, "We'd rather have supervision keep employees informed. If an employee has a question we will get the answer for him."[2]

Though it is stingy with objective information, the company is very generous with propaganda. One publication, *Better Living,* has a circulation of 30,000–40,000 in Delaware—more than any periodical distributed in the state, other than the DuPont-owned Wilmington daily newspapers. (*Newsweek* had fewer than 7000 subscribers in Delaware in 1968.) All DuPont publications are heavily censored by management to safeguard "trade secrets" and to ensure their managerial point of view. The subject of labor unions is taboo. A photo of polluted water near an oil refinery was held up until the word "Texaco" was airbrushed from the oil tanks. When *Better Living* took excerpts from the company's 1969 annual report, it excluded extremely positive data that might lead workers to expect more money and extremely negative facts that would foster anxiety among workers.

In these highly edited, often distorted publications, DuPont tries to convince employees that they have an effective voice in corporate policy making. DuPont continually assures employees that even in a giant corporation they are well cared for. The first page of one DuPont magazine emphasized that DuPont management takes great pains "to make sure that all its individual members shall experience no bar to personal satisfaction and a sense of accomplishment. For DuPont believes all people have a right to seek these rewards in whatever organizations they loyally serve."[3] It dispels any concern that the "individual . . . may lose his individuality" as being "more theoretical than factual." Since the truth falls short of this utopian stronghold of rugged individualism, DuPont tries to outflank reality by distinguishing the "voluntary conformity of behavior which constitutes good manners," which it claims is found at DuPont, from the "enforced conformity of thought which represents an invasion of personal rights."[4] It also sloughs off as abnormal those "infrequent" occasions when DuPont will "fail to meet the legitimate expectations of some employees, . . . since the best of supervisors are fallible."[5] In any case, if someone wants to leave

DuPont, there is always the "one advantage of an enterprise economy that the escape hatch is always close at hand." [6] DuPont claims to make efforts to ensure that it is not found guilty of "inadvertent sabotage of individual creativity and initiative." [7]

> To guard against this, DuPont management seeks to keep channels of communication open, to encourage the individual to speak his mind, and to place a premium on his imagination. The most jealously guarded right in DuPont is the right of the individual to hold his own opinions.[8]

The attempt to make the corporation appear like a huge, happy family has been taken to ridiculous extremes. One DuPont publication valiantly attempted to show that the low-income employee is not much different from his highly paid boss. Under a picture of bathers lolling under palm trees was the caption:

> Recreation of families with $100,000 income varies more in degrees than in kind from that of families with less income. Facilities they use usually differ little; people at all income levels make use of resorts and beaches.[9]

The company's elaborate efforts to convince its employees and the public of its benevolence and fair-mindedness, while impressive, do not square with realities in Delaware or elsewhere. In fact, as the following pages will show, DuPont comes very close to the very totalitarian, monolithic organizations its literature decries:

> In totalitarian countries today, the monolithic power of the state tends to the destruction of individual rights and personal dignity. . . . In the democratic society, the checks and balances of various institutions tend to ensure that the organization careless of the general welfare will be brought up short.[10]

To increase the role of workers in corporate policy making and to give them access to appropriate information, the Delaware Study Group proposed to DuPont management that workers' representatives be added to the company's board of directors. Such participation by workers in management has been tried, with varying success, in several European countries. In France, a plant committee composed of representatives of employees and employers is consulted on matters of organization and administration. In Germany, a system of codetermination has been instituted whereby nonmanagerial workers elect plant and office "works councils." Blue- and white-collar workers are represented on each council, but not management. The councils help determine wages, benefits, hiring and firing, and grievances. They also share authority with management over policies such as mergers or changes in production processes. These works councils in turn elect half the members of middle-level managerial and supervisory boards, and half the top-level "economic committee," which advises management on important economic matters for the company. Workers directly elect at least one-third of the directors of all large corporations in Germany. In Yugoslavia, workers' councils are the highest authority in a company, functioning somewhat like a board of directors. The council elects a managing board which assists with day-to-day plant management. The government of Norway recently announced an industrial democracy scheme whereby a "company assembly" would be interposed between management and the stockholders. One-third of the assembly (which would appoint the board of directors and review important management decisions) would be elected by workers.

Some variant of these approaches might be most appropriate for a large American company like DuPont. But neither C. B. McCoy, president of DuPont, nor Irenee du Pont, Jr., a vice president of the company, felt that nonmanagerial employees should have *any* representation in decision making. Irenee du Pont said nonmanagerial employees by definition could not develop both deep knowledge of company workings and a talent for directing large groups. This negativism precludes the democratic checks and balances DuPont claims are necessary for democracy, for there is no way employees can be sure their views are being given proper weight. The recent layoff of over 4000 DuPont workers in different parts of the country is a case in point. Without representation at decision-making levels, workers could not effectively argue for alternative cost-cutting moves.

According to Irenee du Pont, an employee who exhibits significant managerial skills is automatically put into management. The effect of this policy is to remove leaders from the ranks of workers. At Edgemoor, for instance, almost all union presidents during the past decade have become supervisors. This debilitates the already weak unions two ways: it gives union officers an incentive to water down opposition to management, and it siphons experienced leaders from the nonmanagerial work force.

### *White-collar Workers*

Most of the white-collar employees in DuPont's Delaware facilities are well-educated people with scientific or engineering backgrounds. They are competent to develop their ideas, market their talents, and make independent judgments on complex technical issues. But conditions of employment at DuPont prevent scientists and engineers from acting as conscientious professionals. Like many white-collar workers, they suffer from being unorganized while operating within a homogeneous, immobile job market. One student of management stated the problem facing professionals working for large corporations this way:

> The control structure of professions differs sharply from that of a typical bureaucracy. Within a profession, the source of discipline and reward is primarily the informal and essentially egalitarian structure of the colleague group. But within bureaucracies, discipline lies in an authoritarian hierarchy.[11]

Because of the company's much greater power, DuPont has been able to impose numerous working conditions to keep its white-collar employees in a state of dependency. They do not have a contract to define the rights and duties of employee and employer, giving both parties the advantages of definiteness and security. For an employee, the contract would guarantee him employment for the duration of the contract. Employers would be assured some continuity of an experienced work force. Without such a contract, DuPont employees are at the mercy of corporate whims, and this fact lies at the root of their dependency.

DuPont employees do sign an employee agreement with

the company (see Appendix 2), but this agreement constrains only the professionals, not the company. It establishes three rules: the employee shall never use or disclose any confidential information of the company without written permission, except as required by his duties for DuPont; the employee must promptly disclose all inventions made during his employment and must give DuPont full rights over his discoveries; upon the termination of his employment, he must promptly return all confidential materials relating to DuPont business.

The first clause of the employee agreement may severely hamper technicians' job mobility. Many DuPont employees are trained in a specialized area in college and graduate school; on taking a job with the company, they work in an even narrower area. The more expert an employee becomes in an area, the more he may be limiting his options because he cannot use elsewhere information or techniques learned at DuPont. Thus, the employee's skills are no more marketable than when he left college; in fact, he is worse off because his specialty is narrower and most employers prefer to hire recent graduates. DuPont itself hires 95% of its professional employees directly out of school.

The story of Donald Hirsch shows the practical application of the employee agreement to a man the company wants to keep. Hirsch, a key man in the development of a chloride process for manufacturing titanium dioxide, decided to quit and work for American Potash; he had not been able to get into the managerial stream at DuPont. Before Hirsch began working at Potash, DuPont obtained an injunction that limited Hirsch's employment with Potash. DuPont argued that Hirsch would inevitably use DuPont trade secrets in developing a chloride process for Potash, even though Potash had already agreed to purchase rights to a British process. Hirsch was not allowed to work for Potash in the chloride process field, his specialty. Not many such cases are needed for a firm like Potash to decide that it is not worth the threat of a lawsuit to hire a man like Hirsch or the expense of defending him, as Potash did. Nor is it long before other scientists realize that, as they make new discoveries, they have to accept DuPont as a lifetime employer.

The second clause of the employee agreement gives all results of an employee's creativity that relate to the "business or activities" of DuPont to the company, even if these discoveries are made *at home after working hours.* Since DuPont's business includes 1500 products which are in turn used in thousands of other products, almost any invention is "related to the business or activities of the Employer." Due to its size, DuPont can shelve patented ideas indefinitely. The company told the Delaware Study Group that it had no idea how many of the 3200 American and 10,700 foreign patents obtained by DuPont since 1965 have been used or might be used in the future. In addition to the dissatisfaction an unused patent may give its creator, this policy prevents public benefit from many undeveloped inventions. Whether DuPont releases a patent is now left to its own discretion.

With no rights guaranteed in the employee agreement, an employee with a problem has no recourse but the company's three-step grievance procedure. First, the employee discusses his problem with his immediate supervisor. Second, he can speak with any member of his line supervision, including the head of his laboratory, service, or production group. Third, if he feels that no satisfactory answer to his grievance has been or can be obtained through the line organization, he may discuss that matter with the site manager or someone designated by the site manager. This system is totally lacking in due process protection. The employee cannot confront his accuser or cross examine witnesses. He has no appeal to an independent body; appeals are made totally within a structure controlled by management. Employee complaints often concern the very supervisors to whom, under the grievance procedure, employees must bring problems.

Even aspects of the employment relationship designed to benefit employees further employee dependency. Among these are the bonus plan, the pension plan, and the system of performance reviews. Bonuses are earned for outstanding work during a year. Many technical employees earn a bonus year after year, and bonus payments may account for up to 30% of a professional's income. The bonus is paid in four equal annual payments, starting the year after the bonus is earned. If an employee quits or is fired before being paid all of his earned bonuses, he loses all outstanding bonus payments. Moreover, management reviews the employee's eligibility to receive each of the four installments. It is much easier to discipline a worker by cutting his bonus than by cutting his salary. DuPont management fully intended that bonuses be weapons against employees. One writer commented on the genesis of the bonus system during the first quarter of this century:

> In those meetings [of the High Explosives Department of DuPont] too, some of the beginnings of the famous DuPont bonus plans were developed. Bonuses were used as a means of disciplining the men in their general behavior and observance of rules, especially safety rules, and of holding the men from temporarily more lucrative employment.[12]

The DuPont pension plan is an extremely effective means of binding employees to the company. An employee is not awarded a pension unless he works for the company for at least ten years.* Nor are pension rights transferable from DuPont to other chemical companies or businesses. The long period of service required and the nontransferability of pension rights decrease an employee's job mobility. Further, the pension plan contains a cancelation clause:

> If the Board of Benefits and Pensions, after a hearing at which a former employee who was retired or otherwise terminated shall be entitled to be present, shall find that he has, at any time, willfully engaged in any activity which is harmful to the interest of the Company, all rights to any payments under this Plan attributable to his service shall be forthwith cancelled.

The chilling effect of this vague clause is obvious. If, as some executives maintain, the clause is merely meant to prevent former employees from spilling trade and business secrets, there is no reason for its all-inclusive sweep. Former DuPont executive Russell W. Peterson felt compelled to obtain the company's written exemption from the cancelation clause when he was elected governor of Delaware; he wanted to maintain his pension rights, despite what he

* Until 1971, pension rights vested after 15 years.

might do as a governor that could be construed as "harmful to the interest of the company." Former employees who talked with the Delaware Study Group were often afraid to have their names mentioned in this book lest the company cancel pension payments. Note also that final determination is not subject to outside review except in the courts—an expensive procedure for a pensioner. Nor does the former employee have any rights when he appears before the Board of Benefits and Pension; this procedure is devoid of due process protection in the same way as DuPont's grievance procedure.

The annual performance review and appraisal is another mechanism which can easily be used against an employee, even though it is purportedly for his benefit. At these reviews, employees discuss their future in the company with one or more of their supervisors. Two researchers from Harvard Business School found this kind of review to be "harmful to the low-rated men and of little help in boosting the performance of higher-rated men." [13] According to several DuPont employees, reviews are often used to coerce resignations from employees who have fallen into disfavor with a supervisor. Performance reviews are also used to divide employees. Rather than evaluating all employees individually by an objective standard, supervisors evaluate an employee's "attitude" toward DuPont and his productivity relative to other employees in his skill groups. This method of comparative evaluation encourages conflict and rivalry in employee groups.

Other subtle mechanisms reinforce the divisiveness produced by the performance review. For instance, DuPont does not provide information for employees about general wage levels within the company. This policy of secrecy prevents employees from perceiving individual complaints as group deprivations and from banding together on these issues. In 1968 DuPont found that its rate of resignations had gone up; one reason, corporate officials found, was "salary administration. Many of our people are greatly concerned about their lack of information in this area." [14] But the company response was not to provide more information to its employees. It merely reiterated its shopworn statement: "Our company policy is to pay in the upper bracket of salaries paid in the better-paying companies for positions of equivalent responsibility."

These policies together make the employee powerless in his dealings with the company. An insecure employee is susceptible to company pressures; he is more likely to shape his own attitudes and behavior to conform to what he thinks his superiors expect of him. Lacking the legal protection of an employment contract, even independent thinkers may find themselves slowly molded by the company's efforts to foster dependency.

DuPont justifies its treatment of white-collar workers with two types of assertions: first, that DuPont is good to its employees; second, that dissatisfied employees can always leave. The first is a matter of opinion, and DuPont's is inherently biased and flies in the face of strong contrary evidence. The second is wishful thinking. Most scientists or engineers have no sources of employment other than companies like DuPont. Sometimes large corporations may be reluctant to hire someone with specialized expertise who was either fired by DuPont or who resigned. Also, employees become so tied down in Wilmington, so constrained by pension plan and attenuated bonus payments, that to leave would impose great professional and financial burdens.

Extensive evidence contradicts DuPont's assertions of its own fairness and goodness, and more would probably be available were the company less secretive; furthermore, the lack of an employment contract, the inadequate grievance procedure, and the broadly defined trade secret doctrine probably reduce the number of complaining white-collar workers still further, because they are unprotected against employer reprisals.

A Ph.D. chemist, whom we shall call Paul, joined DuPont's plastics department in 1948; he received a bonus for outstanding work for 12 years. In 1962 the laboratory director of the fabrics and finishes department (F&F) urged Paul to transfer to his department; Paul did so with the understanding that, for a reasonable period, his old job would be kept open. He received even larger bonuses for three more years until a new director took over in 1965. Paul got no bonus that year because, the new man explained, he did not finish a certain piece of work. Paul felt the director himself had caused the delay. At his next performance review and appraisal in 1966, he received a poor rating. Feeling that his personal relationship with the new director was steadily worsening, Paul asked to be transferred out of F&F. The suggestion was never taken up. His performance reviews grew worse; in February, 1970, he was notified that he would be fired in two months unless his work improved. Although he had received bonuses his first three years at F&F, the notice began: "Since transferring from the Plastics Department in 1962, your performance has varied from unacceptable to marginally acceptable." Paul asked the man who had recommended him for three bonuses in F&F to defend his performance; the man never responded. In April, at age 50, Paul was fired.

With no contract or independent grievance procedure, Paul had no effective way to appeal his dismissal for what, in his opinion, were unjustifiable reasons. At 50, his possibilities of finding further employment as a chemist are slim. Furthermore, DuPont's trade secrets policy makes other companies reticent to hire men like Paul for fear of a lawsuit claiming unfair competition.

Outside the plant, DuPont similarly restrains white-collar workers. According to the company, an employee's outside life is entirely his own: "There is a sharp dividing line between the company's area of interest and [the worker's]. . . . Beyond that line DuPont does not intrude." [15] But for years, DuPont has run an extensive campaign to inculcate its viewpoint on business and politics in employees. It promoted its viewpoint through the *DuPont Facts Book,* "designed to help you convey an accurate picture of DuPont and of American industry. Every opportunity should be taken to discuss these facts with friends, community groups, and others." [16] Employees were encouraged to use "data employed in speeches by other DuPont men" [17] in their conversations. DuPont developed a course, HOBSO,* to "inoculate blue-collar employees against creeping socialism." [18]

In the early 1950s, DuPont politics were openly conservative. The January, 1950, copy of *Management News-*

* HOBSO is the acronym for How Our Business System Operates.

*letter* offered free copies of Flynn's *The Road Ahead,* which detailed, said the newsletter, how British socialism was failing and why national planning is bad. The back cover of the May–June, 1952, edition of *Better Living* had a picture of Karl Marx and Groucho Marx, with the caption "which Marx gets the biggest laugh?" The text read:

> The Marx, named Karl, founder of communism, was a dour character who lived in the 19th century. A deadpan kind of comic of the Buster Keaton-Ned Sparks type, his act was to say funny things as though they weren't funny at all. . . . Groucho can stick to romantic roles, where both he and his countless admirers will have more fun. We'll stick to Karl. He's the biggest laugh of all times.

The November–December, 1952, *Better Living* contained a photo essay, showing a DuPont employee and his wife in a bungalow surrounded by luxuries. Then they were shown clumping about in drab, ill-fitting clothing, with glum expressions and slumping shoulders—their lot if they were Russian workers. The level of communication was sufficiently primitive to insult the intelligence of DuPont employees.

DuPont encourages employees to participate in politics. As Crawford Greenewalt said when he was president of DuPont: business people have not been "active enough in their own behalf." [19] While other elements in society have resorted to "shrill cries," Greenewalt argued, the business community has "all too often pleaded its case in whispers." To rectify the low level of business impact on government, Mr. Greenewalt endorsed

> the principle of political participation of business people, for it is obviously essential that their point of view, representing the largest and most widespread influence in our national life, should be clearly expressed. . . . Businessmen are already beginning to see that government, like parenthood, requires personal attention.[20]

For all this encouragement, however, DuPont sometimes harasses employees who take the "wrong" side of public issues. Harassment can include ostracism, giving employees meaningless tasks, or subjecting them to intense and unpleasant supervision.

One good example of harassment for political activity involved several DuPont employees who opposed the building of an oil pipeline by a joint venture of oil companies. The confrontation between company and employees began in 1963, when Colonial Pipeline's Texas to New York pipeline reached the area of Pennsylvania bordering on Delaware, where many DuPont employees live. Residents of the area organized in opposition. Their research found that the pipe was thin, poorly welded, brittle, and inadequately protected from corrosion. Using x-ray photography, the landowners determined that 10 welds out of a sample of 41 were unsatisfactory. With these photographs and testimony from several DuPont engineers who provided expertise to deal with technically sophisticated problems of pipeline safety, the landowners filed a complaint with the Public Utilities Commission (PUC) in Pennsylvania.

The DuPont Company's interest in the pipeline conflicted with the public's interest in safety. DuPont sold tetraethyl lead and explosives to the oil companies, and explosives to the pipeline contractors. DuPont therefore tried to stop the engineers, even though they worked against the pipeline primarily on their own time. One division manager refused to allow an employee to testify before the PUC. About five employees were told by their supervisors to curtail their involvement in the issue. Another employee was invited to the house of a tetraethyl lead sales supervisor and told to stop harassing the oil companies. An officer of the American Society of Mechanical Engineers told a DuPont engineer he would make a good ASME officer if he quieted down.

All but one of the DuPont employees gave in. A DuPont engineer, whom we shall call Ed, was warned by his division manager not to go into New Jersey to look at the pipeline and, generally, not to fight the pipeline. One Sunday afternoon when Ed was away from the Wilmington area, he stopped at a spot in New Jersey where the pipeline was not yet buried. The next week, after DuPont learned of the trip, his division manager told him that he had disobeyed orders and might be fired. Ed demanded to talk to his chief engineer. At a subsequent meeting with several superiors, the chief engineer put Ed on probation before he even had a chance to defend his actions. Ed received no bonus that year, cutting his salary 30%. Soon thereafter, he quit.

The Delaware Study Group was often told about employees penalized for involvement in political affairs. Much of this harassment cannot be laid to explicit company policy, but it derives from the company's refusal to protect employees from arbitrary behavior by supervisors. During the 1964 presidential campaign, two DuPont scientists who actively supported Lyndon Johnson received abusive telephone calls from employees in their department, and after the election one was told by a supervisor, who had tried to shield him from pressure, that these political activities had hurt his relations with the company.

DuPont's employee agreement sometimes forces employees to keep silent about harmful or defective products. In 1970 the Federal Trade Commission (FTC) charged that DuPont Zerex antifreeze may aggravate the clogging of car radiators, and asserted that the television advertisement for Zerex used an invalid demonstration and failed to note that Zerex "could or might cause damage to automotive cooling systems." DuPont defended its advertisements by denying the FTC allegations. According to the company, all complaints had been investigated and dirty and corroded cooling systems, not Zerex, caused the damage. However, several months before the FTC charges were made public, a former DuPont chemist familiar with some of DuPont's research on Zerex told the Delaware Study Group that he knew Zerex antifreeze was clogging radiators. He did not make his information public: he would have received a bad recommendation from DuPont for his next job application, and the company might have charged him with violating his oath of confidentiality. Those who know most about a product are forbidden through the employee agreement to divulge information considered to be confidential that would expose possible product defects.

## *Blue-collar Workers: DuPont and its Unions*

Labor unions are a countervailing force within corporate government designed to hold management accountable to employee interests and give nonmanagerial employees a voice in decision making through collective bargaining. The United States Industrial Commission, created by Congress in 1898, stressed the importance of industrial unions in its 1902 report:

> By the organization of labor, and by no other means, is it possible to introduce an element of democracy into the government of industry. By this means only can the workers effectively take part in determining the conditions under which they work.

But DuPont's blue-collar workers have only weak, independent unions to represent their interests. The economic power of DuPont unions is so tiny, particularly next to the power of DuPont's over $3 billion in annual sales, that one DuPont union officer remarked: "We're not company dominated. We're so weak that the company doesn't have to dominate us."

DuPont has tried to "render labor unions unnecessary in the eyes of employees," according to John Oliver, head of DuPont's employee relations department. Throughout its history, DuPont has maintained an image of the "benevolent" employer. In the 1800s DuPont provided company-owned housing for its workers. It established a bonus plan in the early 1900s, and one of the first industrial pension plans in the country. These provisions helped DuPont build an image of altruism. Present blue-collar workers, heir to the myth, have been led to believe that as the company gives, so it may take away—unilaterally and capriciously. The dialectic—the workers' gratefulness and their fear of reprisal—permits DuPont to abuse and co-opt unions with impunity.

### OPPOSING UNION ORGANIZATION

DuPont is one of the few large U.S. corporations without an international union representing most of its employees; no single international union represents DuPont employees at more than four plants in the country; no plants in the Delaware area are affiliated with an international union. Thus workers have no access to nationwide labor expertise—professional negotiators, plentiful strike funds, and research facilities—which an international union could provide. The company defeated a recent attempt by employees at the Experimental Station outside Wilmington to join Oil, Chemical, and Atomic Workers, AFL-CIO, an international union.

Workers from the Experimental Station asked the OCAW to help them organize lower-level employees at the station. After learning of the organization drive, management introduced a new progression and classification system for nonsalaried laboratory personnel, alleviating a problem which had generated interest in the union. Workers who had received nothing more than overall wage adjustments for 10 or 15 years were suddenly given raises.

Still, interest in the union increased throughout the spring of 1969. In June, DuPont created a new position of site manager, to be responsible for employee relations and administration of the Experimental Station. The company chose William Eckstein, a gregarious and amiable individual with a reputation for fairness in his dealings with unions, who met workers for coffee and bowled with them. Eckstein initiated a series of management information bulletins to help "improve communication." After the organization effort failed, the bulletins came out quite infrequently. Eckstein succeeded in making it clear that DuPont would deal firmly with the union, while bolstering the image of management as the friend of employees.

As a second tactic, DuPont organized supervisors and research scientists against the union. Meetings were held to educate research personnel about the disadvantages of the union. After these lessons, the white-collar workers carried the company's campaign against the union to the blue-collar workers.

DuPont's third tactic was to argue that OCAW could offer the workers no benefits that DuPont would not give them. One management information bulletin included a detailed comparison of the salaries and benefits of employees at the Experimental Station with those of employees represented by OCAW at the nearby Avisun Corporation film plant. The comparison did not show that DuPont was significantly larger and richer than Avisun. A second bulletin cited the lower wages paid at a DuPont facility in

Alabama where the OCAW represents employees. It did not point out that the cost of living and wages in Alabama are far lower overall than in Delaware. Nor did it say that OCAW represents only a single DuPont plant and has no leverage to overcome DuPont's policy of paying wages based on general community wage levels. The second bulletin also compared the Birmingham union member's total *yearly dues* since 1960 to the wage increases for the same period—but expressed only in *cents per hour,* thus conveying the misimpression that wage increases were less than the amount of union dues. Furthermore, it never connected the seemingly low wage increases to DuPont's own wage policy.

Finally, the company began to revise employment policies in the *Handbook for Employees.* Management promised to correct most grievances through these revisions, according to employees. The company solicited workers' suggestions, but only a few minor changes based on the suggestions were incorporated. DuPont thus created a façade of responsiveness to dissipate support for the union.

Management's token changes and skillful propaganda apparently worked. In October, 1969, the union began distributing cards among employees for signatures that would authorize the union to hold a representation election. Records of the card signing indicate that signing progressed at a good pace until a rumor was circulated that the signed cards would lead to recognition of the union rather than to a representation election. Less than two months after OCAW began distributing cards, the union gave up.

Employees at the Experimental Station are as powerless as they were before. No blue-collar employees have served on the 17-man committee that has been rewriting the *Handbook for Employees.* No blue-collar employees serve on the committees that determine policy at the Experimental Station. Several employees, both pro-union and antiunion, told the Delaware Study Group there was little indication management would institute further improvements like the ones it made to undermine the union's organization attempt.

At Edgemoor, DuPont managers used less subtle methods when they feared the replacement of the independent union by an international. Officials of the 550-member independent Edgemoor union notified the plant manager in February, 1969, that they wished to begin negotiations on a new contract to replace the one due to expire on April 30. In March, before negotiations began, the union told management it planned to include advisors from other unions in its negotiating committee. The DuPont Edgemoor union had no members who worked full time on union matters or who were experienced, professional negotiators. To enhance their bargaining power, therefore, the executive committee of the union voted to have John Oshinski—regional director of District 50 of the United Mine Workers—assist the contract negotiating committee.

Oshinski accompanied the union committee to the second negotiation meeting on March 31. On the advice of the DuPont legal and employee relations departments, the Edgemoor plant manager announced he could not negotiate while Oshinski was present, and walked out of the meeting, along with the management negotiating team. The union considered this a "refusal to bargain," an unfair labor practice, and charged the company with a violation of the National Labor Relations Act.

DuPont was subsequently found guilty by the National Labor Relations Board because it would not negotiate in Oshinski's presence. The trial examiner stipulated:

> It is well settled that, absent special circumstances, it is a violation of Section 8(a)(5) [of the National Labor Relations Act] for an employer to condition bargaining on a change in the identity of the Union's negotiator or in the composition of the Union's bargaining team.

The NLRB also rejected DuPont's argument that the union conspired with Oshinski to permit the old contract to expire, thereby preparing for a takeover of the Edgemoor union by Oshinski's international:

> The fact that a particular bargaining tactic is pursued in order to pave the way for an ultimate change in the parties' bargaining relationship, including abdication in favor of another union, does not justify refusing to bargain at all. In a strikingly similar case (*Minnesota Mining and Manufacturing Company,* 173 NLRB 47, enforced 72 LRRM

2129, C.A. 8, 1969), the Board adopted the following findings of the Trial Examiner: "Whatever may be the Company's fears, and howsoever accurate its prognostication and its discernment of the Union's ultimate aims, the Company here and now is under a duty to bargain with whatever representatives the Union chooses to send."

For six months DuPont had effectively blocked the union at Edgemoor from cooperating with an international union and from bargaining on a contract. That it lost the decision was of little consequence to DuPont at this point. Management had won time. During negotiations, management unilaterally gave a wage increase while refusing to include wages in the contract or in contract negotiations with the union. The union thus had no role in setting the wage hike, decreasing its usefulness in the view of employees. DuPont encouraged the election of a slate of union officers widely viewed as promanagement. Those union leaders challenging the traditional impotence of DuPont unions were removed. The new officers voted not to include Oshinski or any international union in the negotiations. The new contract, signed in January, 1970, was so weak that the union's attorney, Joseph Craven, stated in an interview with the study group that the employees would have been in a stronger position if they had not signed it.

### DIVIDE AND CONQUER

Just as DuPont has kept its independent unions from affiliating with international unions, so it has undercut union power by keeping the unions at each DuPont facility isolated from each other. DuPont has fought every union move to strengthen the Federation of Independent Unions–DuPont Systems (FIU–DS). The federation's 17 member unions nominally seek to bargain nationally about the DuPont industrial relations plans.* However, in the face of management opposition, the federation has become merely a way to exchange information among members. A good example of DuPont's battle against the federation occurred

* The industrial relations plans are the vacation plan, disability wage plan, length of service rules, group accident and health insurance plan, special benefits plan, pension and retirement plan, contributory and noncontributory group life insurance plans, salary allotment insurance plan, and the thrift plan.

at the Carney's Point Works, across from Wilmington on the Jersey side of the Delaware.

Carney's Point employees have been represented by an independent union for 27 years. In 1956 the union adopted a new name, the United Chemical Workers, with no objection from the company. In 1959 the United Chemical Workers held an election to determine whether to join the federation. Two days before the vote, the plant manager at Carney's Point wrote each employee, predicting, "Joining the Federation under its present constitution and in view of its present activities, could spell the end of the Carney's Point Union as an independent bargaining agency." Nevertheless, the Carney's Point union has remained a member of the federation for the past 11 years and retains its autonomy.

In February, 1968, the union voted to add "Local 4, Federation of Independent Unions–DuPont System" to its name. The change did not alter the relationships between the union and the federation nor between the union and management; it involved no change in union leadership or membership. However, DuPont refused to recognize the new name. On July 18, the company wrote the union:

> As we clearly stated in our second meeting of July 11, 1968, we are most anxious to proceed with the negotiation of all the incumbent Union's proposals other than the said "NAME CHANGE" proposal; and we again affirm our desire to continue our meetings with you in an attempt to consummate and execute an extended Bargaining Agreement with the United Chemical Workers, the traditional representative of our employees.

When union and management agreed on a new contract in late September, the company refused to sign the contract if the union used its new name. A management note to supervisors, marked Personal & Confidential and dated October 3, 1968, indicates how far the company would go to bypass the name change:

> It is most important for you to keep in mind that we cannot legally, nor are we willing even if it were legal, agree to a contract with any group purporting to represent the employees other than the United Chemical Workers.

Professor Clyde Summers, a prominent expert in labor law, characterized DuPont's muscle-flexing in this instance as an "outrageous example of management shoving a weak union around, like a strong man clobbering someone else just to remind him how strong he is."

To verify member support for its new name, union leaders decided to hold a representation election supervised by the National Labor Relations Board, rather than spend time and money litigating an unfair labor practice charge. During the weeks before the election, management distributed a torrent of propaganda. In "Memos to Management," "294 Messages" (short, spicy diatribes that could be dialed over the telephone from home or work), "Carney's Point Work Fact Sheets," and letters to employees, management tried to create the impression that the new name represented an entirely different union. But DuPont did not stop here. The union was portrayed as a new outside force trying to dominate the workers.

The workers did not give up. By a margin greater than three to one, they accepted their union's new name. DuPont still refused to sign the contract, even though the NLRB found the United Chemical Workers, Local 4, FIU–DS, to be the successor to the United Chemical Workers. The union once again went to the NLRB with an unfair labor practice charge; when the board issued a complaint against DuPont, the company agreed to implement most provisions of the 1968 agreement. But the settlement was reached after the 1968 contract had expired in 1970. The Carney's Point union has worked without a contract for over three years and has been unable to negotiate a new contract with management.

### REFUSAL TO BARGAIN

By maintaining a weak union organization, the DuPont Company has sufficient power to be more than just a tough bargainer. With impunity, DuPont can and does refuse to bargain over legally *mandatory* subjects of collective bargaining, that is, over wages, hours, and other terms and conditions of employment that cannot be set by management without first bargaining with the appropriate union.

The federation, originally intended to unite the independent unions to map out strategies for dealing with DuPont, has attempted in vain to bargain on behalf of member unions for the companywide industrial relations plans. The plans include pension and insurance benefits, ruled as mandatory subjects of bargaining by the federal courts;[21] a federal court of appeals has ruled that a refusal to bargain over such topics was "an attempt to bypass the union, and an attempt to disparage its importance and usefulness in the eyes of its members," and as such, was an unfair labor practice.[22]

In response to the federation's attempt to bargain, the company argued, in a letter dated August 21, 1969, that it preferred to bargain with each local unit about the industrial relations plans, and that

> it is [our] opinion that effective bargaining has regularly taken place with each appropriate local unit, since no Union at any location is required to accept the Industrial Relations Plans and Practices.

But according to the DuPont method of negotiating, the plant manager, who ostensibly is bargaining with the union, has no authority to alter or change these plans. According to union negotiators, the Carney's Point manager has said he could not bargain for changes in the industrial relations plans; he must pass any request on to top management in Wilmington. The only recent change in the pension and retirement plan, for example, was presented as a management proposal to stockholders at an annual meeting, as required by company bylaws.

When the Niagara Falls union asked if industrial relations plans could be bargained about on a local basis, management referred to the catch clause in the employment contract which states that the plans are subject

> to such modifications as may be hereafter adopted generally by the company to govern such privileges, provided, however, that as long as any one of these company plans and practices is in effect within the company, it shall not be withdrawn from the employees covered by this Agreement.[23]

This clause is in every union contract with DuPont and prevents the changing of a single plan at any plant. When the Niagara Falls union asked if the local plant manager could change a plan at the union's request, the plant manager replied that *all* of the plans had to be scratched if any change in *one* of the companywide plans was contemplated.

The DuPont Company also refuses to bargain over wages with unions during contract negotiations or to include wages in the employment contract, while at the same time it unilaterally hands out wage increases to employees. At Edgemoor in April, 1964, DuPont offered the union wage increases ranging from 18¢ to 22¢ per hour. On the same date, the same wage offer was made to at least five other plants in the Delaware area. The unions were not bargaining together at the time. Again, in April, 1971, plants in the Delaware area received the same wage increase even though the unions had not requested one. Wage hikes sought by unions have been granted only if the request coincided with a management decision to give a wage increase. Several years ago, the union at DuPont's Newport plant sought a wage raise before management offered one. The plant manager refused to talk to the union, saying they were due for a big raise in a few months. And, in 1964, the union at the Carney's Point plant asked for an across-the-board raise of 5¢ per hour; the plant manager said he could not grant it. Ten days later, the company gave an 8¢-to-10¢ per hour wage hike that had been planned for several months. Clearly, DuPont unions are futilely trying to bargain with plant managers who have no power to negotiate over wages.

Rather than bargaining with unions over wages, DuPont sets wage increases according to the general wage levels in a community. John Oliver, head of the Employee Relations Department, explained in an interview with the study group:

> The company policy, which is the only involvement we have, is that the DuPont Company shall pay wages in the upper bracket of wages paid for similar work in the community in which the individual performs his duty for DuPont, and this varies depending upon the community variability.

But wages are a mandatory subject of collective bargaining under the National Labor Relations Act. DuPont's refusal to bargain for wage increases with each separate union during contract negotiations is an unfair labor practice; so is the company's action to unilaterally set general wage increases.[24] As the United States Supreme Court said in *NLRB* v. *Crompton-Highland Mills:*

> The opening which a raise in pay makes for the correction of existing inequities amongst employees and for the possible substitution of shorter hours, vacations or sick leave, in lieu of some part of the proposed increase in pay, suggest the infinite opportunities for bargaining that are inherent in an announced readiness of an employer to increase generally the pay of its employees.[25]

Numerous regulations of plant working conditions, contained in the supplement to the union contract or in the plant rulebook, *Administrative Plans and Practices,* are subject to unilateral change by management and are never discussed with the union. DuPont management wants to be free to change agreements with unions without having to bargain. In an interview with the Delaware Study Group, John Oliver, head of the employee relations department, acknowledged:

> There are issues frequently that management is willing to agree to under today's circumstances, but are not willing to include in the contract which in turn obligates them to bargain over those issues or changes in those issues, really as a future contract is bargained. And I may be willing today to operate under this set of circumstances on those issues, but I want to be free to informally change those agreements with the unions if the circumstances are such that I feel as a manager I can no longer live with those. So I'm willing to contract for some and I'm willing to agree to some under today's circumstances, but not contract for them.

While a desire to keep some policies and practices out of the contract is perhaps a reasonable position for both the union and management, such exclusions must be the result of negotiations, or they are an unfair labor practice.[26]

At Edgemoor, the company avoids bargaining on many vital issues by hiding them in the supplement. Employees have no share in deciding what goes into the supplement. The union is not normally consulted on changes and does not get copies of revisions made in the supplement. The supplement contains policies on items such as overtime, call-in provision, and split-week scheduling—which should not be considered management prerogatives. *Administrative Policies and Practices* for the Newport plant also contains numerous provisions normally bargained for collectively: clothing allowances, safety shoes, vacation policies that differ from the companywide vacation plans, certain wage practices, and job advancement tests. While the Newport contract contains provisions that are uniform throughout DuPont, *Administrative Policies and Practices* contains provisions peculiar to the Newport plant. These variations on companywide policies are usually the stuff for local-level bargaining; yet these are precisely the items *not* bargained for locally at DuPont. Safety rules, like vacation plans, are mandatory subjects for collective bargaining.[27] For DuPont not to bargain about the exclusion of these and other subjects of collective bargaining from the union contract or the bargaining process is an unfair labor practice.

In addition, DuPont refuses to bargain about an "agency" shop arrangement, whereby all employees in a plant who benefit from union efforts pay union dues. DuPont unions have repeatedly sought such a clause, but DuPont management at both the Carney's Point and Newport plants has told those unions that the DuPont Company would never agree to an agency shop, regardless of what the union was willing to give up in return. The federal courts have already held that union security clauses, such as an agency shop provision, must be bargained about by employers when presented by a union for negotiation.[28]

The overall effect of DuPont's bargaining tactics are strikingly similar to those of General Electric, known as "Boulwareism." In declaring GE's labor tactics an unfair labor practice, the United States Court of Appeals said:

> The Board found that GE's bargaining stance and conduct, considered as a whole, was designed to derogate the Union in the eyes of its members and the public at large. This plan had two major facets: first, a take-it-or-leave-it approach ("firm, fair offer") to negotiations in general that emphasized both the powerlessness and weakness of the Union to its members, and second, a communications program that pictured the Company as the true defender of the em-

ployees' interests further denigrating the Union, and sharply curbing the Company's ability to change its own position.[29]

HOW TO BREAK A STRIKE

As a result of the tough bargaining practices of DuPont management, both legal and illegal, DuPont unions cannot mount any *successful* economic pressure, such as a strike, against the company. From October, 1970, to March, 1971, a DuPont union did strike DuPont. The story of the strike against DuPont's Niagara Falls plant exemplifies how DuPont uses its economic power to break a strike and cripple independent unions that challenge its authoritarian approach to labor relations.*

DuPont showed its usual unwillingness to bargain during negotiation sessions between the union and Niagara Falls plant management in August and September, 1970. Management responded to only one of the union's 18 to 20 contract proposals and made a "final offer" to the union on September 21, refusing to negotiate over any counteroffers from the union. The 1100-member union rejected management's contract proposal on October 1 and went on strike. When the strike did not dissolve quickly, a new production process planned for the Niagara Falls plant was shifted to a DuPont plant in Illinois, cutting back the number of jobs available at Niagara in the future. The company flew in supervisors and scientists from Chambers Works and research facilities near Wilmington to work as strikebreakers. Outfitted in company-provided work clothes, they worked, ate, and slept in the plant for two-week tours of duty. They would return to Delaware for two weeks, then go back to Niagara Falls. They were paid extra wages and given special vacation benefits. One Delaware researcher for DuPont who worked at Niagara Falls during the strike told the study group that he and other employees had no alternative but to "volunteer" for the Niagara assignment.

The Federation of Independent Unions, to which the Niagara union belonged, and Chambers Works blue-collar employees, from whose plant strikebreakers were drawn,

* The story of the Niagara Falls strike is important for an understanding of why no Delaware unions have struck the company in recent history, and how the divided Delaware unions would be unable to aid each other if a strike against DuPont were ever to occur in the state.

failed to support the strike effectively. Short sympathy demonstrations were held in the Delaware area in March, 1971, by unions at Edgemoor, Newport, Repauno, and Carney's Point. These demonstrations were held on lunch hours with no work stoppages or slowdowns. Delaware area unions made only small financial contributions to the essentially nonexistent strike fund. But at Chambers Works, blue-collar employees worked as "temporary foremen" to replace the supervisors who were away strikebreaking.

Management put out a barrage of propaganda about how fairly DuPont was treating the strikers to keep employees from rebelling about the strikebreaking. A letter sent on February 19, 1971, to employees of Chambers Works reported that the first Niagara strike vote passed by a small margin, but neglected to mention that 800 of the 1100 members of the Niagara Falls union had later voted to continue the strike. The memo then justified the use of strikebreakers by arguing that 1000 Chambers Works employees would be laid off if the Niagara plant stopped operating. The last line of the memo said, "Jobs at the Niagara Falls Plant are being protected [by management continuing to operate the plant with supervisory personnel] so that there will be something to return to when the strike is settled." However, after the strike was settled, 70 workers at Niagara Falls immediately lost their jobs, and numerous employees were demoted.

During the strike, Niagara supervisors had called union members known to be promanagement (or at least not strongly pro-union) to encourage them to elect a new slate of officers who would end the strike. A group of dissident, promanagement union members forced a union vote on management's return-to-work offer. When union leaders called for a vote in February, management's proposals were rejected by a margin of 600. After the long session of strikebreaking, however, the situation changed. Dissident leaders, again with active management encouragement, ran for election in March and won the top three positions in the union. The new union president is a close associate of the plant manager, and his brother is a member of DuPont management. Negotiations were resumed in April, 1971. The former negotiating committee for the union was reelected on April 5, but the new president dissolved the committee and proclaimed himself sole negotiator. He made no proposals at the April 7 meeting with management; he merely accepted everything management offered or demanded. The contract was signed on April 12, 1971. The only changes from management's original "final offer" of September, 1970, were in the date for the observance of Good Friday, a new Blue Cross–Blue Shield plan that was never discussed with the union, and a slight change in the new grievance procedure.

### POWERLESS EMPLOYEES

DuPont's efforts to undercut a strong union front and its refusal to bargain in good faith have severe psychological implications for blue-collar employees. In negotiations with unions and during labor organization efforts, DuPont capitalizes on employees' knowledge of their unions' weakness. Employees see DuPont as their only possible benefactor. Company literature portrays unions as outsiders who threaten the personal relationship between the worker and DuPont. The company implies that benevolent employee relations policies will continue only so long as unions are excluded from decision making. DuPont allegedly screens job applicants for union attitudes, thereby acquiring a disproportionately large number of employees with negative or neutral attitudes toward worker organizations. Moreover, the lack of rules governing the workplace leads each employee to hope for special breaks from supervisors, increasing his sense of subjugation to the corporation and decreasing any sense of a community of interest among employees. DuPont's continued opposition to the Federation of Independent Unions–DuPont System and to the affiliation of any independent DuPont union with an international union is designed to maintain this isolation and division within the community of DuPont employees.

At the same time, favorable aspects of employment at DuPont reinforce the psychology of powerlessness among employees. Most DuPont industrial plants are highly modernized, with continuous, enclosed operations and few open batch operations that expose workers to highly hazardous conditions. A study of production workers in an automated chemical plant similar to most DuPont operations showed that while alienation of workers from their jobs was less intense than that of workers in an automobile assembly plant, their degree of loyalty to and dependency on the corporate employer was greater.[30] Since working conditions at DuPont are relatively decent, the company is free of many abuses that have traditionally provoked union organizing. Through DuPont's highly publicized safety program, resulting in relatively safe working conditions, indoctrinated employees feel that DuPont is doing them a favor. As a result, DuPont blue-collar employees tend to work for DuPont for life, unless they are fired early.[31] With second and third generation blue-collar workers from the same family employed by DuPont, many employees feel almost fated to be at DuPont for life and have little incentive to fight for their interests within the company.

These positive reinforcements are buttressed by a series of harsh penalties which workers see imposed upon those who fight hard for unions or against the company. The workers' perception of these penalties is rooted in the extremely antiunion position conveyed to workers by top management. John Oliver, director of the employee relations department, told the study group that if there were no labor unions at DuPont plants, it "would be the ideal that I think would be best for the DuPont Company, and I at the same time feel that it would be best for the employees."

DuPont management has on occasion made its policies regarding pro-union employees quite explicit. In a letter circulated to supervisors at Carney's Point by the employee relations department, DuPont lays out a procedure to "get rid of unwanted employees":

> In some cases, a little risk is preferable to months and even years of frustration. And in suggesting this we refer, frankly, to cases involving employees, who, in management's judgment, are unsatisfactory and unwanted, for one reason or another. Most such employees fall into one or more of these four categories. . . .
>
> 4. In *non-union* companies, employees whose pro-union attitude and activities make them unsatisfactory employees, but whose work and conduct are at least average or better and must, therefore, be regarded as satisfactory.

> Management's problem in all these cases is to get rid of these unwanted employees and make it 'stick.' . . .
>
> Management alertness plus prompt, decisive action can be achieved only if and when three things are done—
>
> 1. These unwanted, marginal employees have to be *identified* in the minds of those management people who (a) are in a position to *see* or *hear* opportunities to take action and (b) who, in the company's normal practice, participate in decisions involving dismissal.
> 2. The persons referred to in point (1) above, have to be made aware of the fact they are expected to *coordinate swiftly* when and as opportunities to take action against marginal employees occur.
> 3. When opportunities to take action against marginal employees do occur, those who *recognize* the opportunity and those who *participate* in the decision have to have the *will* to act promptly and decisively.[32]

As a result of these positive reinforcements and negative penalties, DuPont has built up a love-hate relationship with its workers, symbolized by the nickname "Uncle Dupie." Workers expect the company to take care of them; they begin to believe the company line that there is no need for a union because DuPont is so good to its workers. On the other hand, workers live in fear of their uncle; they know better than to step out of line. Because of this unequal relationship, workers are deprived of the right to make important decisions affecting them and to participate in a system of industrial democracy. While DuPont may provide workers with benefits or wage increases, these workers can neither choose which benefits they want nor demand the wages they need. DuPont has made a calculated trade-off, conceding money in the form of decent compensations in exchange for a great amount of power over workers.

In addition to enduring psychological debilitations and losing participatory rights, DuPont workers do not receive the best possible material benefits in the trade-off. For example, before the OCAW attempted the organization drive at the Experimental Station, employees had no job security, no sharing in patent fees, and no uniformity in job classifications or rates of pay. They still have none of these. Even the highly touted DuPont industrial relations plans leave much to be desired. Company officials do not consider the cost of living when determining support payments made through the pension and retirement plan. Pensioners with a fixed income are helpless when faced with a rising cost of living. Employees are entitled to a pension only after 10 or more years of employment. Pension rights are not transferable to other chemical companies or any other business.

The DuPont thrift plan provides that for every $1 the employee puts into low-interest-paying U.S. savings bonds, the company will put 25 cents into a trust fund for the purchase of DuPont stock. Savings under the plan are limited to $37.50 per month. Other companies in Delaware have better plans. Sun Oil, which has a plant near several DuPont facilities in the Wilmington area, pays 50 cents for every employee dollar. Employees can put up to 10% of their salary into the stock purchase plan. DuPont's noncontributory group life insurance plan provides only $3000 worth of life insurance for employees with five or more years of service in the company. Members of the UAW working at one of the two auto assembly plants in Newark, Delaware, receive from $7500 to $14,500 (depending on their salary) in life insurance paid by the company. Benefits begin after the first month of employment. One of the regular DuPont-sponsored voluntary health insurance plans does not cover employees for their first six months' employment and excludes employees' children who are over 18 years of age. Employees at Electric Hose and Rubber Company, a small company in Delaware, are represented by an AFL-CIO union. They receive fully paid hospitalization insurance, covering children up to age 23 if they are in school; coverage begins after 30 days' employment.

# *Part* II

# The DuPont Family

CHAPTER 4

# Preservation and Power of DuPont Wealth

The DuPonts of Delaware descended from Pierre Samuel du Pont, a nobleman in the court of King Louis XVI during the late 18th century. When Louis was dethroned by the French Revolution, the DuPonts gained prominence in the ranks of bourgeois liberals, but later fell from power as the revolutionary leadership shifted to more radical forces. Pierre Samuel was jailed and escaped the guillotine only by the timely death of Robespierre.[1] After talks with a banker who owned land in America, Pierre Samuel decided to move there. A family biographer explained Pierre's plans:

> He would found a veritable state of his own—Pontiana would be an ideal name—a vast development upon which he would build houses, schools, roads, and waterways, lay out great farms and cultivate all manners of crop, perhaps even start manufactories.[2]

In 1802 the family settled on the Brandywine River in Delaware, and, with help from Thomas Jefferson, a close friend, began to manufacture gunpowder. As the company prospered, the family built its own versions of medieval estates throughout what is now New Castle County. The DuPonts remained in Delaware "in the French tradition . . . unlike so many other rootless millionaires' families who left their source of wealth and settled for the social whirl of New York and Newport."[3] Halfway between New York and Washington, the family could make short trips to consummate financial deals or obtain political favors. At the same time, the family enjoyed Delaware's open woodlands and streams, unthreatened by growing metropolises.

Soon after the turn of the century, the family faced a crisis upon the death of Eugene du Pont, president of the powder company. Since none of the officers wanted to take Eugene's place, they planned to sell the company. But Alfred I. du Pont, a young executive, felt strongly that the company should continue to be handed down from one generation of DuPonts to the next. With the help of two cousins, T. Coleman and Pierre, Alfred bought the company.

This triumvirate was sundered in 1915 when a tremendous family battle raged over control of the company. It began when T. Coleman du Pont, who had became inactive in company management because of ill health, offered to sell 20,000 of his DuPont shares to the corporation. Coleman's proposal went to the company's finance committee, where Alfred and William du Pont said the asking price of $160 per share was too high. Shortly thereafter, Pierre, who had been acting head of the company, made a secret, personal offer to buy all of Coleman's 63,000 shares at $200 per share. Pierre quietly enlisted the support of his brothers, Irenee and Lammot, two other DuPont family members, and company treasurer John Jacob Raskob, who secured large bank loans through J. P. Morgan.

Alfred first learned of Pierre's deal from a newspaper. In a confrontation with Pierre, Alfred argued:

> Don't do this thing! . . . you have accomplished something by virtue of the power and influence vested in you as an officer of the company. . . . For that reason the stock which you have acquired does not belong to you but to the company which you represent. I therefore ask you to turn this stock over to the company.[4]

Pierre at first refused to sell to the company, but in a sudden about-face agreed—as long as John P. Laffey, DuPont general counsel, approved the transaction:

> As if delivered by genie, the rubicund Mr. Laffey appeared, with marked copies of law books under his arm. Mr. Laffey read from the books in a sonorous voice; then gravely gave his opinion that the company could not legally purchase the Pierre-Coleman stock except out of its surplus funds. These, he said, were insufficient.[5]

In December, 1915, Francis I. du Pont, joined by Alfred and other family members, filed suit against Pierre's syndicate in federal court. In response, the company's board members, now controlled by Pierre, removed Alfred from his post as vice president and member of the finance committee. Later the board took Alfred, Francis I., and William (who did not join the suit, but testified for Alfred's side) off the slate of directors up for reelection. The federal district court ruled that Pierre's syndicate had violated its fiduciary obligations to the company, and ordered a stockholder vote on the disposition of Coleman's stock, a remedy which Pierre turned to his advantage. While neither Pierre nor Alfred had a majority of stock (leaving out Coleman's shares), Pierre's group had much more stock and more resources to seek stockholder votes than Alfred's group did. After a wild scramble for proxies, Pierre won easily.

The feud between Alfred and Pierre spread beyond the confines of the family, the company, and the courts. Alfred, a progressive Republican, precipitated the fiercest political struggle in Delaware's history by successfully opposing Coleman's Republican machine. Alfred won control of the Delaware GOP convention, crushing Coleman's bid for the U.S. Presidency. He then stopped Henry A. du Pont's election to the U.S. Senate by supporting a third-party candidate, who drew enough votes to let Democrat Josiah O. Wolcott win the election. In 1921 Coleman turned the tables on Alfred, however, when Delaware's Governor Denney, who had been put into office by Coleman's Republican machine, lured Wolcott from the U.S. Senate into the state's highest judicial post. Denney then named Coleman to replace Wolcott—an episode known in Delaware history as "The Dirty Deal." Although Alfred was disillusioned with politics, he still campaigned against Coleman in the next senatorial election. When the candidate backed by Alfred, Thomas A. Bayard, beat Coleman, Alfred felt that the "cancer" of DuPont control in Delaware had "been removed for all time." [6] Despite Bayard's marriage to a DuPont, his campaign slogan had been: "Are we a free people or shall we permit ourselves to be crushed under the weight of DuPont wealth?" [7]

The two DuPont factions fougnt with their money for public support, giving away school buildings and highways. After a group founded by Pierre released a study on the deplorable conditions of education in Delaware, Pierre offered to spend $4 million, half the cost of replacing a hundred of the state's dilapidated school buildings. The program was passed over strong opposition from many communities that objected to paying the other half. In 1930 Pierre supplied $12,582.89 to survey the state's fiscal and business needs; a standardized cost accounting system resulted. The state legislature reimbursed Pierre the next year. Alfred supported legislation for an old-age pension plan. When the bill was originally defeated in 1929, Alfred set up a private pension plan, paying an average of $16 a month to about 1400 poor, elderly residents of the state. In 1930 Alfred was appointed to a special Old Age Welfare Commission and used his position to get candidates elected. The legislature enacted an old-age assistance program in 1931.[8] Alfred, more progressive than Pierre, was responsible for one of the most radical reforms in Delaware tax history, the graduated inheritance tax. He characterized the state's tax laws as being "framed for the sole purpose of assisting such [wealthy] men to pay as little as possible, and it is to the minimum that they intend to stick if permitted to do so." [9] After Alfred left Delaware the graduated inheritance tax was repealed.

The feud left a deep schism in the once united family. Those who stood with Alfred stayed out of the DuPont Company. Some remained in Delaware, others drifted away. Alfred eventually left to rebuild his empire in Florida. Francis I. du Pont, who originally brought the lawsuit against Pierre's syndicate, moved to New York, where his stock brokerage company became one of the country's largest. After merging with another Wall Street broker, the business was bought from Francis's heirs in 1971 by Texas millionaire Ross Perot, who had rescued it from ruin. Some of William du Pont's heirs set up large horse-breeding farms, complete with private race tracks, in Delaware, Pennsylvania, and Maryland near the Delaware border. Others ran the family's bank, Delaware Trust Company. Even today, family members who do not attain high posts in the DuPont Company tend to leave Delaware. Pierre S. du Pont IV said that his father always considered family members "suspect" who did not rise in the company, even if they made millions in other businesses.

The burgeoning DuPont Company was left to Pierre and his allies. Along with the company presidency, Pierre donned the mantle of *paterfamilias.* According to one author, "The clan has always produced at least one *paterfamilias* in each generation, who usually ran the business and ruled the family with an autocratic hand." [10] With the power, prestige, and resources of his dual role, Pierre moved vigorously into local and national politics.

Pierre's pet project was the American Liberty League. With the help of Jacob Raskob and Alfred Sloan of General Motors, Pierre's Liberty League published ultraconservative literature including pamphlets entitled "Government by the Busybodies," "The Way Dictatorship Starts," and "Abolishing the States." To help the Liberty League's efforts to defeat Franklin D. Roosevelt in 1936, DuPont executives gave $1 million to Alfred M. Landon, the Republican candidate. A New York newspaperman wrote: "Never before in political history as far as observers could recall, has a campaign been so dominated by a single family or has any family donated a comparable sum in an effort to elect its man to the Presidency." [11] The Democrats stated: "The American Liberty League should be called the American Cellophane League because first it is a DuPont product, and second you can see through it." [12]

The most recent clan leader, a favorite of Pierre's, was his nephew, Henry Belin du Pont. For 40 years, H.B. held such a long string of directorships that he personified Du-

Pont influence in Delaware. He was a director of the DuPont Company, Wilmington Trust, the *News-Journal,* Christiana Securities, and Atlantic Aviation Company. H.B. established the Delaware State Planning Commission, sat on the state Goals Commission and the Delaware Planning Council, headed a special advisory committee to the governor, served on the New Castle County Soil and Water Conservation District Commission, was school board president of the Alexis I. du Pont Special School District for 30 years, and was president of the family's Longwood and Welfare foundations, director of the family-held Eleutherian Mills–Hagley Foundation and Winterthur Museum, trustee of the University of Delaware and St. Andrews preparatory school, and chairman of the powerful Greater Wilmington Development Council.

The impact of Pierre's victory in the family feud has continued to be a major factor in Delaware. With the exception of DuPont's current president, Charles B. McCoy, top company officials have generally been members of the original syndicate, their sons, or men who married into Pierre's side of the family. Other lines of business in Delaware are also dominated by descendants of Pierre's allies. For instance, W. W. Laird, Jr., a land developer, inherited a large part of his extensive holdings from his father, William Winder Laird, who bought the land with a fortune built on shares given to him by Pierre during the feud.

Similarly, government offices now bear the mark of the victors. The sons of Lammot du Pont, Pierre's brother and a member of the original syndicate, are key figures in Delaware's Republican party. Lammot's grandson, Pierre S. du Pont IV, was elected to the United States House of Representatives in 1970. Likewise, heirs of DuPont executives, won over by Pierre's large gifts of stock, are now prominent in state politics. The current mayor of Wilmington financed his campaign out of a family fortune built by his father, Harry Haskell, who sided with Pierre.

Alfred I. du Pont summarized the situation before he left for Florida: "The golden tentacles of the wealthy class have been quietly laying hold of the whole state of Delaware." [13] And as one distinguished social historian made clear:

> The clan DuPont . . . has sunk deep roots in one of the nation's smallest states, which it has controlled down through the years as perhaps no other family has ever done in America.[14]

## *Preservation of Family Wealth*

The current generation of DuPonts is worth between $2 billion and $7 billion. Most of these people have not earned the money; they are millionaires at birth. The descendants of both factions of the feud have become multimillionaires.* For Delaware citizens the passage of DuPont billions from generation to generation poses serious problems. A democratic system cannot tolerate men buying their way into office. Nor does highly concentrated wealth bring about a beneficial plurality of investment. Finally, a system of wealth by birthright can hurt the local economy. Even President Herbert Hoover advocated inheritance taxes to "thaw out frozen and inactive capital and the inherited control of the tools of production."[15]

The DuPont billions are preserved within the family by two general types of federal and state laws: those protecting the income of the super-rich during their lifetime and those enabling persons who have accumulated wealth to pass it on at death.

The structure of the Delaware income tax exemplifies protection for the lifetime income of the super-rich. Taxpayers in the highest income bracket are supposed to pay state income tax at the rate of 11% of income.** But with various tax credits, deductions, and exemptions, the progressive nature of the tax virtually ends at $30,000. People making $31,000–49,000 paid 6.4% of their income in tax

* For example, the eight children of Irenee du Pont, Sr., Pierre's brother and a member of the original syndicate, were given stock holdings in Christiana Securities alone worth over $400 million. Similarly, Robert R. M. Carpenter, who received his first Christiana Securities shares from Pierre, bestowed upon his four children enough of these shares alone to pay yearly dividends of about $1 million per child. On the other side, William du Pont, who backed Alfred in the feud, left his children $28 million in 1928 plus extensive land holdings currently worth $10,000 per acre. William du Pont's estate, willed to his grandchildren, has increased in value to over $300 million.

** Because of the state's fiscal crisis, income taxes in the upper brackets were raised in July, 1971. See Chapter 14.

TABLE 4-1.
*Genealogy of the DuPont Family*

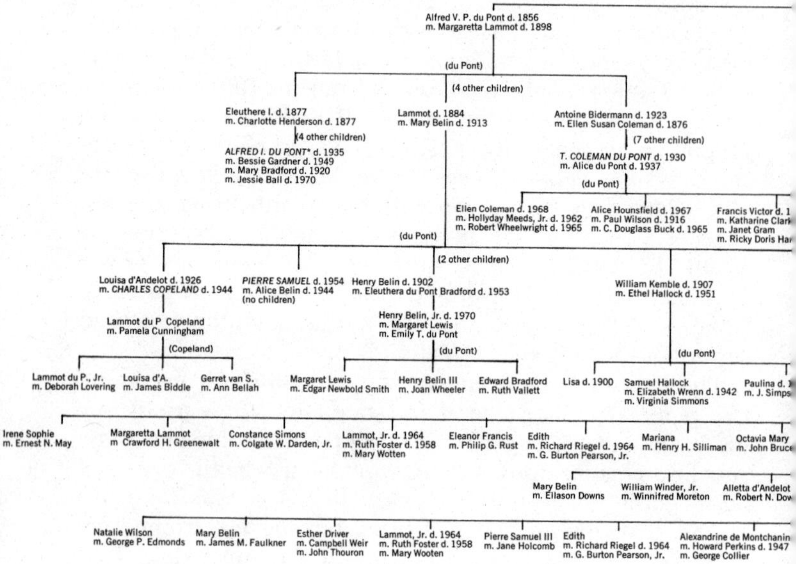


Participants in 1915 struggle in capital letters and italicized

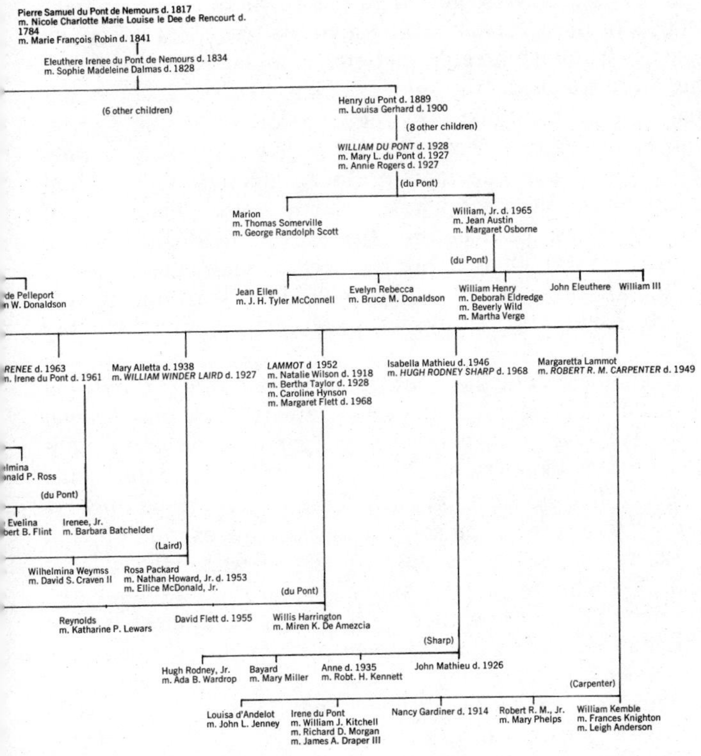
Pierre Samuel du Pont de Nemours d. 1817
m. Nicole Charlotte Marie Louise le Dee de Rencourt d. 1784
m. Marie François Robin d. 1841
Eleuthere Irenee du Pont de Nemours d. 1834
m. Sophie Madeleine Dalmas d. 1828
(6 other children)
Henry du Pont d. 1889
m. Louisa Gerhard d. 1900
(8 other children)
WILLIAM DU PONT d. 1928
m. Mary L. du Pont d. 1927
m. Annie Rogers d. 1927
(du Pont)
Marion
m. Thomas Somerville
m. George Randolph Scott
William, Jr. d. 1965
m. Jean Austin
m. Margaret Osborne
(du Pont)
Jean Ellen
m. J. H. Tyler McConnell
Evelyn Rebecca
m. Bruce M. Donaldson
William Henry
m. Deborah Eldredge
m. Beverly Wild
m. Martha Verge
John Eleuthere
William III
de Pelleport
n W. Donaldson
RENEE d. 1963
n. Irene du Pont d. 1961
Mary Alletta d. 1938
m. WILLIAM WINDER LAIRD d. 1927
LAMMOT d. 1952
m. Natalie Wilson d. 1918
m. Bertha Taylor d. 1928
m. Caroline Hynson
m. Margaret Flett d. 1968
Isabella Mathieu d. 1946
m. HUGH RODNEY SHARP d. 1968
Margaretta Lammot
m. ROBERT R. M. CARPENTER d. 1949
lmina
nald P. Ross
(du Pont)
Evelina
bert B. Flint
Irenee, Jr.
m. Barbara Batchelder
(Laird)
Wilhelmina Weymss
m. David S. Craven II
Rosa Packard
m. Nathan Howard, Jr. d. 1953
m. Ellice McDonald, Jr.
(du Pont)
Reynolds
m. Katharine P. Lewars
David Flett d. 1955
Willis Harrington
m. Miren K. De Amezcia
(Sharp)
Hugh Rodney, Jr.
m. Ada B. Wardrop
Bayard
m. Mary Miller
Anne d. 1935
m. Robt. H. Kennett
John Mathieu d. 1926
(Carpenter)
Louisa d'Andelot
m. John L. Jenney
Irene du Pont
m. William J. Kitchell
m. Richard D. Morgan
m. James A. Draper III
Nancy Gardiner d. 1914
Robert R. M., Jr.
m. Mary Phelps
William Kemble
m. Frances Knighton
m. Leigh Anderson

after exemptions, deductions, and credits; those making $200,000–222,000 pay 6.8%—a small difference. Those earning from $15,000 to $17,999 paid 4.3%—only 2.5% less than those in the $200,000–222,000 bracket.[16]

In 1970, Delaware abolished one of the most progressive aspects of the Delaware tax system, its treatment of capital gains as ordinary taxable income. (Capital gains income is the profit made on the sale of assets like stocks or bonds that an individual does not regularly offer for sale.) Delaware now follows the federal practice of taxing capital gains at a lower rate than ordinary income, and DuPont millionaires, much of whose income comes from capital gains, pay less than before. In 1965, individuals with incomes of $800,000 or more reported capital gains of about $600,000 per person, while individuals earning in the $8000–8999 range enjoyed capital gains of only $75 per person.

While the income taxes of the corporate rich are reduced by local and federal laws, they pay no levy on personal property. There are two types of personal property: tangible objects, like cars, machines, or furniture; and intangible property, like stocks and bonds. Delaware is one of only six states that taxes *no* personal property, an exemption that works to the obvious benefit of people who have a great deal of it. The immediate families of the 13 DuPonts on the company's board together own over a million shares of Christiana Securities, worth over $150 million; these, like the lavish appointments of many DuPont chateaus and vast holdings of jewelry, go untaxed. There are arguments against a personal property tax, chief among them being the extreme difficulty of administering it, but it cannot be denied that the absence works to the particular benefit of the Delaware upper class. This benefit is compounded by *real* property taxes—taxes on land and houses—in the state. For the average citizen, his house and lot represent the bulk of his property, so the bulk of his property is taxed. But for a DuPont, the value of mansion and grounds is usually a tiny percentage of his total property, and only that tiny percentage is taxed. For example, H. B. du Pont owned real property worth $6.1 million, yet his total property holdings—real, tangible personal, and intangible personal—amounted to $56 million; he paid property tax on just over 10% of his property.*

Finally, Delaware does not have a stock transfer tax, another tax benefit for the wealthy. If there were a tax on the transfer of stock, those who regularly trade shares would be affected, while the bulk of stock owners, who do not buy or sell stock often or in great quantities, would not. Moreover, the wage tax in Wilmington entirely exempts dividends from stocks and bonds. While the blue-collar DuPont worker must pay the 1% wage tax on his $7000-per-year salary, the DuPont family member working in Wilmington pays no tax on the $200,000 per year he might derive from dividends on his shares of Christiana Securities or DuPont stock.

Delaware law also shields DuPont millions from taxes at death. Although Delaware taxes on very large estates are about the same as most other states',** there are numerous ways to avoid the state's inheritance taxes. The simplest way involves giving money to heirs at least six months before death. Delaware had no gift tax until the state's fiscal crisis in 1971.

Delaware is too generous in assuming that if a donor lives longer than six months after making a gift, the gift was not an attempt to avoid estate taxes. The federal government and 42 states require more time; 20 states demand three years. Of all the mechanisms for transferring wealth, the large gift is most restricted to millionaires. While a fair number of people can bequeath several hundred thousand dollars, only the super-rich have the financial security to give away large sums *before* their death. In a typical recent year, Delaware residents paid one dollar in federal gift tax for two dollars in federal estate tax, while the national average was one to eight. The difference between these two

* Making this situation still worse is the gross underassessment of real property in New Castle County, discussed in Chapter 12. Notably, the large estates and mansions are much more likely to be underassessed, or to be severely underassessed, than the houses and grounds of less wealthy families.

** For net estates of $2.5 million and $5 million, there are respectively one and two states with lower tax rates and 27 and 35 states with the same tax rate. On the other hand, those persons with estates of $25,000 pay more tax in Delaware than they would in most states. See Appendixes 3 and 4.

ratios suggests that Delaware's wealthy have been giving away more money than the rich in most states. In fact, the DuPonts have always taken advantage of the absence (until 1971) of a Delaware gift tax and the federal government's favorable treatment of such gifts. For instance, R. R. M. Carpenter, Pierre's brother-in-law, had only 11,520 shares of Christiana and 20 shares of DuPont common in his estate upon his death in 1949. But between 1918 and 1948 he established 21 trusts for his family, which included 357,000 shares of DuPont and over 700,000 shares of Christiana Securities and saved his heirs nearly $9 million in federal estate and inheritance taxes as well as over $1 million in Delaware inheritance taxes. Pierre S. du Pont gave away from $200 million to $400 million before his death. By bequeathing nearly all of his remaining $58-million estate to his own Longwood Foundation, Pierre paid only $586,162 in estate and inheritance taxes to the state of Delaware.

Unique Delaware trust laws also save taxes for the rich. When a millionaire sets up an irrevocable trust in Delaware before his death he pays only state and federal gift taxes. The beneficiary of the trust pays no state inheritance tax at the death of the donor. As long as the principal is not distributed, the beneficiary can live off the dividends and interest from the trust without paying estate taxes. Moreover, the exemption from estate taxes on trusts lasts through four generations, one more than allowed by any other state. Until 1951, this provision of state law allowed wealthy Delawareans to avoid federal estate taxes as well; before that time, the DuPonts could avoid paying any state or federal estate tax for a whole century. Although Congress closed this federal loophole, state loopholes gape conspicuously. For instance, DuPont decedents still can avoid $800,000 in state death taxes by establishing a $5-million irrevocable trust if they exercise all powers of appointment, $200,000 more than in other states. Because of these favorable legal provisions, the DuPonts have put 50% to 70% of their money into trusts, according to Wilmington bankers.

If a Delaware resident purchases bonds from a political subdivision of the state—for highways or schools, for example—the state and federal governments do not tax the interest from these bonds. Furthermore, government bonds are not taxable assets of an estate. These provisions are put to work by the DuPonts. In 1949 R. R. M. Carpenter held $7,100,000 in state and municipal bonds, with a large percentage from Delaware. He paid no income taxes on most of the $150,000 to $200,000 annual interest he received from the bonds, and he reduced his death taxes by over $5 million. Similarly, $2.5 million in municipal and state bonds reduced H. B. du Pont's inheritance taxes by almost $2 million.

Foundations are one of the most important ways DuPonts preserve their wealth for themselves and their heirs. During his lifetime an individual who donates money to a foundation can deduct from his taxable income base up to 20% * of his gross annual income. The higher the income bracket of an individual, the greater the tax saving he can receive. For example, someone in a 25% tax bracket saves only $25 in taxes for a $100 contribution. But if a DuPont with an annual income of $100,000 makes a $100 contribution to a foundation, his income tax saving is $60 if he files a joint return and $69 if he files a separate tax return. Although he appears to have given up $100, the cost to him is really only from $31 to $40. By giving the money to a family foundation run by himself or his relatives, he retains control over the full $160.

There are more sophisticated methods of contributing to foundations to increase tax savings. An individual can contribute to a foundation securities or property which have appreciated in value, and then deduct the contribution at the current appreciated value, without paying income or capital gains taxes.

DuPonts may also establish foundations to avoid taxes at death. The funds of a very wealthy DuPont are subject to a 77% maximum federal estate tax plus a very small Delaware estate tax upon his death. If a DuPont gives his money to his children before he dies, this gift is subject to a 50%

* A person can deduct from his taxable income base up to 50% of his gross annual income for contributions to organizations qualifying under federal law, limited to churches, schools, hospitals, publicly supported charities such as the Red Cross, states and subdivisions of the states, and fund raisers for schools.

federal gift tax. Instead, as DuPont family members get older, they set up foundations and appoint their children to the foundations' board of directors. For example, when Irenee du Pont, Sr., established the Crystal Trust Foundation with a bequest of $33 million from his estate, he avoided $25 million in federal estate taxes or $16.5 million in federal gift taxes. He also reduced his Delaware estate and inheritance taxes by several million dollars. The Crystal Trust is now run by Irenee du Pont, Jr. Similarly, when Henry B. du Pont bequeathed approximately $7 million in stocks to various foundations and other tax-exempt organizations, his executors saved about $5.4 million in federal estate taxes or $3.5 million in federal gift taxes. H.B. gave some of his stock to several foundations which were controlled by other family members.

Family-run DuPont foundations provide a cheap way to influence those Delaware institutions that are the source of family wealth. DuPont foundations own at least 108,000 shares of DuPont common stock and over 900,000 shares of Christiana Securities, which means one-twelfth interest in the News-Journal Company and a significant voting block in the Wilmington Trust Company. If family members held these shares in their own portfolios, they would have to pay income and estate taxes on the dividends and shares. But foundations for years paid no taxes; the Tax Reform Act of 1969 now requires them to pay a general tax of only 4%. By putting stock into foundations, family members acquire tax-free voting power in Delaware economic institutions through their roles as foundation directors, and direct control over the use of the foundation money.

### *The Charitable Subgovernment*

The power the DuPonts obtain for themselves through foundations is enormous. DuPont family foundations * give away over $12 million each year, mostly within Delaware. Contributions made by or through the foundations

* There are 36 in Delaware, with assets totaling over $400 million. This figure includes only foundations either with assets over $200,000 or making grants over $10,000 annually.

to various charitable, educational, cultural, and scientific groups are supposed to contribute to the common welfare. Foundations are given special tax-exempt status under federal and state tax laws because they claim to serve a general public purpose. But this tax loophole for the wealthy decreases public revenues, and the money stays in private hands for allocation to allegedly public purposes.

In theory, granting special tax status to charitable foundations should promote pluralism by allowing nongovernment groups to distribute money for the public good. But in Delaware, the DuPont family exercises a virtual monopoly over the private, noncorporate dollars available for charity. Worse, DuPont foundations—unlike the Ford Foundation, with its more diverse board of directors and many programs which are quite separate from the corporate goals of the Ford Motor Company—are run almost exclusively by family members, who concentrate their grants within Delaware and in close coordination with DuPont interests. As a result, an exclusive group wields tremendous power under the banner of noblesse oblige, and the private DuPont foundations are an extension of family power.

Power in the foundations lies with the donor-appointed boards of trustees. DuPont family members constitute a majority of the trustees in 31 of the 36 foundations.* Trustees who are not family members are either close friends of the donor like the family lawyer or executives in DuPont-controlled businesses. And the boards are self-perpetuating; the trustees reelect themselves and replace deceased or retired trustees with other family members. The boards of the various foundations themselves interlock; 30 of the 36 foundations share trustees with other foundations. The trustees also link foundations to the rest of the corporate establishment. The five trustees of the Bredin Foundation, for example, are all DuPont family members and personally link the foundation, through top executive positions, with the DuPont Company, Wilmington Trust Company, a DuPont brokerage house, and six other DuPont foundations. The DuPont foundation network is loaded with potential abuses of the public interest,

* See Appendix 5 for a list of DuPont foundation trustees.

and an examination of how the money is spent shows that the foundations have lived up to this potential.

The top 20 groups receiving foundation grants are listed in Table 4-2. These institutions received almost three-quarters of all the funds distributed by the 36 foundations in 1968. Many of them are worthwhile endeavors, deserving charitable support. But when charitable organizations become dependent upon DuPont foundations and DuPont family donations for a substantial part of their support, the unequal distribution of power within the state is worsened. Charitable organizations in the community are not supported by the community as a whole, or by a wide variety of individuals with different, often competing interests. Rather, a single wealthy family can influence and often control the charitable efforts of the entire community.

TABLE 4-2.
*Top Twenty American Agencies Supported by DuPont Foundations (1968)*

| | *Amount Received* | *Name of Agency* |
|---|---|---|
| 1. | $2,692,000 | University of Delaware* |
| 2. | 1,383,000 | Alfred I. du Pont Institute* |
| 3. | 930,000 | Friends School* |
| 4. | 541,000 | Tatnall School* |
| 5. | 502,000 | Wesley College* |
| 6. | 493,000 | Eleutherian Mills–Hagley Foundation* |
| 7. | 338,000 | Boys' Club of Wilmington* |
| 8. | 251,000 | United Community Fund of Northern Delaware* |
| 9. | 245,000 | Jewish Community Center* |
| 10. | 207,000 | Nanticoke Memorial Hospital |
| 11. | 176,000 | Greater Wilmington Development Council* |
| 12. | 170,000 | Wilmington Medical Center* |
| 13. | 153,000 | Tower Hill School* |
| 14. | 143,000 | The Pilot School |
| 15. | 130,000 | Children's Home* |
| 16. | 125,000 | Massachusetts Institute of Technology* |
| 17. | 125,000 | Institute of International Education, New York |
| 18. | 121,000 | Delaware School Auxiliary* |
| 19. | 116,000 | Children's Beach House, Inc. |
| 20. | 114,000 | Delaware Wildlands, Inc.* |

* One or more DuPont family members on board of trustees

As a result of autocratic rule in the foundations, the distribution of foundation grants is determined by the interests of family members. All the major recipient institutions are of particular interest to family members, who often are their founders or directors. The University of Delaware and the Wilmington Medical Center have long been dominated by the family, while the private schools on the list, like Friends or Tower Hill, provide an alternative system of education for the corporate elite. The Greater Wilmington Development Council is controlled by DuPont Company executives; the Nanticoke Hospital serves the families of DuPont employees at its nylon plant near Seaford. The Jewish Community Center is the only group which seems out of place, but the exception illuminates the rule. Before 1968 no foundations gave to the drive for a new Jewish Community Center. But in 1968 Irenee du Pont, Jr., was named head of the foundations and industry division of the fund-raising campaign of the Jewish Federation of Delaware; that year DuPont foundation grants totaled $245,000.

Instead of paying taxes to the government, the DuPont family has created its own government through personal gifts and foundation grants. The $12–13 million given in 1968, for example, went for a wide variety of traditionally public functions—hospitals, schools, and community action programs. In the same year, the officials of Wilmington and New Castle County each spent about the same amount—$16 million and $9 million—to carry out their local government functions.

The difference between foundations and local government is that foundations are operated on the personal preference of the donors. In local government, elected officials make budget proposals which are subject to public debate and officials are accountable to the public for their actions; but the directors of a foundation make no budget proposals to the public, do not ask for public debate, and are accountable only to the donor.

There is much for which to indict this system. First, it is impossible for DuPont foundations to make thorough and objective appraisals of grant applicants. Most have only one or two paid employees, who normally do not work full time and may work for several foundations; three foundations—Christiana, Ederic, and Holpont—share one employee. The foundations often do not have their own offices; they operate out of the desk of the single paid employee or the trustee who serves as president, usually located in the DuPont or Wilmington Trust buildings. The trustees normally do not spend much time looking at grant applications. The trustees of large foundations meet only once a month, while the boards of smaller foundations meet as infrequently as twice a year. Each trustee of the Bredin Foundation, for example, spends two to three hours per month on foundation business. The Bredin Foundation receives about a thousand requests for money per year. Even if the work were split among the trustees, each would spend an average of less than 10 minutes on each application.

Without an adequate staff or intensive work by board members, DuPont foundations hand out large sums of money through an informal system of contacts, increasing the power of individual trustees and other insiders. Directors give out grants on the basis of generalities like "charitable cause" or "public good," instead of specific guidelines. Foundations do not give reasons for turning down a request; some foundations do not even reply to rejected grant applications, according to the people working for the foundations. Trustees' meetings tend to be formalities where previously made decisions are ratified. DuPont foundations frequently make contributions in lieu of a direct gift from the person who set up the foundation. H. B. du Pont often personally promised money to a group which soon received a check from his Welfare Foundation; the Crystal Trust Foundation plays the same role for Irenee du Pont, Jr.

Second, DuPont foundations often make donations to organizations which are themselves part of the corporate establishment. Over one-half of the DuPont foundations contributed to the corporate-controlled United Fund of Northern Delaware (see Chapter 2). Similarly, the DuPont foundations contribute heavily to the Greater Wilmington Development Council, a DuPont-dominated group. DuPont foundations donate money to organizations which themselves have family members on their boards. Of the 20 agencies that receive grants from the greatest number of

DuPont foundations (see Table 4-3), all have DuPont family members on their boards of directors. DuPont foundations seem deliberately to conspire to give to organizations the DuPonts control, thus assuring that the charitable subgovernment is monolithic and isolated, beyond the purview of the public.

TABLE 4-3.
*Agencies Supported by Several DuPont Foundations*

| *Number of Foundations Contributing in 1967, 1968, or both* | *Agency* |
|---|---|
| 19 | United Community Fund of Northern Delaware* |
| 17 | Wilmington Medical Center* |
| 15 | Delaware League for Planned Parenthood* |
| 13 | Delaware Wildlands, Inc.* |
| 12 | Boys' Club of Wilmington* |
| 12 | Greater Wilmington Development Council* |
| 12 | Tower Hill School* |
| 12 | University of Delaware* |
| 11 | Block Blight, Inc.* |
| 11 | The Pilot School |
| 10 | Friends School* |
| 10 | Historical Society of Delaware |
| 10 | Tatnall School* |
| 10 | YMCA* |
| 8 | Methodist Country Home* |
| 8 | Tri-County Conservancy of the Upper Brandywine, Inc.* |
| 6 | Christ Church* |
| 6 | Henry F. du Pont Winterthur Museum* |
| 6 | Jewish Community Center* |
| 6 | Old Brandywine Village, Inc.* |

* DuPont family members or executives on boards of trustees

The lack of information generally available about DuPont foundations effectively protects this subgovernment from outside pressures. Except for Winterthur Museum and Eleutherian Mills–Hagley Foundation, the DuPont foundations are not listed in the Wilmington telephone book. Prior to the 1969 Tax Reform Act, citizens could learn about foundation activities only by reading the 990-A Internal Revenue Service forms at an IRS office in Pennsylvania or the Foundation Center Library in New York City.

The 1969 Tax Reform Act requires all foundations with assets over $5000 to publish an annual report in addition to the IRS form. The availability of the report must be advertised in a local newspaper. A spot-check of seven DuPont foundations in July, 1971, a full year and a half after the act went into effect, revealed no annual reports and no advertisements. Employees in the office of Christiana, Ederic, and Holpont foundations told a representative of the Delaware Study Group that only the 990-A IRS form was available for public disclosure. Officials at three DuPont foundations—Welfare, Crestlea, and Red Clay Reservation, Inc.—would not give out any information without foundation treasurers present.

Even the IRS records on DuPont foundations give a grossly inaccurate picture of them. The 1964 returns for the DuPont foundations indicate total assets of $420 million for the 36 foundations. This figure is significantly below the actual value of the assets they control. The ledger value of cash and investments of Eleutherian Mills–Hagley Foundation, for example, was about $16 million; the market value was over $25 million. Foundations that are beneficiaries of trusts do not list the trust assets as foundation assets; Copeland-Andelot foundation lists no corporate stocks or bonds as assets, yet the foundation receives an annual income of about $200,000 from stocks held in five trusts.

Rather than serving the public interest or encouraging pluralism in decision making, DuPont foundations have fostered community dependency on their own arbitrary policies. This dependency takes two major forms: some private groups change their programs to suit a DuPont family member, and some governmental bodies rely on foundations to perform public functions.

Private groups seeking funds usually must turn to individual DuPonts or their foundations if they cannot receive government backing. The only other major funding source in the state is the United Fund, which is controlled by corporate executives. Faced with this narrow range of choices, community groups may be forced to meet the whims of DuPont family members. When Peninsula Methodist Homes and Hospitals was planning a rest home for New Castle County, for instance, the head of the organization went to Henry F. du Pont to buy a piece of his land and to discuss financial support. Henry agreed to support the project—if the rest home were built in colonial style and if he were allowed to approve the plans. Peninsula Methodist Homes and Hospitals met these conditions and got the land for well under the going price in the area. DuPont foundations provided a large portion of the money needed to build the home.

On the other hand, DuPont family members have withdrawn funding when they dislike the programs undertaken by a community group. Professionals working for a Catholic organization, financed heavily by DuPonts, raised fundamental questions about corporate power during the nine-month National Guard occupation of Wilmington; some lost their jobs in the organization because a fund-raising expert determined that their activities threatened continuing DuPont support. One community organization in Wilmington lost the support of a DuPont family member who objected to its pollution study. A Protestant group, pressing local businesses to participate in Project Equality (see Chapter 3) lost the financial support of some members of the corporate elite.

Perhaps the best example of a DuPont withdrawal of funding because of disagreements with a community group is the story of Organization Interest (OI). OI was established in 1969 by black ex-convicts to aid other released prisoners in finding housing, jobs, and schooling. OI developed an outstanding reputation within the Wilmington black community, where most of its clients lived. Late in 1969 the Correctional Council of Delaware (now the Delaware Council on Crime and Justice), a white group working with ex-convicts, asked OI to come under its control. OI refused and lost most of its funding.

The directors of OI sought help from William Henry du Pont and his wife, who had been actively concerned with ex-convicts' problems. Mrs. du Pont, a director of the Correctional Council and Boys' Home of Delaware, had crusaded against the horrible conditions in the Ferris School for Boys, a juvenile detention center in New Castle County. Mr. du Pont agreed to provide Organization Interest with $24,000 for the next year, in quarterly payments of $6,000. According to OI, du Pont also promised to pay the $13,500 salary of a professional director. Du Pont denies making this promise and never did pay the salary. He paid $21,000 of the $24,000 but abruptly stopped payments in September, 1970. He gave no explanation for pulling his support away, but later claimed that OI was spending his money improperly and not accounting to him for expenditures. OI directors stated that du Pont never asked for any accounting when he first promised his donation; he only wanted to be kept periodically informed of the group's progress. As to misspending funds, the Wilmington Council of Churches handled all money for OI and carefully monitored expenditures.

In September, 1970, the directors of OI asked du Pont to fulfill the rest of his pledge. They supplied him with the accounting reports. The directors and officers of OI held a series of private meetings with du Pont. He agreed to make his final $3000 payment. In November, OI asked du Pont for the following promises in writing: that his financial commitment would be fulfilled (including payment of the director's salary); that Herbert Porter, the ex-offender who had founded OI, would be kept on the staff at least three months; and that the old board of directors would be retained until a new board was appointed. In response, du Pont said: "Nobody in his right mind would go along with those demands." [17] Organization Interest abruptly folded.

DuPont family members have used their money and grants from their foundations to purchase new public policies. A case in point is H. B. du Pont's transformation of Delaware Avenue. H.B. first bought an apartment building at the intersection of Delaware and Pennsylvania avenues. Soon afterwards, the Midtown Study, a consultant study done for the corporate-funded Greater Wilmington Development Council, recommended a park on the site. The apartment building was torn down and a park was built. To transform the avenue into the "Gateway to Wilmington," H.B. lobbied for the widening of Delaware and the supporters of the boulevard used the Midtown Study's data before the Wilmington City Council. Despite protests from property owners along the avenue that the special zoning ordinance would stifle development and necessitate renovations as well as demolition, the city council went along. Delaware Avenue property owners unsuccessfully petitioned the Wilmington planning council to change the new plan. The planning council's action was described even by the *News-Journal* as "a bow to the GWDC and other interests that want Delaware Avenue made into an elegant boulevard." [18] With the private park and public zoning ordinance, H.B. created by private fiat a public memorial to himself—the "Gateway to Wilmington" leading to DuPont's new Brandywine Building.

Institutions tied to DuPont foundations have even taken over explicitly public roles. One example is the Health Planning Council (HPC)—begun in the midsixties as a private group to help DuPont foundations and major Delaware corporations choose among grant applications from medical facilities. While the council had no legal enforcement powers, its executive director says that hospitals, Blue Cross–Blue Shield, and other health care agencies in Delaware sought approval before formulating their plans for growth. When New Castle County tried to establish a public hospital planning committee in 1967, it was defeated on the grounds that the HPC already existed. But HPC was never representative of the citizens served by Delaware's health institutions. Among its 22 directors in 1968 were 3 DuPont executives, a former executive, a DuPont family member, a corporate lawyer, the chairman of the family's News-Journal Company, and an ex-senator with a reputation for being extremely pro-DuPont. In 1968 four of these men were on the seven-man executive committee of HPC. In the absence of a public group, the Health Planning Council was designated by the federal government in 1969 as the group to do comprehensive health care planning for New Castle County and health facility planning for the entire state. Under the federal Comprehensive Health Planning Act of 1969, the council's board had to be expanded to include representation of Delaware consumers; three new board members were named. HPC now handles funding requests and planning for federal as well as private monies going to health care facilities in the state, and no medical facility can receive federal money until the HPC approves its plans.

As a result of DuPont funding for so many private and public functions, a peculiar psychology has evolved in Delaware about foundations and family largess. Whenever groups need money, they think DuPont; local, state, or federal governments are not fully developed as viable sources of funds. Community organizations try to get a DuPont on their boards, and if they succeed his influence is disproportionately large. Some of it derives from organizations' deep fear that DuPont funds will be pulled out if they take a wrong step. When a liberal church group tried to garner support among its members for open-housing efforts, several DuPont employees refused to participate because they feared the DuPont Company and DuPont family members would be opposed to the policy. Many community leaders told the study group they felt confined by DuPont funding even though no one had brought overt pressure against them. When a DuPont serves a community agency, it is often unclear whether he is interested in the agency's work or distribution of his money. In sum, as one community leader said:

> Paternalistic giving is an unviable system where community groups are always begging or living in fear while the rich are always being pestered and disconcerted by policies pursued by community groups.

### THE SUBGOVERNMENT IN ACTION: TWO CASE STUDIES

For many years, the DuPont family provided most of the financial support to Delaware's private hospitals. But as the costs of medical care soared, even DuPont pocketbooks could not keep pace. The three hospitals—Delaware State, Wilmington General, and Memorial—began to merge in 1963, to avoid staff, facility, and equipment duplication. The merger also allowed the family to centralize control over the hospitals.

The merger created the Wilmington Medical Center, the fifth largest voluntary general hospital in the country. The three boards of directors merged, forming an unwieldy board of trustees that included some representatives of was in the executive committee, 9 of whose 12 members were connected with the DuPonts. As the hospitals approached a complete merger, conflicts arose between the DuPont-oriented board and the hospital staff. As a result, the Wilmington Medical Center became a three-headed monster and derived few benefits from the centralization.

Late in 1967, a number of doctors met with key hospital administrators to discuss the shortcomings of the merger. A statement of the proceedings said:

> It was the impression of most of the physicians that merger had been initiated in order to give us (a) increased utilization of joint facilities, (b) eliminate competition among the hospitals with emphasis on increased help from large donors, (c) better patient care and improved medical attention. It was felt that to this date merger had been almost a complete failure. . . . It is definitely felt by a great many physicians that the Board of Trustees is not well acquainted with our problems as often they only air problems with physicians who are truly not representatives of the overall feeling.

The best survey of attitudes among medical personnel at the center (302 of 475 questionnaires were returned), done in 1969, indicated widespread discontent with the DuPont-interests outside corporate and family circles. Real power sponsored merger (see Table 4-4).[19]

TABLE 4-4.

*Results of Survey of Wilmington Medical Center Medical Personnel*

| | *General Improvement* | *Little or No Change (%)* | *General Decline* |
|---|---|---|---|
| Quality of patient care | 14 | 42 | 34 |
| Administration of facilities | 15 | 39 | 32 |
| Patient's evaluation of services | 9 | 49 | 28 |
| Professional autonomy | 4 | 58 | 27 |
| Control of out-patients | 9 | 58 | 18 |
| Status of individual doctors | 9 | 63 | 18 |
| Availability of specialized equipment | 19 | 63 | 8 |

Similarly, a review of the tenure of the center's first director, Ernest Shortliffe, shows the conflict between health care personnel and the DuPont family. In 1963 Dr. Lewis Flynn recruited Shortliffe for the job of administrative chief, reporting to a joint hospital management committee. Shortliffe diligently set about consolidating the management of three hospitals to bring about the anticipated gains in efficiency. He began consolidating such specialized functions as obstetrics (fused into one facility at Wilmington General), pediatrics (centralized in Delaware State Hospital), and surgery plus general ward medicine (also at Delaware State).

Shortliffe ignored the wishes of certain old-time hospital donors—Mrs. R. R. M. Carpenter and her daughter. Both women, scions of the archconservative Carpenter family, were furious when Shortliffe closed down obstetrics in Memorial, "their" hospital. Carpenter's daughter demanded the return of the lounge furniture she had given to the obstetrics wing of Memorial Hospital. Shortliffe ignored her, but the board gave in, and ordered Shortliffe to satisfy her whim. (Presumably, the furniture remains to this day in her barn.)

In short, politics influenced the merger: functional consolidations were stalled by the quibbling of family members loyal to their favorite hospitals, or enacted so carelessly that the overall quality of patient care declined or stayed the same. To make matters worse, members of the joint board of the three hospitals began to worry about losing support from major donors like the Carpenters. Shortliffe would not compromise, and demanded a free hand in effecting the merger, so the board forced Shortliffe to leave by abridging his authority in ways he could not accept. Shortliffe believes the Carpenters not only demanded his ouster, but blocked him from at least one subsequent job.

To replace Shortliffe, the board chose John Perkins, who had been a good fund raiser, utilizing his close ties to the corporate establishment while president of the University of Delaware. Perkins had left the University of Delaware to become head of Dun and Bradstreet. Perkins says he yearned to be back in Delaware and accepted the post. He had never run a medical facility, but the directors thought he was qualified because of his administrative background and a short tenure in the Department of Health, Education, and Welfare.

Although Perkins was acceptable to the DuPont family, he had trouble with the doctors. Though a newcomer to medicine and hospital administration, Perkins ran a very authoritarian medical center, according to many doctors. In July, 1970, Dr. Martz, the director of medical education, reported the results of a survey he had taken of doctors. One statement read: "Administration will take over and run things to the detriment of staff," and 62 respondents agreed (20 strongly so), while 37 disagreed (4 strongly so).

Recent events have disclosed more problems for the Wilmington Medical Center. A study by Sociometrics, an independent consultant, showed that the center was providing low-quality care to poor patients. While this study was being done, the center, whose fees were already the highest in the state, raised its rates an average of $13 per day so that a private room for an average stay would cost an additional $104. St. Francis hospital charged $82, and Riverside, $63 per day, $10–30 below the Center.

As highly educated and prosperous doctors could not overcome the limitations imposed upon them by DuPont support, so ghetto dwellers could not avoid the built-in problems of community dependence on foundations, as the case of the Neighborhood Improvement Program (NIP) clearly illustrates. NIP, a social action program designed to uncover the roots of ghetto problems, was run by Russell Peterson, then a top executive in the DuPont Company, and H. B. du Pont, chairman of the Greater Wilmington Development Council, which provided NIP staff.

With H. B. du Pont's backing, NIP never had financial problems. As the head of the DuPont clan, H.B. opened the coffers of personal bank accounts and DuPont foundations to it. Although community groups in Wilmington ghettos had been living on a shoestring budget for years, all H.B. had to do to raise money was summon a small group of businessmen and family members to lunch at the Hotel DuPont. One luncheon guest described the scene:

> There were about ten of us around a table with H.B. One person from GWDC spoke for a few minutes on the goals of the NIP program. Then H.B. explained that three-quarters of a million dollars was needed to run the program and started around the circular table. By the time he got to the end of the circle, the NIP was oversubscribed. And the luncheon was only cold cuts.

They approached this social action program like a business venture, choosing neighborhoods that were poor, but not the poorest, to improve their "return on investment," and formulating a set of numerical goals and a schedule for meeting them. One community leader described the businessmen's technique as follows:

> Peterson saw that there were so many dilapidated housing units in Wilmington, so he set a goal to wipe out all local blight and then divided by the number of years of the NIP program. The goals had nothing to do with the realities of low-income housing problems. It was like Peterson was phasing out a DuPont department whose products had become obsolete.

The goals of NIP were to be met by organizing neighborhood service centers. The businessmen assumed that people were poor mainly because they did not have proper access to existing social service agencies; the service centers supposedly would meet that need. But the crucial problem, as the NIP experience showed, was that the social agencies lack the resources to help the poor.

Once the program began, problems of community dependency quickly surfaced. Peterson and H. B. du Pont first had to choose community groups to sponsor neighborhood centers. This choice gave Peterson and H.B. tremendous influence over the program, since several groups were seeking sponsorship in each neighborhood. In northeast Wilmington, conflict between two would-be sponsors stalled the program almost a year. Eventually, NIP chose a settlement house started and still partly financed by W. W. Laird, a DuPont family member. The other group was a grass roots organization whose members felt they understood residents' needs better than the bureaucrats in the settlement house.

The corporate elite kept tight control over the sponsoring groups. NIP demanded detailed reports and accountings of all activities and expenditures, and tried to overrule programs it disliked. When one community center hired a painter to work with local youths to improve the neighborhood, the NIP staff said it had not given prior approval to the project and withheld the $1500 needed for it. The central NIP staff insisted that one neighborhood center take an OEO law office, though local residents thought a nearby area needed the office more.

As community groups in NIP began to think that reform of the local political structure was a prerequisite to improving their condition, they became more suspicious of DuPont-related funding. The businessmen wanted to improve communication with social service agencies. In contrast, community leaders wanted to bring political pressure on public officials to allocate more resources to the ghetto. As one community leader in NIP said:

> Professional and neighborhood people knew where the money came from and we were always sensitive to the NIP's informal and formal requirements to stay out of politics. We knew political activity is necessary for change in the long run, but in the short run we needed money to keep our program going.

The community's increasingly political stand upset NIP. During the third year of the program, NIP cut the budgets of the community groups, effectively telling them to go into debt or change their program. At least one center went into debt because it would not break promises to local residents.

In the end, NIP was an exercise in tokenism. It tried to improve education, housing, and job training, and to do so quickly. In education, NIP accomplished nothing. Concentrated activity in education was scheduled for the program's final year, by which time the corporate group was trying to get out.

Housing programs proved equally unsuccessful. NIP hired Block Blight, a housing rehabilitation group with William Foster du Pont on its board, to run the program. Block Blight was an exercise in mismanagement. It got badly into debt because it paid for contracts before completion. William du Pont, Jr., had promised $35,000 to pull the group out of financial trouble, but died before making the gift, and the money never came. The NIP's own report concluded that less than 5% of home improvements made during the program were carried out by Block Blight. Community groups still receive requests to repair or finish work Block Blight had supposedly done.

Job recruitment, the allegedly successful component of NIP, illustrates the total inadequacy of NIP's commitment to neighborhood needs. The main component of the recruitment program, carried out jointly with the YMCA, was to interview neighborhood residents for industrial jobs in the "familiar setting" of the three NIP centers. By January, 1968, the program was in shambles. The Conference of Neighborhood Service Centers announced that only 23 out of 66 participating companies actually hired anyone.[20] The conference accused the companies of being more interested in their public images than in providing jobs.

By the end of the Neighborhood Improvement Program in 1969, members of the corporate elite were out of the social action field entirely. Corporate executives explained to the neighborhood people that the program was intended to run for only three years. When the three years were up, the NIP staff understood the problems of urban poverty and left. Meanwhile, the neighborhoods continued to struggle with their problems. To carry out some of the unfulfilled goals of NIP, community groups like Westside Conservation Center had to beg for money from some wealthy patron, a foundation, or some city agency. Now the corporate establishment's main link with the neighborhood groups of NIP is its originally misplaced preoccupation with the research on urban poverty. According to the *News-Journal,* Greater Wilmington Development Council "plans to start work next year on setting up a system of social indicators to measure effectiveness of social action efforts."[21]

CHAPTER 5

# DuPont Chateau Country and the Delaware Upper Class

The DuPont family has always been tightly knit. Not only has it intermarried—Pierre Samuel and Henry B. du Pont married their own cousins and, says one author,[1] "one paterfamilias was forced to issue an edict against the practice"—but the DuPont family remains tied to one state, Delaware, and one neighborhood within that state. In addition, the DuPont family has always been very class-conscious. Blood relation to the DuPonts plus long-standing connections with high officials in the DuPont Company are prerequisites for membership in the state's upper class. DuPont Company directors have historically married DuPont women.* Other factors differentiating the Delaware aristocracy are education in certain private schools, membership in certain elite clubs, and residence in "chateau country."

* Hamilton McFarland Barksdale m. Ethel du Pont, 1890; Charles Copeland m. Louisa d'Andelot du Pont, 1904; W. W. Laird, Sr., m. Mary Alleta Pelin du Pont, 1904; R. R. M. Carpenter m. Margaretta Lammot du Pont, 1906; Rodney Sharp m. Isabella du Pont, 1908; Crawford H. Greenewalt m. Margaretta Lammot du Pont, 1926.

To prove upward social mobility exists in Delaware, DuPont family members constantly point to Charles McCoy and Walter Carpenter, Jr., the only presidents of the DuPont Company who were not DuPont family members. But McCoy's father had been a top DuPont executive for years, and McCoy attended an elite private school in Wilmington. McCoy's sister married the secretary of the DuPont Company, and one of his sons is married to a granddaughter of Margaretta du Pont Carpenter. Similarly, Walter S. Carpenter, Jr., was the close friend of Irenee and Lammot du Pont, as well as a yachting partner of Pierre S. du Pont. His son, Walter S. Carpenter III, a director of the company, married into the DuPont family two years before Walter, Jr., became president of the DuPont Company. His brother, R. R. M. Carpenter had married into the family and been a DuPont Company director for 34 years.

The DuPont-centered class is clearly the most influential in Delaware. It includes most of the important businessmen, many powerful politicians, and almost all the wealthy landowners. Obviously it does not contain all the wealthy or powerful persons in the state. Many high-income families have not gained entrance into the upper class, though they want to; some do not care to "join" and wish no contact with the DuPonts. But the crucial point is that many powerful and wealthy Delawareans are relatives, schoolmates, fellow club members, or neighbors of the DuPonts. The influence of each member of the upper class reinforces the importance of the others; the existence of class multiplies the sway of the DuPonts, and the presence of the DuPonts increases the prominence of the others.

## *Private Schools and Social Clubs*

One distinguishing characteristic of Delaware's upper class is private education at one of four elite schools in the Wilmington area: Tower Hill, Tatnall, Friends, and St. Andrew's. Members of the corporate elite dominate the administration of the four, which together serve less than 1% of the state's precollege school enrollment, through financial ties or board memberships. W. W. Laird, a DuPont family member, has been the chief benefactor of Tatnall; Felix du Pont established St. Andrew's, and DuPont-related foundations have financially supported Friends. Tower Hill is the most elite of the elite, with Pierre S. du Pont III at the head of a board that includes many family members.

With their close ties to the DuPonts, the four private schools have created a system surpassing public education. While public schools in New Castle County are facing severe social and financial problems, the private schools provide an almost luxurious education for an almost all-white student body. Though many school districts spend about $600 per pupil per year, the private schools charge $1500 a year in tuition alone.

Both private and public school officials say their regular sources of income—taxes or tuition—are hopelessly inadequate. The private schools have the advantage, however, in searching for outside funds. During a recent three-year period, the DuPont Company gave $170,000 to the Wilmington public schools in the wake of riots that followed the assassination of Martin Luther King. In the same period, the Crystal Trust gave $250,000 to Friends and $100,000 to Tower Hill, and Longwood Foundation gave $600,000 to Friends and $500,000 to Tatnall. Both foundations have been run by men holding high positions in the DuPont Company—Irenee du Pont, Jr., and Henry B. du Pont. Presumably they helped set the company's contribution to the Wilmington schools while their foundations were providing over eight times as much money to private schools.

Community leaders insist that influential DuPonts have not been committed to educational reform because they have no personal stake in the public school system. Rodney Layton, a DuPont family member, headed the city's Urban Coalition, which was supposedly dedicated to improving local teaching facilities, but he sent his children to Tatnall. While prominent government officials like Wilmington mayor Harry Haskell make crucial decisions on public education, their offspring attend private schools.

The elite schools also drain off the most promising students from the public school system through their (limited) scholarship programs. A consultant report done for three private schools says that because of this brain drain "the public educator is apt to see the selective independent school as a potential threat to his own efforts to improve the quality of the program for his own district."

Like elite schools, social clubs isolate the upper class from the masses of the state. The wealthiest and most powerful residents of Delaware sit around one large round table each day for lunch in an old brownstone house—the Wilmington Club. Of the 259 resident members, about one-fourth are DuPont family members and an additional one-sixth hold top posts in the DuPont Company, including 14 of the 25 company directorates. The 4 officers of the Wilmington Club for 1970 included the president of Wilmington Trust, a DuPont family member, and a DuPont Company executive. There has never been a black member of the club. Dr. Luna Mishoe, the black president of Delaware State College in Dover, has never been asked to join; the white presidents of the University of Delaware get honorary membership. Italians, Poles, and Jews are also excluded, although a Jewish judge once became an honorary fellow because all members of the Delaware Supreme Court are granted this privilege.

A rung below on the social ladder is the Wilmington Country Club, built on land purchased from the late Henry F. du Pont. Four-fifths of the DuPont Company directors are members, and the club's officers are mainly from the DuPont family, the DuPont Company, Wilmington Trust, or Delaware Trust. To limit membership, the Wilmington Country Club has established rigid induction procedures. All applications must be accompanied by letters from eight members, which are posted on the clubhouse bulletin board "to permit members to submit comments to the [Membership] Committee." [2] One person on the membership committee said in an interview, "The Wilmington Country Club makes every effort to insure its exclusivity"—which means no blacks, Jews, Poles, or middle-class workers. Membership costs are very high—a $3000 initiation fee plus $340 annual dues.

The Vicmead Hunt Club established at the turn of the

century, is the center of foxhunting for the upper class. Vicmead was named after two du Ponts, Mrs. Victor du Pont and Mrs. Hollyday S. Meeds, Jr. (formerly Ellen C. du Pont). While Vicmead has hosted important family events like the 1937 marriage of Franklin D. Roosevelt, Jr., to Ethel du Pont, it is primarily a hunt club. The hunts are held in the southern part of New Castle County, around the Chesapeake and Delaware Canal.

The most recently formed upper-class social club is the Bidermann Country Club, which began operation in 1965. According to George Weymouth, DuPont in-law and the first president of the club, Bidermann was started for two reasons—to cater only to golfers in an intimate and informal atmosphere and, more important, to protect the DuPont family's Winterthur Museum from the inroads of residential buildings and traffic.[3] Bidermann was set up in 1963 in cooperation with Henry F. du Pont, who gave a small group of the upper class a 50-year lease on 160 acres of Winterthur land including his own personal nine hole course. The club was so exclusive that it accepted only 200 members at the start. All but one of the initial officers were DuPont family members; the lowest ranking officer was a fellow horseman of the DuPonts.

Aside from their class and race discrimination (few Italians and now Jews are members of the DuPont clubs, though many have the money), social clubs have provided a very private forum for decision making on important public matters in Delaware. One Delawarean told how he was approached in the locker room of the Wilmington Country Club by a prominent member of the upper class who held a high public office. The official asked the man about a problem in the Wilmington area. Apparently pleased by the response, the public official appointed the man to an important committee to study the problem and make policy recommendations. Social club contacts are most important for realtors, bankers, and lawyers, because their professions depend more heavily on personal relations than on free-market transactions. One important Wilmington realtor told how his club memberships were an integral part of his business:

> I deal mainly with high-priced residential properties, so I depend on the DuPont Company executives for a large part of my business. The company has a policy of transferring supervisors and middle managers in and out of Wilmington about every five years, so I have a tremendous incentive to develop personal friendships with company officials. I maintain my contacts mainly through playing golf and drinking at the bar of the Wilmington Country Club. . . . These contacts have paid off well. I get many of my best referrals from the DuPont Company, especially the textile fibers department which has the largest number of transfers in the Wilmington area. You see, social contacts are the key. You know ——— ———; he can't break into the high priced housing market because he does not belong to the right clubs.

Social clubs are also important for local bankers. At a party in one of Wilmington's country clubs, one bank officer received an early tip that Columbia Gas System was moving its headquarters from New York City to Delaware. As a result, his bank obtained part of the Columbia Gas account. One Wilmington bank president stated in an interview that bank policy required all officers to join at least one country club. While the bank preferred to have officers join the Wilmington, Bidermann, or Greenville country clubs, the few Jewish executives join the Brandywine Country Club. According to the bank president, bank officers were encouraged to befriend real estate agents and attorneys because they would be most likely to have information valuable to the bank.

The connection of social clubs to the legal community opens up possible conflicts of interest. Twenty-eight lawyers, 15 of whom are from large corporate firms associated with DuPont interests, are members of the Wilmington Club. Six federal judges in the Wilmington area as well as all the justices on the Delaware Supreme Court and Chancery Court are honorary members of the Wilmington Club. The club provides a perfect meeting place for lawyers with the judges who are hearing their arguments. According to several attorneys, after they argued a case against an upper-class lawyer in court during a morning session, the presiding judge and opposing counsel have walked out together to the Wilmington Club for lunch.

## *Chateau Country*

From the public viewpoint, the most important aspect of the Delaware upper class is its land holdings. Seventy families within the DuPont clan alone own 13,000 acres of the most attractive land in northern New Castle County. The land and buildings are worth over $200 million.

The land holdings and dwellings of the upper class vary in style and quantity, though all the residences meet an aristocratic standard. Irenee du Pont, Jr., owns about 520 acres of land around his 55-room mansion. Henry Belin du Pont owned a mansion on 357 acres of land, worth together nearly $3 million, as well as another 510 undeveloped acres. Wilhelmina du Pont and Donald P. Ross live on 63 acres in Christiana Hundred * and own another 940 acres in Mill Creek Hundred with a 3-acre private race track. While some estates are smaller, they too are tremendously valuable, often worth several hundred thousand dollars. The mansion of Pierre S. du Pont IV, built on a 5.8-acre site adjacent to his father's 165 acres, is worth from $300,000 to $500,000. Many other DuPont estates, like Pierre's, are contiguous to the homes of immediate relatives. For instance, Henry H. Silliman, Jr., lives on an 18-acre estate worth over $100,000 near the 11-acre estate of his mother, Marianna du Pont Silliman.

Outside the lavishly furnished family estates, a wall of green isolates the DuPonts from the rest of the county (see Map 1). To the north and northwest is the Pennsylvania border and land held by other DuPonts. To the southeast is a greenbelt between the DuPonts and Wilmington—387 acres of the DuPont Company Country Club and Experimental Station, the 860-acre Winterthur Museum (former home of Henry F. du Pont), 136 acres of the exclusive Wilmington Country Club, 280 acres of the Alfred I. du Pont estate (now a hospital for crippled children), 93 acres of the DuPont family's Eleutherian Mills–Hagley Museum, a municipal golf course turned over to the city by William du Pont, Jr., and some open land owned by the

* The "hundred" was the primary electoral and administrative unit of government in colonial times; the term is now merely descriptive of different areas of the county.

University of Delaware. To the northeast, the 2000 undeveloped acres of Woodlawn Trustees buffer the upper class against suburban encroachment. To the southwest are vast expanses of open land without adequate roads or public utilities, the Hercules research facility and country club, and another 1700 acres of DuPont Company land; all protect the DuPont estates from encroachment by the city of Newark, Delaware, and more of suburbia. The consequences of this greenbelt include grievous misallocation of land resources and recreational facilities, overcrowding in sectors beyond the greenbelt, diminished property tax revenues, and rigid stratification of social classes into their respective ghettos—poor and rich alike.

To maintain their elegant isolation, DuPont family members have fought hard against public measures designed to promote rational, planned development. The estate owners have persuaded county officials to keep public sewers needed for residential development out of chateau country. As one county official said, "This is the trade-off the rich make with the county. They pay for the few sewers and the septic tanks needed to service their mansions and we don't push development. If we put sewers in, then they would be subjected to great pressures to increase the density."

Similarly, the DuPonts obtained a special dispensation from the planned unit development (PUD) provision of New Castle County zoning regulations. Planned unit development calls for the integration of commercial and residential uses, especially low-income housing, as opposed to the current pattern of expensive residential areas isolated from other kinds of housing and from commercial strips. Since the DuPonts in Greenville, the heart of chateau country, did not want PUDs in their neighborhood, they hired their own consultant to justify the need for only low-density land uses. Despite the strong objections from professional planners, the County Council passed what is commonly known as the "Greenville Amendment." The amendment sets an absolute limit of four units per acre for PUDs in Greenville, while PUDs throughout the rest of the county may have densities as high as nine units per acre.

To further guarantee the pristine residential isolation of

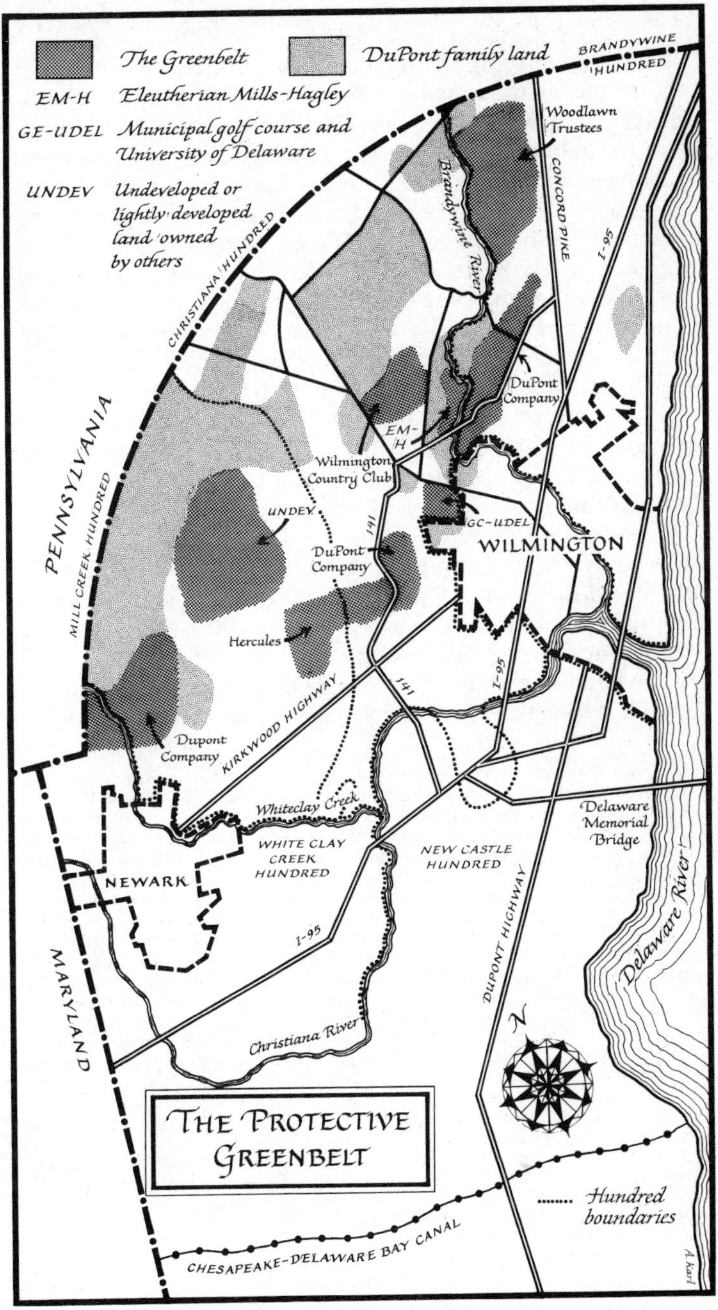

The Greenbelt
DuPont family land
EM-H Eleutherian Mills-Hagley
GE-UDEL Municipal golf course and University of Delaware
UNDEV Undeveloped or lightly developed land owned by others
BRANDYWINE HUNDRED
Woodlawn Trustees
Brandywine River
CONCORD PIKE
I-95
CHRISTIANA HUNDRED
PENNSYLVANIA
MILL CREEK HUNDRED
DuPont Company
EM-H
Wilmington Country Club
UNDEV
GC-UDEL
WILMINGTON
DuPont Company
141
Hercules
KIRKWOOD HIGHWAY
141
I-95
Dupont Company
Whiteclay Creek
WHITE CLAY CREEK HUNDRED
NEW CASTLE HUNDRED
Delaware Memorial Bridge
NEWARK
I-95
DUPONT HIGHWAY
Delaware River
MARYLAND
N
Christiana River
THE PROTECTIVE GREENBELT
Hundred boundaries
CHESAPEAKE-DELAWARE BAY CANAL
A. Karl

chateau country, the DuPont family has tried to buy up all the prime industrial sites left in the county.* The Chesapeake and Delaware Canal, for instance, would be attractive for industrial development with its nearby water supply, relatively low land prices, and distance from residential neighborhoods. But the canal area is also the center of the Vicmead Club's foxhunting. The canal zone was of special concern to H. B. du Pont, whose wife is an avid hunter. One Saturday morning the head of the Water Resources Center at the University of Delaware was suddenly called to the university's main office where he found the university president and H. B. du Pont waiting for him. H.B. told the professor that the Water Resources Center would do a study on the availability of water in the canal area within 100 days because both Union Carbide and Shell Oil were planning to establish plants there. H. B. du Pont asked the professor how much money would be required to finance this study. After a moment's reflection, the professor arbitrarily threw out the figure $50,000. H.B. replied, "You've got it," according to a witness. Within 100 days, the report came out showing that existing water demands in the canal area were too high for both Shell Oil and Union Carbide to establish plants. The results were presented to the state

* With the rise of pollution as a public issue, the upper class now rationalizes its isolationist practices with a conservationist logic. But DuPont-family groups like Delaware Wildlands have not opposed the White Clay Creek dam, a DuPont Company project strongly criticized as an environmental debacle by independent conservationist groups like the Sierra Club (see Chapter 11). Nor has the upper class brought its influence to bear upon the DuPont Company to stop polluting air and water (see Chapter 2) or prevent DuPont executives from weakening Delaware environmental law (see Chapter 13). A more credible explanation for upper class isolationalism would be political. In the 1930s, DuPont prevented the Fords from buying Delaware land for an auto factory, reportedly because the Fords threatened DuPont domination of Delaware. Currently, the upper class seems bent on undercutting the political challenge inherent in a strong blue-collar movement by buying up industrial land, which is then never developed. With the blue-collar population of Delaware thus limited, DuPont-related candidates can ride to victory on the ballots of the corporate middle class. This political explanation for upper-class isolationalism derives considerable support from the company's acrimonious battle against strong unions (see Chapter 3), the state's failure to promote industrial development (see Chapter 13), Governor Peterson's decision to ban all heavy industry from the Delaware coast (see Chapter 14), as well as the failure of the DuPont-dominated Greater Wilmington Development Council to aid industrialization of the city's Cherry Island and port areas (see Chapter 8).

governor who approved the conclusions. In response to the study (as well as for other reasons), one of the companies has since withdrawn its plans, and the other has yet to build.

While H. B. du Pont used his foundation to thwart industrialization along the canal, Delaware Wildlands, a DuPont-funded private group, has been buying up prime industrial land in the state. In 1967 Delaware Wildlands paid $1 million for a 2020-acre farm bordering on land belonging to Shell Oil in southeast New Castle County. The Wildlands purchase prevents Shell from expanding. Soon after this purchase, Delaware Wildlands paid about $1 million for a 2300-acre tract of potentially industrial land at the mouth of the St. John's River in Kent County, on the south Delaware coast.

The two purchases, while laudable from an environmental viewpoint, have unfortunate side effects. Unlike other environmental groups Delaware Wildlands has circumvented public processes completely to stop industrial development. With its great economic power in Delaware, the aristocracy is able to make a public decision like stopping industrial growth, and implement it on its own terms; other interests must petition state or local governments. The upper class in Delaware has chosen to oppose most forms of industrial development through its very private but quite effective use of economic power. As a consequence, it has unilaterally resolved the dispute between environmentalists and job seekers.

Yet, the very existence of these private facilities has reduced the interest of the powerful upper class in public recreation, though the DuPonts have donated a little land for parks. The recommended national land standard is 90 acres of open space for every 1000 members of the population.[4] New Castle County has a total of only 9240 acres of publicly owned lands for parks, equal to 25 acres of open space per 1000 residents, or a net deficit of 24,000 acres, according to the recommended standards. The country clubs and private family lands together amount to 18,000 acres of prime park land in the country, but all this acreage is very private.

Another result of DuPont family isolationism has been a

great decrease in the property tax base for New Castle County. Family estates like Winterthur do not pay property taxes because they are now held by tax-exempt groups dominated by the DuPonts. The large holdings of Delaware Wildlands are tax-exempt. In 1970 alone, the total land holdings of tax-exempt groups related to the DuPonts reduced the New Castle County tax base by over $7 million.

Moreover, upper-class families have grossly underpaid New Castle County government for the extensive estates still held in private hands. As Chapter 12 explains in detail, DuPont family lands benefit from a county property assessment system that assesses and taxes large residential landholdings at a lower assessment rate per acre than smaller holdings. As a result, middle- and lower-middle-class residential property owners in the county pay a disproportionate share of property taxes. The DuPonts have also benefited more than most property owners because increases in the market value of land are not reflected in increased assessments. The DuPonts own the most valuable, least developed land near populated areas in the county. They have escaped millions of dollars in property taxes because assessments have not changed in 15 years, a period of rapidly rising land values in the DuPont area of the county.

## *Private Interest Before Public Plans*

As H. Rodney Sharp, a DuPont family member, was flying his private plane one day, he saw an attractive plot of county land near the intersection of Interstate 95 and Delaware Route 7. After consultation with H. B. du Pont, Sharp purchased this large tract of land with du Pont and turned it over to du Pont's Welfare Foundation. While the tax-exempt Welfare Foundation held title to this 591-acre tract, the county planners carried out extensive public hearings on a comprehensive land use plan for the county. Neither du Pont nor the Welfare Foundation publicly objected to the designation of the 591-acre plot as part of the county's prime industrial zone.

Several years later, representatives of the Welfare Foundation offered 200 acres for construction of a hospital complex by the Wilmington Medical Center. The Welfare

Foundation asked the county to rezone the whole 591-acre plot for institutional instead of industrial uses. According to the county planners, the requested rezoning would destroy the land use balance in the county. Public services such as sewers and roads could not cope with the center's projected level of demand. And the request for rezoning struck at the heart of the county's comprehensive plan. The county planners said:

> It is not merely that the request deals with almost 600 acres of land—in itself obviously of major consequence—but, more pointedly, if granted, is bound to influence the use of at least an equal amount of land in the same general vicinity, thereby affecting future planning and development in the county for many years to come.[5]

When faced with the objections of the county planners, Dr. John Perkins, the executive director of the Medical Center, told the study group he had always been one of the strongest advocates of planning in the Wilmington area. When asked if this belief conflicted with his flagrant contravention of professional judgment on the Medical Center move, Perkins replied that the question "made him cry crocodile tears." In August, 1970, Ralph K. Gottschall, the chairman of the Wilmington Medical Center board, had not read the consultant reports evaluating the merits of a move to the county, although some of these reports had been out for months.

Like the county planners, city officials strongly criticized the proposed move by the Wilmington Medical Center. If the Medical Center were located in the county, there would be only one branch left open in the city. Some doctors in the center predict a discriminatory system of medical care—ghetto blacks going to a second-rate city facility while suburban whites attending the new complex in the county. When the study group interviewed Perkins in August, 1970, he said the center was providing excellent service to the black community of Wilmington and would continue to do so after it located in the county. Several months later, a consultant study by Sociometrics jointly sponsored by the city, county, and Medical Center after much community pressure, concluded that medical services to the Wilmington poor were completely inadequate; the study specifically noted the inability of the poor to get to medical facilities without cars, a problem that obviously would worsen if the center moved to the county.

In response to the medical problems of the urban poor, Mayor Haskell suggested that the center should expand into the two cemeteries adjacent to the center's existing hospitals. Mayor Haskell, in a study group interview, pointed out that the cemeteries could be moved at a relatively low cost whereas the hospitals would lose a tremendous capital investment by moving.

All parties to the dispute at last agreed to commission a study by Frederick Guttheim. According to a member of the County Planning Board, Guttheim introduced the results of his survey recommending the county site by saying that his wife had thought that the conclusions were not supported by the data. She was right. Guttheim asserted that other industrial plots could replace the Welfare Foundation land; after years of intensive study, the county planners have not found another site, and Guttheim didn't propose any. Guttheim presented a traffic analysis by the state highway department to show the roads at the intersection of I-95 and Route 7 could cope with the Wilmington Medical Center. But he had asked the highway planners to choose only between two sites—both at the intersection of I-95 and Route 7. In fact, highway department officials strongly opposed the center's move to this intersection. They said there would have to be expensive large-scale changes in the county's transportation plan, which would be almost impossible to accomplish in a way that would be safe for car drivers. Posing another solution to the transportation problem, Guttheim predicted a major breakthrough in the technology of mass transit in the next 10 to 15 years. Again, there was no specific analysis of the serious planning problems in making the county site accessible to hospital employees and city residents, who are mainly poor blacks, without cars. Guttheim did not even ask the transit company in the Wilmington area about the possibility for mass transit to the site.

In the final round, the center announced its rejection of the cemetery site because of "complications."[6] While the county planners publicly denounced the Guttheim report as an intellectual fraud, Rodney Layton, a DuPont family member and corporate lawyer, filed a brief with the county government in favor of the center's proposed move. In December, 1970, the county council approved the Medical Center's request for rezoning the county tract. Thus, county residents have lost job prospects and tax revenues, city dwellers may suffer drastic reductions in medical services, and the Welfare Foundation will have undermined the public planning processes in both governmental units—all through the chance flight of H. Rodney Sharp and the personal whim of H. B. du Pont.*

## *Social Class and New Castle County*

Through the operations of the DuPont-biased land market, together with the impact of elite private schools and exclusive country clubs, New Castle County has become a rigidly divided class society. It is the product of a free land market that is not free, an equal opportunity education system that is not equal, and a socially mobile society that is immobile. The rigid class divisions of New Castle County follow the four geographical divisions marked on the county map (see Map 2): the Brandywine area (#1), the DuPont area (#2), the airport area (#3), and the southern canal area (#4).[8]

The median family income for the whole county was $6823 in 1960. The DuPont quadrant was by far the wealthiest, with median yearly incomes over $20,000; followed by the Brandywine area, where annual family earnings range between $12,000 and $15,000; then the airport area, with most families in the $7000–8000 range each year; and finally the southern canal area, where annual median incomes in 1960 were just below $4000.

* Ironically, the Health Planning Council announced in September, 1971, that New Castle County will need an additional 255 hospital beds by 1980—345 *fewer beds* than predicted by John A. Perkins when he was urging the county to rezone the Welfare land.[7] The center's proposed 600-bed hospital in the county may be either postponed or reduced in size. Or a cynic might think the 600-bed hospital will be built anyway. It would present a "good reason" for the Medical Center to reduce services in the city.

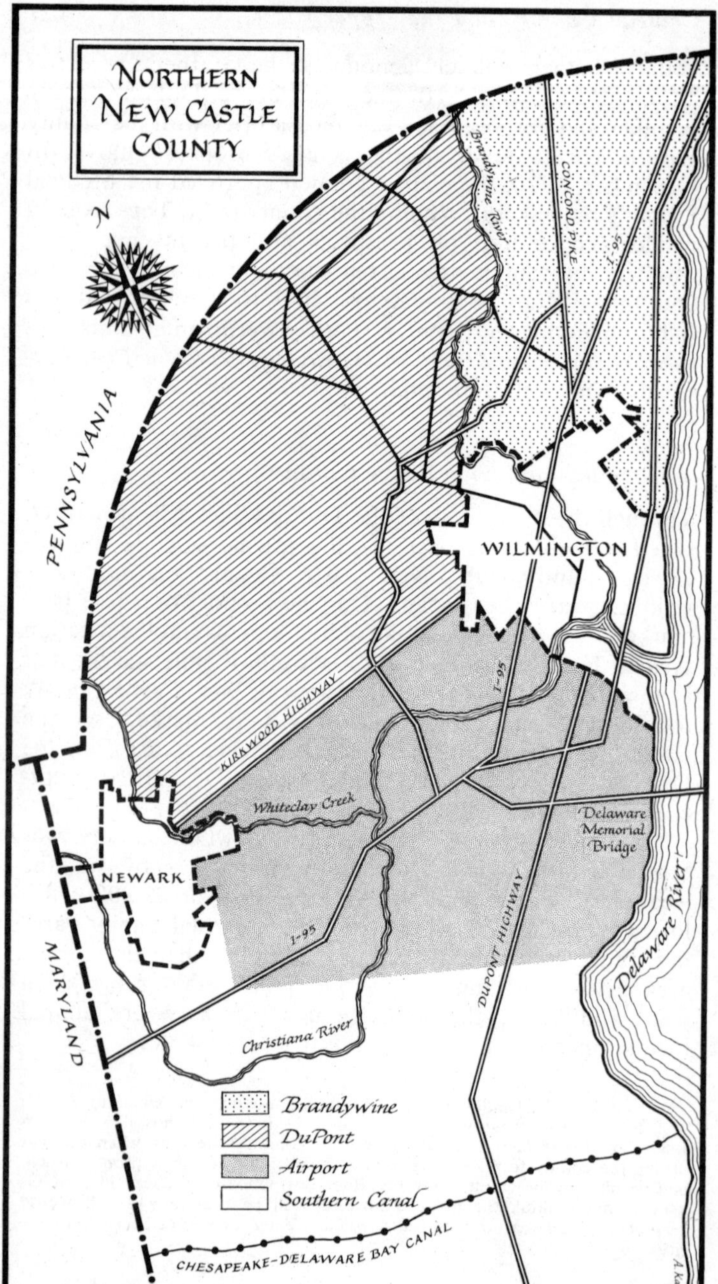
NORTHERN NEW CASTLE COUNTY
N
PENNSYLVANIA
MARYLAND
Brandywine River
CONCORD PIKE
I-95
WILMINGTON
KIRKWOOD HIGHWAY
Whiteclay Creek
NEWARK
Delaware Memorial Bridge
DUPONT HIGHWAY
Delaware River
Christiana River
Brandywine
DuPont
Airport
Southern Canal
CHESAPEAKE-DELAWARE BAY CANAL
A. Karl

In terms of the quality of housing, the highest rates of housing dilapidation are in the southern canal area, with significant percentages of dilapidated housing units in the airport section. In contrast, dilapidation is virtually nonexistent in the DuPont or Brandywine sections. The statistics on inadequate plumbing and overcrowding present a similar pattern. In some areas in the southern canal zone, 30–40% of the houses lack plumbing facilities. In some census tracts in the southern canal zone and the airport section, a large number of units had more than 1.01 persons per room; in Brandywine and DuPont overcrowding is practically nonexistent.

The combination of income and housing quality determine to a large degree the caliber of schools for each area, since education is funded by a school tax based on the assessed value of property in the school district. In Brandywine, the valuations for homes range between $20,000 and $28,000; Brandywine is known for the finest public schools in the state. DuPont similarly has plenty of money to support educational facilities because the homes are mainly in the $35,000-plus category and many children attend the elite private schools. In contrast, the value of homes in the airport and southern canal sections are in the $8000–9000 range, and the families do not have high enough salaries to afford a steep tax rate. For both these reasons the schools in the southern canal zone and the airport zone have very low levels of expenditures per pupil (see Chapter 14).

While recreational needs are supported by the countywide real property tax rather than a districtwide levy, a great discrepancy still exists between sections. Brandywine Hundred contains 24 public parks or recreational facilities plus two large private country clubs, several private swimming clubs, and the vast forest reserves of Woodlawn Trustees. But New Castle Hundred in the airport zone contains only 13 public parks or recreational facilities, even though the residents in this area cannot afford private club memberships. Even the DuPont quadrant, with its very low population density, numerous private country clubs, and private swimming pools, has more public recreational facilities than New Castle Hundred. The southern canal zone, whose residents depend entirely on the government for recreational facilities, has only four public park areas.

One of the most striking divisions between sections is the ethnic distribution. Most residents of the DuPont section are white Anglo-Saxons. Like DuPont, most parts of Brandywine are white, with Jews concentrated in a few pockets. In the airport zone, Italian or Polish working-class suburbs, like Minquadale or Collins Park, are rigidly set off from all-black suburbs, like Rosedale or Oakmont. In the canal zone, blacks live in small adjuncts to towns composed mainly of poor whites.

# Part III

# Corporate Agents

Corporate agents are private groups so controlled or dominated by the DuPont family or company that in effect they represent DuPont interests. Corporate agents may be businesses owned by the DuPont Company or family, such as the News-Journal Company, or non-profit groups with DuPont control over purse strings and board membership, like the Greater Wilmington Development Council.

The formal separation between corporate agents and the DuPonts gives agents an important role. Because they seem to be independent, many people do not realize that they are controlled by or closely interlocked with the DuPonts. An editor of the *News-Journal* explained the nature of these interlocks in an article of July 4, 1969:

> James A. Grady's presidency (until this spring) of the Greater Wilmington Development Council and Roger W. Fulling's direction of Downtown Wilmington, Inc., are two examples of this approach in practice. Not only does final authority and responsibility in the or-

> ganizations they lead or led not rest in their offices, but the "representative" boards and executive committees to which they report do not have final authority or responsibility. Certain key individuals or groups within those organizations are in turn reporting back to other groups or individuals, either within the DuPont family or company or both. It is those last groups or committees that say yes or no.

With the appearance of independence, corporate agents can assume functions which family members or company executives could not carry out directly. While the DuPont family can hardly write news stories on itself, it can make sure that the *News-Journal* keeps unfavorable comments off the front page; it would be outrageous if the DuPont Company itself wrote the state's general corporation statute, but a small group of corporate lawyers can represent the company's interests when writing legislation. While corporate agents may occasionally disagree with the DuPonts, in the long run the interlocks of personnel and interests are strong and effective.

# CHAPTER 6

# *Money and Morals: Bankers for the Corporate Establishment*

The DuPont family has owned controlling interest in two of the four major banks in the state since the early part of the 20th century. Family and company control the board of directors of both banks. Alfred I. du Pont bought almost all the Delaware Trust Company stock in 1916 and sold it to William du Pont a few years later. The family and company have held controlling shares in the Wilmington Trust Company since its formation in 1901. The other two major banks in the state are personally tied to the corporate elite. In 1969 the 26 directors of the Bank of Delaware included 3 DuPont executives, 2 family members, and board members of 3 DuPont-dominated firms. While the state holds a majority stock interest in Farmers Bank of the State of Delaware, 2 of the 25 directors in 1969 were family members and one was a DuPont executive.

As of June 30, 1969, the combined total assets of all Delaware banks was $1.67 billion. Of these assets, the Wilmington Trust Company held 27%, the Delaware Trust held 11%, Farmers Bank held 18%, and the Bank of Delaware held 15%. The four largest banks thus control 71%

of the state's total bank assets and the two DuPont banks, Wilmington Trust and Delaware Trust, hold more than half of these. The total assets of the five national banks in Delaware were less than one-tenth the total assets of the Wilmington Trust Company and only one-twentieth the combined assets of the two DuPont banks. The 25 savings and loan associations in Delaware are also quite small, with combined assets of only $48.5 million, as compared to Wilmington Trust's $450 million.

By all objective standards, then, the Wilmington Trust Company is the largest and most important bank in the state. Its position in the banking community is like that of the DuPont Company in the industrial community. It is an integral part of the company and family empire. Of the 24 directors of the Wilmington Trust Company, 13 are DuPont family members or DuPont Company executives. The family owns some 25% of the bank's stock, easily a controlling block. As the major stockholders and a majority of the board of directors, the DuPont family and Company control the money in Wilmington Trust. Stockholders' equity * in Wilmington Trust is only 3% of the total assets of the bank. This means that the DuPont establishment can manipulate assets worth at least 130 times its investment in the bank.

Not surprisingly, DuPont family members use the Wilmington Trust for the bulk of their deposits and for their trust funds. The DuPont Company, too, does most of its Delaware banking there, with only token deposits in the three other major Delaware banks. The funds for both the DuPont Company pension and retirement plan ($1.8 billion) and the DuPont thrift plan are held by Wilmington Trust, although the family-dominated finance committee of the company makes all investment decisions for both funds.

The DuPonts who control the Wilmington Trust use it in the interests of family and company. The bank serves as trustee of the family trusts. The trust department is big business at Wilmington Trust. In 1969 it had the 12th

* Equity means the initial sale price of stock, which goes to the company issuing the stock. When a stockholder sells stock to a third party, the price of the stock may differ from the initial sale price, but the difference affects the stockholder only. The company still holds only the initial sale money.

largest trust department in the United States, although the bank's total deposits ranked only 143rd. Its trust assets were worth $5.7 billion, almost 10 times the trust assets of all other Delaware banks combined. In the same year, Wilmington Trust derived 18% of its total income from the trust department, as compared with 9% at the Delaware Trust and 11% at the Bank of Delaware. Wilmington Trust derives a higher *percentage* of income from trusts than even the Morgan Guaranty Trust Company in New York, which has the largest amount of trust assets in the country.

The trust department of the Wilmington Trust Company is directed toward the very rich, although some trust department employees will work on the small trusts of ordinary people. But according to one trust officer at the bank, top management frowns upon this practice and actively solicits large trust accounts through national advertisements. In its commercial publicity, the Wilmington Trust cites the bank's "specialized experience in the management of substantial personal property" and Delaware's "exceptionally favorable" trust laws.[1]

The special concessions of the Delaware tax law, outlined in Chapter 4, have attracted some of the richest families in the country, including the Mellons of Pittsburgh, the Millikens of New York, and the David K. Bruce family. The DuPont family, too, takes full advantage of Delaware trust law. According to a source in the Wilmington Trust Company, family members put 50–70% of their wealth into trusts prior to their death. Family trusts contain 5% of all outstanding DuPont common stock as well as 50% of all Christiana Securities common, which represents control of another 15% of DuPont stock. A family member may also put stocks into a trust account for a charity or foundation, which receives the income from the stock while the family still holds the stock's voting rights.

The DuPonts retain control over stock held in trust, though when a trust is established, the grantor usually gives the bank as trustee complete powers over the trust principal, including the power to vote proxies of the trust's stock and to sell the stocks originally in the trust. The bank normally sends copies of proxies to the trust beneficiary or to the grantor, if he is still alive, for voting directions, and the grantor can restrict trustee voting power. He may, for instance, *require* the bank to obtain consent of a person chosen by the grantor before voting stock in the trust fund.

Family members guard their trusts through board memberships. The Wilmington Trust, with so many family members on its board, seldom offends DuPont interests. One family member told the study group that he is a director of another local bank to look after a large trust held there for his benefit. Both DuPonts on the Bank of Delaware's board are members of the board's Trust Committee, which supervises all trust matters.

Grantors can protect the family's interest in retaining DuPont and Christiana stock by requiring approval of a person appointed by the grantor before any trust assets are sold. Wilmington Trust must consult with both H. Rodney Sharp, Jr., and Bayard Sharp before selling any property held in trusts established by their mother, Isabella du Pont Sharp. The grantor may impose other restrictions on the bank's power to trade stock in a family trust. Eugene Eleuthere du Pont stipulated that DuPont Company stock put in trust under his will could be traded only if the company's financial condition were bad enough to *require* it. When Pierre S. du Pont bequeathed his entire estate in trust to his Longwood Foundation in 1954, he provided that the trustees could not trade or sell Christiana stock for any stock but DuPont common.

### *The Story of "Motsey" Copeland and His Friendly Bank*

It is difficult to document instances of special favors done by DuPont banks for family members. But it is clear that such abuses occur in the small world of Wilmington finance. The recent bankruptcy of Lammot du Pont Copeland, Jr., appears to be one.

Copeland, Jr., a Harvard-trained securities analyst for the DuPont Company, began building a financial empire in the early 1960s, often working through his holding company, the Winthrop Lawrence Corporation. In 1965 he earned $756,984 in personal income. He owned $10 million of life insurance and a $550,000 home in Delaware. In

1969 he purchased the Citizen News Company, owner of 39 Southern California suburban newspapers. His other investments included a toy manufacturing company, a van line, and college dormitories. Copeland's California newspapers paid him $13,000 monthly in consulting fees, while he was receiving over $300,000 annually from more than 70 trusts established for his benefit by his father and grandfather.

To finance his empire, Copeland, Jr., took out loans from over 46 banks and insurance companies. When Copeland, Jr., declared assets of $25.7 million and liabilities of $59.1 million in his bankruptcy petition on October 20, 1970 (one of the biggest personal busts in history), he caught all his creditors by surprise—except the Wilmington Trust Company.

In April, 1969, Wilmington Trust loaned Copeland, Jr., $3,718,925, secured by $500,000 in collateral and a $3,350,000 guarantee from his father, who was also a director of Wilmington Trust and board chairman of the DuPont Company.[2] When the note came due a year later, it had an unpaid balance of $3.4 million. The Wilmington Trust, upon the advice of William S. Potter, DuPont in-law and attorney for Copeland, Sr., sought and obtained judgment on this loan in a Wilmington court on June 19, 1970. Under bankruptcy law, any creditor that enters judgment less than 120 days before a petition of bankruptcy is filed must join other creditors in a court-approved general settlement of all claims. Conveniently, the date on which the Wilmington Trust entered judgment was 121 days before Copeland's petition was filed.

Bank officials claim that the perfect timing was pure coincidence. It is hard to believe that they did not know that Copeland, Jr., was about to file bankruptcy, since both the bank and Copeland, Jr., used the same Wilmington law firm and his father was on the Wilmington Trust board. Whether or not bank officials knew that Copeland, Jr., intended to file for bankruptcy, Wilmington Trust effectively protected over $3 million of his assets, including his $550,000 Wilmington home, from his other creditors. These assets were protected by the lien obtained by the bank through its timely action.

Moreover, Wilmington Trust refused to execute the $3.4 million judgment until three days after Copeland, Jr., filed his petition of bankruptcy; it sold his collateral—$410,000 worth of stocks and bonds.[3] By waiting, the Wilmington Trust hid the financial woes of Copeland, Jr., from other creditors. The creditors would not be likely to learn about the June, 1970, judgment, since there are only about 70 subscribers to the publication in which the sole public notice of the judgment was made. The publisher, the Bank Credit Bureau, is located in Wilmington with an unlisted telephone number. The Wilmington Trust's judgment against Copeland, Jr., was so secret, in fact, that he was able to get a $1 million loan from the Union Bank in Zurich, Switzerland, one month after the judgment had been obtained.[4]

Copeland, Sr., must have known that his son was in serious debt. He had personally provided over $4 million to shore up his son's crumbling empire. But he used his financial influence to help his son borrow more. As director of the Chemical Bank in New York, Copeland, Sr., helped his heir obtain a $3 million loan from Chemical Bank. And when Wilmington Trust executed the judgment against Copeland, Jr., it sold his collateral but did not collect the rest of the money, $3 million guaranteed by the bank's director, Copeland, Sr. Instead, it sold the judgment—to a syndicate headed by Copeland, Sr. It is a virtue to be good to one's children, but the behavior of Copeland, Sr., raises serious legal and ethical questions. By encouraging two banks to give multimillion-dollar loans to his son, Copeland, Sr., may have abused his position as director of these two banks. The directors of Wilmington Trust may have breached their fiduciary duty to the bank's shareholders when they refused to liquidate immediately the $3 million guarantee given by Copeland, Sr., for his son's loan at Wilmington Trust. The father's decision to remain a director of the bank after the guarantee was not liquidated might be viewed as self-dealing, since the other directors would be reticent to force him to pay the debt if he were still one of their associates on the board.

In the whole incident, the family interests were in direct opposition to the legitimate rights of bank stockholders, other creditors, and the public. Wilmington Trust should have informed other potential creditors of the bank's June judgment against Copeland, Jr., so as to stop the spread of uncollectable loans being given out to him. Its silence made it possible for him to obtain another $1 million loan after defaulting on the $3.5 million at Wilmington Trust. Non-DuPont family stockholders and depositors of Wilmington Trust were left out of this closed-interest-group arithmetic. Their deposits and shareholder interest were jeopardized because Wilmington Trust did not liquidate Copeland's tremendous debt immediately. Needless to say, an ordinary person defaulting on a large loan at Wilmington Trust would have received less consideration. Lammot du Pont Copeland, Jr.'s middle name didn't hurt him.

Nor, for that matter, did bankruptcy. Substantial portions of Copeland, Jr.'s assets are tied up in trusts. He used the $13 million in trust assets and $311,000 in trust income to inflate his own financial statement when securing loans around the country.[5] But when he filed the bankruptcy petition, he correctly listed these trusts as "spendthrift" trusts which could not be attached by his creditors, in accordance with another Delaware law favoring the corporate rich.* With this trust income, young Copeland will be bankrupt and earning $300,000 per year.

## *Information and Private Control*

While the Wilmington Trust pays special attention to certain of its wealthy clients, Delaware banks provide little public information about their own activities. For private and public groups to evaluate a bank's work in a community, they need access to specific data on bank policies for use by independent analysts. While some data are available on Delaware banks, most of it is in aggregate form. To permit intelligent analysis, such data should be broken

* Title 12, Section 3536, of the *Delaware Code:* "Every interest in trust property or the income therefrom . . . shall be exempt from execution, attachment, distress, for rent, and all other legal or equitable process instituted by or on behalf of such creditors." The "spendthrift" clause does not allow the beneficiary to assign his interest in the trust in such a way that is unassignable according to the trust instrument. By listing the trust assets in his financial statement, Copeland, Jr., was incorrectly implying that such assets could be used to pay off any debts.

down into categories that are fairly precise. Loans, for example, should be broken down to show the amounts going into local retail businesses, local manufacturing, consumer installment loans, national corporations, and so on. This information is not available.*

The special ties between the DuPonts and the Delaware banks have created a level of secrecy far beyond what is needed to protect the privacy of bank depositors. Wilmington Trust officials say a trust "is not open to public inspection as is a will after the death of the testator; therefore the disposition of the bulk of the trustor's property is kept confidential." Therefore the bank refused to provide our study group with information on trusts or trust investments, which are held mainly by DuPont family members. In 1970 a Wilmington Trust stockholder asked to see a list of stockholders. He was interrogated at length by several lawyers before being allowed to exercise his stockholder rights to obtain such minimal levels of bank information. According to Lewis S. Munson, chairman of the board of Wilmington Trust, the bank even refused to give certain information to Congressman Wright Patman's House Banking Committee

* Although both the Federal Reserve Board and Federal Deposit Insurance Corporation (FDIC) have complete accesss to a bank's records, they publish only generalized figures similar to the balance sheets given in annual reports. The more detailed reports of the bank examiners are highly confidential; each page of each report carries a warning that severe criminal penalties will be incurred if the report is shown to anyone except a bank officer. The aura of secrecy is so strong that a bank's lawyers hesitate to read examiners' reports, even with permission of the bank officers.

The Securities Exchange Commission (SEC) and the underwriters of a bank's stock are the only other outsiders to receive detailed information on a bank's activities. Both groups receive "composition statements" giving a detailed breakdown of the bank's assets and liabilities according to the specific categories necessary for a comprehensive evaluation of a bank's policies in terms of its financial security or community impact. The public does not have access to these reports except when the bank rejects a recommendation of the examiners. In such a case, Federal Reserve officials may publicize those parts of the examiners' report supporting the rejected recommendation. The SEC may also publish such data if a bank merger is proposed.

The concealment of examiners' reports and composition statements from the public is not needed to protect the competitive position of banks. The data in these reports circulate informally among financial institutions. Through personal contacts bankers know the degree to which their competitors are in the auto loan business, the types of people to whom they grant mortgages, or the degree to which they are making loans on the local or national market. This is especially true in a small city like Wilmington.

for an investigation of bank trust activities until required by subpoena to reveal the data.

The Bank of Delaware and the Delaware Trust Company cooperated with the study group; they gave data concerning the types of loans in their commercial and consumer loan portfolios, dictating some of the material directly from the reports of federal bank examiners. When members of the study group posed the same questions to officials of the Wilmington Trust, they were told that no such data existed—in spite of the fact that the same bank examiners audited its accounts and presented similar detailed reports. The Wilmington Trust even refused to name its main corporate clients and insisted that it had no idea what corporations banked with other banks in Wilmington. Officials in other banks, however, freely admitted that such matters were common knowledge in local banking circles.

A bank has a duty to protect the legitimate private interests of depositors and other individual customers, but when it carries secrecy to the extremes as the Wilmington Trust does, it implies it has something to hide. And the Wilmington Trust does.

Delaware's banking commissioner, John W. Green, supports the secrecy fetish of local bankers. In an interview with the study group, Green did not analyze the information problem in terms of the public interest; instead, he defended refusals to disclose many types of information, such as the amount of money in different loan categories, because such disclosure is not in the best interest of the banks. More important, Green has tried to hinder efforts by members of the public to get information about Delaware banks. When an attorney sought data from Farmers Bank, of which he was a shareholder, Green warned that the attorney might be subject to criminal prosecution under a Delaware law that prohibits "willfully and maliciously making . . . any false statement, rumor, or suggestion . . . which is directly or by inference derogatory to the financial condition . . . of any bank."[6] This warning is in line with the commissioner's general policy of replacing strict regulation with friendly accommodation for Delaware banks. He goes to their social functions and, in general, tries to cultivate close personal contacts with the money men. In an interview, Green said he would like to have the authority to evaluate the impact of bank lending policies on the community; for example, he would like to know whether banks are making loans locally or going out of the state in search of high yields. But since Green's appointment in May, 1970, he has let his good intentions slide, while abdicating any real regulation of Delaware banks.

### *Banks and Community Needs*

In terms of bank loan policies, the needs of the corporate elite are directly opposed to the interests of the public. DuPont family members do not normally require bank loans to buy a new car or home. Pierre Samuel du Pont, for instance, had four cash accounts with Wilmington Trust, totaling $1,135,000 in 1954. Lammot du Pont, Jr., maintained balances of approximately $2.5 million in his Wilmington Trust checking accounts. Irenee du Pont, Sr., had nearly $8 million in four cash accounts at Wilmington Trust in 1964. Accounts of this size provide immediate access to large sums, so that family members seldom need to borrow money and pay interest. Because of the large demand deposits maintained by family members, the Wilmington Trust has to keep enough cash on hand to meet their special needs as well as the normal cash needs of other depositors. As a result, the Wilmington Trust Company keeps from 10% to 15% more of its assets in cash and short-term federal funds than do all other banks in Delaware, thus denying the local economy the benefit of millions of dollars that might have been given out as loans. In 1969 Wilmington Trust had cash and notes payable on demand from other banks equal to 37% of demand deposits. This cash account, totaling $113,598,000, was 24% of the total assets of the bank, while the comparable percentages for the Delaware Trust, Farmers Bank, and Bank of Delaware were 8%, 8%, and 15%. Wilmington Trust says in its 1969 annual report that it

> maintain[s] a high degree of liquidity and normally has funds in excess of reserve requirements. These funds are invested on a day-to-day basis by purchasing securities

under agreements to resell or by selling federal funds to other banks.[7]

These short-term notes have a comparatively low rate of return; their main function is to keep large sums available on short notice. If the cash account were reduced by 10% of total assets, in line with the policy at other Wilmington banks, $66.8 million would be released for possible investment in the community * and the account would still be above the 7% of bank assets that must, by state law, be held in cash accounts.[8]

Moreover, what money the Wilmington Trust does lend is not put into the local economy. Instead Wilmington Trust puts a large part of its assets into government and corporate bonds. In 1969 the value of securities held by Wilmington Trust was 60% of the loans then outstanding, as compared with 42% at the U.S. Trust Company of New York, 23% at the Philadelphia National Bank and 26% at the Girard Trust Company of Philadelphia. The other large banks in Delaware, with the exception of the Bank of Delaware, have similarly high percentages of assets in investment securities. These policies do not harm the DuPont Company. It never borrows from domestic banks, financing all its American investments through profits, and DuPont employees can easily obtain personal loans in Delaware banks. DuPont employees are assumed to be good credit risks and often do not even need a company credit reference to get a loan.

But the ordinary consumer has trouble getting banking services. He may have to present several letters of recommendation and may never be approved as a credit risk. One member of the Delaware study team found that a local bank would not even pay the face value of a cashier's check, which is supposed to be as negotiable as cash; the bank insisted on calling the study group member's home bank at his expense. But it is exactly the ordinary customer, not the DuPont family member, who at times requires

* Some of the $66.8 million may represent either funds in the process of being collected ("float") or funds deposited to the account of the Wilmington Trust at correspondent banks. But the bank's own admission that it maintains excess cash reserves suggests that a large portion of the money may be resting idle in the bank's vaults or invested in short-term federal notes.

banking services for basic needs—housing, a small business, and some social mobility. Moreover, ordinary customers are faced with an increasingly limited range of banks from which to obtain banking services since, within the last two decades, the four large banks in Wilmington have bought out many of the smaller banks throughout the state.

### HOME LOANS

DuPont-related banks play a major role in determining the costs and the location of homes for individual families in New Castle County. Since few families can buy a house with cash, and since mortgage loans are usually given out only to local residents, Delaware residents have to borrow from Delaware banks. Many families want mortgages insured by the Federal Housing Administration, as such mortgages allow a longer pay-back period and require a lower down payment than other mortgages. But there are only two banks in the Wilmington metropolitan area that deal seriously in FHA mortgages. One is the Wilmington Trust Company, which bought out the largest home finance company handling FHA mortgages in the state. The other is the Wilmington Savings Fund Society, with a board of directors filled with members of the upper class. If either of these two banks will not finance plans for home purchase, then many families are in effect prohibited from building. The home finance company bought out by Wilmington Trust had a reputation for approving applications for FHA loans on much more stringent standards than those established by the federal government. Wilmington Trust has continued that policy. As one Delaware developer said about Wilmington Trust's officials: "They don't want guys with A ratings; they want triple A ratings."

Even when a local bank decides to finance a home mortgage, it charges interest at a rate calculated by its own evaluation of the mortgage application. In every bank there is a standard interest rate for conventional mortgages and for FHA loans—somewhere between 6% and 9%. But banks in every state tack on charges called discount points; each point is equal to one-tenth of the standard mortgage rate. Discount points are given completely at the bank's discretion according to vague criteria of desirability. Those connected with the corporate establishment have a better chance of obtaining a low number of discount points (or no points at all) than, say, a black man who works in a black construction firm. Although Delaware's usury laws prohibit interest rates over 9%, a recent addition to the Delaware statutes exempts discount points from the law. The addition of discount points to a standard loan rate usually brings the rate over the 9% mark, and sometimes to as high as 13%. Delaware banks hide this extra cost of the mortgage from homebuyers by charging the discount points to the developer instead of the loan recipient. Then the developer passes the added cost on to the family through a higher purchase price.

The system of collaboration between realtors and bankers in the Wilmington area imposes even higher prices on the purchaser of a home in Delaware and increases the granting of loans. The experiences of homebuyers whom we shall call Mr. and Mrs. O'Keefe are typical for the Wilmington area, according to local architects and realtors.

Having done well in his job, O'Keefe talked with a local contractor about building a home in the Wilmington suburbs. Since the contractor was not giving him what he wanted, O'Keefe went to an architect, who drew up plans and put them out to public bid. The next day a local realtor told the architect that the original contractor could not possibly compete with other bidders because he owed the realtor a commission for being introduced to this home purchaser. The commission, which runs between 4% and 4½% of the cost of the land and the house, in this case amounted to $3400. When the bids were opened, an Italian-American contractor was low bidder. The next day the original contractor went to O'Keefe and offered him a better mortgage interest rate, since both the contractor and the real estate agent were on the board of one local bank. Moreover, he told Mrs. O'Keefe, surely she did not want an Italian building her house in such a fancy neighborhood; but the couple did not yield. However, at the bank where they had large sums of money deposited, O'Keefe was told no funds were available for loans and, besides, it was a bad time to borrow. The architect checked with other bankers in town. All of them said it was an excellent time to borrow because the standard rate was between 6½% and 7% and was on the rise. Finally, O'Keefe yielded to the realtor's wishes and agreed to have the original contractor build the house. He then easily obtained a home loan from the bank that had originally rejected him.

Besides granting individual home loans, Delaware banks seriously influence the local housing market by their financing policies for large developments in both high- and low-income ranges. While local banks are generally ready to finance a high-income housing development, pressure from the DuPont family may create complications. Several years ago, a group of Delaware businessmen planned a residential development near several large DuPont estates. They worked on the plans for over a year and arranged for $250,000 financing from a local bank. But just as they were ready to build, their financing fell through. Although no one would say exactly who was responsible for the withdrawal, there were strong indications that influential estate owners had blocked the project because it would have marred their scenic views. No more details about the incident are available, since one of the businessmen involved did a substantial amount of work for family members who had opposed his project. He refused to give any more information to the study group because he would lose too many customers among the Delaware upper class, but he admitted that the withdrawal of financing was unfair.

In the field of low-income housing projects, Delaware banks have refused to accept financing obligations under almost any circumstances. Delaware has a severe housing shortage (see Chapters 10 and 14). To alleviate this shortage, the banks could promote rehabilitation of many substandard or abandoned buildings in the city of Wilmington. But according to many local businessmen, Delaware banks for years have been unwilling to underwrite "spot loans" * for housing rehabilitation. One prominent developer with a long history of financial success told how DuPont-related banks would not help him finance the rehabilitation of a

* "Spot loans" are made individually for each house being rehabilitated at the time the remodeling work is ready to be done, rather than a lump sum being given for an entire rehabilitation project of numerous housing units.

small office building near downtown Wilmington because it fell into the spot loan category.

The construction of new low-income housing units is another key to improving Delaware's housing supply. Federal programs that provide 100% financing and interest rate reductions are available; however, a nonprofit housing sponsor needs "front money" to pay for such expenses as preliminary design *before* he can obtain federal financing. Front money is usually estimated at 10% of the total cost of a project. To help nonprofit groups obtain front money, the head of the Wilmington Housing Authority proposed in 1964 that local banks establish a revolving fund which would lend money to nonprofit sponsors until they could obtain full federal financing. But the local banks have not taken a single step in that direction.

### SMALL BUSINESS LOANS

Delaware banks, busy kowtowing to big companies like DuPont, have neglected small business in the state, according to officials of the Small Business Administration. The SBA, which works with local banks to provide more risk capital for small firms, has two types of financing programs. The first provides direct loans to small businessmen. The second asks local banks to make the loan with SBA's guarantee (up to 90%). The SBA naturally prefers working through local banks to making direct loans, since its limited money can go much further if used to guarantee loans. Its assistance to local businessmen is severely limited if local banks will not participate. Yet during 1966 and 1967, the Delaware banks did not provide any SBA loans, forcing the local SBA office to make 23 loans totaling $1.25 million directly to Delaware applicants. During 1968 and 1969, banks supplied 9 out of 26 SBA loans (35%) totaling $308,000 out of $644,500 loaned; in 1970 they helped fund only 11 out of 48 SBA loans (23%) or $479,000 out of $1,400,950. In Philadelphia during the same period, SBA officials say that banks provided 80% of the SBA loans. The only Wilmington bank that has shown any significant cooperation is Delaware Trust, which made 7 of the 11 SBA-guaranteed loans in 1970, for a total of over $200,000.

In 1967 SBA officials tried to convince Wilmington

Trust to participate in SBA loans, only to be told that the bank was "all loaned up." That is, the board of directors had decided it would be imprudent to invest any more of the bank's assets in loans. At that time, Wilmington Trust's total outstanding loans were only 51% of its total deposits; the average for the four largest Delaware banks was 58%. Nor has the percentage of loans at Wilmington Trust increased significantly since. Wilmington Trust has denied small businessmen the benefit of millions of dollars that could have been prudently invested in guaranteed loans without jeopardizing the interest of the bank's depositors and shareholders. In a state as small as Delaware, an investment of that size could make a significant difference for the local economy.

### MINORITY BUSINESS LOANS

Americans like to view their society as socially mobile. But in practice upward mobility depends on access to education, jobs, and financial resources. Banks can thus play an essential role in bettering the lot of the economically disadvantaged. With only a few exceptions, Delaware banks have refused to play the role. Although the banks claim they never have discriminated, black community leaders offer many examples of Negroes denied home loans for no apparent reason. One black leader told of an experienced black public school teacher who approached the bank where he had long conducted his financial affairs, asking for a home improvement loan of $4000. Bank officers said they would give him only $1000, and that only if he first raised the other $3000 on his own.

The difficulty black entrepreneurs encounter in obtaining loans can be seen clearly in the experience of Melvin Perry. Perry, a black college graduate, incorporated with some friends on April 3, 1968, under the name of Autolab Automotive Service Center. His venture was designed to provide high-quality automotive repair service to the Wilmington area. Atlantic Oil Company agreed to furnish him with equipment, and several experienced mechanics working at other autodiagnostic centers agreed to work for him. The corporation registered with the Securities Exchange Commission in 1969. By December 31, 1969, it had received

$73,297 as payment for stock already issued; CONRESCO, a Connecticut small business investment corporation licensed by the SBA, agreed to loan Perry $100,000.

Perry then asked the Wilmington banks for $155,000 to build the service center on land the corporation had already purchased. He then had assets of $61,375, only $3,442 of which were subject to claims which would be superior to any loans the bank might make. He had agreements with Atlantic Oil Company and CONRESCO as evidence that other corporations found him worth backing. The local SBA was willing to guarantee any loan made to Perry up to 90% or, alternatively, to put up 75% of the loan if the banks would put up the remaining 25%. A bank's total risk exposure would have been limited to $15,500 in the first case or $38,500 in the second. Despite all this, both the Wilmington Trust and the Delaware Trust turned him down, as did two small savings funds.

Finally, Perry sought advice at a local organization established to aid minority businessmen. A staff member, a retired DuPont employee, took Perry back to the Delaware Trust and got him the loan after a brief, amicable meeting. The message was clear: even one of the most liberal banks in the state, Delaware Trust, would deal with him only if he was introduced by people with the right connections.

Responding to the small civil disturbances over the assassination of Martin Luther King, Delaware banks modified their irresponsible and indifferent attitudes toward racial minorities. In cooperation with the DuPont Company, they agreed to make available $500,000 in credit to a new community fund, the Wilmington Business Opportunity and Economic Development Corporation, established by the Black Alliance in 1969. WBOEDC would review loan applications from blacks, referring those considered acceptable to a credit steering committee composed of representatives of the four major banks and the Peoples Bank and Trust Company, a small community-oriented bank in Wilmington. Loans approved by the credit steering committee would be processed by one bank, which would allocate part of the loan to each participating bank. Staff from each of the banks, DuPont, and other corporations would counsel recipients of WBOEDC loans. And DuPont, Atlas, and

Hercules corporations promised $150,000 for an insurance fund to repay the banks if any loans were defaulted.

By September 28, 1970, only three loans, totaling $22,000, had managed to get through WBOEDC's intricate structure. During the same period the banks gave away between $12,000 and $15,000 to defray the overhead costs of WBOEDC. The ratio of loans funded to contributions was thus less than two to one.

The three loans that were granted were selected from over 39 applications—11 of the 39 were disallowed, 2 more were approved but had not yet been funded, and 19 were still being processed on September 28. Seven applicants withdrew before making a formal application. The small percentage of applicants receiving loans was in large part the responsibility of John L. Lane, Jr., the first executive director of WBOEDC. Lane applied standards only slightly less stringent than those of the banks and relied on bank credit reports. He would overlook marginal credit records only if there seemed to be strong signs of growth. His standards were strict, he said, to ensure that blacks referred to the banks would be fine credit risks who would demonstrate to the banks that black capitalists are competent. Since Lane left WBOEDC in 1971, loans have increased substantially.

The failure of WBOEDC becomes even more evident in light of possible uses for the $150,000 cash and $500,000 credit which the fund is currently tying up. Under an SBA program to set up Minority Enterprise Small Business Investment Companies (MESBICs), the federal government will contribute twice the capital invested by private sources. The MESBIC can then invest these funds, equal to 3 times the original private investment, in minority enterprises. These funds can also be used in conjunction with bank loans which the SBA will guarantee up to 90%. Since the guaranteed bank loans can be up to 4 times the money invested by the MESBIC, the total amount of capital channeled into minority enterprise will be 5 times the MESBIC investment and 15 times the amount of the original private investment.[9] If the $150,000 invested in WBOEDC by DuPont, Hercules, and Atlas corporations had been put into a MESBIC, a total of $2.25 million could have been generated for economic development in the black community. If one adds in the $500,000 kept out of circulation for ready loans, the figure rises to $9.75 million.*

The question, then, is why the MESBIC program was not utilized in Wilmington, since much more capital could have been raised for the black community, given the *same level* of contribution from the Delaware corporate establishment. Some people connected with WBOEDC say the MESBIC alternative was considered and rejected as being inflexible. But in discussions with us, they didn't seem to realize the tremendously advantageous multiplier possibilities of MESBIC. John Lane, while director of WBOEDC, offered a different explanation. He said in an interview conducted in 1970 that Wilmington had its own minority investment company, rather than a MESBIC, because of an anti-federal government attitude within the Wilmington business community. Lane's statement is supported by the historical aversion of DuPont-linked banks to the federal Small Business Administration. The SBA officer for Delaware explained to us that Delaware bankers generally have felt they could take care of Delaware's problems without federal interference. In 1967 the local SBA officials met with the SBA's Delaware advisory council, representing most of the major financial interests of the state. The consensus of the council was that SBA was not needed in Delaware.

### LOCAL GOVERNMENT FINANCING

A final important aspect of bank policy in Delaware is the relation between the financial community and government. From time to time, local governments or public agencies must borrow money to finance large civic projects. Typi-

* As opposed to the ineffectual WBOEDC, MESBIC would have also opened up a vast new array of possibilities. MESBIC offers the investors a return on their capital in the form of dividends or a long-term appreciation in the value of its stock. MESBICs also have a privileged tax status, allowing investors to "pass through" their income to their shareholders without paying a corporate income tax. Thus investors avoid double taxation at both the MESBIC and shareholder corporations. The government grants various other tax advantages in order to maximize the MESBIC's chances of earning a good profit. The potential profitability of the MESBIC, combined with the large sums it can funnel into the black community, make it clearly superior to the nonprofit corporation that was actually set up.

cally, long-term borrowing is done by a bond issue sold through investment bankers. Since the interest on the bonds is free from federal and state income tax, the purchasers are normally banks and wealthy individuals (often represented by bank trust officers). However, a fundamental conflict exists between the government body and the initial underwriter, especially in the case of revenue bonds supported by charges made to the users of the project. The public body must carefully weigh the annual burden placed on the project so that the public will be charged the lowest rates. The investment banker, on the other hand, is concerned with writing into the bond agreement safeguards for the investors and speedy repayment provisions.*

An example of the inherent conflict between public and private interests arose in the financing of the Wilmington Parking Authority, a public agency established by state law to finance parking facilities in the city of Wilmington at a lower cost to the public than could be provided by private industry. In 1956 the parking authority issued bonds for $2.15 million, paying an interest rate of 4¼% to construct the Midtown Parking Center. The bonds were to mature in 40 years, interest to be paid semiannually. But the bond resolution severely fettered the discretion of parking authority officials. It required that parking rates be fixed to yield enough annual income to pay operating expenses and 140% of the amount necessary to pay debt service. Current

* In the case of long-term bond issues for revenue projects, investment bankers insist that the rate covenant (the promise made by the local government agency regarding the basis on which it will fix the user rates) contain certain protections against a reduction in use of the facility. This is called "cover," and the amount of cover is a matter of bargaining between the local government unit and the underwriter. The underwriter tries to arrange the required user charges so that, after payment of operating expenses and the required interest and principal on the bonds, there is a substantial surplus. The underwriter then requires that the surplus be used to retire bonds ahead of the fixed schedule. The underwriter will try to have the excess funds pledged to the repayment of bonds in what the lengthy document called the "Bond Resolution" or "Trust Indenture" refers to as the "Bond Redemption Fund" or some similar name. The underwriter pushes for early retirement of bond issues because, as interest rates rise generally, the price at which an investor can sell bonds previously purchased in a lower interest rate market will decline. Also, the investor can reinvest, at a higher rate of return, the money repaid to him sooner than anticipated. On the other hand, the issuing body wants to have the greatest freedom in using these surplus monies for other public purposes.

expenses must be set in accordance with a previously adopted budget approved by the consulting engineer, who must be satisfactory to the underwriters. Most important, the bond resolution said that all surplus funds must flow into the bond redemption fund to redeem the debt, even if way ahead of schedule. The bonds will be paid off 21 years ahead of schedule.[9]

Thus, the provisions of the bond resolution go much further than protecting the legitimate interests of bondholders in receiving payments on schedule. This bond resolution forces the parking authority to give up ahead of schedule revenues needed for additional facilities. To finance more parking lots, the parking authority will have to borrow money at rates higher than 4¼%, since the interest rates have been increasing. Moreover, the inflexibility of the bond provisions blocked the city government in its efforts to allocate some of the parking authority's yearly surplus for municipal services. Many bond resolutions provide that the surplus monies may be used by the public body for "any lawful purpose"; this bond resolution requires that all surplus monies be used only to redeem the bonds.

CHAPTER 7

# *Lawmakers and Lawbreakers: Counsel for the Corporate Establishment*

There are four major law firms in Delaware: Connolly, Bove & Lodge; Morris, Nichols, Arsht & Tunnell; Richards, Layton & Finger; and Potter, Anderson and Corroon. These four firms do most of their work for large corporations and wealthy individuals. For example, Morris, Nichols, Arsht & Tunnell represents the DuPont Company and Christiana Securities; William Potter was attorney for the estates of William, Jr., Pierre S., and others in the DuPont clan.

Members of the four big firms have both personal and institutional ties to the corporate elite. Some are DuPont family members by birth or marriage. Many serve as directors of other groups in the corporate establishment. Corporate lawyers are on the DuPont-controlled boards of the Greater Wilmington Development Council and the University of Delaware. Almost all the corporate lawyers belong to the upper-class clubs.

To these ties, corporate lawyers add close connections with public government. For years, state agencies were represented by private lawyers from large firms, paid handsomely for their work while they obtained the additional benefits of information and political contacts. For example, Alexis du Pont Bayard was the special attorney for Delaware Turnpike from 1962 to 1969. Three of Bayard's partners held similar posts in other state agencies. Samuel Arsht was attorney for the state highway commission for 12 years. Arsht was receiving a $12,000 annual retainer from the state plus fees for extra work, like the $40,000 he got representing Delaware in a suit over the placement of Interstate 95 in Wilmington.

While state agencies now hire their own lawyers, attorneys from the top four law firms retain close links with the court system. Potter, Anderson & Corroon has sent at least six judges to Delaware courts, including the current chief justice of the Delaware Supreme Court. Richards, Layton & Finger—which represents the family's Wilmington Trust, News-Journal, and Atlantic Aviation companies—has supplied two judges to the Delaware Superior Court. From the DuPont Company's law firm—Morris, Nichols, Arsht & Tunnell—have come two federal district court judges and an associate justice of the state supreme court. A former justice of the state supreme court is George B. Pearson, a DuPont family member; earlier in his career, a current justice lobbied for DuPont on the General Motors divestiture bill discussed later in this book.

With a separate chancery court to decide most business-related cases, Delaware has gained a national reputation for a promanagement judiciary. When U.S. Steel decided to incorporate in Delaware, it cited as a key reason the "substantial body of case law, decided by a judiciary of corporate specialists." [1] A $2-billion telephone company, according to a Delaware corporate lawyer, moved its state of incorporation to Delaware for the case law *and* the favorable attitude of chancery court judges. New York lawyers who specialize in shareholder suits against management told the Delaware Study Group that Delaware courts tend to discourage such stockholder suits. Or in the words of William Potter, a DuPont family member and corporate lawyer: "Delaware has judges who provide a good business climate."

## *Special Law for Special People*

Solving the legal problems of the rich—tax avoidance, for one—is practically a separate legal specialty in Delaware. As Irenee du Pont, Sr., neared his death, the corporate elite faced a serious problem—how to reduce taxes for a man who pulled down $16 million a year and would leave an estate worth over $200 million. The guardian-executors of the estate (Irenee du Pont, Sr., had been declared mentally incompetent and his three executors-to-be were named as guardians by the chancery court during his lifetime) were all prominent in the corporate elite: Irenee du Pont, Jr., his son and vice president of the DuPont Company; Crawford H. Greenewalt, his son-in-law and chairman of the company's board; and Ernest N. May, another son-in-law. To find a way to avoid taxes, the guardians hired Samuel Arsht, a partner in the DuPont Company's law firm—Morris, Nichols, Arsht and Tunnell.

Their first problem was Xanadu, Irenee's stately pleasure dome in Cuba. Irenee at one time operated Xanadu as a plantation, but it served only as a winter vacation spot from the 1930s until Fidel Castro confiscated it in 1961. Because of the confiscation, the Washington, D.C., law firm of Ivins, Phillips and Barker * pressed a *business* loss claim of $1.6 million from Irenee's 1961 taxable income. Since Xanadu was clearly personal property, the Internal Revenue Service rejected Irenee's claim.

While Arsht worked on tax problems of the estate in Delaware, Fleming Bomar, a partner in Ivins, Phillips and Barker, met with IRS officials in May, 1963. The IRS offered to settle its $2.1 million claim for back taxes for only $1.1 million, but Bomar wanted better. Bomar had two possible approaches: through the State Department, which was planning to seek reimbursement for expropriations of Cuban properties owned by Americans, or through Congress, where a special amendment to the Internal Revenue

* Ivins, Phillips and Barker is a medium-size Washington law firm that has handled tax problems for DuPont family members for many years.

Code might be passed to cover the loss. The guardians and their attorneys chose the Congressional route because, as Bomar put it, "It [will] be difficult to keep the DuPont name in the background if a claim for damages is filed with the State Department." [2]

So the family and its lawyers engaged Bomar as a lobbyist. Bomar, a lobbyist for the American Automobile Association, did not register as a lobbyist for the DuPont family before lobbying on their behalf, as required by federal law.[3] Jay Glasmann worked with Bomar on the problem, and he, too, failed to register as a DuPont lobbyist.* Nor did Bomar, Glasmann, or their law firm report compensation received for any year between 1960 and 1965, when Bomar and Glasmann were lobbying for the DuPonts.** Greenewalt and Bomar decided to approach a U.S. senator from Delaware, John J. Williams, because Williams held a strategic position on the Senate Finance Committee. Greenewalt had some doubt about Williams's willingness to help, because the senator had earned a reputation as the "conscience of the Senate" from his criticism of Bobby Baker's scandalous financial dealings. Greenewalt also knew that Senator Williams had refused to support past DuPont efforts to secure special interest legislation from Congress after the Supreme Court ordered the DuPont Company to divest itself of its General Motors holdings. Greenewalt's doubts were dismissed, however, by a report from Bomar on a fruitful meeting with Senator Williams, who "was in a good humor and seemed unusually sympathetic to our problem." [4]

Senator Williams agreed to help the DuPonts by introducing and supporting an appropriate amendment to the Internal Revenue Code. Bomar wrote to Greenewalt that Williams

> suggested the best procedure was to wait until the President's tax bill passed the House and was being considered

* Glasmann, also a lawyer with Ivins, Phillips and Barker, did register in 1969 as a paid lobbyist for the Wilmington Trust Company. He represented the bank during consideration of the 1969 Tax Reform Act.

** The penalty under federal law for failure to file a report with Congress for any quarter in which compensation is received for lobbying activities is a fine of not more than $5,000, or imprisonment for not more than 12 months, or both. 2 *U.S. Code,* §310.

by the Senate Finance Committee. He would then seek to attach the amendment to that bill in Committee. He wished to be certain that the amendment would be attached to a bill that would go to the White House and which would not be vetoed, and he thought the President's tax bill was the appropriate vehicle.[5]

Bomar and Williams "tentatively agreed that no mention would be made of the DuPont name in connection with the legislation. If possible, the only name mentioned will be that of Castro." [6] Bomar promised to write the amendment to cover Cuban property owned by Americans "whether or not for profit" so that inclusion of the Xanadu loss would not be blatantly obvious. The family and their attorneys feared the furor that might well be raised in Delaware over this unethical and illegal use of an unregistered lobbyist to obtain special legislation. One guardian, Ernest N. May, protested to all the heirs of Irenee, Sr., in 1964:

> I did not want to expose the Irenee du Pont name and family to the machinations of influence-peddling and political footballing.
>
> It may be true that "the name of Irenee du Pont was kept out" of the legislative process, but how many Xanadus were there in Cuba? At best the situation was one elephant and some mice.[7]

On February 7, 1964, Senator Williams introduced and secured Senate approval of an amendment to the Internal Revenue Code providing that "losses of property which arise from expropriation, intervention in or confiscation by Cuba, shall be deemed to be losses from 'other casualty.' " [8] When the study group first questioned Senator Williams about the amendment as well as the meeting with Bomar and Glasmann, the senator said he did not remember the particular occasion, but that it was possible the two lawyers did discuss the problem with him. As to any amendment the two lawyers may have asked him to introduce, Williams argued that their interest must have been only coincidental with an amendment proposed by the Treasury Department. After making serious efforts, however, the study group was unable to verify that Treasury had initiated the amendment.

One former Treasury official, who was in office at the time, said it was "highly unlikely" that the Treasury had proposed the amendment. He felt Williams had gone to Treasury for comments only after the amendment had been drafted.

In a later defense,* Williams argued that the amendment was fully considered and approved by the Senate Finance Committee, had the support of the Treasury Department, and benefited many persons other than Irenee du Pont. However, Williams first introduced the bill on the Senate floor and secured its passage in February, 1964, before the Finance Committee had considered it. The committee discussed the bill in June, 1964, when Williams gained approval for adding an effective date. Committee approval of the June changes, presented as a "perfecting amendment" by Williams, was virtually assured, since the amendment had already been passed by the full Senate. Moreover, according to a Congressional staffer, the need to add an effective date to the bill indicated that the February bill was written either by Bomar or by Williams himself. This staffer, with long experience on tax legislation, told the study group that someone accustomed to drafting tax legislation, such as a Treasury official, would not have left out an effective date.

Treasury support of the February amendment was also less than Senator Williams claimed. When Williams introduced his floor amendment, Senator Long said:

> Mr. President, this is a matter with regard to which the Treasury Department would like to cooperate to reach a proper solution of problems relating to Cuban expropriation. While we have not been able to determine the matter conclusively, we hope to do so in conference. In the event we cannot arrive at an adjustment, I hope the Senator will not be intransigent.[9]

In urging quick passage of his floor amendment, Senator Williams himself said that the Treasury was less than enthusiastic about the amendment:

* After a preliminary draft of this book was released in December, 1971, Senator Williams issued a 10-page response to our statements concerning the amendment.

> First they thought the desired result could be accomplished by regulation or that we should wait until a general bill dealing with this subject came over. This is too important to wait, and I hope the provision I am proposing can be inserted in the bill.[10]

Finally, Senator Williams argued that records of the State Department's Foreign Claims Settlement Commission showed that Irenee du Pont was not the only American to own property in Cuba. Commission files indicate that decisions were rendered on almost 5000 individual confiscation loss claims. According to Williams, du Pont's estate amounted to less than 1% of the aggregate value of the "individual" (as opposed to corporate) claims. But this information bears no relationship to persons who actually received an income tax deduction under the Williams amendment. In fact, we made a further examination of the claims commission files and learned that a large portion of the "individual" claims were actually business losses (deductible under the Internal Revenue Code before Williams's action), such as Arthur Vining Davis's $4-million claim for 200,000 acres held for future subdivision, or a $2-million claim for a 9500-acre Isle of Pines guest ranch and development site. The largest individual, nonbusiness claim allowed by the commission was $536,000, and according to claims commission records, the person who filed this claim *did not* file a tax loss claim under the Williams amendment. The 86 largest claims commission awards for real and personal property averaged only $15,000; thus, the $1.5-mil-million Xanadu residence represented an elephant in the midst of a few large dogs and a lot of mice. Furthermore, the short filing deadline of the Williams amendment (six months) effectively prevented many persons from filing tax deduction claims. All of the 5000 individual claims decided by the Foreign Claims Settlement Commission were filed at least six months after the Williams filing deadline for tax loss claims. The Irenee du Pont estate was one of few to benefit from Senator Williams's amendment, effectively making the amendment "special legislation," even though it was written as "general legislation," as suggested by Bomar.

Arsht quietly began to obtain relief for the estate under

the new law, despite Ernest May's admonition that "there is still one thing left the Irenee du Pont executors can do, and that is NOT to take advantage of the new legislation."[11] After Arsht and Bomar held a number of conferences with the Internal Revenue Service, a deduction of around $2 million from the 1961 tax debt was allowed for loss of the Cuban property.

To cut estate taxes further, Arsht used the Delaware courts. After their appointment in January, 1963, the three guardian-executors (heirs themselves) needed a way to reduce the taxes to be paid out of the $200-million estate. One idea was to make a big charitable contribution from assets of the estate. But first, a major obstacle had to be hurdled. Since the estate was under guardianship, the chancery court had to approve any gifts made from the estate. A Delaware statute authorized the chancellor to approve charitable contributions by guardians of up to 10% of the yearly income of the ward. But Arsht and the guardians wanted to make contributions far in excess of 10% of Irenee, Sr.'s $16-million income of 1962. Furthermore, Delaware lacked a statute that would authorize the chancellor to approve noncharitable gifts—an option the guardians greatly desired because they contemplated making gifts out of the estate to themselves and the other heirs. Arsht told the guardians the chancellor lacked statutory authority to approve this kind of gift:

> I am investigating whether the charitable contributions statute should be amended to remove the 10% limitation and also whether a specific gift authorization statute should be enacted.[12]

Before approaching the Delaware legislature, however, Arsht talked with Chancellor Seitz of the Delaware Chancery Court to feel out his reaction to the idea of making sizable gifts to the heirs out of the estate prior to Irenee's death. Arsht reported:

> The meeting was fruitful and I am encouraged to hope that he [Seitz] may be persuaded (by law on the subject with which I was armed) to approve gifts of Mr. du Pont's property to his children and/or grandchildren.[13]

Arsht, thus encouraged, pursued court action instead of legislation.

Chancellor Seitz's positive response was important, not only in view of Delaware law, which Arsht easily could have had amended anyway, but because of its potential weight with the U.S. Internal Revenue Service. Arsht indicated that if the guardians decided to make the gifts,

> it would, of course, be most desirable to obtain the Chancellor's specific approval or authorization before the gifts are made because it would preclude the Internal Revenue Service from even contending that the gifts were invalid, with whatever consequences might follow if the contention were sustained.[14]

Arsht continued his research and presented a memorandum to the guardians on May 3, 1963. He recounted the tax advantages that would accrue to the estate if the guardians made the gifts, while pointing out that

> difficulty may arise in obtaining the approval of the Court of Chancery to make such gifts. Our research has failed to discover a court decision which directly upholds the authority of a guardian to make gifts of the principal of the ward's estate to the heirs of the ward in order to achieve estate tax benefits.[15]

Being a veteran of the Delaware chancery court, however, Arsht was optimistic enough to state:

> Despite the paucity of authority supporting the guardians' power to make gifts of principal, the authority is sufficiently strong, in my opinion, to support an application to the Court of Chancery.[16]

Chancellor Seitz approved the petition on the morning of October 17, 1963, and Arsht called a meeting of the guardians within an hour to have them sign the deed of gift in trust. The deed transferred 160,000 shares of Christiana Securities, worth $33 million, from Irenee, Sr.'s estate to trusts established for the eight heirs. When Irenee, Sr., died two months and two days later, the heirs were able to realize a savings of nearly $10 million in federal estate taxes.

These examples point out what the corporate rich can get from lawyers if they want to pay for it. Arsht was paid over $800,000 for his work, and Bomar at least $10,000. While the DuPonts clearly benefited from these legalistic maneuvers, the public lost tax revenue, the secret lobbying for special legislation corrupted the legislative process, and the perpetuated concentration of private economic power undermined public policy. But the efforts to avoid taxes on Irenee du Pont's estate were only little evils compared to the undue influence corporate lawyers have on laws in Delaware.

## *Corporate Law and Corporate Lawyers*

The DuPont establishment has long played a major role in shaping Delaware's corporate law. In 1897 the DuPont Company wanted to incorporate. Since the state's constitution precluded a general incorporation law, a constitutional convention was called. A leader in the fight for a "liberal" * incorporation provision was Edward G. Bradford, a DuPont in-law and Delaware legislative leader. Several other members of the convention were prominent in DuPont affairs, and at least one DuPont man, Charles F. Richards, served on the convention's committee on corporations.[17] In 1899 a few local lawyers, together with two New Yorkers, maneuvered the passage of a new corporate law for Delaware—a blatant attempt to gain more business by attracting firms from other states.

Since then, Delaware has taken pride in being the friendly home of the American corporation. Many large firms exploited the advantages of the Delaware law. But as the state and its lawyers grew fat on incorporation fees and corporate litigation, other states began to pass laws in an attempt to outbid Delaware's largesse. In 1963 the Delaware legislature responded to this threat by appropriating $25,000 for the secretary of state to revise the General Corporation Law. The appropriation was used by a small group of corporate lawyers who, almost without consultation with public officials, wrote a new law. It was passed by the legislature with virtually no debate (see Chapter 13).

* A "liberal" corporate law provides a maximum of rights and powers for the corporation and its management and a minimum of responsibilities to stockholders and the public.

Delaware law has always favored corporations. *The Red Book of Delaware Corporate Procedures,* published by the Corporation Service Company in Wilmington, lists the major "advantages" of the Delaware corporation laws:

1. No taxation upon shares of stock held by nonresidents and no inheritance tax upon nonresident holders.
2. No corporation income tax in Delaware for companies not doing business in Delaware.
3. No "Blue Sky" laws.*
4. Stockholders, directors, and/or committee members may act by unanimous written consent in lieu of formal meetings.
5. Voting trusts and stockholder voting agreements may be created.
6. Stockholders' liability is limited to stock held in the corporation.
7. No minimum capital required.
8. Corporation may be incorporator.
9. Only one incorporator required.
10. There is a statutory subchapter dealing exclusively with closed corporations.
11. Contains America's most advanced provision for indemnification of officers and directors.

The philosophy of this law is that businessmen, not state legislators, should formulate corporate statutes. Within the large area not preempted by federal or constitutional requirements, practically every provision of Delaware law now allows corporate managers to formulate their own provisions for governing their corporation. Section 216 says that the firm's certificate of incorporation or bylaws may specify the votes necessary for a quorum. Even sections of the corporate code which set up a general legislative scheme for regulating corporate action may be bypassed by a corporation's own bylaws or certificate of incorporation. For instance, shareholders have the power to make, alter, or repeal bylaws (§109a); but the certificate of incorporation may confer this bylaw power on directors. The only limits to corporate power are the imagination of the directors and the consciences of Delaware judges—already well known for their receptivity to corporate interests.

* Blue Sky laws regulate issuance and transaction of stocks not listed on federally regulated stock exchanges.

The write-your-own-law approach is a boon to corporate lawyers in Delaware. Since corporations are encouraged to tailor the certificate of incorporation and the bylaws to meet their own unique situations, there is a great need for expert legal counsel in drafting these documents. With years of experience in helping corporations avoid any responsibilities to stockholders, consumers, or the public, the Delaware bar is the obvious choice of the many firms incorporating in the state.

STOCKHOLDERS' RIGHTS

While the new General Corporation Law gives corporate directors extremely broad power, it severely limits stockholder rights. In theory, the annual meeting provides stockholders with an opportunity to obtain information about corporate decisions and to voice their views on past and projected policies. The 1967 Delaware statute provided that annual meetings could consider only the business designated in the notice of the meeting (§211[b]), which is written and controlled by management. A 1968 amendment to the law enables stockholders to raise points at the annual meeting. But in light of other provisions, this amendment is only a token advance. The new law allows a corporation to do away with stockholders' meetings completely (§228).

The new Delaware statute impinges on other basic stockholder rights. Section 242(a) allows directors to cancel accrued dividends that have not yet been declared. In effect, directors, though they may have the money, can refuse to pay what they owe stockholders. Stockholders cannot propose amendments to the corporate charter; only a management resolution can (§242[d][1]). Minority stockholders get no legal protection. There is no right of cumulative voting,* a means of concentrating votes for directors that helps minority stockholders gain representation.

The Delaware law is particularly destructive of stockholders' rights in the area of mergers. Stockholders may suffer financially in the confusing and complex legal gyra-

* For example, a stockholder with one share is entitled to five votes in the election of five directors. Using the method of cumulative voting, the stockholder could cast all five votes for one candidate.

tions involved in mergers or they may just want to retain a large interest in a small company instead of a small interest in a very large conglomerate. For these reasons, the law in many states requires corporate directors to submit any merger proposal to all stockholders. But the new Delaware law allows corporate directors to effect a merger with another company as long as the certificate of incorporation remains intact and less than 15% of the same class of stock in the surviving corporation is involved in the merger plan (§251). The provision permits gross abuse by corporate directors, who can buy up other companies by succcessive small mergers without ever putting the question to a vote of the shareholders of the surviving corporation and without allowing appraisal rights.

Appraisal rights permit stockholders to demand the appraised or market value of their shares, instead of participating in the corporate merger. The new law completely denies appraisal rights to a shareholder if the corporation is registered on a national securities exchange or if its stock is held by more than 1999 shareholders. If a stockholder knows of his appraisal rights and wishes to exercise them, he must file an objection 20 days prior to the date of the merger vote. But the directors need not inform him of the proper procedures for preserving his appraisal rights.

### DIRECTORS' PRIVILEGES

The Delaware incorporation law lets directors receive unusual types of compensation and even be reimbursed if they breach their fiduciary duties to their company. The compensation to "corporate executives, officers, and employees" may be paid through "pension, profit sharing, stock option, stock purchase, stock bonuses, retirement benefits, incentive and compensation plans, trusts and [other] provisions." (§122[15]). According to Professor Ernest Folk, a legal consultant to the authors of the new General Corporation Law, the statute is so broad that it can "permit financial aid to dependents of corporate personnel as an aspect of compensation, pension and incentive arrangements for employees." [18] Despite the broadness of the provisions, the law provides no assurance that the compensation plans will be commensurate with the duties, if any, of the recipient. Someone who is only marginally attached to the company may draw a full salary, and no one need to be told of it. Moreover, the general corporation law allows corporate directors to make loans to other directors, officers, or employees without interest and without security, as long as the loan "may reasonably be expected to benefit the corporation" (§143). Again, disclosure is not required.

A key protection for corporate directors is reimbursement, generally called indemnification, for damages incurred because of breach of their fiduciary duty. Since federal law on fiduciary duties has become more strict, directors have become increasingly worried about possible suits for mismanagement or abuse of their positions. On the other hand, those interested in honest and prudent corporation management have become increasingly alarmed at the way indemnification clauses have insulated corporate directors. Professor Folk wrote in 1966: "The aid-to-directors movement has now so exhausted itself in an orgy of indulgence and favoritism that little more remains to be done on the state level."[19] But in 1967, Delaware legislators showed Professor Folk that there were still more goodies left to give. The Delaware law now allows corporations to repay any expenses (including attorneys' fees), judgments, fines, and amounts paid in settlement of any suit incurred by a director or officer who is either sued or threatened with suit when the director or officer "acted in good faith and in a manner he reasonably believed to be in or *not opposed to* the best interests of the corporation, and, with respect to any criminal action or proceeding, had no reasonable cause to believe his conduct was unlawful" (§145a. Emphasis added.)

By protecting officials in actions "not opposed to" the company's best interests, Delaware law opened up a whole new area of indemnification. Specifically, "not opposed to" is applied to personal transactions made on inside information, recently ruled illegal in the famous case of *Securities Exchange Commission* v. *Texas Gulf Sulfur*.[20] From the public policy viewpoint, there is no reason to indemnify directors guilty of insider trading, for this practice undermines the workings of the stock market. From the standpoint of stockholders, the company should not use its assets to aid an executive exploiting company information for private gain.

The law allows indemnification of directors who win court cases on a technicality, though grave abuses of fiduciary duty have been shown (§145[e]). Section 145(d) allows a company to indemnify a director even if he is found guilty: "independent counsel" or "disinterested directors" may determine that the officer acted in good faith and that he had reasonable cause to believe that his behavior was not contrary to company interests. The problems with this section lie in the "disinterested director," who might act out of fear that the board's next vote may be on whether or not to provide his indemnification, and the "independent" counsel who might act in hopes of being hired on the next indemnification question. Moreover, even if the court found a director "liable for negligence or misconduct" that could not possibly be construed as an act of good faith even by "independent counsel" or "disinterested directors," he may still be indemnified if a court determines that reimbursement is the most equitable path available (§ 145[b]). Given the well-known receptivity of Delaware courts, this provision may prove to be important.

Since a director may theoretically still be denied indemnification if he loses in court, the general corporation law provides a legal mechanism that allows directors to avoid entering a courtroom (§145[c]). Under this provision, directors are reimbursed for expenses if they settle a suit out of court. Thus a plaintiff may be bought off, damages limited, and publicity reduced—at company expense. Such settlements prevent persons with similar claims from learning that they have a legal cause of action, while undercutting suits brought in the name of the whole corporation (stockholder derivative suits) by paying off the stockholder who organized the suit. Furthermore, out-of-court settlements permit important corporate issues to be decided by informal negotiation instead of systematic court investigation. Section 145(e) provides a pay-as-you-go plan under which corporate directors can be advanced money by the corporation to defend a suit in exchange only for a promise to pay. But of course there need be no worry about repayment; the director can settle out of court and then be indemnified.

Section 145(f) destroys the last regulation of indemnification. This section allows many types of indemnification clauses, illegal under other provisions of the statute, to be established by a corporation bylaw, agreement, or vote of the "disinterested directors." Professor Folk recommended that an old provision like section 145(f) be eliminated because its breadth "invites misuses of corporate powers for improper indemnification." [21] Yet the new section 145(f) is much broader than the former statute. Directors may be indemnified "as to action in another capacity"—whatever that means. Under this statute directors can surely be indemnified for work in a subsidiary, but can they also be indemnified in their capacity as automobile driver?

Section 145(g) is the capstone of the system; it authorizes the corporation to purchase indemnification insurance for a director or officer,

> against any liability asserted against him and incurred by him . . . Whether or not the corporation would have the power to indemnify him against such liability under the provisions of this section.

Moreover, the state refused to regulate in any way the issuance of these insurance policies. This section of the Delaware statute allows corporations to insure a director or officer for any amount of money that he may have to pay in connection with any lawsuit or threatened lawsuit, civil or criminal, whether he is found innocent or guilty.

### CORPORATE LAWYERS

In contrast to the general thrust of the new Delaware statute against stockholders' rights and in favor of corporate management, a few provisions seemingly do protect stockholders' interests. However, these provisions were aimed at serving the self-interest of Delaware corporate lawyers. First, the revision commission ruled out provisions requiring security deposits to insure payment before a stockholder could file suit on behalf of a corporation (a derivative suit). Such a security provision has been a major barrier to stockholders' derivative suits in New York State. While the lack of such a provision obviously favors stockholders in Delaware corporations, it was omitted mainly because Delaware lawyers did not want to discourage lawsuits from being brought in the state. As Professor Bishop has written,

> It might . . . occur to a cynical mind that this curious anomaly of the Delaware law may not be wholly unconnected with the fact that the prosecution or defense of a derivative suit in a Delaware court requires the retention of Delaware counsel.[22]

The sequestration provisions similarly serve the interests of Delaware lawyers, while coincidentally benefiting stockholders. The sequestration clause says the stock of out-of-state directors may be seized to compel their appearance in the Delaware courts. To avoid the sale of their seized stock, nonresident directors have to hire a Delaware lawyer to defend them in state courts. Of course, corporate directors are not too pleased with this sequestration clause. But sequestration can be avoided by concealment of shares under front-names or merely by nonownership of stock. On the other hand, Delaware has no "long-arm" statute to allow Delaware lawyers to serve process on corporate directors wherever they are. Maintaining a delicate political balance between Delaware lawyers and corporate directors, the general corporation law encourages corporate defendants to employ local lawyers in Delaware courts by a sequestration clause, while not coercing the appearance of directors by a "long-arm" statute.

In short, the corporate law in Delaware isolates the managerial elite from the rights and responsibilities of ordinary citizens—special law for special people. A DuPont chemist who blows the whistle on a hazardous DuPont product by making use of inside information breaks his Employee Agreement with the company. But a DuPont executive who makes a fortune on the stock market by using inside information does not violate his fiduciary duties to stockholders.

The new Delaware corporate law was a great success. Immediately after it passed, Delaware's rate of incorporation jumped from 300 to 800 firms per month. Among the post-1967 newcomers are International Telephone and Telegraph, Lorillard, North American Rockwell, Delta Airlines, Gulf & Western Industries, and Borg-Warner. Over half of the 100 largest corporations in the United States and one-third of all the corporations listed on the New York Stock Exchange are now chartered in Delaware.[23] Delaware lawyers benefit from the influx of new firms, who pay large fees for incorporation papers and large retainers for representation in Delaware's procorporation courts.

Delaware got these companies—and Delaware lawyers got their business—by insulating management from challenges by stockholders, employees, consumers, and the public. While the corporate elite claim that the state benefits from increased revenues, the income from incorporation fees merely reduces the pressure for increases in Delaware taxes on local corporations and wealthy individuals. Moreover, to the extent that the state does reap additional revenues through its new General Corporation Law, it does so at the expense of the American public. The additional tax revenues, if any, go only to Delaware, while the law insulates corporate management from legitimate challenges of American citizens in all parts of the country.

## *Inequality of Legal Services*

The system of government in America is based on redress of grievance by law rather than by violence. To make that system work, the law must be equally accessible to all—which means lawyers must be equally accessible to all. The state must provide free counsel for criminal defendants who cannot afford counsel. As the U.S. Supreme Court explained in *Gideon* v. *Wainwright:*

> From the very beginning, our state and national constitutions and laws have laid great emphasis on procedural and substantive safeguards designed to assure fair trials before impartial tribunals in which every defendant stands equal before the law. This noble ideal cannot be realized if the poor man charged with a crime has to face his accusers without a lawyer to assist him.[24]

The *Gideon* decision helped, but legal services for the poor remain woefully inadequate all over the nation. With only a handful of exceptions, lawyers sell their services to the highest bidder; they are a free-market service, bought like automobiles or bananas. In Delaware, where the law, like everything else, is strongly dominated by the DuPont-oriented elite, the legal problems of the poor are particularly grave. If a Delaware resident is poor, he is lucky to obtain any legal representation.

Worse, auctioning legal services has skewed the base of legal resources in Delaware. Since wealthy individuals have continually paid large sums to the four major law firms, their lawyers have become highly skilled in estate and tax law. Because Delaware is home to many corporations, it is home to many specialists in corporate law. On the other hand, since neither public nor private groups have strongly supported the concept of legal services for the poor, very few lawyers in Delaware are experts in consumer advocacy, civil rights, or pollution litigation.

There are several more reasons for the lack of "peoples' lawyers." Delaware has no state law school which could provide a cheap legal education, student-run legal services for the poor, and independent, critical evaluation of state laws by law school professors. Thus, Delaware draws its attorneys from out of state through recruitment practices that only wealthy firms can afford. As a result, most new lawyers come to Delaware for the lucrative work for corporations and rich individuals. Finally, according to several Wilmington lawyers, Delaware has a long history of discrimination against black lawyers. Today, out of over 300 private attorneys practicing in the state only 3 are black. Considering the obstacles of the state's racial discrimination and its neglect of the needs of minorities, many black and progressive lawyers no longer even try to gain entry to the state bar.

Compare the legal staff of the DuPont Company with the resources available at legal aid and public defender programs in Delaware.* The DuPont legal department has

* In general, legal aid programs handle civil suits for the poor, and public defenders handle criminal cases.

150 attorneys. Many of them deal with patents and other specialized corporate problems. Four attorneys work primarily on the company's pollution problems; four or five devote full time to company property tax assessments. Another group performs the bulk of the lobbying activities for DuPont and watches relevant legislation. On important issues, this group arranges for DuPont representatives to testify on proposed legislation: contacting committee members or legislators, preparing testimony, and briefing DuPont representatives before they testify.

In contrast, until recently almost no legal services have been available to plaintiffs or defendants who could not afford attorneys. The Legal Aid Society, established by the Delaware bar in 1946, did not employ a full-time attorney until 1969. Legal Aid merged with the poverty program's Community Law Service in 1970, to form the Community Legal Aid Society (CLAS), which has three full-time and two part-time attorneys for all the poor of New Castle County. The other two counties of the state—Sussex and Kent—have no legal aid societies. New Castle County has only one full-time attorney plus five lawyers serving part time as public defenders; Kent and Sussex counties have one part-time public defender each, and Sussex County did not get its public defender until 1970.

The disparity between the legal resources of the rich and the poor has led to gross differences in the development and elaboration of Delaware law. In the corporate field, Delaware is well known for the precision of its law, because so many business cases have been litigated in its courts. But in poverty law, there is a dearth of court decisions. Only recently have legal aid lawyers begun to attack some obvious inequities in Delaware law. The CLAS got the state's one-year welfare residency requirement declared unconstitutional. The first full-time attorney of the Legal Aid Society attacked the Delaware statute allowing confessed judgments to be written into time-payment purchase agreements. By this legal device, a creditor can write into a sales contract a provision whereby the creditor, if the buyer fails to meet a payment, can automatically get a lien put on the buyer's property. The buyer signs away his right to be represented in court and to be given notice of the seizure of his property or the lien on his income.* Still unchallenged are dozens of bizarre statutes and practices in Delaware law. For example, some Delaware courts do not waive filing fees or appeal bonds for indigents in civil suits. If a plaintiff loses a civil suit in the magistrate court and wishes to appeal, Delaware law requires him to post a bond equal to the amount of the lower court's judgment against him; yet the courts go further and charge *double* the judgment, thus discouraging, and for many poor people prohibiting appeal.

By bringing class actions instead of fighting many individual cases, the few poverty lawyers in Delaware could close the gap between corporate and poverty law in the state more efficiently. Through a class action, similar claims of numerous people can be litigated together, greatly reducing the costs to each individual plaintiff. The corporate establishment dislikes class actions. After a legal aid lawyer brought a class action against the confessed judgment statute, the trustees of the Legal Aid Society, including three attorneys from corporate firms, suggested that he devote more time to individual casework and office administration. According to the legal aid attorney, the trustees brought subtle pressures against his engaging in significant legal reform efforts, although they did not prohibit such efforts.

Not only does the legal elite discourage efficient strategies like class actions, but corporate lawyers themselves do not contribute to the legal defense of the poor. Legal service lawyers have unsuccessfully asked the corporate bar for help on several occasions. Potter, Anderson and Corroon flatly refused to do work *pro bono publico* (for the public good) on a regular basis. Richards, Layton and Finger did not reply to a legal aid lawyer's request for help. While one legal aid attorney got two days' assistance from Morris, Nichols, Arsht and Tunnell on the confessed judgment

* For example, the buyer may have been a day late on the 30th of 50 payments for a refrigerator, but the creditor may take away his appliance without refunding the 29 previous payments or attach his income without notice and with no representation in court on the part of the buyer, if the contract so states.

suit, the firm would make no long-term commitment to help.*

Similarly, legal aid lawyers obtain little assistance from the legal departments of DuPont and other chemical firms. According to the DuPont Company, only one-third of its attorneys have been admitted to the Delaware bar; thus, few can represent a state citizen except by special motion to the court. Letters to the legal departments of DuPont, Atlas, and Hercules, asking them to devote the time of one attorney to the Community Legal Service, got a negative response from each company, although one attorney from Atlas has helped considerably on his own time. The DuPont Company has contributed old furniture to the legal aid office.

Although a DuPont Company lawyer is a board member of the community law program in Wilmington, DuPont has no formal *pro bono* program to encourage its attorneys to represent the poor. IBM, by contrast, assigns an attorney on a rotating basis to work full-time with the Westchester (N.Y.) County legal services office. All attorneys with IBM are given a set number of hours they can spend on *pro bono* work at company expense. While DuPont attorneys may occasionally be appointed as special public defenders (mostly by the federal courts), DuPont attorneys are, on the whole, nine-to-five suburbanites who do not identify with the Wilmington legal community outside of the four major corporate law firms.

Nor did private liberal groups in the past contribute greatly to reducing the gap between legal services for the poor and rich. The Wilmington chapter of the American Civil Liberties Union (ACLU) was not very active, even in civil rights. Some attorneys could not remember any time during the early 1960s when the ACLU took a strong stand on a controversial issue. In fact, the ACLU was one of the few liberal groups that refused to support the Delaware Conference on Equal Housing in 1966. Recently the ACLU

* When a legal aid lawyer talked with a partner of a large corporate law firm about counseling the poor, the partner said his firm already was substantially involved in *pro bono* work. The work turned out to be for the Wilmington Medical Center, a DuPont-dominated organization (see Chapters 4 and 11).

has become more active. For example, in 1971 it filed suit against the state board of education for drawing Wilmington school district boundaries in a way that brings about de facto segregation. And while the ACLU represented blacks arrested during the 1968 riots, Delaware still abounds with legally sound causes of action for constitutional litigation. In many cities, the disparities between municipal services in different neighborhoods is so great as to raise grave constitutional questions under the equal protection clause. Delaware law on municipal annexation bases votes on the amount of property owned and not on the one man, one vote principle required by the federal constitution.[25] Similarly, the procedures of housing and welfare agencies in the state are constitutionally suspect under the due process clause, as shown by a recent ruling in the federal courts.[26]

The last hope of poverty lawyers in Delaware is the state bar association. But according to the president of the bar, bar committees have little impact outside corporate law. Dominated by the senior partners from the big corporate law firms, the state bar has done very little for noncorporate interests. It has no committee dealing with consumer problems. It has not tried to establish a regular *pro bono* system for Delaware law firms. It has few programs for educating young people or adults about their legal rights and responsibilities. And it does not train paraprofessionals who could aid regular lawyers in the Community Legal Aid Society. Moreover, the bar is making little effort to provide free legal aid in Sussex and Kent counties or to expand legal services in New Castle County. According to a Wilmington attorney, the bar association has negligently failed to pursue legal reform in the areas of race relations, bail, public housing, or welfare. While the Delaware Bar Association and members of the corporate bar have served their corporate clients well in providing the most permissive incorporation law in the country, they have made only minimal efforts to help more needy groups in the state.

CHAPTER 8

# Urban Renewal, Incorporated: Greater Wilmington Development Council

The Greater Wilmington Development Council (GWDC) was formed in 1960 as a nonprofit corporation to help solve Wilmington's urgent urban problems. Its bylaws state that GWDC's purpose is

> to identify and analyze the physical, social, cultural, and governmental problems of the Greater Wilmington Area; to determine the priority for dealing with these problems; to develop solutions to these problems for the long-range good of the people and the community; and to bring action to bear on the recommended solutions, primarily through coordinating and strengthening existing agencies and organizations—both public and private—so that the Greater Wilmington Area will be a better place in which to live, work, and do business.

Toward these goals, GWDC has two subsidiaries, Downtown Wilmington (to shepherd a regional shopping center plan) and the Greater Wilmington Housing Corporation (GWHC, a nonprofit housing sponsor). In practice, GWDC is the urban development agent for the business elite; in the words of Irenee du Pont, Jr., "GWDC is the businessman's approach to community affairs."

Wilmington businessmen came late to an interest in urban renewal. In 1954, some local corporate executives called the Wilmington Housing Authority's first urban renewal project a form of communism. But in 1960, the business leaders looked down from their elegant skyscrapers upon a deteriorating city that threatened their future. The mayor and business leaders called a meeting to form the Greater Wilmington Development Council. Within eight days, GWDC had 246 members.

The DuPont family and company played important roles in GWDC. H. B. du Pont, vice president of the company, chaired the GWDC board for many years; in fact, as one businessman remarked, "H. B. was GWDC." His prestige, wealth, and access to foundations gave him tremendous influence over GWDC. His aide-de-camp was James Grady, the head of DuPont's General Services Department and president of GWDC. When H. B. died, his place as chairman of GWDC was taken by Irenee du Pont, Jr., also a vice president of the company, and Grady became chairman of the board of the newly formed Greater Wilmington Housing Corporation. When Downtown Wilmington was created, the DuPont Company donated the full-time services of one of its engineers, Roger Fulling, to head its day-to-day operations. As the *News-Journal* editorialized with unwitting honesty, GWDC is an organization of the "community's top business and professional people, who have drawn together out of enlightened self-interest as much as anything." [1]

## *GWDC and the Business Community*

From the start GWDC was in no way representative of the city's population. The interim committee on organization which mapped out the structure of GWDC after the first meeting, was composed of two DuPont and two bank executives. The first president of GWDC was J. H. Tyler McConnell, a DuPont family member and president of Delaware Trust Company. He ran the council at regular meetings in his office, which were attended by Grady and William E. G. Weisbrod of DuPont, another bank president, and one other business executive. When the council's first full board of 46 was chosen, some attempt at representation of Jews, blacks, and noncorporate interests was made, but it met with little success. Corporate dominance was not avoided and has continued to the present, especially among the officers and in the executive committee.

The most serious gap in GWDC's board was the absence of the city's young, well-educated black leadership. Those blacks who have been on the GWDC board (and even held minor offices) have repeatedly been described to the Delaware Study Group as "house blacks" or "Uncle Toms." According to a former top staff member of GWDC, for years the names of young, liberal blacks were put before the council's nominating group, only to be struck down. When GWDC finally changed its policy, they were unwilling to join. Some felt GWDC had insulted them; to others, GWDC had become so well known as a business front that liberal blacks could not join and retain their credibility in the black community.

After the 1968 civil disturbances, a Wilmington chapter of the big-business-based national Urban Coalition was formed as a counter organization to the GWDC. It was supposed to have a broad cross section of whites and blacks and act "like a Supreme Court sitting over smaller groups" in the community.[2] Each racial group nominated 25 members to represent its racial community. The whites chose almost entirely from the ranks of business executives and the wealthy. In protest, the blacks requested that some liberal, nonestablishment figures be on the white side, and named five men whom the blacks would find satisfactory. These five have never been asked to join. Even the first executive director of the coalition has been quoted as saying "the local coalition is a reactionary organization and nearly failed in its first year to initiate anything." [3]

If a GWDC or Urban Coalition board member is also an executive of a large corporation, does he serve GWDC as a corporate representative or as a public-spirited individual? Many corporate executives, including John Oliver, head of DuPont's Employee Relations Department, explicitly say they are half corporate representative and half individual member. When a representative on GWDC retires from a firm, he is replaced on GWDC by another high-level executive. For example, when Ed Crumm retired from his position in Hercules, he also quit as president of GWDC and appointed another Hercules executive to replace him.

The absence of middle- and lower-echelon corporate executives from the council's board is striking. In part, this absence can be explained by the professional demands placed on an ambitious young executive. Too, DuPont's policy of transferring young executives every few years lessens a junior executive's ability and incentive to get involved in GWDC. But the young executives' main handicap is that, by definition, they are not prominent business men. As one corporate executive told the study group:

> If you want to get something done in an organization in Wilmington, then you have to get the ear of the big shots. If you were a socially concerned executive thirty years old, you could not get a seat on the Urban Coalition or GWDC. These organizations feel they need the big men to be successful.

The obvious question is, what does a corporate officer do when GWDC or the Urban Coalition formulates a policy which is against the interests of his firm? John Oliver, asked this question by a study group interviewer, never got a chance to answer; Irving Shapiro * cut in to say:

> Let me give you an answer . . . just to get out of the world of theory. The Board of Governors or the Board of Trustees of the Urban Coalition includes the president of the DuPont Company. If that board takes a policy position, obviously there isn't going to be any conflict for employees who are also involved.

A more subtle way business controls GWDC is the use of corporate methods in the development council's operations, such as inflexible agenda prepared in advance and

* At this time, Shapiro was the assistant general counsel of DuPont and the official liaison between the company and the study group. He attended all the official, taped interviews with company employees. Shapiro is also a director of the Urban Coalition in Wilmington.

complicated rules of order. These procedural devices implicitly determine the organization's priorities, and this procedural emphasis allows corporate officials to stifle consideration of substantive issues important to the community. Community leaders have not been able to get certain issues considered because GWDC officers put them at the bottom of the agenda, which the committee never gets to. A member of the Urban Coalition said that Puerto Rican issues are often put at the bottom of the agenda. Community leaders have been prevented from criticizing corporate policy because their remarks were ruled outside the scope of the agenda. When the black members of the Urban Coalition called an emergency meeting to discuss racial strife in Wilmington High School, the corporate executives spent the first 45 minutes of the unproductive session arguing that the Urban Coalition could not meet because an agenda on Wilmington High School had not been prepared.

## *GWDC and Community Groups*

Pluralism holds that democratic decision making can occur if many private groups compete on equal grounds to influence public policy, each group representing its own interest. But GWDC has always outmuscled other community groups. With DuPont backing, GWDC is much richer than other private organizations in Wilmington (except for the United Fund, also controlled by the corporate establishment). GWDC raised about $2.5 million between 1962 and 1969 for routine work alone, not including large foundation gifts for special projects.

To compensate for its greater power, GWDC could make serious efforts to canvass other community groups before bringing its resources to bear on public decision. It does not. Rather, GWDC tends to go outside the community, hiring consultants who come to Wilmington for short times, rely on already gathered data, and talk mainly to city officials or corporate executives. Only rarely do they attend meetings of community groups or their leaders. A former GWDC staff member explained the council's penchant for consultants:

> When an executive has a decision to make, he goes to the guy under him or the service department in the relevant area. He looks for a decision-maker similar to himself. In community affairs, if he does not know locally where to get the same type of decision from a guy in the same social situation, then he goes to a consultant vaguely familiar with that area. An executive is more likely to follow this route than go to the community because he does not usually know many people in the community.

The GWDC has also arranged trips to see how other cities handled problems; there, like the consultants they bring to Wilmington, they rely on corporate executives and city officials. Most of the trips have been made to New Haven, Connecticut, partly because H. B. du Pont owned a house nearby, where he kept his yacht. Although council members probably know more about New Haven than any other city they have visited, when interviewed by the study group none had any idea why that city's urban policies are now under serious attack from many sides. GWDC members talked only with Mayor Richard Lee and his aides, who painted a rosy picture of Lee's approach to urban problems.

At the same time that GWDC was going outside Wilmington for advice, it prevented outside groups from moving in. The National Urban League is a case in point. The late Whitney Young's assistant, Alexander Allen, was very interested in starting an Urban League chapter in Wilmington. A committee of local business and community groups appointed a working subcommittee including two DuPont executives to determine whether a Wilmington chapter was needed, and unanimously decided in favor of one. The subcommittee's report was never given to the committee, and the chapter was never started. Acccording to one member of the committee, executives cooled to the idea when they found out that Young wanted broad community support for the group.

GWDC even tried to co-opt the federal Office of Economic Opportunity (OEO) program proposed for Wilmington. A broadly based community group, hoping to sponsor the program, met at the YMCA to study what programs and organizational structure the community wanted. But GWDC, without informing the YMCA group, went to Mayor John Babiarz and asked that OEO be put under its aegis. The mayor used the competition between groups as a reason to turn down both groups, and appointed his own assistant to develop the OEO program.

To maintain its dominant position in community development, GWDC levies an informal tax, enforced by peer group pressure, for each project. The tax, imposed on all member corporations, is based on the number of hourly wage employees each has locally. The informal tax, coupled with gifts from wealthy individuals and DuPont foundations, permits members of the corporate elite to operate as an alternative local government, controlling funds used for public purposes. And, since the council is tax-exempt under federal and state laws, contributions are tax deductible, providing a major tax loophole to corporations and wealthy individuals. Moreover, state law gives corporations up to $50,000 in direct tax credits for contributions to groups like the GWDC that qualify as organizations devoted to community improvement under the state's Neighborhood Assistance Act. The DuPont Company and DuPont family have been the major beneficiaries of these tax provisions as they apply to the council. According to the figures of GWDC and the DuPont Company, the company has contributed about one-third of GWDC's lifetime budget. Most of the rest were tax-exempt gifts made by DuPont foundations or family members. Through this series of tax deductions, corporations and wealthy individuals retain control over money used to make or affect public decisions. The vast amount of gifts made by the DuPont Company and family through the GWDC allows the DuPonts to have a substantially greater impact on public decision making than other private groups in the state.*

Public taxes and GWDC dollars are used to accomplish similar city functions. The major difference is that

* Conversely, if the DuPonts did not give their money to GWDC and other groups they controlled, but chose to keep all the money inside the family or corporation, the tax benefits would be lost, but not the political power. The DuPonts have a significant portion of the private funds in the state that can be allocated to nongovernmental public groups and functions. By not giving, the family and company would effectively be determining that fewer or none of these groups should operate.

the allocation of public tax revenues is controlled by public officials—either elected or appointed (and thus responsible to elected officials)—while GWDC money is controlled by the corporate elite. Under the GWDC taxing system, DuPont pays 30–40% of these "taxes." DuPont can effectively control GWDC simply by threatening not to pay. Since DuPont family members control the GWDC board, they control the distribution of its revenues. It is not surprising, then, that the council's programs often reflect the interests of members of the elite and conflict with the interests of the rest of the Wilmington community.

While DuPont interests control GWDC, it in turn controls the purse strings of several community groups. A good example of the inherent political conflict created by GWDC funding is Delaware's Opportunities Industrialization Center (OIC), a job training program. The Delaware OIC is the only one in the country started by businessmen instead of community groups; it is also the only OIC run with private and state funds rather than federal grants. GWDC set up the OIC and funded it for several years. Recently, to gain more independence, the community people in OIC tried to raise funds from other sources. But several corporate executives predict that OIC will soon be forced back into the GWDC fold, since private donors will not respond to OIC's independent overtures. While the OIC has been able to get on the federal payroll, the money comes through a contract with DuPont, Hercules, and Atlas for training workers for them. According to several executives, the three corporations are using OIC as a training agent because the companies can receive federal money without having the "government getting into their books."

## *GWDC and City Government*

GWDC is so involved in the traditional work of urban government that many local public decisions are not made democratically through the municipality, but undemocratically through GWDC, or some mixture of both. As one former GWDC staff member said: "Local business objects to national planning because the control is exercised by the federal government. But these same executives go for planning in Wilmington because they can exercise the control here."

Indeed, practically every new urban concept in Wilmington originated in GWDC and was then carried out by public planners. Generally, a standing committee would originate an idea; GWDC's executive committee would discuss and approve it; then the officers and staff would inform the mayor. The mayor in turn would ask GWDC to finance the consultant study it had suggested, and it would. Thus the façade of public decision making was retained, while GWDC made the city's decisions.

The GWDC also sponsors consultant studies for individual corporations in the guise of publicly oriented reports. A good example is GWDC's Midtown Study. Its ostensible purpose was to figure out "how to accommodate traffic and parking changes generated by the imminent completion of Interstate 95." [4] But the real purpose, according to several GWDC staff and board members, was to analyze the traffic and land use problems DuPont would face if it built a new office building in midtown Wilmington. The report recommends several expenditures, such as the building of parking garages and the widening of roads, which would make a midtown location more attractive to DuPont. But the report does not say that the garages will very probably have to be subsidized by the city. Nor does it intelligently discuss the alternative of providing parking through zoning requirements that would force businesses to build their own off-the-street parking. This is an obvious strategy, required by federal renewal programs. Since the GWDC consultant report was the only study then available, the city accepted all its recommendations. Not until several years later did the city's fiscal committee show how the Midtown Report completely neglected questions relating to the city's best interests: "The fiscal dimensions of the alternatives either were not considered or not included in the report, nor is there any mention in this report that perhaps nonresidents of the city stand to gain most from its proposals." [5]

On occasion, GWDC consultant studies have been accepted by public bodies as the final word, even when their conclusions were clearly wrong. For example, the Greater Wilmington Housing Corporation hired Charles B. Reeder, DuPont's chief economist, to study housing in Wilmington.[6] Reeder concluded that the city had a 6.7% vacancy rate in housing, a statistic often quoted by public planners and in city documents. The statistic is extremely misleading. Reeder does not distinguish between low- and high-income units, so it is unclear what part of the vacancy rate could be utilized by the poor. A close examination of Reeder's charts shows that 10.5% of the city's units are substandard; if families now living in substandard units moved into all the vacant units, 3.8% of the families would still be living in substandard units. Therefore, the vacancy rate for *standard* housing in the Wilmington area is *minus* 3.8%. Indeed, in interviews, employees of Wilmington Housing Authority's relocation office insist that it is almost impossible to obtain low-income housing in the city.

Since GWDC is the only funding source available for most studies, it can manipulate consultants without fear. In 1963 GWDC hired the Department of Urban Affairs at the University of Delaware to study the downtown area. The university group, which GWDC members consider very competent, concluded that shopping should be developed mainly for office workers on their lunch hours. But GWDC decided that Wilmington needed a large regional shopping center. Since the university group was clearly against this alternative, GWDC hired another consultant firm to study downtown. Not surprisingly, this consultant firm concluded that Wilmington did need a large-scale shopping mall.

To carry out the recommendations of its consultant reports, GWDC first encouraged acceptance of the concept of public planning and then created governmental planning agencies. It prompted the city to begin a planning department. It helped establish the New Castle Transportation and Land Use Planning Group, which became the county plannning office; it hired a consultant to recommend that Delaware join the Penn-Jersey Transportation Study. GWDC hosted regular meetings of area planners to coordinate the implementation of its own ideas. It even created a model for comprehensive metropolitan planning in which GWDC, together with the University of Delaware, were supposed to serve as the "steering committee."

In sum, GWDC so overwhelmed competing private interests and became so influential in traditionally public spheres that in many ways it served as a parallel city government. This system of indirect rule had several advantages for the corporate establishment. Local government decisions could be made behind a façade of neutrality. Under the corrupt practices laws, corporations cannot contribute to political candidates but they can give to a nonprofit private organization like GWDC. Participation in the private development council permits politics without public accountability. As one former GWDC staff member said:

> Businessmen feel more comfortable in GWDC than in city government because they are not used to having their authority challenged; they are accustomed to working in hierarchical systems more on the model of enlightened dictators.

Since GWDC was mainly an alter ego for the local government, it rapidly declined in 1968, once Harry G. Haskell, a member of the corporate elite, became mayor of Wilmington. Haskell hired a top GWDC staff member as his administrative assistant. H. B. du Pont resigned as board chairman, and the executive director was asked to leave. An interim director, a lower-level DuPont employee, took charge of winding up old programs without initiating any new ones. Between 1968 and 1970, the only active group in the GWDC constellation was Downtown Wilmington, Inc. In line with the new fusion of corporate establishment and city government, half the board of Downtown Wilmington was appointed by the GWDC and half chosen by local government units. The executive head of Downtown Wilmington has always been a full-time DuPont employee on leave from the company. Only very recently has GWDC begun to evolve a new role for itself within the corporate local government. As a fitting start, it hired the city's chief planner to become its executive director.

## *GWDC's Social Action Programs*

GWDC's major programs have been in education, youth groups, and housing (for GWDC's role in the Neighborhood Improvement Program; see Chapter 4). When GWDC established its priorities in the mid-1960s, it placed a major emphasis on education. After GWDC's connection with the Neighborhood Improvement Program failed to improve local school systems, the development council hired a clergyman, Robert Stoddard, to work full time on education. Stoddard first proposed to apply the techniques of corporate executive job counseling to career guidance for students in a local high school—a revealing decision. But the local school officials in 1968 were not enthusiastic about this proposal; they reportedly felt that GWDC was meddling in their business.

Next Stoddard read a book about metropolitan approaches to education in Hartford, Nashville, and St. Paul. Early in 1969, he called corporate executives and several top school officials together to discuss metropolitan educational policy. The group formulated three goals: improve city schools, promote racial integration of city and county schools, and develop a statewide research council. Stoddard says he "concentrated on the first two goals." GWDC's education committee established an elaborate organizational model with information input, public relations, and sensitivity training "to make sure the members of the committee were communicating," according to Stoddard. Stoddard then talked to experts in education in Philadelphia, Boston, and, on his vacation, Leicester, England. He found that "none of those educational authorities had enough expertise in developing an interdisciplinary approach to the committee's three goals."

Without having created a single program, as explained by Stoddard, the GWDC committee suddenly "decided that it had no business going so far so fast because we were not a representative group." So the committee hired a small public relations firm to find out public opinion on education. This firm was not from Delaware and had no expertise in education. GWDC officials told the public relations firm not to say that it was from GWDC, unless asked directly. Now the committee is starting work on the third goal, a statewide educational research council. As Stoddard said, "Since we figured we were so well underway on the first two goals of improving city schools and promoting integration, we could go on to the third goal."

GWDC's involvement with youth groups was equally fruitless. It supported the Wilmington Youth Emergency Action Council (WYEAC), a group of black street youths whose aim was to bring about a wholesale change in the distribution of power and wealth by organizational means rather than violence. WYEAC sought to develop political consciousness in the black community to replace the corporate establishment in Delaware government. Officially GWDC supported WYEAC because it was, according to a GWDC report, "persuading the gang leaders that there is a better 'pay off' in learning to work with the community than in a life of conflict, hostility, or sullen apathy."

GWDC's involvement with WYEAC was extremely controversial, since Governor Charles Terry continually accused the WYEAC of plotting armed rebellion. Some prominent black politicians say GWDC supported WYEAC in an effort to split young blacks from adult black political movements. While there is no evidence that this was GWDC's intention, it did split the black community politically. Rather than having to work through political leaders of the black community, WYEAC members had direct access to the corporate establishment through GWDC.

Several members of WYEAC and many knowledgeable observers in Wilmington say GWDC supported WYEAC to reduce the chance of riots in the city. It was widely believed that during 1967 black ghetto youths were often the key elements in provoking the riots in many American cities. By co-opting WYEAC, so went the argument, the Greater Wilmington Development Council hoped to minimize or prevent violent ghetto outbreaks. Although GWDC officials roundly deny that their intent was to use WYEAC to keep the community cool, there is some direct evidence to support this position. For example, in August, 1967, amid widespread fear that riots would spread to Wilmington, WYEAC met with officials of various public and private agencies, including James Grady, the president of GWDC at the time. At this meeting, WYEAC emphasized the real potential for violence and the inadequacy of its federal funds. At one point in the meeting, according to several sources, Grady asked WYEAC members: "What do you want, the whole city?" That night, on behalf of GWDC, he offered WYEAC $15,000 to buy vans. Grady telephoned H. B. du Pont on his yacht to confirm the expenditure, and the figure appears in the 1967 budget as a disbursement for the "WYEAC project."

By the interpretation of most blacks, GWDC's support of WYEAC was a way to protect the corporate establishment, not to promote the interests of the black community. In contrast, GWDC officials construe their support of WYEAC as an effort to meet the urgent needs of ghetto youths. GWDC describes the youth group experiment as a success. The development council approved WYEAC's programs on job placement, black culture, recreation, and summer youth employment. The GWDC reports explain that these programs "were imaginative and were aimed at real problems in their neighborhoods," as well as "constructive in their objectives and potential effects in the city." They found only two problems: the youth needed more professional guidance, and the group could not operate effectively under Governor Terry's violent attacks.

Yet GWDC did not follow up the WYEAC experiment or enter the field of youth programs again. It could easily have provided WYEAC or any of a number of Wilmington youth groups with more professional guidance. After the threat of civil riots diminished and WYEAC leaders, like Chezzy Miller, themselves became part of the black power structure, GWDC dropped its support. Even so, many of its ideas were carried on by other organizations. The YMCA undertook a youth program; Model Cities is carrying out WYEAC's idea for a "university of the streets"; and Mayor Haskell helped establish the Martin Luther King Center, which grew out of WYEAC's black culture projects.

By far the most successful social action program of GWDC has been the Greater Wilmington Housing Corporation (GWHC), the best-funded and best-staffed nonprofit housing sponsor in Delaware. GWHC has a $500,000 grant from H. B. du Pont's Longwood Foundation and it holds a yearly fund-raising campaign, which netted over $100,000 in 1969. But relative to its resources, GWHC has contributed little housing to the Wilmington area. From its start in 1968 to the summer of 1970, it had undertaken only two substantial projects. First, GWHC worked with a local developer to put up Madison Gardens, a complex of 24 moderate-income housing units in the city. The project was financed by loans solicited by the developer from DuPont and three other large corporations. GWHC officials extracted a promise from the Wilmington Housing Authority to purchase Madison Gardens so that the funds could be returned to the four firms.

But the Wilmington Housing Authority, which planned to use federal funds for the purchase, has not yet bought Madison Gardens, for a reason that points up a serious failure of GWHC. When federal funds are used for public housing, federal law requires a housing agency to build or buy one low-income housing unit in a nonblack area for each unit built in a black area.[7] In Wilmington this means low-income housing must be built in the county, as no suitable sites are available in the city. Since the county council will not build any public housing in its jurisdiction, only a private, nonprofit sponsor like GWHC could break the freeze. GWHC could build low-income units in nonblack areas of the county and lease them back to the public housing authority, thus increasing the ratio of county to city low-income units and freeing the city to obtain more federally funded public housing. Although GWHC was well aware of its potential role in breaking the freeze on city public housing and was talking about erecting units in the county in the summer of 1970, the organization had not purchased any county land as of the spring of 1972.

GWHC's second housing development is in the Asbury Church area, part of the Poplar Street urban renewal project. About 15 years ago, the city tore down almost 1000 low-income homes and turned over part of the land to a private developer. The developer built a few luxury town houses; his plans called mainly for moderate and luxury dwellings on the rest of the land, though a few low-income units were added under community pressure. Before starting its Asbury Heights project, GWHC officials knew that the developer was thinking of giving up his option on the Poplar Street land, because old, run-down houses nearby were not conducive to his unfinished plans for moderate and luxury housing. If the developer had given up his option, the city could have used the land for low-income units. But by building Asbury Heights, the GWHC eliminated the "offensive" housing and the private developer decided to continue with his original plan. James H. Gilliam, the GWHC administrator of the project, recently became the vice president of the company owned by the same private developer.

Moreover, GWHC has continued the Poplar Street tradition of throwing low-income families out of their homes without providing adequate replacement housing or relocation payments. In its Asbury Heights development, GWHC has constructed only 81 living units so far, though another 52 units are planned. All are for moderate-income families. They replaced 53 buildings (number of living units unknown), inhabited by low-income families. GWHC paid only moving expenses to relocated families and individuals. If the city had done the project, it would have provided relocated families with payments of up to $1000 over a two-year period.

### *The Downtown Shopping Center*

While GWDC has not lived up to its education, youth, and housing plans, it is forging ahead on a regional shopping center in downtown Wilmington, to be completed by 1976. The proposed complex will include a luxury hotel, entertainment facilities, garages, a connector from the interstate highway, and a shopping mall with two department stores and up to 100 other stores. The project is masterminded by Downtown Wilmington, a GWDC spin-off; Roger Fulling, a DuPont executive loaned full time to GWDC at no cost, runs it.*

The city's own planning department had a far different, less grandiose plan for the same plot of land. It resembled

* Since this was written, Fulling has been replaced by Peter A. Larsen, executive head of GWDC.

the policy suggested by the University of Delaware Division of Urban Affairs in a 1963 consultant report financed by GWDC, which concluded that Wilmington should concentrate on expanding its present shopping facilities, but should avoid a regional shopping center plan. GWDC officials, not content with the city's modest plan, hired another consultant who would tell them what they wanted to hear. While the GWDC consultant study was in process, the city hired Realty Consultants, a group of prominent local real estate agents, to find developers for the land. The group found one, John Rollins, and he drew up and submitted plans. Meanwhile, the Wise-Gladstone report done for GDWC arrived, calling for a regional shopping center; Rollins's proposal was rejected because it did not conform to the corporate plans. Another round of soliciting developers' proposals was begun, this time under the auspices of Downtown Wilmington. Rollins, a self-made businessman who had always been at odds with the DuPonts, did not bother to try again. Many prominent corporate and public officials feel that H. B. du Pont's dislike of Rollins had a major role in the defeat of his proposal, but no one has absolute proof.

Downtown Wilmington chose Fusco Corporation as the developer. After a year and $28,000 worth of studies and plans, Fusco withdrew from the downtown project, and was reimbursed when Downtown Wilmington obtained "an interest-free loan from a private individual." [8] The search for a developer began again; Pan American Development Corporation got the nod. Wilmington Housing Authority's deputy director for urban renewal said: "Basically we didn't have a choice. We'd really scoured the field looking for people that would be interested." [9]

### THE SHOPPING MALL: CAN IT WORK?

GWDC's proposal for a mammoth shopping center is based on the retail analysis of the Wise-Gladstone study. The city has accepted the plan, though it has not done an independent analysis of the potential retail market at the shopping center. The Wise-Gladstone study in turn based its plan on the assumption that the huge mall would serve New Castle County, the two southern counties of Delaware, and parts of Maryland to the south and west, Pennsylvania to the north, and New Jersey to the east.

It is unclear whether shoppers would ever travel from such distances to patronize the Wilmington mall; but it won't be necessary for some of them. Pan American Development Corporation is also building a big shopping center to the southwest of Wilmington. Although Pan American has promised to give priority to the mall, the suburban shopping center will cut sharply into the shopping population the Wise-Gladstone study had envisioned. In a personal interview with the study group, George Rubin, a vice president at Pan American, said that the downtown shopping mall will draw only from the city and its northern suburbs.

Even if we put this basic assumption of the consultant report aside, the basic arguments in the report are unpersuasive. The key to a successful downtown shopping center with the ability to woo suburban housewives away from convenient outlying shopping centers is the lure of big-name department stores, as Downtown Wilmington's Fulling concedes. Rubin of Pan American Development admitted to the study group: "We cannot make any money on the department stores; they know that you need them badly." He added that Fusco, the original developer, had had trouble finding department stores to move to Wilmington. Thus the crucial question is, Is Wilmington an attractive site for big department stores?

The Wise-Gladstone report says yes, although no department stores have rushed into downtown Wilmington on their own. The report reaches its conclusion by comparing a downtown site to several other locations. The fallacy is that all the locations analyzed were also in the city; the report completely ignores the possibly greater attraction of a suburban site. Wise-Gladstone suggests that department stores will find Wilmington attractive because the market is growing. But so is the number of suburban department stores, including such prestigious names as Strawbridge & Clothier, Sears Roebuck, and John Wanamaker.

Yet Pan American Development Corporation and Downtown Wilmington remain optimistic about hooking department stores. While no announcement has been made revealing which department stores will take the bait, the developer has hinted that he's caught two. And Fulling has named some stores that he claims are interested. The *Evening Journal* checked on his claim and reported:

> A number of department stores—John Wanamaker, Strawbridge & Clothier Co., Gimbel's, Garfinkle's and Hess Bros., listed by Fulling as being interested in Wilmington—were also contacted. None acknowledged interest. And two, Wanamaker and Strawbridge, expressed a positive disinterest.[10]

In addition, no less an authority than James Rouse—a nationally famous mortgage banker who has built many shopping centers and is now developing the new city of Columbia, Maryland—told Fulling, who has never built a shopping center, that the plot is not a financially viable location.

PUBLIC BURDENS

The GWDC plan now includes a spur from the interstate highway system feeding into a 5000 car parking garage. It is instructive to note that the discarded city plan included a transportation center to concentrate rail, bus, and air connections, aimed at alleviating the transportation problems of the 40% of the city households without cars. GWDC substituted the costly highway connector and garage serving suburban commuters. The corporate establishment's support of the GWDC plan solidified when Pan American Development Corporation said it would not develop the shopping center unless the garage and highway were built. Furthermore, since the available land is just big enough for the shopping center, the garage will be built underground, a particularly expensive approach.

Although the corporate-backed GWDC is promoting the garage and the developer is demanding it, the public is expected to pay for it. Not that that is unusual. A study done in 1970 by an engineering consultant firm showed that 80% of those using public parking facilities were in Wilmington for business and work.[11] Joseph T. Walsh, attorney for the parking authority, "agreed that parking lots already in Wilmington are a subsidy to industries and business for which parking requirements were waived."[12]

The projected revenues from the mall garage will not be enough above costs to render parking revenue bonds attractive investments without other guarantees.[13] So the Wilmington Parking Authority has asked the city to pledge its full faith and credit to back the $23 million in bonds needed to finance the garage. (A special law was passed by the state legislature giving the city the authority to make the pledge.) This means that the city will pay if the parking authority defaults.

Use of public funds for the garage is essentially a public subsidy of the private interests promoting the shopping mall. City Councilman Thomas Maloney has opposed such a pledge from the city because it will lower the city's credit rating and limit its ability to undertake additional projects. In 1971 the city council passed Maloney's resolution asking the Wilmington business community

> to demonstrate its solid support of downtown development by undertaking efforts to guarantee the bonds, purchase the bonds, or otherwise provide a method of effective financing for the commercial-retail center's parking facilities.[14]

The business community's response was firmly negative.

The connector between the interstate highway system and the mall, the second condition of the developer, will also be paid for entirely by the public. If the federal government agrees to finance the $20–22 million plan, it will pay half the connector cost and 90% of the costs for the I-95 interchange. Delaware must pay the remaining $5–10 million. The city will have to pay the costs of relocating 63–77 families and individuals, as well as 30–38 small businesses just for the connector. Also the city tax base will lose forever the large strip of land required for the highway. Finally, the city will have to bear the traditional costs of any renewal project: its share of sewer and road installation, land acquisition, as well as tax loss because of the time lag between demolition and project completion. If we assume that the shopping center constitutes half the redevelopment area, we can estimate these traditional costs. Sewers and roads will cost the city about $220,000. The city's share of land acquisition costs will be about $650,000.

The real estate left untaxed between demolition and completion, at a conservative estimate of 10 years (the land has been vacant for several years already), is worth about $15 or $16 million; according to information supplied by the city Department of Planning and Development, nearly $1 million in property and other taxes have been lost already, and project completion is at least five years off. The city planning department says the shopping mall will eventually cost the city over $30 million.

Yet the shopping center will contribute very little to Wilmington's tax base. The Wise-Gladstone study generously estimates that the assessment base will be $15 million, including associated retail, restaurant, entertainment, and recreation facilities as well as the shopping center itself. According to the Wise-Gladstone report, this sum translates into only $390,000 a year in tax receipts. The city would also get wage taxes from shopping center employees earning over $6000 a year. For the employees of all stores in the mall at an average annual income of $10,000—this would total about $50,000 a year.*

### PRIVATE POWER, PUBLIC FUNDS

As GWDC greatly changed the nature of the shopping center complex, so corporate power altered other components of the city's redevelopment plan to fit the GWDC scheme. The city, says Councilman James Sills, "unwittingly allowed local corporate and business interests, through Downtown Wilmington, Inc., to usurp its power and virtually dictate the planning process." [15]

The original city proposal included a high density housing complex for the elderly next to a large hospital. Peninsula Methodist Homes and Hospitals, which runs two other homes for the elderly in Delaware, was to develop the facility. The corporate establishment vigorously supported the plan. Peninsula Homes threw a fund-raising dinner attended by Mrs. H. B. du Pont and other family members; it arranged to buy land from a DuPont family member; it lined up funds through family foundations. But once GWDC's report proposing the huge regional shopping cen-

* Other employment aspects of the shopping mall will be discussed below.

ter was published, the corporate establishment backed out. (Ironically, the GWDC report had also recommended housing for the elderly and expansion of medical facilities.) The city was forced to build housing for the elderly elsewhere, and lost the chance to use the land for much-needed health care services. The same H. B. du Pont who helped replace Peninsula's elderly housing and hospital with a shopping mall was instrumental in getting Wilmington Medical Center to begin cutting back its hospital facilities in the city (see Chapter 4).

Both the original city and the GWDC plans proposed luxury hotels. The city's plan called for a motel, the Wilmingtonian, to be built on Delaware Avenue between Interstate 95 and the central business district. The GWDC proposal put a luxury hotel in the shopping center. Both the city and GWDC thought a new hotel would succeed. For many years the Hotel DuPont has been the only major hotel in the city; originally built by the DuPont Company to house business visitors, the hotel now attracts visitors for all corporate affairs, and is very profitable. During the work week the Hotel DuPont works at almost 100% capacity. So good are the chances of the new hotel's success that the present developer of the shopping mall intends to build the hotel immediately, even if plans for the rest of the complex fall through.

Yet the corporate establishment killed the city's plan for the Wilmingtonian Hotel. When the Wilmingtonian was proposed, there were attacks from three corporate fronts: the Hotel DuPont, the newspapers, and the banks. One former city official says Hotel DuPont staff members called the city to discourage the sale of city land to the Wilmingtonian. James Grady, head of DuPont's General Services Department, which runs the hotel, says that, to his knowledge, no survey showed a need for the Wilmingtonian. Interestingly, however, Grady was then president of GWDC, whose consultant reports praised the plans for the Wilmingtonian. When the city sold the land to the Wilmingtonian, a suit was brought in the Delaware courts by several people, including an employee of the News-Journal Company and a DuPont employee. The suit accused the city of selling the land to the Wilmingtonian too cheaply. The newspaper, of course, endorsed the suit. The Delaware Supreme Court decided against the Wilmingtonian, on grounds which neither plaintiff nor defendant had argued. The court noted that the sale of land included an agreement for the city to supply ingress and egress to the plot but that since Delaware Avenue was a state road, the city had no legal power to make this agreement. So the land was put out to public bid again, and again the Wilmingtonian, topping its earlier offer, bid highest. Studies done by the nationally known real estate firm of Horwath and Horwath had shown that the location was perfect. But the developer could not get financing for construction of the hotel. Delaware Trust, the Bank of Delaware, and Wilmington Trust refused to support the project. After the search for financing failed, the developer sold the land to IBM, which built an office building on it.

There are several explanations for these events. Many people claim that the Wilmingtonian was not built because the developers were Jewish and Italian entrepreneurs with no links to the corporate establishment. As one former high city official stated: "If the developer had been from the right social background, the corporate guys would have given their OK." Others feel that it was a political attack by the Republican newspaper on the Democratic administration. By charging that the sales price was too low, the paper was able to embarrass the city government. (The city chairman of the Democratic party was part of the Wilmingtonian group.) A third explanation is that Hotel DuPont did not want competition, while the IBM building, built in place of the Wilmingtonian, continued the white-collar atmosphere desired by the corporate establishment. Whichever explanation one accepts, the fact remains that corporate interests wielded their power to thwart the city. Only when the business community got behind the plans for a hotel in GWDC's regional shopping center did the hotel proposal go unopposed.

Although GWDC argues in its own bulletin that "all efforts should be made to protect and reinforce the fabric of community life that churches provide," GWDC's plan necessitated the demolition of three churches, all with black congregations: Shiloh Baptist, Mother African Union

Methodist Protestant, and Ezion. Two of these were of historical significance: Mother AUMP was the first black church in the country; Ezion has just celebrated its 165th anniversary.

Shiloh was wiped off the planning maps by GWDC. The church was pressured not only to discard expansion plans but also to move out of the area. To persuade the church to move, Mayor Haskell raised some money among his corporate friends to help the church relocate, and a DuPont family member was engaged as architect. Officials of Mother AUMP were willing to move if they got a plot in the same neighborhood. As one prominent spokesman for Mother AUMP said, "There seemed to be something approaching a moral commitment to make land nearby available." After prolonged negotiations, the corporate establishment gave in and provided the land. To deal with Ezion, GWDC at first offered to place a plaque marking the site where the church once stood. Since this offer did not satisfy Ezion, H. B. du Pont's Welfare Foundation bought a new plot relatively near the old site for the church; Mayor Haskell chipped in a personal check for $20,000 to $30,000 to sweeten the pot and appointed the recalcitrant pastor to the parking authority—an appointment the pastor considered "one of the most blatant attempts at co-optation" he had ever seen.

Finally, according to GWDC, to integrate the shopping mall into the rest of the Wilmington retail district, it will be necessary to develop an area nearby with a complex of stores, offices, and luxury apartments. This area, says Downtown Wilmington, is a "key anchor" of the whole development scheme. Perhaps not coincidentally, when the Wise-Gladstone consultants were preparing their study, the Rockland Corporation, the holding company of DuPont family member W. W. Laird, was quietly buying up the land and preparing to build just such a store-office-apartment complex. GWDC took Laird's plan and tacked it on to its own, glorifying it as in the public interest. Though Laird decided to drop the project and sell the land in June, 1971 (reportedly at a nifty profit), GWDC's action to promote his private interest is more evidence of its finely tuned cooperation with the corporate elite.

COMMUNITY RESPONSE

The downtown renewal plan is held out to Wilmington residents as a source of jobs for low-skilled workers, breaking the cruel cycle of poverty. The estimates of employment opportunities for low-skilled workers range from 1000 to 3000, but this figure must be understood in view of a number of factors. The number of jobs lost through the relocation of 30–38 businesses must be subtracted; the number of jobs that might have been generated on the land now being used for the highway connector must be subtracted; a comparison must be made between the jobs that would have been generated by the city's original plan and the jobs to be created in the GWDC complex; there must be an evaluation of how many jobs could have been created if the same amount of time, energy, and money went into recruiting new firms for Wilmington; and, because retail clerks are not highly paid, the personal income lost by not attracting higher-paying industries must be subtracted from the salaries generated by the mall. These analyses have not been made. The shoddy Wise-Gladstone report remains the only major study of the downtown center.

Nor is it clear that what jobs are created will go to those who need them most. A recent article in the *Evening Journal* states:

> He [Fulling] says no guarantee can be made that a certain set percentage of Civic Center jobs would go to minority group members because the shopping center is to be built and staffed privately. He will not hear of "offending" any developer by asking that a fair-share agreement be made.[16]

Meanwhile the nearly 1000 housing units that were torn down for what is euphemistically called urban renewal—primarily the shopping center complex—have not been replaced. It is revealing that GWDC, which followed the Wise-Gladstone study so closely in formulating the mall plans, ignored the study's findings on the tremendous need for housing in Wilmington. But Downtown Wilmington wants high-income families, not poor families, in the city. In the same vein, the plan for the area around the downtown complex calls for high-rise luxury apartments. According to Fulling,

> GWDC and Downtown Wilmington cannot let the Wilmington environment go bad; we have too much invested here—in people, buildings, and prestige. We do not like bringing foreigners to the chemical capital of the world that looks bad.

In March, 1971, five center-city neighborhood groups filed a complaint with the federal Department of Housing and Urban Development. The groups charged that the failure to replace low and moderate income housing violated the Housing Act of 1949. They asked that the federal government cease funding Wilmington's renewal projects, which of course includes the shopping complex. The neighborhood groups also charged that, "every effort has been made to avoid public debate and citizen participation" [17] in the downtown project.

An opportunity for "public debate and citizen participation" occurred in July, 1971, when federal highway authorities held a hearing on the proposed connector from the interstate highway system to the shopping center. The *Evening Journal* summed up the hearing in its headline on the following day, "Connector Given Its Lumps—Officialdom: Yea; But the Public: Nay." The story reported that "the connector had a major setback with its rejection by the vast majority of groups and individuals" [18] Only one community group stood with state and city officials. All the others, supported by only a few public officials, expressed opposition. They cited air pollution, noise levels, isolation of neighborhoods, and the lack of public input into the plans. But the greatest criticism centered around the city's priorities. A labor group carried a banner which read: "No connector. Better housing, schools, and hospitals for the poor instead of profits for the rich." The sentiments were widespread. City Councilman James Sills, Jr., a leader in the fight for housing, said, according to the newspapers, "there should be 'no connector, no civic center, and no revitalization of downtown Wilmington' until tangible and satisfactory plans are developed to solve the city's housing, economic, and educational problems." [19] Sills made a suggestion feared by the corporate establishment that the community "use the connector with all the cunning we can muster to help turn this city around." [20]

Fear that the community might stop the connector, and hence the whole regional shopping center conditional on the connector, has been growing. Corporate executives talk of deliberate sabotage, and the newspapers have written that the project is a fragile dream that could be shattered. But the connector, and hence the shopping center, passed one major hurdle when the state Advisory Council on Highways approved the route, claiming,

> It is not within the realm of this council to challenge the redevelopment program. We must decide on the best way to solve transportation problems that can be expected with the anticipated economic growth.[21]

After the public hearings, the *News-Journal,* which still supports the mall, wrote:

> It is becoming fairly obvious that if the federal government really pays attention to the feelings of community organizations such as the Model Cities Neighborhood Council, Wilmington is not going to get federal money for the downtown connector.[22]

The Department of Transportation, however, did approve the plan.

CHAPTER 9

# The DuPont Dailies: The Voice of the Corporate Establishment

The DuPont family has a virtual monopoly over news in Delaware. Through Christiana Securities, it owns 100% of the News-Journal Company, which publishes the *Morning News* and *Evening Journal*. The two papers have a statewide circulation of 140,000. The next largest Delaware paper has a readership of only 20,000. The most widely read out-of-state papers are even smaller: 2300 for *The New York Times;* 5100 for the *Philadelphia Bulletin;* and 11,200 for the *Philadelphia Inquirer*. The two DuPont papers provide practically all the local news used by Delaware radio stations. There is no commercial television station in Delaware. The only independent broadcast news source in the state is a small, educational television station.

The *Morning News* and the *Evening Journal* do not compete. The *Evening Journal* may carry a few articles that could not get into the morning paper. Sometimes editorials in the *Morning News* are slanted more toward business, *Evening Journal* editorials toward the community. A headline may be reworded or a paragraph added. Otherwise, the two papers are essentially identical.

The DuPonts launched their domination of Delaware newspapers when Colonel Henry A. du Pont acquired the *Wilmington Evening Journal* during the first decade of this century. Alfred I. du Pont, a family renegade who battled against T. Coleman du Pont's business and political leadership, countered by secretly purchasing the *Journal*'s major rival, the *Wilmington Morning News,* in 1911. For nine years Alfred, having also bought six downstate papers, fought his cousin Coleman through his news media. However, in 1920 Alfred encountered financial difficulties and had to surrender his heavily subsidized *Morning News* to Pierre S. du Pont, an ally of Coleman.

Most competitors of the DuPont press have either failed or been bought out by the DuPont papers.* There are a few specialized and small-town papers in Delaware, but the only non-DuPont daily is the small *Delaware State News,* circulation about 20,000, which has survived despite the *News-Journal*'s campaign to undermine it. When the *Delaware State News* was first issued in Dover, *News-Journal* salesmen threatened to pull their papers from any newsstand which stocked it. The *News-Journal* then gave downstate advertisers reprints of a story in *Editor &*

* The *Every Evening* was an early Wilmington newspaper with Democratic ties, in contrast to the DuPont's Republican allegiance. In 1918 a DuPont syndicate headed by a friendly Democrat, Josiah Marvel, bought it. At first, the DuPonts tried to create the appearance of independence for *Every Evening* by leasing the paper to its former editor. But heading the Every Evening Printing Company was William Coyne, a vice president of the DuPont Company and a Christiana Securities stockholder. The editor had to consult with Coyne on many things, especially family and company matters. No DuPont except Republican Coleman was treated unkindly.[1] In 1933 the DuPont family dropped the thin guise of autonomy and merged *Every Evening* into its Delaware newspaper empire.

After World War II, some Democrats attempted to restore news competition to the state by reviving the Wilmington *Sunday Star*. The *Star* died after a few issues because it could not obtain sufficient advertising support, even though it was the only Sunday paper.

By refusing to give funds to a newspaper in need, the DuPont family and company can force community papers out of business. The *People's Pulse,* once the major newspaper of Wilmington's black community, requested help from Delaware's United Fund, a charity group dominated by DuPont family members and company executives. In explaining why it could not aid the *Pulse,* the United Fund argued that "with appropriate management, it can be self-supporting." But in fact, according to a prominent black leader in Wilmington, a corporation with a large plant in Delaware had pressured United Fund to refuse the paper's request because corporate officials disapproved of its content. The *Pulse* folded in December, 1970.

*Publisher* which grossly understated the *Delaware State News*'s circulation. Even after the editors of the *Delaware State News* protested the reprint's glaring inaccuracies and vindictive tone (the *News-Journal* had printed "not more!" after the circulation figure), *News-Journal* salesmen continued to circulate the reprint to *Delaware State* advertisers.

The editors of the *News-Journal* defend their monopoly with two arguments. The chairman of the *News-Journal* board argued in 1968 that rising publishing costs have forced consolidation of papers which share the same printing press. But the Seaford *Leader,* for example, shares printing facilities with other small papers in southern Delaware and Maryland. The *News-Journal* itself publishes two papers on a press which could just as easily be shared by two independent papers.

The chairman's second argument is the remarkable one that competition is bad—because it would engender

> rabid partisanship and lurid sensationalism which too often accompany the fight for readers among many papers in a single town. . . . The good old days were not so good after all for a public which found each paper printing a different highly colored version of the news according to its partisan bias. . . . Monopoly papers, by and large, feel a far greater obligation to print the news objectively and to give space in their columns to opposing points of view.[2]

Maybe monopoly papers "by and large" are objective, but not in Delaware.

## *The Family and the News*

The DuPont family controls the board of directors as well as the stock of the News-Journal Company. Two family members on the board of Christiana Securities—Irenee du Pont, Jr., and R. R. M. Carpenter, Jr.—are directors of the *News-Journal.* Henry H. Silliman and Richard P. Sanger, both married to DuPonts, join their in-laws on the board. Sanger is also president and editor-in-chief. Completing the nine-member board are Chairman Charles L. Reese, Jr., son of a famous DuPont chemist; Robert H. Richards, Jr., a devoted family lawyer; Frederick Walter, the *News-Jour-*

*nal*'s general manager; J. J. B. Fulenwider, a retired executive from Hercules, Inc.; and Ralph K. Gottschall, president of Atlas Chemical Industries.

The family chooses editors it can trust. If an editor grows too independent, the family acts decisively to curb his power, as Creed Black, editor from 1960 until 1964, found out. Family and company interference in the papers' affairs frustrated him. At one point, Black complained to a friend that he had "to keep a genealogical table next to the phone to tell the pecking order of people calling in to complain." He urged that the *News-Journal* be sold to new owners. Ben Bagdikian's article, "Wilmington's Independent Newspapers," in the Summer, 1964, issue of the *Columbia Journalism Review,* documents the numerous instances of owner interference with the *News-Journal.* Bagdikian showed "what happens when an owner fails to understand the role of the monopoly newspaper and the discipline of news." [3] The *News-Journal* owners, according to this article, "seemed increasingly rigid in their demands for ultraconservative orthodoxy and family convenience, both in the news columns and editorials." To discredit the article and reassure the newspaper staff, H. B. du Pont sent a memo to newspaper employees on July 29, 1964, claiming that the Bagdikian article showed "a childish petulance in reciting the out-of-context remarks of various directors and represents nothing more than an attempt to find trouble where no trouble exists."

But H.B.'s own actions proved Bagdikian correct. Even before the article came off the press, the *News-Journal* board had created a new editorial position superior to Black's to limit his power. The board plucked Charles M. Hackett from a high post in the DuPont Public Relations Department to fill the new slot, reputedly at more than the $75,000 annual salary DuPont had given him. Black resigned over Hackett's appointment, in which he heard the death knell of his autonomy. Black tried to publish his letter of resignation in the *News-Journal;* H. B. du Pont blocked it. Philadelphia papers, however, printed the letter the day Black posted it on a newsroom bulletin board. It ran in part: "I, for one, need no further evidence that the ownership wants the *Morning News* and *Evening Journal* operated as house organs instead of as newspapers." The *News-Journal* printed the letter two days later, but only after H. B. du Pont had been given a chance to reply. Characteristically, the article began: "The independence and integrity of the *News-Journal* papers were reaffirmed yesterday by Henry B. du Pont."

History corroborates Creed Black's side of the argument. For years, the *News-Journal* has so effectively guarded the family's interests that Delaware residents have learned to rely instead on the Philadelphia papers for facts about DuPonts. Even *News-Journal* reporters scrutinize the *Bulletin* for Wilmington news and often publish follow-up stories from *Bulletin* leads. One *News-Journal* reporter noted that family items get triple checking, and treatment is always restrained. Even if nothing is cut from the stories, DuPont family vigilance creates anticipatory self-restraint which amounts to censorship. One *News-Journal* staff member described how stories on the bankruptcy of Lammot du Pont Copeland, Jr., were handled: "The city editor was asked to read the stories to higher-ups. They didn't change a single thing in the stories, as far as I know, but the word sure got around."[4] The *News-Journal* has never explained how its courthouse reporters "missed" the June, 1970, judgment against Copeland obtained by Wilmington Trust; reporters make daily checks of court decisions in Wilmington.

The *News-Journal*'s shielding of family members can be well documented. In the fall of 1970, its papers carried no account of William Henry du Pont's abrupt cut-off of funds from Organization Interest (OI), a self-help project for released prisoners. Thomas DeBaggio, an independent journalist in Wilmington, thought the omission strange, particularly since the *Philadelphia Bulletin* had run a feature story exploring OI's problems on its Sunday Wilmington page,[5] and the *News-Journal* had run several stories on OI before. DeBaggio wrote a story for the *People's Pulse*, then the dominant black newspaper in Wilmington, detailing William Henry du Pont's withdrawal of support. He gave a copy to several reporters at the *News-Journal*, but none were "interested." In an effort to stop the story in the *People's Pulse*, William Henry du Pont called Mayor Harry

Haskell, several black community leaders, a black city councilman, and even the Maryland printer of the *Pulse*. The story was held up for several weeks, but it finally appeared in the *Pulse* as written. Not a word surfaced in the *News-Journal*. Three months later, however, the *Evening Journal* ran a front page story on the crusade of William Henry du Pont's wife against the horrible treatment given juvenile offenders in Delaware jails.

When the *News-Journal* cannot avoid an event which might prove embarrassing to a DuPont, it works hard to break the news as gently as possible, as in reporting the bankruptcy of Lammot du Pont Copeland Jr. Suits against Copeland began piling up as early as July, 1970, but the Wilmington papers carried only short back-page notices. Meanwhile, a Chicago grand jury was investigating Copeland's Winthrop Lawrence Corporation for possible charges of fraud. No notice appeared in the *News-Journal,* even though a two-column article in the June 27 issue of *Editor & Publisher,* a national magazine regularly read by *News-Journal* staff, carried the full story, including the fact that Copeland, Jr. had testified before the grand jury prior to June 12, 1970.[6] When Copeland's bankruptcy petition was filed in October, 1970, the *Evening Journal* read, "Copeland Jr. Asks Court for Help on Debts," the best possible headline under the circumstances. The first story about the investigation ran on November 13, 1970, when the grand jury subpoenaed Copeland's financial records. But the article said pointedly that Copeland "willingly accepted service of the subpoena . . . and is cooperating fully with the government." [7] When national news media began to publicize the bankruptcy, many papers carried background stories and investigative reports, often on their front pages. But no such in-depth reporting appeared in the *News-Journal*.

Two months later, the *News-Journal* ran a multicolumn story on Copeland to "bring the overall picture into focus." The article was blatantly pro-Copeland. The *News-Journal* blamed Copeland's financial fiasco on the "slumping economy," Copeland's trust in shady business partners, and even his inexperience in the intricacies of building a financial empire, although Copeland had worked as a securities analyst for the DuPont Company. The "comprehensive" article conveniently omitted several important facts. It never noted that Copeland had extracted a $13,000-per-month "consulting fee" from his faltering West Coast newspapers, made no reference to the Chicago grand jury investigation, obliterated the news that the Wilmington Trust protected some of Copeland's assets from other creditors by a complex legal maneuver, did not speak of the large sums laid out for Copeland by his mother and brother, and did not inquire into possible breaches of fiduciary duty of Copeland's father, whose position as director of two major banks helped his financially troubled son get loans. With consistency, the DuPont-controlled papers continued to protect Copeland when they reported the reelection in 1971 of nine of the News-Journal Company directors, omitting the fact that Copeland, the tenth, had been dropped.

The *News-Journal* likewise protects the pet projects of the DuPont family. The most prominent "sacred cow" is the University of Delaware, which is heavily financed and directed by DuPont family members. The *News-Journal*'s protection of the University of Delaware was noted in the *Delaware State News* in an editorial entitled "University of Delapont":

> The University of Delaware has always been one of the most sacred of the sacred cows in the DuPont pasture called Delaware.
>
> So it was no great surprise that the headline in the DuPont Press in Wilmington was "McCormack Aide Accused of Pressuring U. of D.", instead of the "U. of Del. Admits Bowing To Pressure" which appeared in the state's only independent daily.
>
> And that's what happened.
>
> After pressure was apparently put on the university to admit the son of a purported labor racketeer, the university changed its mind and accepted the boy.
>
> Dr. Robert Mayer, director of admissions for the University of DuPont, claimed a man who said he was Speaker of the House John McCormack asked him on the telephone to "consider favorably the [boy's] application."
>
> Later, Mayer said, he received another call in which a person identified as a National Aeronautics and Space Administration official hinted that a research contract with

the university would be renewed and enlarged if the university admitted the boy.

The U. of D. claims the boy's original application wasn't complete, and that a later interview with the boy and completion of the application changed the university's mind.

An early edition of the DuPont Press said:

"Mayer replied to a question, 'after we decided to admit [the boy] . . . because the last word had been that we would not . . . I placed a call to Speaker McCormack, and I spoke with Speaker McCormack.' "

That incriminating paragraph was left out of a later edition of the DuPP.

The University, if it is to be truly a state university and not a family company university, must come out from behind its closed doors; and out from under protection of the DuPont house organs in Wilmington.[8]

H. B. du Pont and R. R. M. Carpenter, Jr., served both as trustees of the university and directors of the News-Journal Company. Both used their dual positions to protect the university from adverse publicity.

For instance, in early 1965 a new reporter at the *News-Journal* naively began a story based on a complaint by two faculty members about University of Delaware president John Perkins, who temperamentally fired and subsequently rehired a minor university administrator. Perkins was an intimate friend of Henry B. du Pont; editor Hackett promptly ordered the reporter to forget his story.

In the winter of 1967, a reporter uncovered a scandal centering on carelessly prescribed pep pills at the University of Delaware. As soon as university officials heard of the story, they contacted Carpenter, probably the family member who has most often interfered wtih the *News-Journal.* Carpenter promptly phoned Dixie Sanger, *News-Journal* editor, and suggested that the reporter be fired. Carpenter was eventually placated and the reporter kept his job, but when the story appeared on March 23, 1969, it was short, watered down, and buried in a larger story on drug abuse in Delaware. Carpenter also objected when the *News-Journal* printed a letter from 64 University of Delaware students favoring university integration. According to Ben Bagdikian, Carpenter declared that he thought the paper should close the letter column to all students.

University news was again suppressed when a *News-Journal* reporter submitted an article on chemical and biological warfare research, including an account of the University of Delaware's participation. The article explained that four Pentagon contracts at the University of Delaware had been among those in a list of chemical and biological warfare contracts made public by Senator Gaylord Nelson and that a university official had acknowledged the existence of the contracts on Nelson's list and had given information on three others not listed. When the *News-Journal* top brass finished editing the article, the reporter quit in disgust. The story now read as if the university had disclosed the information of its own accord without any pressure from the public release of the Nelson list. Every reference to Democrat Nelson was edited out of the story. Whole paragraphs were deleted, among them these:

> According to Dr. Mosher [the major Pentagon contract recipient at the University], the University's Chemistry Department has felt the pinch of the army's shift in priorities. During an interview this week, he lamented the "drying up" of army funds for his Department's chemical research. No army money is being dished out for chemical research this year, he said. . . .
>
> Belying the talk of the innocent basic research on the part of the scientist is also the fact that most investigators have an excellent idea of what use the military can make of their findings. Mosher and Berglin [University research coordinator] both conceded that the method used in acquiring a military grant almost precludes such ignorance of purpose. . . .
>
> Although not actually involved in the basic development of chemical and germ weapons, an extremely dangerous operation which takes specially constructed lab equipment and buildings, Mosher said he was aware in a general way of the applicability of most of his research. Most scientists would be, he said.

The *News-Journal* wholeheartedly supported the university's bid to prevent state audit of private donations. Since the university gets over two-thirds of its budget from public funds and has the public power of eminent domain, Delaware officials were by law permitted to fully audit the school's books. However, the DuPont-dominated board of trustees pressured for a university exemption from the law to insulate upper-class donors from public scrutiny. In an editorial entitled "Independence for University," the *Evening Journal* proclaimed that the protection of donors was vital to the independence of the University of Delaware:

> One of the major factors behind [the University of Delaware's] growth in physical facilities and prestige has been the enthusiastic support it has attracted from generous donors as an independent institution. . . . We strongly endorse [a bill that] would specifically remove any statutory compulsion for the budget commissioner to assert any control over that portion of the university's budget which is underwritten by income from endowment, gifts, and student fees. . . . Independence is an essential element of greatness in a university—and no form of independence is more essential than political independence.[9]

On the other hand, when the university refused to renew the contracts of several professors involved in "unapproved" political activity—an antiwar petition—the *News-Journal* reported the events; but no editorial appeared criticizing university officials for possible infringements of constitutional guarantees of free speech. When the university backed down slightly and offered Professor Edward Kaplan a teaching post for the next year if he could not find another job, the *News-Journal* would not print the story. As Kaplan said:

> It's strange that the News-Journal papers were perfectly willing to let the world know I had been muzzled and then canned last winter, but that they have now turned so shy and retiring about letting the state know that their bosses (and ours) have had to back down, if only a little.[10]

Like the University of Delaware, the Wilmington Medical Center, heavily financed by the DuPonts, is a DuPont sacred cow. One former *News-Journal* reporter was in fact told that all stories on the Wilmington Medical Center were to be checked for "accuracy" by the center's own public relations chief.

When the merger that created the center (see Chapter 4)

was being planned in 1963, ample coverage was given to the consolidation committee, headed by a family member, and its efforts toward merger of the three hospitals. But when a *News-Journal* staffer interviewed several physicians critical of the proposed merger, his report was emasculated by editing. Later in the fall of 1963, a noted *News-Journal* columnist spoke with several irate doctors; his report on these conversations never even appeared. These doctors were not a small nucleus; a survey later showed that the *majority* of the hospitals' doctors were opposed to the merger on the basis of valid medical concerns.

In December, 1970, an assistant to Mayor Haskell gave a *News-Journal* reporter a copy of an affidavit from the parents of two young boys who had been refused emergency service by one of the center's hospitals and had died en route to another hospital. No mention of the center's refusal of service ever appeared, even though there were several articles about the boys' deaths.

### *The Company and the News*

Christiana Securities, the DuPont holding company which owns the News-Journal Company, also has controlling interest in the DuPont Company. Some directors of the DuPont Company have also been directors of Christiana Securities and the *News-Journal* at the same time, among them H. B. du Pont and Irenee du Pont, Jr. Most significant, H. B. du Pont moved Charles M. Hackett from a high post in the DuPont Public Relations Department to the specially created top editorial post in the paper, where he served for six years.

H. B. du Pont once declared in the *News-Journal* that "these papers have never been and never will be operated as a house organ for any organization." But the transfer of Hackett from the DuPont Company to the *News-Journal* reminded Delawareans of an old nickname for the papers—the "Daily Better Living"—after a DuPont Company house organ, *Better Living.* At least one prominent DuPont family member partially accepts this characterization; asked if the *News* and *Journal* were DuPont Company house organs, Alexis I. du Pont Bayard said, "In rare instances, yes." In a transparent effort to recast Hackett as the guardian of the public interest, the *News-Journal* wrote after his death:

> Anyone on the outside who criticized a story of a reporter to Mr. Hackett was virtually pushed against the wall to substantiate his criticism.[11]

In fact, the situation was just the opposite: when anyone on the paper criticized the DuPonts, Hackett virtually pushed *him* to the wall.

One *News-Journal* staff member wrote an article in February, 1970, on the sudden, early retirement of eight DuPont department managers within a year; he noted that only seven such retirements occurred between 1959 and 1963. When the reporter called a DuPont executive for comment on this story, he was told to check back shortly. The executive promptly phoned editor Hackett in apprehension; Hackett dutifully called the reporter into his office to ascertain what kind of news slant he would take. Assured of the reporter's conciliatory tone and low-key presentation of the facts, Hackett permitted the story to run.

DuPont press releases are often printed intact. Stories about the company often consist of uncritically accepted statements of DuPont spokesmen. A *News-Journal* editor, Les Cansler, once wrote to the *Delaware State News* about press releases:

> I fear that our city editor pays little attention to releases, except when they come down from the DuPont Building. Then he quivers with awe and follows instructions to a "T." [12]

Indeed, until recent years, the *News-Journal*'s treatment of the DuPont Company was entirely uncritical. The editorials on the DuPont–General Motors antitrust case provide a perfect example. In 1954, when the federal district court found the DuPont Company and family not guilty of conspiracy and antitrust violations, the DuPont newspapers said the case had been "preposterous," a "wearying persecution of an outfit that has too great a stake in free competition to abuse it in the business world of today." [13] Another editorial on the same day referred to the government prosecutors as "Doubting Thomases of the Department of Justice, as it was spawned under the New Deal."[14] When the federal government appealed the trial court's decision, the *News-Journal* ridiculed the move, referring to lower court Judge LaBuy's opinion as,

> The most complete exoneration that any defendant could have hoped for in an antitrust action of this sort. . . . [We have a] suspicion that politics has played as large a part as the hope of a reversal in the decision to appeal. Nothing is surer than that Democratic orators would have taunted the Eisenhower Republicans with favoritism to big business. . . . This would hardly excuse the continued harassment of the DuPont family, the DuPont Company . . . unless there is sound legal logic for the appeal.[15]

Another editorial suggested that the government's suit against DuPont was not legally sound:

> It is hard to avoid the suspicion that the government's decision to appeal the DuPont antitrust case is based on less than good legal reasons.[16]

When the U.S. Supreme Court reversed the lower court and found the DuPont Company guilty, the *News-Journal* emphasized that the decision hinged upon a finding that DuPont's ownership of General Motors stock created "a reasonable probability that the acquisition is likely to result in the condemned [trade] restraints."[17] Exactly the same observance appears in the *DuPont Facts Book*, a DuPont Company publication for its employees. A reader of both the *DuPont Facts Book* and the *News-Journal* would have been entirely misled as to what the Supreme Court really found. The DuPont publications were quoting merely the *threshold* test of whether a violation of Section 7 of the Clayton Act occurred. Actually, the Supreme Court decided that DuPont had gone far beyond this threshold and found the company guilty of abusing and exploiting its formal ownership position:

> The fact that sticks out in this voluminous record is that the bulk of DuPont's production has always supplied the largest part of the requirements of the one customer in the automobile industry connected to DuPont by a stock interest. The inference is overwhelming that DuPont's

> commanding position was promoted by its stock interest and was not gained solely on competitive merit. . . . But the wisdom of this business judgment cannot obscure the fact, plainly revealed by the record, that DuPont purposely employed its stock to pry open the General Motors' requirement for automotive finishes and fabrics.[18]

News items or editorials dealing with issues in which DuPont's role is less than laudatory are often run with no mention of the company. An editorial on the problems of Project Equality, a private church-sponsored campaign to promote equal employment opportunity, failed to note that the DuPont Company had refused to participate in the program.[19] In another instance, the *Evening Journal* carried a story on Senate hearings investigating possible links of certain meat additives to cancer.[20] The story in the Wilmington papers omitted a central fact which appeared in the *Wall Street Journal*'s account: DuPont is one of the two largest manufacturers of the additives.[21] But when the DuPont Company devoted the June, 1971, issue of *Better Living,* its largest corporate magazine, to explain the company's commitment to help save Wilmington, the *News-Journal* bestowed extravagant praises on the company. In an editorial quoting the article and applauding DuPont's "leadership," the Wilmington paper "warmly welcomed" DuPont's commitment to the city's problems.[22]

*News-Journal* editorial policies on general business issues often closely follow the DuPont Company position. The *News-Journal* editorially opposed Campaign GM, an effort by public interest lawyers to reform corporate decision making by placing representatives of consumers, environmental organizations, and minority groups on the General Motors board of directors. Moreover, the Wilmington papers never told the readers that a DuPont stockholder had presented a similar proposal in the proxy for the 1970 DuPont stockholders' meeting, though the *News-Journal* found space to report a DuPont stockholder's accusation that the man who had proposed the DuPont committee on corporate responsibility failed to appear at annual stockholders' meetings. On the question of potential dangers posed by big business, the *News-Journal* has echoed DuPont's words. A 1957 editorial approvingly quotes a speech made by Lammot du Pont Copeland before the Associated Press Managing Editors Association:

> 'While large companies try to be fair and decent in order to survive, even if they were selfish and evil, the nation would still have to have them because it cannot survive without them.'

The editorial went on to say:

> That goes to the heart of the issue. For great tasks must be done. Without big businesses to perform them, they will either go undone or government will do them. If they go undone, the nation will be weakened. If government does them, the free enterprise system will no longer exist.[23]

During the 1960s, a decade when giant conglomerates swelled through mergers, not a single editorial appeared in the *News-Journal* pondering the potential danger conglomerates posed to America's competitive system by concentrating economic power. Instead, the DuPont papers plugged their theme of the necessity of big business. One editorial, entitled "War Against Mergers," talked about the necessity of having big, varied businesses (often generated by mergers) to meet changing technological needs of society.

Unions normally receive poor coverage and treatment by the *News-Journal*. Very little coverage was given the long strike by DuPont employees at Niagara Falls in 1970, even though quite a few of DuPont's Delaware employees were commuting to Niagara Falls to work as strikebreakers.

In line with DuPont policy, the *News-Journal* considers a graduated corporate income tax to be detrimental to competition. After quoting with approval Lammot du Pont Copeland's claim that a graduated corporate tax threatened the free enterprise system, the papers concluded: "Certainly it is obvious that if we want to eliminate large enterprises, this is one way to do it."[24] The *News-Journal* even joins DuPont in decrying the graduated income tax on individual incomes. The paper once argued that the federal tax structure, because it was developed during the Depression, was designed "to achieve goals far different from the needs of the economic normalcy we now enjoy." Tax provisions have "penalized investment in order to achieve a greater distribution of income. . . . The tax structure, with its high and rapidly progressing rates, is still draining off consumer and investor money." [25] It is as if the editors were in the dark about the multiple loopholes which the corporate and individual rich have carried out of the federal tax laws to reduce their taxable income.

As the *News-Journal* has sided with the DuPont Company on its own economic affairs and its general business views, so the paper has given favorable treatment to the company's pollution policies. The *News-Journal* supported DuPont lawyers who lobbied for a variance section in the enforcement provisions of the 1966 Delaware Water and Air Resources Act. This corporate-planned administrative mandate lowering standards for industry was vague enough to be open to grave abuse; however, the *News-Journal* argued that "variances should be permitted under the terms that were specified by industry representatives who suggested changes in the bill." [26] When DuPont began barging millions of gallons of acid waste out to sea instead of dumping them into the Delaware River as it had done for decades, the *News-Journal* glorified the company's decision without revealing its deficiencies. Editorially, the DuPont papers saw the barging as "one firm's dramatic answer to a vast modern problem." [27] An editorial in 1969 approvingly quoted a speech by DuPont's president and added: "To be sure, not all U.S. industry has shown the kind of pollution control leadership the DuPont Company has demonstrated over the years." [28]

But the *News-Journal* conveniently glossed over some crucial facts about DuPont's pollution policy. It failed to inform the reader that numerous DuPont plants around the country, in states like West Virginia and Wisconsin, were major polluters, worse even than the manufacturing plants near Wilmington. Furthermore, the paper did not explain that in the metropolitan Wilmington area DuPont's Chambers Works still has only *primary* treatment for industrial waste and the Edgemoor plant still dumps 262,500 pounds of acid waste *per day* into the Delaware River with only primary treatment. Ironically, the *News-Journal* itself had described the deficiencies of primary treatment. In a

1964 editorial, one of the papers accused the state Water Pollution Commission of not moving against polluters. The editorial mentioned that the primary treatment given wastes by Wilmington and Delaware City was not sufficient to remove bacterial pollution from sewage. It went on to say:

> The commission is not without power to move against pollution in any form including the nonbacterial type from industrial discharges.[29]

On June 30, 1970, the *News-Journal* ran a photo of water pollution caused by a spill at the Chambers Works plant. The picture, shot by an independent photographer, bore a caption explaining DuPont's involvement in a pilot waste treatment project and quoting the company's assurances that the spill was a harmless, freak accident. The information which appeared was supplied to a reporter by the DuPont public relations department in a telephone conversation. No editorial was written condemning DuPont for the spill or calling for stricter enforcement of laws or urging DuPont to clean up its mess. The DuPont-controlled papers chose to ignore the fact that DuPont's daily waste continued to receive only primary treatment and was still being pumped into the Delaware River.

Likewise, the *News-Journal* blindly repeats DuPont's public relations material on pollution. DuPont's public relations department counters criticism of the company's role in environmental matters by citing the amount of money DuPont has spent on pollution equipment. It does not relate that figure to the extent of DuPont's pollution damage or the monetary value of pollution control machinery still needed for company installations; nor does it cite the net value of that investment after accelerated depreciation and other tax write-offs. The *News-Journal* proudly quotes the company's figure on pollution expenditures whenever a story is run on ecological damage caused by a DuPont plant. For example, when the government brought a court action against DuPont for polluting in Indiana, the *Evening Journal* headline read: "DuPont Co., Sued as Polluter, Notes $1 Million Outlay." [30] Times are changing somewhat, however, as evidenced by recent articles [31] discussing the facts about pollution caused by various Du-

Pont plants and other industrial facilities—but still no editorial policy.

## *The News and the Community*

Some of the worst abuses of the DuPont monopoly of news in Delaware involve community issues—the reporting of political campaigns and the coverage of important local projects. The owners of the *News-Journal* have used the paper as their political mouthpiece and as a forum for conservative causes. To keep the paper's viewpoints in line, family members seldom hesitate to criticize articles or change editorials. Robert R. M. Carpenter, Jr., a DuPont family member on the news company's board, has issued numerous complaints about the political viewpoint of the *News-Journal* to the editorial staff:

> On an editorial praising President Kennedy's Supreme Court appointments: "Why should we devote space to one who is an enemy of private enterprise and the capitalistic system?"
>
> When editors asked him if his complaints about their comments on a bill by Representative McDowell mean the paper should oppose everything McDowell was for, the answer was, "I would say, Yes."
>
> When an editorial criticized some Republican choices of candidates: "Are we endorsing the Democratic Party by criticizing the Republican Convention? . . . Could we not become a house organ for the conservative cause?"
>
> On an editorial noting that French Socialists had outmaneuvered French Communists: "Should the *News-Journal* take the position of favoring actions of any socialist party? I believe it is a grave error for a subsidiary of DuPont to follow the philosophy of the ultraliberal whose objectives are destruction of capitalistic systems." [32]

In 1961 the *News-Journal* editorialized against the official showings of the right-wing propaganda film, "Operation Abolition," by Delaware State Police. This blatantly political film of dubious factual accuracy, the paper felt, set a dangerous precedent for political indoctrination. However, H. B. du Pont ordered the *News-Journal* to stop protesting.

Toeing a similar political line, Robert H. Richards, Jr., a

*News-Journal* director, family lawyer, and one time Republican National Committeeman, complained that an ordinary news story about a Democratic rally should have been written as a pro-Republican story; he even wrote one of his own to show how it should be done, adding: "This is a matter, if properly handled, could, in my opinion, have been very useful to the Republican Party and their success at the polls in November." [33]

Some newspapermen have refused to consider working on the *News-Journal* because of the political use made of the papers. In 1960, when the *News-Journal* was hiring a new editor, one applicant, an editor from a prominent newspaper, asked what would happen if he wanted to endorse a Democratic candidate for office; he was told that the board of directors would decide such an endorsement. He quickly declined the job.

As a result of family political watchdogging, the paper has reflected DuPont views and endorsed a Democrat only when the candidate's conservatism overrode his party affiliation. A notable example was J. Allen Frear, an ultraconservative Democratic senator from Delaware. The *News-Journal* once approvingly likened him to the renowned reactionary, Senator Harry Byrd of Virginia. In a May 29, 1959, editorial, the *News-Journal* praised Frear for the legislation he introduced during his tenure in Washington, especially bills concerning the cellophane and General Motors antitrust suits. So, in 1960, owners of the news company had a difficult time deciding whether to support the Democrat Frear or the Republican Caleb Boggs for the U.S. Senate. In the end, they hit upon double endorsement as a suitable compromise. In 1962, however, the editorial staff members were so appalled by the Republican candidate for the U.S. House of Representatives that they wanted to support the Democrat, the lesser of two evils. But the staff's endorsement editorial was rewritten at a meeting of the Christiana Securities board of directors. In the revised version of the editorial, the only Democrat endorsed was the candidate for state auditor.

In 1964 the *News-Journal* editors wanted to support the Republican party through editorials focusing "on an objective appraisal of the chances of the various candidates."[34] H. B. du Pont was against this idea because it would "leave editorial writers free to snipe at candidates for the Republican nomination for President."[35]

When the leadership of Delaware's Republican party shifted to "Rockefeller liberals," the tension between the political views of the owners and the staff was reduced. The staff could support Governor Russell W. Peterson and Mayor Harry G. Haskell both as members of the corporate elite and as corporate liberals. The DuPont-controlled papers now accord these politicians the same uncritical treatment DuPonts' conservative friends have traditionally received. Of course, the paper supported Pierre S. du Pont IV for U.S. Congressman. It played down Pierre's family affiliation, however, to avoid the implication that he was a tool of DuPont family or company interests.

The downstate *Delaware State News* carried a revealing editorial concerning the *News-Journal*'s slanted coverage of Governor Peterson:

> Last week, the Associated Press wire carried a story saying Delaware had borrowed $14.1 million to meet current operating expenses.
> The morning DuPont paper didn't carry the story. Nor did the evening paper.
> Instead the morning paper carried this headline over another story: "Governor's Anti-Litter Aides Named."
> And this one: "Youths Told of Peterson's Concern Over War, Crime."
> And this one: "State GOP Chief raps Democratic 'Politics.' "
> The evening edition followed up with "Peterson Lists Some Savings." (The story included a $12-a-year magazine subscription which had been canceled [sic]. Big Deal!)
> And "Peterson To Speak In St. Louis." But still no room for the $14 million.[36]

The *News-Journal* showered Governor Peterson with editorial praise for his efforts to reorganize state government. But after Peterson's new governmental machine led the state into a deficit of over $30 million, its papers had no editorial condemning his incompetence. The absence of editorial criticism is even more striking in light of the paper's own news reports. In the middle of the financial crisis, a *News-Journal* news article began:

> If state government had not been so permissive toward corporations which did not file annual reports, the current fiscal crisis might have been avoided, the chief financial analyst in the Peterson administration conceded yesterday.[37]

When a group of Puerto Rican youths took over an office of the Wilmington Housing Authority to press demands for better housing, the *News-Journal* protected Mayor Haskell. An editorial underscored Haskell's statements that the city had built many public housing units over the last two decades; it ignored the fact that in that period the city tore down more housing units than it put up. A representative of the Puerto Rican community delivered to the newspaper a statement rebutting many of Haskell's words and the paper's coverage of the incident; the newspaper refused to print the statement.

The *News-Journal*'s reflection of DuPont views on community issues shines beyond politics to local projects. First, the *News-Journal* refrained from considering serious questions involved in the controversy surrounding DuPont's purchase of 1200 acres for a county reservoir on White Clay Creek (see Chapter 11). Did the county need a dam or did DuPont need water for industrial expansion at its Glasgow site? Was the plan for the dam feasible in light of ecological and social factors? Instead of asking these questions, the *News-Journal* said:

> For this, DuPont certainly deserves the public's thanks, for while its own interest was the original and primary consideration in acquiring the land, the public's interest was also well served.[38]

After the state acquired land adjacent to DuPont's site to use for a park, DuPont earmarked some of its land for a park, also. In an editorial praising the DuPont offer, the *News-Journal* failed to note that DuPont had done so only on the condition that the county first build the reservoir on the company's White Clay Creek land.[39] This condition amounted to corporate blackmail, but the *News-Journal* had a different view. The paper shared the DuPont Company's consternation with a slow legislature:

> The very obvious need for a White Clay reservoir ought to be matched by prompt action in the legislature. The people and industry of the county cannot afford to let the stream keep flowing wastefully to the ocean.[40]

By 1968 the *News-Journal* had lost all patience with careful consideration of the very complex issues; it editorially commanded the county to "Build That White Clay Dam."[41]

The desirability of the dam was not quite so obvious to everyone. Reports and analyses done by University of Delaware economists, including Paul Seidenstat, Charles Tremblay, and Francis Tannian, criticized previous consultant studies for making incomplete cost benefit analyses, especially of the ecological costs of inundating the White Clay Valley. The county asked a local nature group, the Delaware Nature Education Center, to forecast the ecological effects of a reservoir on the White Clay. DNEC did a survey of flora and fauna in the valley and concluded that a reservoir would cause no serious ecological damage. The *News-Journal* immediately endorsed the report and urged:

> There is no longer any valid excuse for New Castle County Council to delay a firm decision on the proposed dam.[42]

A month later the DuPont papers purported to present a complete summary of the various dam reports, concluding:

> A decade later the evidence suggests that it [the dam] is still desirable, on balance, but that it is much more necessary now than it was when the issue first arose. The time has come for New Castle County to proceed with White Clay Creek dam.[43]

The editorial failed to remind the reader that the water shortage prophesied by the Army Corps, DuPont Company, and other early reports had not only failed to materialize, but also looked more and more remote. Nor did it mention any of the several reports showing the dam to be either infeasible or unnecessary.

Not once in the nine years since the dam project was first urged by the DuPont Company did the *News-Journal* publicly ponder whether the company, a private organization, was in effect making, or unduly influencing, a public decision. In an attempt to discredit a letter to the editor bringing out this line of argument, the *News-Journal* attached comments from a DuPont vice president and the director of the Delaware Nature Education Center.

Tellingly, the *News-Journal*'s firm support of the DuPont Company on the White Clay Creek dam proposal has not been consistent with its stand on other public issues. In 1966, when the Delaware governor proposed that the state buy land 5 to 10 years before it was needed for highways and other public uses, the *News-Journal* urged the state to maintain flexibility in its capital improvement program:

> At first glance, land acquisition so far in advance could seem to be at odds with this procedure. Early purchase of land for highways or buildings not scheduled to be built for several years would seem to freeze the state into a definite commitment to go ahead and build when the time arrived. . . . Conditions change, and the highway that was projected seven or eight years ago may not be needed today after all.[44]

DuPont's purchase of the White Clay Creek land and its designation of the area as a dam site before a public body had decided whether a dam would be useful or necessary is clearly subject to the same criticism. Yet that criticism was never voiced by the DuPont papers.

The *News-Journal* has also swung its support behind community projects of individual DuPonts. For example, in 1966, when H. B. du Pont decided to turn a major street from chateau country to Wilmington into a boulevard, complete with a little park he would donate to the city, the papers "cast [their] vote for the boulevard." The papers never reported H. B.'s role in the project, nor that it was primarily designed to provide a gateway to DuPont's planned Brandywine Building, or that property owners along the boulevard would be severely damaged by the zoning restraints brought about by H. B.'s proposal. Rather, according to the *News-Journal,* the plan was

> found to have considerable merit by a lot of Wilmingtonians. . . . Wilmington has a beautiful plan for the western gateway to the midtown area. . . . And we hope that the city administration, which hasn't made its comment about the plan yet, will demand that the plan be followed to the letter, at least where streets and boulevards are concerned.[45]

The papers gave ample coverage in 1969 to the opening of H. B.'s little park. A caption writer who described the site as a "once barren piece of land" [46] apparently had forgotten that an eight-family apartment building and a fountain built in 1872 had once occupied the area.

Predictably, the papers' editors and owners have often slighted the black community. H. B. du Pont once told the editors of the *News-Journal:*

> A continual overplaying of integration in our papers certainly plays right into the hands of the radical element of our population. . . . Many of the writers on your staff seem to have a degree of dedication to certain causes which would make them appear to be quite far to the left.[47]

One recent example of the subtle way the *News-Journal* shortchanges Delaware's black citizens also illustrates the papers' protection of University of Delaware officials. After an honors day ceremony at the university was disrupted by black students protesting discrimination, the *News-Journal* ran a story on May 19, 1970, making casual reference to a telegram sent to the university by 68 prominent black citizens. They had protested the disciplinary procedures given the black demonstrators and the exclusion of a representative of the state's human relations commission from the proceedings. The very next day, a rebuttal by university president Arthur Trabant was run in a prominent place in the newspaper. Angered by Trabant's assertions that the black demonstration was violent and by the university's failure to follow proper judicial procedures, a key leader of Wilmington's black community who had signed the telegram dashed off a reply. This reply, however, was not printed until nine days later.

Since the death of top editor Charles M. Hackett in 1970, reporters and the editorial staff of the *News-Journal* have begun to be less dependent on the corporate establishment. Several aggressive reporters have written in-depth investigative articles critical of the corporate elite, and the editorial board seems less responsive to family and company interests. For example, in July, 1971, the *Evening Journal* ran a series of articles on the GWDC-backed shopping mall and parking garage in downtown Wilmington. The series gave comprehensive, objective coverage and raised some doubts about the center's prospect for success. Recent articles on the Wilmington Parking Authority, the New Castle County Housing Authority, mass transit, and pollution have also covered issues that formerly would have been ignored or gingerly treated. If all formal ties between the family and the newspapers can be broken, and if the informal pressures of the DuPont-dominated milieu can be resisted, perhaps the staff can provide the kind of independent news coverage Delaware needs.

# *Part* IV

# Local Government

CHAPTER 10

# A Tale of Two Cities: DuPont in Seaford and Wilmington

The impact of corporate power on local government is experienced daily in communities across the country. In Delaware, the DuPont Company and its family of owners have directly affected two—Seaford and Wilmington. In Seaford, DuPont operates a large nylon plant with about 4,000 employees. At its office headquarters in Wilmington and nearby research and manufacturing facilities, it employs 29,000 workers. The total capital investment in DuPont's Delaware locations is about $600 million.

Two presidents of DuPont provide criteria for judging DuPont's relationship with communities in which it operates. First, according to Charles B. McCoy, DuPont contributes to a local community according to the proportion of the work force it employs. Second, in Lammot du Pont Copeland's words:

> Business is a means to an end for society and not an end in itself, and therefore business must act in concert with a broad public interest and serve the objectives of mankind and society or it will not survive.[1]

McCoy's formula and Copeland's rhetoric have clashed directly with a more fundamental criterion for DuPont's involvement—profitability. And the important question is whether corporate profit at community expense is still the company's guiding light.

## *The Nylon Capital of the World*

DuPont dubbed Seaford, near the southern border of Delaware, "The Nylon Capital of the World" after building the world's first nylon plant there just before World War II. Seaford was then a small, rural town without industry, surrounded by flat farmlands and pine forests. Seaford remains small (pop. 5500) and rural—except for DuPont's plant. The nylon plant is the biggest employer around; all other employers of over 10 persons in Seaford employ a total of 500 persons.[2] By C. B. McCoy's criterion, then, DuPont should be making every conceivable contribution to the welfare of Seaford residents.

DuPont is proud of what it has done for Seaford. In a company-sponsored television advertisement in the early 1950s, DuPont got the editor of the Seaford *Leader* to say:

> We know the DuPont plant has directly benefited many of us individually and made Seaford an important part of American industrial life. Frankly, our town has gained a lot by the coming of the nylon plant—economically, civically, and socially. In every way we are a bigger and better community.[3]

But DuPont's installations—even its golf course and country club—have always been outside the city limits. Map 3 shows how the city's irregular western border winds around the DuPont-owned land. Appropriately, one of the borders between town and plant is Nylon Boulevard.

DuPont has avoided incorporation into the town because of Seaford's growth pattern and the state's annexation statute. Instead of annexing undeveloped land adjacent to the town, Seaford has expanded by allowing fringe areas to develop and annexing them then. Annexation of built-up

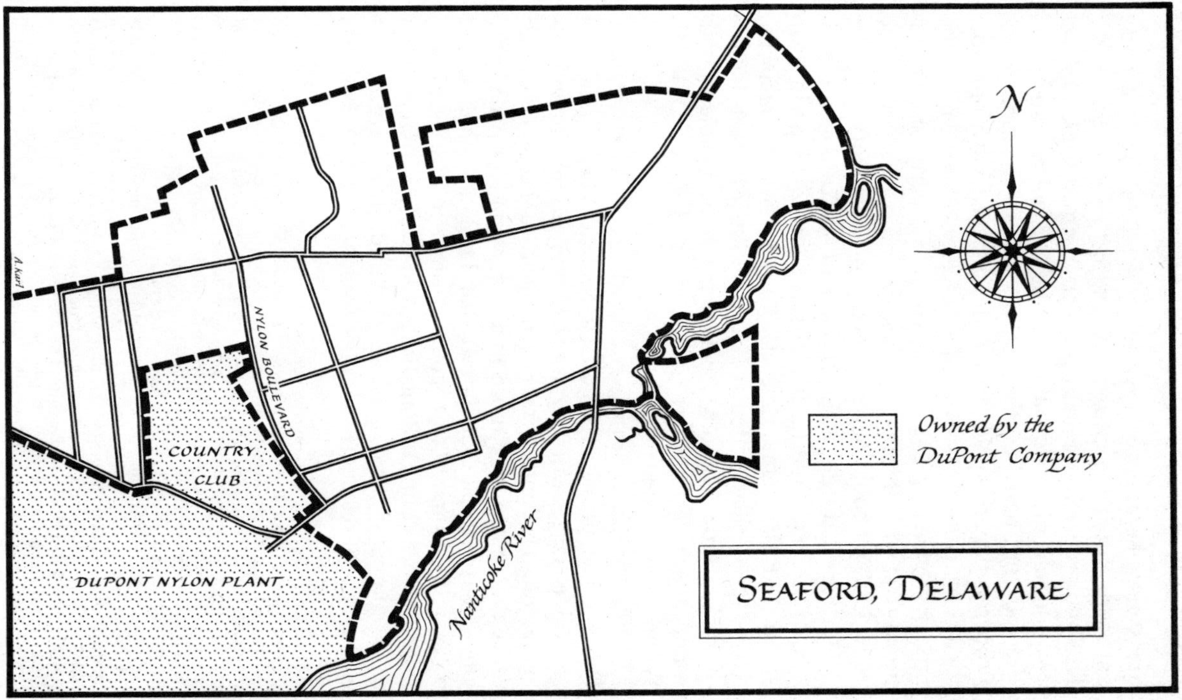
N
Owned by the DuPont Company
SEAFORD, DELAWARE
Nanticoke River
NYLON BOULEVARD
COUNTRY CLUB
DUPONT NYLON PLANT
A. Karl

areas must be approved by the residents of the area being annexed. But if the citizens of Seaford tried to annex the DuPont properties to increase their tax revenues, DuPont could easily block the attempt. In Delaware, annexation votes are not based on the principle of one man, one vote. Property owners in the area to be annexed have one vote for every $100 of asessed value of real estate, while non-property owners get only one vote,* a clearly unconstitutional system.[4] Because its investment in the area is so huge, DuPont could outvote the rest of the county.

Outside Seaford's jurisdiction, DuPont can ignore municipal problems and taxes and feel no need to act in town affairs. At the same time, DuPont is free to reap the advantages—clean water and air, and lots of cheap land—of the Seaford location.** Seaford is also accessible to both water and rail transportation, and is close to DuPont's Wilmington headquarters.†

While Seaford provided everything DuPont wanted, DuPont has provided little that Seaford needs. DuPont's payroll is large, but city officials and prominent citizens agree that DuPont's presence in Seaford keeps out other firms that might pay more and that would provide more jobs. These people had hoped that DuPont's plant would serve as an example to encourage other industries to consider Seaford, but DuPont has given Seaford a reputation as a company town and crippled industrial recruitment efforts. Local residents say other firms feel that DuPont has

* Title 22, Section 101, of the *Delaware Code* states that the question of annexation must be "submitted at a special election to the qualified voters and real estate owners of the territory proposed to be annexed and included in the limits of the city or incorporated town. . . . Each real estate owner shall be entitled to one vote for each $100 of real estate assessed to him on the assessment records of the county in which the territory is embraced. Each qualified voter not being the owner of real estate within the territory, shall be entitled to one vote."

** Miles of pipes and tanks are needed to combine the raw materials for nylon—coal, air, and water. The water is the vehicle used to carry a mixture of hexamethylene diamine and adipic acid through the continuous pipes to form polymers. Water is again necessary for cooling the molten polymers to form ribbons of nylon. The air is used to solidify melted nylon after it has been forced through tiny holes to form nylon threads.

† According to the *News-Journal,* the plant had to be somewhere near Delaware, "because the process was so new, the company wanted the plant near its headquarters in Wilmington so engineering expertise would be readily available." [5]

skimmed off the skilled labor throughout much of southern Delaware, so that they doubt they would find an adequate labor supply.

The DuPont nylon plant also created Seaford's only air pollution problem. The state government does not have enough stations in the area to monitor plant emissions, and the DuPont Company refuses to make public its own emissions data, but John C. Bryson, director of the state's Environmental Control Division, told the study group that a pollution "hot spot" may exist at the DuPont plant.* The Delaware Study Group observed a steady flow of thick white and brown smoke coming from the plant stacks on several occasions. On a calm night a visible smoke cloud hovers over the area. When the wind blows, residents in its path complain of coughing and great discomfort.

DuPont has never paid one cent in property tax to the town of Seaford. Its carefully chosen location just outside the town limits and its ability to control the annexation process have saved it millions of dollars in property taxes. The DuPont Company pays property taxes to Sussex County, whose tax rates are only half those of Seaford. DuPont's Seaford complex is assessed at about $7 million by Sussex County, far below full value. For example, in 1964 the town of Seaford included about 776 acres, almost the size of the DuPont plant, but 20–30% of that was woods, vacant land, or open space, and about 25% was used for schools, streets, and other unassessed public services.[6] Thus, Seaford had about half as many assessed acres as the DuPont plant, but the assessed valuation for the town was $13.76 million, nearly twice the assessment of the plant.

DuPont does pay school taxes, because the plant is located within the Seaford Special School District. But even with DuPont's contribution, Seaford has a difficult time financing education. The town had no kindergartens until they became mandatory by state law in 1968. Recently, Seaford's schools have slipped in comparison to

* Not until 1970 did DuPont install equipment at Seaford to reduce the diamine and finish oil released into the air. The company also switched from coal to oil in 1970 to eliminate a fly-ash problem.

others in the county. This slippage has occurred despite the fact that Seaford school district residents pay higher school taxes than do residents of any other Sussex County school district. Teachers' salaries in Seaford are now from $600 to $2500 below those in New Castle County school districts. Basic to the school district's financial problems is its low assessment base. Seaford school district has an assessment of $1013 per pupil, compared to $13,377 per pupil for the De La Warr district (the lowest in New Castle County), and $55,691 per pupil in Alexis I. du Pont School District (the highest in New Castle County). Even with the state providing 80% of the funds, Seaford schools spent only $630 per pupil (excluding transportation paid by the state and debt service), compared to a statewide average of $793 per pupil, and $915 per pupil in Alfred I. du Pont Special School District. For the Seaford school district to collect the money it needs to provide quality education, the assessment base must be increased—which means, since DuPont's nylon plant is the largest assessed facility in the district—that the plant should not continue to be so grossly underassessed.

In lieu of paying taxes to Seaford or contributing its fair share to the schools, DuPont from time to time makes tax-deductible donations to town government and public groups. The company has given a few acres for a park, $229,000 since 1950 to a local hospital, and small gifts to some social service projects. The DuPont Public Relations Department has been so successful in extolling DuPont's concern for Seaford that residents no longer even expect the company to pay taxes. When interviewed by the study group, Woodrow W. Crosby, city manager of Seaford, agreed that DuPont paid no property taxes to the town. He was then asked if he could think of any possible way in which DuPont could help Seaford more, but was unable to offer any suggestion.

DuPont's charitable donations have a substantial impact on public policy in Seaford. DuPont gives just enough to keep down public pressure for the company to pay local taxes, while reaping federal and state tax deductions. At the same time, the gifts are big enough so that some facilities, such as the private hospital, become dependent on the company's donation. Private funding implies power over the recipient as does public funding, but private funding, even of public projects, is not subject to the public's check. Furthermore, because the company alone decides how the gifts will be distributed, the interests of company personnel are the only criteria for giving. For example, the DuPont Company has contributed nothing to alleviate Seaford's critical shortage of decent housing.

While DuPont pays $70,000 in school taxes based on a gross underassessment of the nylon plant's value, it pays no property taxes to Seaford. But the presence of the huge plant has forced the town's expenditures up. Seaford's tax rate has been rising rapidly; between 1966 and 1970, it went up 50%, according to Woodrow Crosby, the city manager. From 1960 to 1968, the cost of running the street and sewer department more than tripled, police department expenditures doubled, and spending on general and administrative functions rose two and one-half times. According to City Manager Crosby, the demand for increased city outlays was created primarily by the influx of nylon plant employees who had tired of commuting many miles to work and moved their families into Seaford.

Yet these burdens are not borne by DuPont; they are spread among the residents of Seaford. If DuPont paid property taxes to Seaford, the town would have received $85,000 in tax revenue in 1970, even using Sussex County's underassessed value of the plant in the calculations. This missing tax revenue is extremely important because Seaford is a poor town in a precarious financial position. In 1960, 14.2% of the town's families earned less than $2000 per year and 45.6% made less than $6000 per year; the average annual income of families in East Seaford, a black neighborhood annexed to Seaford in 1968, was only about $4300.

The town has avoided debt only because it is one of the few Delaware municipalities with a special grant from Delmarva Power and Light to buy electricity wholesale and sell it to its citizens. This privilege could be used to offer residents cheaper power or, as Seaford has done, to supplement the town budget. In 1969 the town profit from sales of electricity was $156,000, while property tax revenues were only $122,000. Without the electricity profit, Seaford would be deeply in debt, and the pressure on DuPont to join the town and pay its share might become uncomfortably high for the company. Yet DuPont, when it purchases electricity does not buy from Seaford; instead the company has its own direct transmission line from Delmarva Power and Light.

Without property tax revenues from DuPont, Seaford cannot take effective action on certain key issues. Housing, probably Seaford's greatest need, is not met by the town council because of insufficient funds. Almost a third of Seaford's 1900 housing units are deteriorating or dilapidated. In predominantly black areas, the substandard figures are astronomical. East Seaford resembles a South American barrio or African shanty town. A housing survey conducted by Community Action of Seaford, found only 16 standard housing units in East Seaford. A majority of the houses in East Seaford lack both running water and sanitary sewer facilities. The overall population density is an incredibly high 36.5 persons per net residential acre.[7]

A nonprofit sponsor, Better Homes for Seaford, has recently developed plans to build 131 low-rent housing units in conjunction with the state department of housing. The number is far too low to meet the problem, and construction will only intensify racial segregation in the housing market: all the new housing is to be located in or next to racially impacted areas of East Seaford. In addition, according to the Seaford city manager, the city cannot meet its local share of public housing costs or provide sewers, roads, or water lines for new public housing. If the DuPont plant were part of Seaford and contributed to its tax base or if it were reassessed to increase county revenues, funds might be available. In the meantime, city and county residents must rely on federal housing programs and private resources. To build a large number of units and break the pattern of residential segregation in line with federal regulations,* a substantial commitment of private funds would have to be made to build housing outside the town in a non-racially impacted area. DuPont could help provide these funds but has chosen not to.

Nor has DuPont exerted itself in the struggle against poverty and discrimination in Seaford. When DuPont opened its nylon plant, it hired very few blacks, though 10–20% of the local population was black. Its job ladder was segregated; those hired were menial laborers. The country club DuPont built for its employees was closed to blacks. The company did not desegregate its Seaford facilities until 1962. For years, the company helped find homes for the many employees it transferred in and out of Seaford; in this role DuPont participated in the blatant racial and economic discrimination practiced in the local housing market. When a controversy over open housing arose in the early 1960s, the DuPont Company reacted by withdrawing entirely from the real estate area, leaving its transferees to find and sell houses on their own. DuPont's withdrawal helped perpetuate the discriminatory realty market. Later events made clear that the company could have been a major force in promoting open housing in the town. After several black DuPont technicians refused to come to Seaford because decent housing was unavailable, DuPont called all local realtors together and told them it would not permit discriminatory real estate transactions involving its transferees. The meeting had a substantial effect on local real estate practices—in 1968, two decades after the Supreme Court had outlawed racially discriminatory covenants in real estate deeds.[8]

DuPont's acquiescence in racial discrimination and Seaford's discriminatory at-large voting procedures are mutually reinforcing. Archaic election procedures are still used to deny blacks effective representation in the town government. While the black population of Seaford, overwhelmingly concentrated in one neighborhood, has now reached about 20%, the town council is elected on an

* Federal housing regulations require a balanced public housing program between racially impacted and nonimpacted areas. If public housing is built exclusively in a racially impacted area, such as East Seaford, federal funds cannot be used unless public housing units are also built outside the impacted area.

at-large basis, thus dissipating the blacks' political power. After the first black candidate ran for the council and lost, the new mayor extended the inequities of the at-large system; he eliminated the practice of assigning each councilman, after election, to represent a certain neighborhood of the city, claiming that it promoted parochialism. The community assignment system was a mechanism, granted a crude one, for representing the interests of individual communities in the town government.

In short, while DuPont uses human resources from Seaford and contributes to many of the city's financial problems, it has buttressed numerous social ills in the city. Rather than making a long-term commitment of resources to the community by seeking annexation to the town and paying property taxes, the company has made sporadic contributions to some community groups. DuPont has not contributed to Seaford according to the proportion of the work force it employs.

## *The Chemical Capital of the World*

Until the 1960s, DuPont ignored Wilmington as it ignored Seaford. DuPont's refusal to exercise its enormous potential for good had a great impact on all aspects of the metropolitan community. Other large companies followed DuPont's lead in neglecting the city's social problems; DuPont foundations ignored city needs; and city government refused to commit substantial public resources for fear of driving away one of its largest tax sources, the DuPont Company.

From time to time, local citizens urged DuPont to become more active in local affairs. In the early 1950s the Wilmington Housing Authority unsuccessfully sought to win DuPont support for the authority's renewal activities. Similarly, the local chapter of the American Institute of Architects made several public calls for planning in the metropolitan area. But the corporate establishment never heard their pleas.

What power DuPont family members used regarding the community was mainly exercised through paternalistic donations that helped retard the development of an effective local government.

The city was run by a part-time mayor operating under

the constraints of an archaic city charter. With such a weak city government, DuPont did not have to worry about city officials undertaking large projects harmful to its interests. If any project was desired, a DuPont handout was required to avoid the cumbersome procedures of the city government. To remain an alter ego for local government, the DuPonts were willing to give thousands of dollars. These contributions were mainly concentrated in projects of particular interest to company or family, like schools, which would not threaten the operations of the DuPont Company or the elegant life style of the DuPont family. But DuPont charity never reached such community needs as antipollution laws, job opportunities for low-skilled residents, or low-income housing in Wilmington.

Through this behind-the-scenes power, members of the corporate elite molded Wilmington to their needs. Wilmington had banks, clubs, a hotel, brokerage houses, newspapers, a playhouse, and a symphony—all DuPont creations. For corporate managers, Wilmington provided an atmosphere conducive to effective teamwork and strong identification with company goals.* As DuPont public relations material makes clear, one of the keys to the company's longevity has been the *esprit de corps* developed because employees live together in a relatively homogenous community.[9]

But years of neglect left Wilmington almost a caricature of the urban crisis. The chemical capital of the world was a rapidly decaying town of 80,000; dilapidated housing spread only blocks from company skyscrapers. Private and suburban public schools were excellent, city schools abysmal. Whites left the city so fast that the city's population plummeted from over 110,000 to 80,000 in 1970. Like many center cities, Wilmington suffered financial difficulty because suburban regions did not pay taxes for services provided downtown, though for years Wilmington residents have paid property taxes to the county as well as to the city. As in many center cities, commercial and entertainment

* President McCoy estimates that DuPont employees in Wilmington, relieved of the pressures of long commuting, work about eight hours more per week than would be possible in New York City. The cost of living is also much lower in New Castle County than in the New York metropolitan area, so DuPont salaries are worth more in terms of purchasing power in Wilmington.

activities have decreased; downtown Wilmington is a ghost town after 6:00 PM.

However, in the 1960s, while remaining aloof in the face of poverty in Seaford, the DuPont Company responded to the urban crisis in Wilmington. The reason for the difference in company policies is simple. DuPont's Seaford facilities are not within town limits, but in Wilmington the company owns 139 acres and seven full blocks downtown—worth at least $200 million. To protect its large investment, the DuPont establishment moved from refusal to use power to very active formulation of public policy. In 1960 the corporate elite formed the Greater Wilmington Development Council (GWDC) which has played a role in the formulation of practically every major community development project in the past decade. Soon afterwards, DuPont assigned some of its employees to the task of examining the company's role and image in Wilmington. Later, it undertook a full-scale study of community relations at all its United States facilities. While refusing to make the results of these studies public, the company has used them as a basis for active involvement in the greater Wilmington area. Employees elected to public office were given 20% time off with pay. The company formed a community affairs committee to coordinate all its social action programs and funded GWDC and other local organizations. In addition, top DuPont executives began to appear in high positions in local policy-making groups.

In 1968, brimming with confidence in Wilmington's future, DuPont preened itself in a widely distributed brochure called "Wilmington." DuPont officials argued that the city did not fit the negative stereotype of "the teeming East Coast." The brochure claimed that Wilmington offered a wide choice of housing, good schools, and cultural resources, that the city was enjoying the benefits of a major slum clearance program, an improving school system, and a superhighway which was relieving traffic congestion. In short, Wilmington was a "city moving ahead."

That same year Wilmington's black ghetto erupted in a small civil riot. Many blacks did not share DuPont's view of the improving condition of the city. In interviews with the study group, black activists expressed the feeling that

DuPont was at the heart of many of Wilmington's most serious problems and that GWDC was a fraud that had usurped their legitimate right to a democratically run local government.

Governor Charles L. Terry reacted to the riot aggressively. He sent in the National Guard and kept it there—from April, 1968, to January, 1969—despite the fact that there was no recurrence of violence. The presence of the guard became progressively more unbearable to Wilmington's black residents; many were afraid to venture out of their homes after dark while jeeps carrying soldiers armed with machine guns roamed the streets. For months DuPont did nothing about the presence of troops. Most DuPont employees scarcely knew the soldiers were there. DuPont employees would leave downtown about five o'clock and the National Guard would emerge from its encampment about six. One corporate executive related to the study group a story of a scuffle in a suburban churchyard between members of an all-white youth group. Someone called the police who were on duty with some National Guardsmen. When the guard arrived armed with machine guns, the suburban parents were shocked and offended to find military forces in *their* neighborhood.

For several months, the DuPont Company approved the military occupation of Wilmington by its silence. Only after the occupation was publicized by Project Communications Network (a church group from outside Delaware) and then by the national media did the DuPonts move to protect the image of the world's chemical capital. By that time, however, Governor Terry could not be budged; he had already planned to run his upcoming gubernatorial campaign by playing on racist fears. With Terry out of their control, the DuPonts supported candidates who were members of the corporate elite—Russell W. Peterson as governor and Harry G. Haskell as mayor. Neither chanced advocating the removal of the guard in his campaign, but after his inauguration Peterson took the guard out.

### CITY EXECUTIVES

For many years, Wilmington was run by a part-time mayor on a shoestring budget. In 1960 John Babiarz, a Democrat of Polish extraction, born and bred in Wilmington, was elected mayor. Through his efforts, Wilmington's outmoded charter was revised and a strong mayoral system created. Babiarz became Wilmington's first full-time mayor in 1966. The new charter did not allow fiscal independence for the city; Wilmington still must seek enabling legislation from the state government to raise funds. A former city official says the Wilmington delegation had to drop a provision for municipal financial independence so that the state government would accept the new charter.

Without financial independence Babiarz was forced to rely on the resources of the corporate establishment. According to a former high city official, DuPont executives and other industrialists were at first wary of Babiarz, who they thought had connections with gamblers. Once the corporate establishment found him honest and hard-working, they worked closely with him on several major city projects, such as the huge downtown shopping mall.

Another example of this cooperation is the planning of the civic center. A 1954 report on urban blight by the Wilmington Planning Commission had led to the Poplar Street renewal project. The city tore down a huge black and poor-white residential area directly east of the city's downtown. Due to the weakness of the old city government and the apathy of the corporate establishment, the land remained vacant for several years. But when DuPont officials saw urban blight as a threat to their downtown investment, they started working with Babiarz to build the civic center on the land. From the viewpoint of the corporate establishment, the civic center offered many benefits. It would be attractive, with its government and private office buildings surrounding a park; DuPont wanted a nice shiny city for its employees and business visitors. The civic center was also consonant with DuPont's concept of a corporate headquarters—a white collar work place. To insure that the design of the civic center would meet with the approval of the corporate establishment, Babiarz let GWDC develop the blueprints, which were then rubber-stamped by the Wilmington Housing Authority.

The close cooperation between the Democratic mayor with an ethnic electoral base and the Republican-dominated corporate establishment may seem odd; but both stood to gain. The mayor wanted a financially viable city, and he liked the idea of large, visible projects which would stand as monuments to his accomplishments. He also wished to avoid corporate dissatisfaction with his policies, which might lead to the locating of new buildings outside city limits. Meanwhile, the corporate establishment, working through Babiarz and the GWDC rather than actually holding public office, could set public policy without being burdened with the day-to-day operations of the city. At the same time, the executives could make public decisions in the privacy of their own clubs.

Not everyone gained, however. In the civic center project, losers included those persons forced from their homes, which were not replaced elsewhere. City taxpayers lost, since a government office building does not pay property tax. The taxpayers would also have to foot the bill for a substantial amount of the costs of the shopping mall, though those to be served by it were suburbanites. In the long run, Wilmington's leadership led only in one direction—and that was not in the direction of people who needed public services.

The Babiarz-elite alliance was not total, however, since each was ultimately accountable to a different constituency. Babiarz emphasized that he was a "man of the people"; the corporate organizations for urban renewal have always been basically elitist. As one former GWDC official said, "GWDC is an organization for the top community leadership, a place for these top guys to cross ideas with each other on city policy." An ex-city official explained the difference this way: "We always viewed the city in human terms; the businessmen were mainly interested in the city in terms of dollars."

The corporate establishment sought even better ties to the mayoralty, and supported Harry Haskell, who defeated Babiarz in the 1968 elections. Haskell, a multimillionaire through his inheritance from his father (once a member of DuPont's executive and finance committees), used his wealth lavishly in his campaign against Babiarz. While Babiarz spent around $20,000, estimates of Haskell's campagin expenditures range from $150,000 to $500,000, an astronomical sum for a city of less than 80,000 people. If Haskell actually spent in the middle range of the estimates, say $300,000, it would be the equivalent of running a United States presidential campaign for $800 million.

Compared to Babiarz, a true native son who really wanted to be mayor, Harry Haskell seems to have backed into the post. The consensus is that he ran to strengthen the ticket for his friend, Russell Peterson, then head of DuPont's Development Department, who was campaigning for governor.

Haskell took advantage of the strong mayoralty system introduced by Babiarz and his own wealth and political ties to build an even stronger power base within Wilmington. Haskell has used his wealth both to exert political influence and to finance activities the city cannot afford. Haskell's favors to Ray Evans, a black GOP politico from northeast Wilmington, provide a good example. Evans once worked at a Wilmington liquor store; with help from Haskell, he purchased the store, according to several sources close to city politics. Haskell himself told the Delaware Study Group that he had guaranteed the mortgage on Evans's house in suburban Brandywine Hundred, worth $30,000 to $40,000. Evans is now a special assistant to the mayor, on Haskell's private payroll. In return for his largesse, Haskell demands certain favors of those he helps. For instance, a young black man working in a local community agency wanted to do graduate work at a nearby university. According to this man, Haskell offered him a scholarship. Haskell later asked the prospective student to participate in Operation Outreach—a favorite Haskell program for sending blacks and policemen on a camping trip together in the middle of the winter. The student refused to go because he thought it was absurd. Later when he called to find out about his scholarship, he was told that the mayor was no longer financing his education.

The mayor's Action Task Force is a good example of Haskell's use of private funds to help run the city. This organization is the equivalent of the mayor's personal welfare fund. As far as can be ascertained, all the fund's money comes from Haskell personally or from DuPont-related contributors. When problems like a fire or a default on a mortgage arise in a section of the city, the Action Task Force comes to the rescue. The gratitude of the recipients contributes to Haskell's power. Undisclosed *quid pro quos* may be exacted, also. The mayor's official programs, taken by themselves, are admittedly worthwhile; but in a larger context they undermine democratic control of city government.

Haskell also tapped corporate treasure chests for contributions to the types of projects which GWDC had been funding. In fact, the funds of the corporate establishment were redirected from GWDC toward the new corporate mayor; DuPont's contribution to GWDC dropped from $237,000 in 1966–67 to $57,000 in the equivalent 1969–70 period. Haskell won political accolades by obtaining private financing from Lammot du Pont Copeland and others for the conversion of an old theater into the Martin Luther King Center, a meeting place for blacks. When the mayor wanted playgrounds, he prevailed upon his friend, Irenee du Pont, Jr., for a large contribution. And, as recounted in Chapter 8, Haskell and his friends coughed up tens of thousands of dollars to encourage three black churches to move out of the way of the shopping mall.

Haskell's political ties, personal wealth, and access to the corporate till make him far more powerful than Babiarz ever was. By cashing some of his political chips, Haskell got the state legislature to approve a 1% wage tax on the salaries of those who work in Wilmington. It is, not surprisingly, a tax that falls heavily on the shoulders of the working man rather than the rich. Unlike the graduated federal income tax, the Wilmington wage tax rate is the same for all income levels over $6000 per year, and it does not apply to income from dividends or municipal bonds, which are held mainly by the very rich. In short, a secretary for the DuPont Company earning $7000 per year may pay more wage tax than a DuPont family member whose income derives mainly from securities. Also, since the wage tax applies only to those who work in the city, it encourages firms to flee to the suburbs. After hearing much protest against the regressive wage tax, Haskell is now backing a surtax on income, proposed originally by the Democrats in 1968, which would be both progressive and countywide.

CITY COUNCIL

The city council consists of 13 councilmen, 10 Democrats and 3 Republicans. Two of the councilmen work for DuPont—William McLaughlin, a group leader in DuPont's business machines section, and Francis Jornlin, a DuPont executive and a member of the elite Greenville Country Club.

Even without much direct representation on the council, DuPont can easily get the favors it needs. Until late 1970, when one full-time and one part-time economist were appointed, the councilmen, working only in their spare time, had no research staff. Thus, when business spokesmen came before the council with extensive facts and figures prepared by experts, they easily influenced council voting. Some councilmen also harbor an attitude of deference to the company—a feeling that the DuPonts have done so much for Wilmington that anything the city can do in return is small repayment. Closely related to this deference are fears that the DuPont Company would leave Wilmington if it were not treated properly; councilmen constantly worry about the location of DuPont's next office building. Furthermore, some councilmen never consider acting against the corporate establishment for fear of losing their jobs or facing other personal reprisals.

The 1969 controversy over the closing of Tatnall Street illustrates the dynamics of the relationship between DuPont and the city council. In question was a strip of Tatnall Street between two of DuPont's major office buildings. DuPont wanted to seal off the street—first to build the Brandywine Building and then to make a pedestrian mall between it and the Nemours Building. Closing Tatnall Street would block off a major southbound street downtown, thus raising serious questions about the city's traffic patterns. The city undertook a small traffic study on the effects of closing Tatnall Street. DuPont outdid it—it hired a former city traffic engineer as a consultant to help design a new traffic pattern. Eventually, the present city traffic supervisor, Walter Neidig, was persuaded that Twelfth Street would be widened so that traffic flow in the area would not be hampered. But the Twelfth Street widening was itself the subject of controversy over dislocation of residents and had not been finally decided. Moreover, as one local citizen, Fred Jacobs, wrote in a letter to the *News-Journal,* the closing of Tatnall Street would "stunt the normal growth of the small business section by making it inconvenient to reach." [10] Jacobs tried to get an attorney to fight DuPont's plan, but none of the four he contacted were willing to take on the case against DuPont.

Instead of selling Tatnall Street to DuPont outright, city officials put it up for open bid, with the requirement that the buyer use it as a pedestrian mall. It was obvious that DuPont would be the only bidder. Councilman Tom Maloney requested an appraisal of the property, and the city council chose the real estate firm of B. Gary Scott, which did appraisals as a sideline. Scott, who worked for DuPont's real estate department from 1957 to 1961, gets many referrals from DuPont and has carried out a few projects for the company in recent years. When Scott turned in an appraisal value of only 6 cents for the land, some people felt it was tainted by a conflict of interest. Scott explained that he meant the land was really worth nothing and the city should take the highest bid—the DuPont bid, of course.

Maloney demanded a second appraisal, as he says is the custom. A bare majority agreed. This time, a full-time appraiser, Walter Barczewski, did the job. In September, 1969, while Barczewski was making his appraisal, DuPont bid $5000. Then Barczewski's appraisal came in at $60,000—$19,000 for ground rights and $41,000 for air rights. In arriving at this figure, Barczewski used the average value of downtown Wilmington land. Barczewski valued only 72% of the air rights because the bid stipulated a pedestrian mall, and he felt DuPont could not build a connector (as it had done between the Nemours and DuPont buildings and between the DuPont and Wilmington Trust buildings) below the fourth floor.

Meanwhile, Maloney and Victor Battaglia, the city

solicitor, went to see the head of DuPont's real estate department. Soon after this meeting, Battaglia switched sides; Maloney claims (and Battaglia denies) that DuPont had put pressure on the city solicitor. In any case. Battaglia told the city council that the second appraiser, Barczewski, had changed his appraisal method and now felt the ground and air rights were worth only $19,000. The city solicitor had a letter from Barczewski that seemed to confirm this change. However, by telephoning Barczewski, Maloney learned that the city solicitor had simply asked the appraiser for a letter stating the value of the ground rights. Barczewski said he followed Battaglia's instructions, including only the ground appraisal; he added that he had not changed his appraisal method.

On December 12, 1969, the council voted eight to four, with one abstention, to sell the land for $19,000. Both councilmen employed by DuPont voted for the measure. If these two men had abstained, the sale to DuPont would not have been approved because the measure needed seven votes to pass. According to Jornlin, the DuPont executive on the city council, the Tatnall Street vote involved no conflict of interesest for him, because he was not involved in the part of DuPont Company which was pushing for the purchase of the street. McLaughlin, the other DuPont employee, said that he was told by Battaglia that he could vote.

DuPont's victory was typical. In part, DuPont won because the council was deferential to it. Several councilmen resented Maloney's challenge to DuPont's offer. They felt the company could be counted on to name a fair price and that DuPont did so much for the city that a challenge was ungracious. Councilmen were aware that DuPont considered the closing of Tatnall Street necessary for the Brandywine Building; several felt that DuPont might not build more offices in Wilmington unless they were given Tatnall Street.

This particular form of corporate blackmail—the implicit * threat to pull out of the city—reared its head once again in September, 1971, when the DuPont Company

* See Chapter 2 for an explicit threat by DuPont to pull out of Chambers Works because of New Jersey's stringent antipollution laws.

obtained council approval to build a tunnel under a city street. Without the knowledge of the city council, DuPont drafted a contract and resolution authorizing the company to tear up a portion of Eleventh Street to build a tunnel connecting the new Brandywine Building to another DuPont facility. The contract did not require DuPont to pay the city for the land or the ground rights to build under city property; it had no lease arrangement and provided no compensation to the city for disruption during construction. It provided only that DuPont pay to build the tunnel and repair sidewalks and streets afterwards.

When the resolution suddenly appeared on the September 16 council agenda, several councilmen objected. To their objections, the sponsor of the resolution, Councilman Harry Thomas, said only that DuPont wanted it passed; he knew nothing about it. Nor did assistant city solicitor Joseph Lichtenbaum know much about the resolution, despite having signed it. He told a *News-Journal* reporter that DuPont had drafted the resolution and he didn't know if anyone had read it.*

Thomas reintroduced the resolution the following week, with no changes. It passed nine to three, with councilman Jornlin, a DuPont executive, voting in favor. No conflict-of-interest cry was raised, however, despite a ruling by the city solicitor's office a month before that Councilman James Sills, employed by the Urban Affairs Division of the University of Delaware, could not vote on anything concerning his employer. The same reasoning did not apply to DuPont employees.

While supporting DuPont's move, the *News-Journal* unwittingly defined the nature of DuPont's corporate blackmail:

> But what the councilmen are forgetting in their initial cool, almost hostile, response to the proposed tunnel . . . is that the city desperately needs tenants like the DuPont Co. for its tax base.

* Lichtenbaum later changed his story and said that he and several others in his office had reviewed the resolution carefully before approving and signing it. This story appeared in the *Morning News* of September 18, 1971, after the reporter had got conflicting stories from lawyers in the city solicitor's office and from Mayor Haskell's press secretary.

> Surely, if DuPont . . . and others are willing to invest their money in city real estate and to counter the trend of building out in the suburbs, then the city leaders (and that includes all councilmen) should attempt to accommodate these ventures.[11]

### *The I-95 Superhighway*

On June 28, 1957, a lame-duck city council, scheduled to go out of office on July 1, voted 7–6 (all 7 yeas were Republican) to put the I-95 highway right through the center of Wilmington. On August 2, 1957, the new Democratic-dominated council rescinded the decision 11–2. But the state supreme court held that the new council could not change the decision made by the lame-duck council.

The decision on I-95 had a profound effect on the future of Wilmington. It benefited downtown corporations and forestalled the development of industry in Wilmington, while causing the demolition of nearly 1000 housing units in a solid working-class neighborhood. According to public officials, three routes were feasible—a route approximating that of the Bancroft Parkway (rejected because it passed close to a fairly wealthy neighborhood), the route presently proposed for I-495, and the route chosen. Route 495 skirted the city on the east—so it was close—and would not require demolishing a significant number of homes; it would also have aided the development of Wilmington's port. The route through the center of town, says Ernest Davidson, chief engineer of the highway department, was chosen to serve downtown office buildings.

The key person involved in the choice was Hugh R. Sharp, Jr., a DuPont family member on the state highway commission at the time. According to Davidson, Sharp, a former commission chairman, regrouped the forces behind the downtown route after it was initially defeated. Another important factor was a local group of advocates for the I-95 route. This group, led by Leon N. Weiner, a local developer, included some members of the corporate establishment. One member of the group said that a lower-level DuPont employee gave so large a donation to the group that he knew the money came from higher up in the DuPont hierarchy.

Although demolition of the residential area in the I-95 right-of-way began around 1961, the highway was not built immediately. There was considerable politicking about the highway appropriations. Since the appropriation had not been granted, the commission could still have reversed the decision and permitted construction of new housing as well as community facilities on the land. To forestall such a reversal, GWDC and the *News-Journal* began a push for "Freeway Now." One of the leaders of this campaign was Russell Peterson. John Burchenal, a DuPont public relations executive, led the state legislators on a tour of the area to dramatize the need for immediate construction. At the same time, the *News-Journal* inundated the public with editorials. The combined effort of GWDC and the *News-Journal* assured the defeat of any attempt to change the location of the highway. The appropriation was passed, and construction began late in 1964.

### I-95, MASS TRANSIT, AND PARKING

While the short-run effects of constructing I-95 were severe for citizens who lost their homes, the long-run effects may be even worse. The construction of I-95 forestalled any large-scale commitment to mass transit in the Wilmington area. Since commuters can get to work quickly on I-95, they have no reason to support mass transit. On the other hand, auto commuting imposes heavy costs on the city. In trying to accommodate heavy rush-hour traffic the city is constructing a spacious street system that will be little used at other times—and will never be adequate in rush hours. A vicious circle develops: as the streets improve, more commuters drive to work, which in turn leads to calls for more street improvements. At each round, pollution costs, borne mainly by Wilmington residents, will get higher.

I-95 created a similar circle of spiraling parking problems. Numerous parking lots were built after completion of the highway—which brought more cars into the city and renewed demands for more parking. To meet increasing parking needs, the city has had to build garages. Two new garages recommended to meet existing needs will cost about $9 million; two more proposed for the downtown renewal area will cost another $29 million.[12] The funds are raised by bond issues which limit the city's ability to undertake other projects. In fact, leading bond-rating agencies told Wilmington city officials that the city's bond rating may fall because of such huge bond issues for parking garages.* An alternative to huge publicly built parking garages would be a requirement that each new building contain its own parking spaces. Federal projects usually pursue this alternative, but Wilmington has not done so.

Several groups clearly gain from the parking authority's strategy: corporations, who do not have to build their own parking facilities; suburbanites, who use the parking (84% of the cars parked in downtown Wilmington got there from the county or further away;[13] 40% of the households in Wilmington do not even own a car); the local DuPont-connected brokerage houses, who earn commissions for selling the bonds; and the very wealthy individuals who reap large benefits from the tax-exempt municipal bonds.

On the other hand, the system of commuter traffic and large parking garages imposes a fantastic burden on the city. According to Wilmington's former city planner, Peter A. Larsen, almost 60% of all city land is used for transportation, a percentage comparable to that of sprawling Los Angeles. Much of that 60% yields no revenue, and the revenue from parking lots is extremely low. The facilities of the parking authority yield no property taxes, no business license tax, no license fees, no wage taxes. Since property taxes are paid on the value of development, privately owned parking lots pay very low taxes even though they occupy prime locations. Moreover, in 1970 Pierre S. du Pont IV maneuvered a bill through the state legislature that would enable the city to grant an exemption from property taxes to private companies that build multilevel garages. DuPont introduced the bill at the request of Richard Hatfield, president of Colonial Parking, in Wilmington. Hatfield explained that he was planning to build a large garage, and the bill

* When a city issues bonds, bonding houses submit bids, naming the interest rate the city would have to pay should their bid win. The city sells the bonds through the bonding house with the lowest bid. The lower a city's bond rating, the higher interest rates it will have to pay and vice versa. A lower bond rating reflects a greater risk that the bonds will not be paid.

was needed for his company to compete with the tax-exempt parking authority. The new law lowers the city's tax base, increases the pressure for wider streets, more highways, and parking lots, and decreases concern for mass transit and urban pollution.

### I-95 AND INDUSTRIAL DEVELOPMENT

By placing I-95 in the center of town instead of along Route 495, the lame-duck Republican city council prevented later administrations from developing the port of Wilmington and Cherry Island. The proposed I-495 runs right by the port and would provide good transportation links to all of Delaware and Maryland, and parts of Pennsylvania and New Jersey. I-95 makes no real connection with the port area. Up to the time of the construction of I-95, the port had been growing rapidly, reaching a replacement value of about $20–30 million. It was providing more and more jobs for low-skilled city residents. As I-95 was being built, the port became a city agency. Burdened by the job of providing parking for the rapidly growing commuter traffic, the city had little time for the port. The development budget for the port was greatly reduced, and staff for the port were not hired in sufficient numbers. The city missed a chance to buy all the land between the port and the Delaware Memorial Bridge, which would have provided the base for serious port development. Although studies were made from time to time, no one took the port question seriously. As the city's port consultant said: "The growth and development of port operations have been remarkable considering the lack of financial and industrial development support and must be recognized as a tribute to the dedicated efforts of the board and its management." [14]

Wilmington's port has great potential. It has always been able to attract a large volume of imports. More warehouse and berth space is needed; ships are now being turned away. Within the last few years, market conditions have produced a great demand for freezer facilities for incoming cargoes; Wilmington could provide them. The mayor's fiscal committee study on ports noted that smaller ports such as Wilmington's are competitive with larger ports, and that the dominant port in the area, Philadelphia, seems to be losing its share of the region's shipments.

Yet so far the city has made almost no effort to build up the port. The newspapers have traditionally rationalized inaction, saying the port is a losing venture, and Mayor Haskell has begun to echo them. But the port is no more a losing venture than the parking authority, which the newspapers never mention in that vein. Both show an operating profit but appear to cost the city money because of debt servicing.* However, according to A. Kirk Mearns, former director of commerce for Wilmington, the port makes a slight profit even after debt servicing. While city officials say that the bonds for port development would be excessive, port development would cost about as much as the $38 million in bonds proposed for the next four parking garages.

While neither the port nor the parking authority pays property taxes, port buildings constructed by private developers will be given to the city after their leases run out. They could be used by the city for a multitude of purposes —public-supported light industry for unemployed, underemployed, or handicapped residents. Or the buildings could be sold to labor-intensive, nonpolluting companies, like assembly plants for consumer goods. Furthermore, industries at the port would pay higher wages than the federal minimum wage paid by retail stores that would locate in the proposed downtown shopping center.

The crucial difference between the parking authority and the port is that corporate employees need parking space, but none of the city's leading corporations make much use of the port. DuPont imports a few raw materials through the port; Atlas sends out small shipments of sorbital. Since the corporate managers have no great stake in the port, they are not interested in its development for the city's benefit. For example, when the study group pointed out to Charles B. McCoy, president of DuPont, that the port could increase job opportunities and city revenues as much as downtown development, he replied: "I don't remember any direct comparison between the port problem and Down-

* Operating profits are used to pay interest on bonds of both authorities.

town Wilmington." Then he was asked how the company set priorities for its involvement in community projects. McCoy replied incredulously: "Do you take it for granted that people sit around trying to dream up a series of choices because you have some facilities you can put in that area [the port]?"

For the port to grow, there must be some industrial development on Cherry Island, a 1500-acre plot of vacant land adjacent to it. In 1962 a committee ruled out making Wilmington a free port * unless the city had more cargo trade from local manufacturing. When Edward Logue, then head of the Boston Redevelopment Authority, came to Wilmington, he said that Cherry Island presented a fantastic opportunity for industrial development. One of GWDC's own reports says Cherry Island "represents one of the largest tracts of underdeveloped land adjacent to an existing city center on the Northeastern corridor," and recommends possible industrial, recreational, and commercial uses for the land.

Recognizing Cherry Island's potential, GWDC set up a New Firm Recruitment Committee, which included some of the most powerful figures in Delaware industry. In 1968 it was headed by Joseph Chinn, president of Wilmington Trust Company, and included the head of Atlas, the president of the Bank of Delaware, plus the president and the chief economist of DuPont. According to a former GWDC staff member, the committee hired a consultant who concluded that the key deterrent to attracting new business was Wilmington's image as a DuPont company town. The consultant recommended that local executives break down this image in meetings with businessmen in other cities. This recommendation was ignored. The consultant also prepared a promotional brochure, "Greater Wilmington, Delaware, Today," which touted the city's advantages as a business location. But there is no evidence that the GWDC committee brought any new industries to Wilmington. A former GWDC staff member explained this lack of success:

* A free port is a place at which foreign and local goods can be combined in a manufacturing process without the levy of an import tax on the goods in process.

> We got tied up in the basic Wilmington problem—how exclusive we should be. While most cities are hungry for industry, Wilmington has a high level of white collar workers. So the new firm recruitment committee was really a way to discriminate among firms that might want to come in.

The corporate elite has no desire to recruit manufacturing, whose largely blue-collar work force might disturb the white-collar atmosphere DuPont wants. Instead, the elite is trying to encourage new firms to make Wilmington their headquarters home.

Corporate executives argue that the real reason the city has not developed industry on Cherry Island is that the island does not have adequate access to transportation—which brings the Wilmington dilemma full circle. The DuPont family and company were instrumental in putting I-95 through the center of the city to serve corporate offices; they opposed the alternative route that would have encouraged industrial development of Cherry Island. Since Cherry Island has not developed, the port cannot be expanded. By reinforcing Wilmington's image as a white-collar company town, the corporate elite has created a self-fulfilling prophecy.

### THE END PRODUCT: A HOUSING CRISIS

If the construction of I-95 is lumped with the plans for the civic center and the shopping mall, the grand result is a monumental housing crisis for low- and moderate-income families. According to the report done for GWDC by Charles Reeder, DuPont's chief economist, I-95 wiped out an estimated 1100 units. The Poplar Street project and downtown renewal schemes demolished another 1000 units. The GWDC report also estimates that about 2000 more units dropped out of the housing market for other reasons between 1960 and 1967. Local housing experts readily admit that most of the over 4000 units destroyed had sheltered low-income families. Yet up to 1967 the Wilmington Housing Authority built less than 2000 subsidized units in the city.

It can be inferred from the statistics in the Reeder report that the vacancy rate for *standard* housing in Wilmington is negative—between minus three and minus four percent (see Chapter 8). While there is some disagreement on the statistical methods used by the Reeder report, the negative vacancy rate is supported by practical indicators of a housing crisis. A study group interview with the relocation office of the Wilmington Housing Authority revealed that it is almost impossible to find a relocation unit in Wilmington for a displaced low-income family. Talks with officials in the city's public housing program revealed that there are at least 2000 families on the waiting list.

Future housing prospects look even worse for families of low or moderate income. According to the Wise-Gladstone report, another GWDC study, about 1400 units will be displaced in the 1970–75 period. The report estimated that in this five-year period, a minimum of 3400 units *over and above the 1100 public housing units then planned* must be built for families who could not afford homes on the open market.[15]

But for several years the city has been forced to cut back even the construction of planned units. According to federal housing regulations, a city must build public housing units outside of racially impacted areas to maintain a balanced program. In the Wilmington area, the only undeveloped land available for a substantial number of low-income units in a nonimpacted area is in the county.

But so far the county has not been willing to accept any of seven proposed sites for public housing within its boundaries. The opposition to public housing has been most vocal in the white areas of the county. To meet the Wise-Gladstone minimum of 3400 units over and above the planned public housing projects, at least 1700 units of public housing will have to be built in white areas of the county before 1975. Nothing indicates that it can be done. Presently, the Wilmington Housing Authority cannot buy 24 units from the Greater Wilmington Housing Corporation because it could not find 24 units to trade off in the county. Recently, the Wilmington Housing Authority lost reservations for 400 units of public housing because "the authority has been unable to get New Castle County's approval on sites in the county outside Wilmington." [16]

The contrasting attitudes of the corporate establishment to highways and housing illuminate the problems created

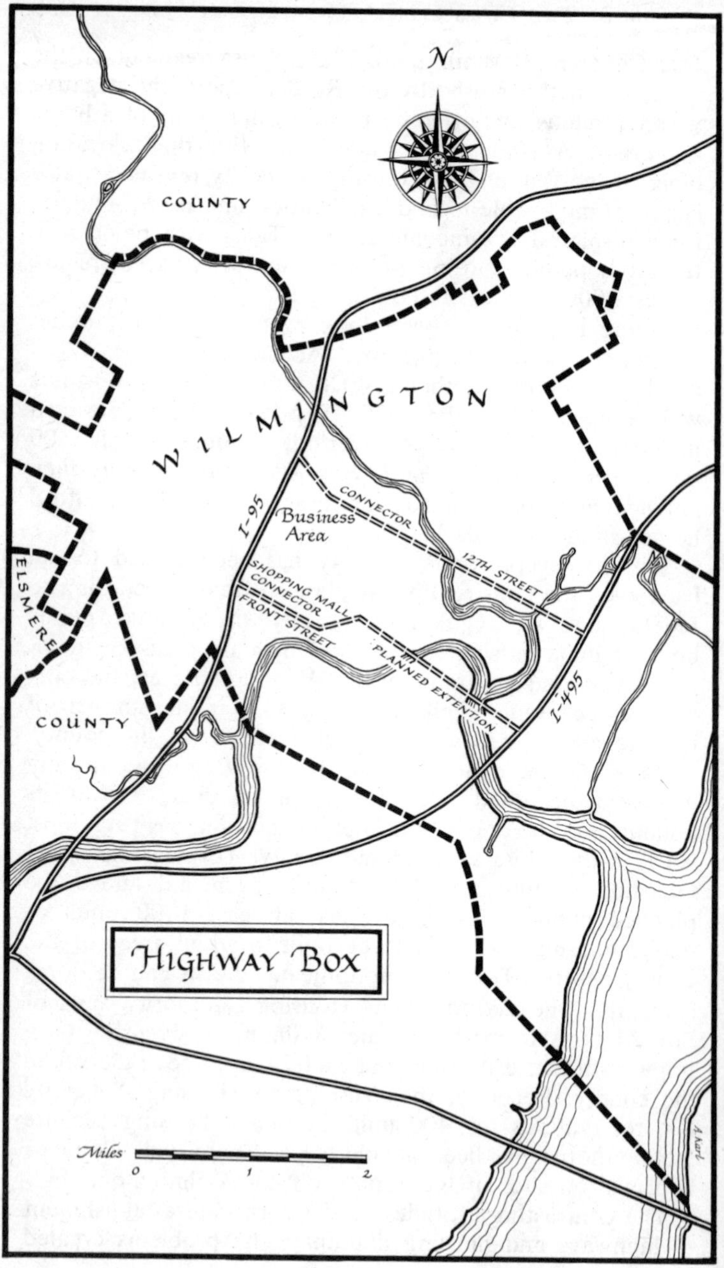
N
COUNTY
WILMINGTON
I-95
Business Area
CONNECTOR
12TH STREET
SHOPPING MALL CONNECTOR
FRONT STREET
PLANNED EXTENTION
I-495
ELSMERE
COUNTY
HIGHWAY BOX
Miles
0
1
2

when a single, private interest controls the use of private resources for public needs. In an interview with the Delaware Study Group, Maurice du Pont Lee said proudly that he had fought to get the highway department to replace every tree that had been removed by the construction of I-95; no one, however, replaced the homes of the families removed by the highway. In the same vein, after GWDC pushed to get I-95 built quickly, it undertook a large project to beautify the highway corridor—for those few households remaining in the area.

The establishment's cavalier attitude toward housing continues to this day. Once I-495 is constructed, there will be two parallel north-south superhighways—I-495 and I-95. So the highway department is planning to build two large east-west roads through the city to connect I-95 and I-495. One connection would be above downtown at Twelfth Street; it would displace up to 180 households. Below the downtown area, there are plans for another connector between I-95 and I-495. The first part of this connector, called the I-95 spur, would displace only a few living units, but it is difficult to estimate how many more families would be displaced by the extension of the spur. Despite nearly unanimous community opposition to the connector, the state's highway advisory group approved it in September, 1971. In short, Wilmington will be boxed in by superhighways (see Map 4). Inside this box will be the corporate business area and a few remaining slums; outside the city will be the homes of whites; and in the interstices between the highway box and the city line will live blacks, Spanish-speaking groups, and some whites. Cutting off most Wilmington residents from the downtown big business district, the highways will be a constant reminder to blacks and whites alike of their powerlessness against Wilmington's corporate goliaths and of a city government unwilling and unable to service their needs.

CHAPTER 11

# Private Land and Public Decisions: County Government

Seaford and Wilmington are company towns; New Castle County is a family domain and the research center for chemical companies. After years of passively controlling the county through its land holdings, the corporate elite has now explicitly taken over the county government.

### *An Ungoverned Land Market*

For many years New Castle County's executive and legislative branches of government were combined in one archaic institution—the Levy Court, composed of three members each serving six-year terms. With only three members to run a county of roughly 200 square miles, the Levy Court was not very active. Many traditional public functions, like garbage collection, were contracted for privately; other governmental functions, such as police protection, were handled by the state. As Professor Francis Tannian, a University of Delaware urban affairs expert said, the Levy Court was a "glorified sewer connection agency."

With so weak a government, New Castle County developed according to the will of the private land market—a seriously defective land market. Upper-class families artificially reduced the supply of land by hoarding undeveloped acreage, while the employees of large chemical firms created a high demand for land. As a result most residents of New Castle County have not been able to buy attractive land.

The extensive land holdings of the DuPont family and related groups are concentrated in one section of New Castle County, the DuPont quadrant (see Map 2). In this area, the upper class and the DuPont Company hold a substantial part of New Castle County's undeveloped land (see Appendix 6 for acreage). The DuPont family and company own over 35% of the "rural" * land in Christiana Hundred, 19% in Mill Creek Hundred, and 13% in Brandywine (see Map 2 for hundreds). The chemical research facilities of DuPont, Hercules, and Atlas are all in the DuPont quadrant, as are several private country clubs. Non-DuPont upper-class families live in Christiana and parts of Brandywine Hundred. Woodlawn Trustees, a builder of homes for the Delaware upper class, holds another 1500 acres, 10% of the rural land in Brandywine.

Meanwhile the demand for land in northern New Castle County has greatly increased. In 1930 only 54,000 people lived in New Castle County outside Wilmington; by 1970 over 300,000 did. This growth was spurred by the construction of DuPont research facilities in the county and office buildings in the city, matched by similar development of the other chemical companies. DuPont's huge work force has nearly doubled since World War II. With no land available in the DuPont quadrant, the increased demand for housing has been channeled directly north and south of Wilmington in Brandywine and New Castle hundreds. This channeling was exacerbated by the routing of I-95. By placing I-95 on a north-south axis, the state highway commission, led by DuPont family member Hugh

* New Castle County classifies land as "rural" if it is neither incorporated nor in a subdivision. It refers to more than just farm and forest land; DuPont factories and research facilities, for instance, are classified as rural.

R. Sharp, encouraged even more building and overcrowding in parts of Brandywine and New Castle hundreds. Meanwhile, the DuPont quadrant, entirely bypassed, remained elegant and isolated.

As a result of family- and company-generated demand, land hoarding destroyed the free movement of the land market in New Castle County. Prices in the DuPont quadrant soared, and hoarding pushed up prices elsewhere. As one prominent Wilmington realtor said: "The land in Delaware is much more expensive than the land right across the line in Pennsylvania because land in Delaware is scarce—it's all tied up in chateau country."

DuPont-related individuals and groups have taken advantage of the defects they helped create in the private land market. For instance, W. W. Laird, a family member with substantial landholdings in the DuPont quadrant, kept prices on land he developed high by feeding plots into the residential market very slowly. Partly because of the "snob value" of living near the DuPonts, Laird and other realtors have been able to sell two-acre undeveloped lots for $25,000 and up. Yet even a potential purchaser willing to pay these high prices has been denied permission to buy one of the lots, for financial solvency is not enough. Local architects told the Delaware Study Group about several families that had to be approved at tea parties before the upper-class realtors would sell them a lot in a neighborhood.

Closely allied to the DuPonts is Woodlawn Trustees, created as a nonprofit group by William P. Bancroft, a wealthy member of a Quaker textile family, who wrote the trustees in 1913:

> The land west of the Brandywine is gradually being bought up by rich people as county seats. My aim is to promote the westerly part of Brandywine Hundred being developed, after reserving what it is desirable should be parks, as a residence district for people of moderate or small means.

Bancroft's aim has been perverted by Woodlawn Trustees. Woodlawn developments get more luxurious and more expensive as they near the Brandywine, "to complement the DuPont estates across the Brandywine River," according to

Philip G. Rhoades, executive director of Woodlawn Trustees. In 1969 the Internal Revenue Service revoked Woodlawn Trustees' tax-exempt status because it was no longer pursuing charitable purposes. Contrary to the intentions of the trustor, Woodlawn's major activity was building $60,000 to $70,000 houses.

Nor has Woodlawn simply kept out those of moderate income. Practically no blacks or Jews live in any Woodlawn development. A DuPont family member told the Delaware Study Group that a few years ago Woodlawn sent out a questionnaire to residents of its developments, asking essentially whether they wanted houses sold to Jews. The answer, we were told, was a resounding no. At least until 1968, the deeds in Woodlawn's developments restricted sales to Caucasians, even though such restrictive covenants were ruled unconstitutional by the United States Supreme Court in 1948.[1] In 1968 the provision was changed to permit Woodlawn to approve any potential purchaser.* The trustees used the deed restrictions to "insure the social compatibility of residents," according to Rhoades. The Delaware Human Relations Commission revealed in 1970 that Woodlawn was still segregating blacks from whites in a rental project run by the trustees in Wilmington.

Like Laird and Woodlawn Trustees, most successful realtors in northern Delaware are tied to the DuPonts and the upper class. A main source of real estate business has been the sale of expensive homes to bankers, lawyers, and high-salaried executives. For instance, Jack Alexander, a major realtor in the DuPont quadrant, handles houses mainly in the six-figure range. Another major boon for realtors has been the frequent transfer of young DuPont executives in and out of Wilmington for four to five year periods. Furthermore, many men have gone into the real estate business after working in the DuPont real estate department, where they gained useful contacts and experience. Even access to land is determined by a realtor's ties

* Through 1968, Woodlawn deeds contained the following clause: "Sale of this property subject to limitations, restrictions, reservations, and conditions set out in deed from Woodlawn Trustees to Rubin Satherwaith, Jr. dated December 10, 1936." The second restriction states: "No lot or part thereof shall be conveyed to, used, owned or occupied as owner or tenant by any person not of the Caucasian race."

with the corporate establishment. Woodlawn, for example, allows only 10 or so selected realtors to work in its developments. One prominent real estate man, Carroll W. Griffith, handles many dealings for W. W. Laird. Through his connections with Laird, Griffith was the first non-family member allowed to purchase DuPont land for development in the Christiana area.

But the real estate business in Delaware has not been open to all comers. There has been only one full-time black realtor in the state, Charles Foreman. He received little cooperation or help in building up his business from white realtors, who would refer only black clients to him. About 1968 Foreman tried to start a project in conjunction with the Ford Foundation to encourage more blacks to become realtors and to promote racial integration in the housing market. However, according to Foreman, the foundation required a corporate cosponsor, and the choice was DuPont. According to John Burchenal, the DuPont public relations executive who handled the request, the company refused to participate, feeling that other community needs were more important; the project collapsed.

Having built up a business through contacts with the DuPont Company and family, realtors themselves perpetuate and exploit the defects in the land market. Their influence has been especially strong in giving DuPont transferees their first tour around the Wilmington area. According to one local executive, realtors directed new employees to the suburb corresponding to their position in the corporate pecking order with lines like, "let me show you where good businessmen live, like employees of your company." At the same time, realtors have imposed extra construction costs on Delaware consumers by their ties with local builders, according to local realtors and architects. After selling a family a lot, a realtor offers a tip on a contractor who is so good that the family will not need an architect. The realtor gets a kickback from the contractor for giving him the business instead of putting the house out to public bid. As a result, home purchasers unknowingly pay 6–8% more than they should for a house.

Instead of regulating the DuPonts' hold on the private land market, the county government, in one of its rare moments of public policy making, reinforced the influence of the family and company. In 1954 the Levy Court began a zoning system which legally affirmed the status quo. The zoning commission, dominated by Samuel E. Homsey, a DuPont family member, did not undertake intensive studies to prepare a zoning map which would have provided the county with the optimum mix of land uses. Instead, it zoned county land according to the already existing patterns of development, while putting all underdeveloped land in a general holding pattern. To break the DuPont grip on the market, landowners and other citizens now had to obtain the approval of both the zoning commission and the Levy Court.

The county government was both unable and unwilling, through zoning or other measures, to rectify two major problems afflicting the New Castle County land market—racial discrimination and sewer development. Since county officials did not police racial discrimination in real estate dealings, in the early 1960s the NAACP began working with the association of realtors toward a *voluntary* agreement on open housing. Over the course of several months a group of liberals, aided by a few businessmen from companies other than DuPont, had almost persuaded the realtors to accept a voluntary agreement on racial integration. The realtors were ready to sign a statement binding all brokers to list houses under open occupancy (if the owner so desired) and to encourage private owners to put their houses on the open-occupancy list. The only drawback was that the association also wanted all the large companies to support the voluntary agreement on open housing. As one realtor said, "We had to present a united front; otherwise we would get hit real hard because a lot of people would go to a broker who did not deal with blacks." Support from the major companies would have forced all brokers to sign the proposal, or so the realtors hoped.

Within a few weeks, the brokers had convinced Atlas and Hercules to accept the policy on open housing; but DuPont's position was unclear. One liberal young DuPont executive indicated to the realtors that the company would be willing to come out publicly against racial discrimination in the housing market. Relying on this assurance, the brokers wrote a press release committing themselves to voluntary open housing. A week later, DuPont reneged. Company officials said they could not take a public stand on housing discrimination, although they would work privately to promote integrated living opportunities for their black employees. The realtors withdrew their press statement and refused to enter into the voluntary agreement.*

The weakness of county government has also brought about a sewer crisis. In November, 1970, county officials announced that a complete breakdown was imminent for its "poorly planned, outdated and polluting sewer system." [2] The economic effects of the sewer crisis may be far-reaching. At this time, the county council was considering implementation of a total freeze on construction in the county because the sewer system could not handle any increased volume in wastes. Furthermore, according to newspaper accounts, "several industries inquiring about sites in Delaware are said to have cooled because of the prospect of plant construction delays caused by the lack of sewer capacity." [3]

The root of the sewer crisis is uncontrolled construction of new installations by DuPont and other chemical companies in the county over the last few decades. These new plants brought thousands of employees into the county who need housing and a wide range of services, including sewers. The county government was simply too weak to cope with the great increases in public needs. As William Conner, the current county executive, said of the former government: "Sewers were built according to what the Levy Court thought it could afford," [4] not along the lines of any rational plan.

DuPont executives have argued that the company's property taxes should have provided enough funds for the county government to build sewers. However, the revenue from corporate property taxes came in very slowly while the demand for public services rose suddenly. Furthermore, the DuPont Company never contributed its rightful share of taxes to the county government (see Chapter 12). Under

* In 1969 the state passed an open-housing law, publicly supported by DuPont and other large companies.

Delaware law DuPont pays no property taxes on its research equipment and office supplies. And the company's land has long been grossly underassessed. For example, the land at the DuPont Experimental Station is assessed at only $699 per acre, while the land at a small shopping center several miles away is assessed at $6224 per acre.

### *The Beginnings of County Government*

By the early 1960s, the county's problems had become so great that there was general agreement on the need for a stronger government. Chemical firms found their employees dissatisfied with an outmoded government which was not providing public services fast enough to meet the rapid growth of the county. In response, Governor Elbert N. Carvel, a liberal Democrat, appointed a commission to propose a reorganized local government. The commission came up with a system with a strong county executive and a county council composed of seven representatives, six from county districts and one, the president, elected at large like the county executive.

To the dismay of the Democrats who had initiated the reform, the county government chosen in 1966 after the reforms were made was overwhelmingly dominated by the GOP and DuPont. The county executive was William J. Conner, who had worked in DuPont's Legal Department from 1947 to 1966. According to Conner, his job for DuPont consisted primarily of traveling from state to state testifying about pollution control bills. When Conner was first elected, he took a leave of absence from his DuPont job. Only when he was reelected in 1968 did he actually resign.

DuPont influence was similarly large in the county council. C. Douglass Buck, Jr., was elected council president. His mother was Alice du Pont, the daughter of T. Coleman du Pont; his father was a U.S. senator and governor of Delaware. Buck, too, was reelected in 1968. Of the six district representatives on the council in 1970, four were DuPont employees, three Republicans (Richard Sincock, Thomas J. Kealy, and Henry Folsom) and one Democrat, Malcolm Gray, a machinist. The only non-

DuPont council members are W. Alva Hollis, a black social worker from central Wilmington, and Joseph H. Toner, who represents working class whites and poor blacks from the southern part of the county. Toner, a painting contractor, worked for DuPont from 1946 to 1954.

The major difficulties confronting the new county government have been related to the tremendous problems created in the private land market. The county has established two well-staffed departments—the planning department, and the department of development and licensing. These, together with the planning commission which oversees both, are supposed to provide an "objective basis" for decisions. But the original chairman of the planning commission was a retired executive from DuPont, the present chairman is a DuPont employee, and the DuPont-dominated council must approve all recommendations from the planning commission or planning department.

A crucial question, then, is whether the DuPont-led government can do an "objective" job when company interests are involved. In March, 1971, Richard Sincock announced that he would not vote on Shell Oil Company's zoning request because DuPont enjoyed a significant marketing relationship with Shell.[5] But Sincock had voted previously on a DuPont Company request for a zoning change in connection with its new Glasgow plant. In an interview with the Delaware Study Group, Sincock said "the issue had been decided against DuPont"; but in fact the rezoning that was approved included the most significant part of the DuPont land.

## *Land Use and the Public Interest*

The most pressing land use issue in the county is the provision of decent housing for low- and moderate-income families in both the county and city. There are about 5000 substandard housing units in the county, twice as many as in the city.[6] Over 50,000 new housing units will be needed over the next decade.[7] In the southern quadrant of the county and below the canal, housing conditions are abysmal. Some families are actually living in converted chicken coops,[8] and many houses have no running water or indoor toilet facilities. A recent newspaper series on county housing pointed out that "there is a housing crisis in the county for not only poor or low-income residents, but for even the average family whose income is less than $12,000 per year." [9] About 70% of the county's families earn less than $10,000 a year and about 50% earn less than $8000; [10] many of them cannot easily buy a house in New Castle County. For the 13,000 families in the county with incomes below $5000 per year,[11] buying a new house is out of the question.

Despite pressure from many groups to alleviate the housing crisis, the county government has responded with only token gestures. In response to pressures from the city of Wilmington to participate in federally funded public housing projects (so that more units can be built in the city), the county council merely passed a resolution that the county would allow public housing to be built if the council approved the site. So the Wilmington Housing Authority placed reservations for 400 low-income units with the federal Department of Housing and Urban Development (HUD), and two developers proposed seven possible sites in the county. Two sites were not acceptable to HUD. Of the others, the county planning department vetoed four and failed to approve the fifth. Now the county council has appointed a commission to study the problem.*

## *Land Use and Corporate Interest*

While the county government has not responded to its housing problems, it has provided for the transportation and office needs of corporations.

The Greater Wilmington Airport is a prime example of public facilities devoted primarily to corporate use. The airport was established in 1941 by the New Castle County Levy Court because of pressure brought by H. B. du Pont,[12] who had had his own aircraft business on his own airfield, but needed room to expand. A publicly subsidized facility

* The New Castle County Housing Authority was formed in late 1971; it has plans to build 900 low-income units in the next two years.

was the logical choice. The county airport is now run by a five-man board. In 1969 two board members were closely related to the corporate establishment; these two also had served the longest. Gilbert Church is a DuPont employee; William J. Christopher was personal secretary to S. Hallock du Pont. When Christopher quit after 1969, DuPont director and family member W. Sam Carpenter III took his place.

Although the airport is supposed to be a public facility serving all local residents, it consists, in large part, of hangar space for private planes. Corporate planes comprise about 38% of airport use. DuPont owns 10 planes and averages about seven flights a day out of Greater Wilmington Airport. Since 1961 DuPont has maintained an office at the airport. Other local companies also use the airport extensively. Columbia Gas, Hercules, and Campbell want to build hangars for their company planes on airport grounds.* A consultant report on the airport said: "The greater use by industries, either for transportation or shipping, is an indication of the importance of the Greater Wilmington Airport . . . to the industrial community." [13] Nevertheless, the county did not even levy landing fees for business planes until 1970.

As corporations intensify their use of the Greater Wilmington Airport, service to the public decreases. As a comprehensive study by Arthur D. Little Company pointed out:

> The increased presence of *general aviation* [private planes] the mainstay of the airport now and over the next decade, will significantly reduce the runway capacity available for commercial aircraft and thus greatly diminish the future attractiveness of GWA as a major air passenger facility.[14]

Recent events have confirmed the consultant's prediction. In 1970 Allegheny and Eastern Airlines each suspended one daily flight into the airport, cutting passenger services remaining at the GWA to a bare minimum. Of the four

* All the DuPont planes and those of other companies were purchased from or are serviced by Atlantic Aviation Company, one of the largest private aircraft sales companies in the country. For many years, H. B. du Pont was the sole owner of Atlantic. Although some of the stock was distributed to executives of Atlantic four years ago, the DuPonts still retain controlling interest.

daily commercial flights in and out of the airport, none are before 10 AM or after 5 PM.

The Arthur D. Little study presented two clear choices for the airport's future. It could serve its corporate customers by expanding its facilities for general aviation and increasing air freight service. Or it could serve the Philadelphia region just as Newark (N.J.) serves the New York City region. In support of the second alternative, the Little report says that in 1967 about 270,000 passenger trips at the Philadelphia airport originated or terminated in Delaware. In the same year, GWA handled only 34,000 trips. The GWA has good road and rail access to the whole region; it is the best existing airport in the region other than Philadelphia; and it is underutilized. By building up a regional air center, the county government would provide easy and quick air transportation for Delaware residents and would bring business to New Castle County. The study suggested, however, that "if the community elects to keep open prospects of a major regional air passenger facility, it should discourage the further development of general aviation." [15]

County residents have never been given a chance to choose between the alternatives. With little public debate and no public hearings, the county government decided to favor corporate interests by increasing general aviation. In an interview with the study group, County Executive Conner said the Little report had concluded that "the future of the airport was in general aviation operations." However, the county did not even adhere to that alternative completely; the report recommends increased air freight service concomitant with development of private flying. Air freight representatives say that they have not found county government receptive to expansion of their facilities and operations.

In sharp contrast to the scant attention paid the decision on the airport's future, extraordinary publicity attended the rezoning application of Columbia Gas System in 1968. County councilman Richard Sincock, a DuPont employee, described it as the "heaviest issue concerning the public interest since I joined the council." In reality, the "public interest" was little more than a family squabble. One branch of the DuPont family sold a plot of land in Christiana Hundred to Columbia Gas, which wanted to move its headquarters from New York to Delaware. It planned to build a campuslike office for 200 employees. This proposal split the corporate community in half. Those in favor were corporate executives, bankers, and the Farquhars, who had sold the land at a million-dollar profit. The businessmen liked Columbia Gas because its corporate headquarters would fit nicely with the white-collar atmosphere promoted by the DuPont Company and local banks. Irenee du Pont, Jr., and J. H. Tyler McConnell, family member and president of the Delaware Trust Company, strongly favored rezoning for Columbia Gas. Even officials of Columbia Gas said they chose the site in part because of the "receptivity of Delaware leaders who have encouraged Columbia and other corporations to locate their main headquarters in the state, since they believe this is the type of growth which Delaware merits." [16]

Opposed were all those DuPont family members who lived near the proposed offices and who were not interested directly in promoting white-collar industry in Delaware. This group included the nucleus of the Carpenter branch of the family, S. Hallock du Pont, and the elderly William F. Raskob, a former secretary of the DuPont Company. This side argued that Columbia Gas would deface the beauty of the Greenville area. After years of tying up the county's prime residential area and thus jacking up land prices, the group now charged: "Exploiters are endeavoring to have this property spot zoned as an area allowing office buildings and light manufacturing."

The county government postponed a public hearing on the Columbia Gas issue several times while trying to arrive at a compromise; when the hearing finally occurred it was lengthy and heated. Then the county council went into hibernation to think the issue out. Finally, the council decided to bow to the business DuPonts, and in 1970 Columbia Gas built an elegant office building, which in no way destroys the aesthetic atmosphere of the nearby DuPont mansions. In essence, the hullabaloo was based on the paranoia of some DuPonts over commercial advances on their secluded estates.

*The County's Future*

The two major decisions for the county council in the near future will involve the DuPonts. The first concerns a dam and reservoir proposed for White Clay Creek, two miles above Newark, Delaware, which would flood acres of wilderness in Delaware and Pennsylvania. The DuPont Company is very directly involved: it owns 95% of the land at the site, which it acquired quietly and systematically.

Although public planning for the White Clay Creek dam has gone on for about 10 years, the idea originated around 1950. The Pennsylvania Railroad owned large areas of suitable land above White Clay Creek and wanted a reservoir to supply the needs of its subsidiary, the Delaware Water Company. In 1956, the Pennsylvania Railroad sold the Delaware Water Company and a year later sold the White Clay Creek land to DuPont, which had already assembled an adjacent plot for its Louviers building and golf course. Company spokesmen contend that at the time of these two purchases, DuPont did not even suspect it was getting into local water resource planning. In an interview with the Delaware Study Group, DuPont attorney Charles E. Welch insisted that the company's interest in White Clay Creek was awakened by the 1960 report from the Army Corps of Engineers on the Delaware River basin. After the Army's report, company executives claim that their own engineering department persuaded DuPont to buy large tracts of land in the watershed area.

However, it seems more likely that DuPont's chronology is carefully reversed. Lyman Darling, now retired, supervised DuPont's 1960 in-house study of the Corps of Engineers's proposal. The inclusion of the White Clay site in the Corps's report, says Darling, was an alteration of its original plan. Darling explains that he read the Corps's report after it had been transmitted to, but before it had been approved by, Washington. This text recommended a dam on the Christiana River. Darling informed the Corps that the Christiana site was full of houses and that the area was situated in a turnpike right-of-way. He took engineers from both the Corps and DuPont out to the

Christiana and White Clay sites. The Army then amended its report to include the White Clay site.

While the dam itself would be in Delaware, the reservoir would flood land in both Delaware and Pennsylvania. Most of the Delaware land is undeveloped, but much of the Pennsylvania land consists of farms and homes. Several of these homeowners were reluctant to sell their property when DuPont real estate agents approached them. According to several in the area, homeowners who refused to acquiesce would sometimes be told that the company would condemn and take the property. DuPont never had the authority to condemn land, but some people believed it and sold.

No one knows for sure why DuPont decided to become a private government over White Clay Creek. Some residents of New Castle County feel that DuPont was motivated by a clear and simple need for more water to enlarge its industrial operations, particularly to expand its Glasgow plant. Others, more charitable, tend to think that the company is trying to ensure that as it grows there will be enough water around to run the employees' dishwashers and fill executives' swimming pools.

C. B. McCoy acknowledged that the decision to buy the land at the reservoir site was made by the DuPont executive committee upon a recommendation from company engineers. Lyman Darling claims to be responsible for that recommendation. He argued that the company's water needs would mount as it grew, until the needs exceeded the available supply; the decision to push White Clay Creek, Darling told the study group, was "just pure selfishness, looking ahead." Darling also told the executive committee that its act would be one of "enlightened selfishness": company officials were easily persuaded that if New Castle County suffered a water crisis, DuPont would be in trouble, too.

While the private government of the DuPont Company was making decisions rapidly, the public government of New Castle County did not hold a single public hearing on the dam issue until late in 1971, despite the intense controversy for several years. Instead, the county has commissioned study after study. Whitman-Requardt and Associates has done several consultant reports for the New Castle County Council, the latest completed in 1967. All of the studies done by the Army Corps of Engineers, the DuPont Company, and Whitman-Requardt stressed that the county faced a water shortage and that a dam at the site on the White Clay would best meet this need. But the activities of the Whitman-Requardt firm raise serious questions about their impartiality. Richard Arnold, project engineer at Whitman-Requardt, told the Delaware Study Group that people from his firm visited the DuPont Company many times while preparing their reports. They were interested in the company's land holdings, private utilities, and engineering data. Whitman-Requardt may have based its conclusions on data gathered by DuPont, because the company has supplied both county officials and its consultants with various studies on water needs as well as with technical plans for the dam complex. Moreover, Whitman-Requardt has done at least two studies on water systems in New Castle County for the Delaware Water Company which stands to profit from the dam's construction. And the DuPont Company is the major industrial customer of the Delaware Water Company. Whitman-Requardt is, in effect, recommending a project to one client (the county) that will benefit another client (the Delaware Water Company) based on the data of a beneficiary of the project (the DuPont Company).

The reliability of the early studies can be questioned from other standpoints. Professor Francis Tannian of the University of Delaware noted that all three of the early reports predicted that the county would be out of water by 1970. However, by 1971 there was not any restriction on water use. Each of the studies stressed the *engineering feasibility* of damming White Clay, but none considered the social costs of the project. As Charles Tremblay argued in his master's thesis for the University of Delaware, Whitman-Requardt used an incomplete cost-benefit analysis. The Whitman-Requardt study does not mention secondary benefits of leaving the river untouched, such as recreation, employment, and increased land valuations. Neither does it include an appraisal of secondary costs of building the dam: potential ecological damage, increased flood danger, the effects of drawdown (the land exposed as the reservoir is drained), interstate negotiation costs, and effects on recreational facilities.

In 1969 the county council commissioned another study, this one by the Roy Weston firm of West Chester, Pennsylvania. The Weston report was described as "the study of studies" by Lyman Darling. It, too, concluded that the White Clay dam would be economically attractive—and it, too, ignored ecological factors.

Next, county officials commissioned a small-scale, short-term study by the Delaware Nature Education Center (DNEC) on the ecological effects of the proposed dam. DNEC is an organization with 500 members and a $40,000 budget. DuPont family members are major contributors; their annual contributions have ranged from $1500 to $15,000, and two family trusts contributed a total of $55,000 over the past several years. After cataloging the region's great variety of vegetation and wildlife, the report concludes that no valid ecological reason exists to oppose the building of the dam and reservoir. The Nature Center stands essentially alone. Other conservation groups, led by the Sierra Club, strongly oppose the project. The Sierra Club is joined in its fight by local wildlife federations, sportsmen's clubs, ornithological societies, and groups devoted specifically to saving the White Clay Valley. Indeed, it is more difficult to believe that flooding 1000 acres would be harmless than it is to believe that DuPont financial support could have directly or indirectly influenced DNEC's report.

Another study—designed, according to the *News-Journal*, to pay particular attention to conservation, including ecology, recreation, and economics—was completed in March, 1971. It was carried out by the University City Science Institute (UCSI), the research arm of the University City Science Center in Philadelphia, on a commission from the Committee of One Hundred, a nonprofit group of builders, industrialists, and merchants dedicated to good government. It, too, is of doubtful objectivity. DuPont is a member of the Committee of One Hundred, and a top official of the science center is a former top staff member of the Greater Wilmington Development Council. One member of the

UCSI research team told the study group that the study was biased and that the group's ecologist, an assistant professor at the University of Pennsylvania, felt that he had been assigned to discover ways in which the dam would benefit the ecology of the valley. In addition, the research team's informal liaison with the Committee of One Hundred and with the county was the former county engineer, John Calahan, who was deeply involved in the planning of the dam and remains committed to it.

Not unexpectedly then, this report supports construction of the dam, but on surprisingly narrow grounds. It calls for immediate construction, primarily because building costs are soaring and lengthy interstate approval procedures will mean a delay even if the county gives immediate approval. On the other hand, it strongly urges the county to consider alternatives to the dam, especially recharging and recycling the county's ample ground water supplies, the use of which has been supported by Robert Varrin, director of the Water Resources Center at the University of Delaware,[17] and would have the least deleterious environmental effects of the various alternatives.[18] Furthermore, the ecological section of the UCSI report gives virtually no support on environmental grounds to building the dam. It points out numerous inaccuracies in the DNEC report, and goes on to say: "No form of life presently existing in these stream and woodland environments would be likely to survive flooding. While mobile animals may be able to migrate, suitable habitat is already occupied by similar animals and the chances for colonizing success are slight." [19] Recreation and open-space needs for the growing population of New Castle County can be better met by preserving the White Clay Creek Valley, not by flooding it, according to the report.[20]

The studies, themselves no substitute for public debate, have not reached any consensus. One member of the UCSI team believes that there is not even a likelihood of a water shortage. Nor have the studies adequately explored alternatives, such as expansion of Wilmington's Hoopes Reservoir, recharging and recycling ground water supplies, tapping the Susquehanna River through a new Mason-Dixon pipeline, or drawing water from a reservoir soon to be built on the Schuylkill River in Pennsylvania. Neither New Castle County nor Pennsylvania residents whose land would be flooded have had a say in deliberations over the dam. Pennsylvania landowners in the watershed area are angered by "the knowledge that the DuPont Company secretly bought land and with the state of Delaware tried to rush the project to completion without consulting the resident landholders of the watershed." [21] The vast majority preferred the natural scenic and recreational opportunities of the valley over the dam and reservoir.

While the county council vacillates, DuPont has been trying to render the White Clay Valley unusable for any purposes except a reservoir. The company has blanketed the area with No Trespassing signs, discouraging recreational use of the wooded valley. Meanwhile, DuPont allows the land to degenerate. The area is untended and unpatrolled. Despite warning signs, abandoned automobiles have been dumped into the stream. The company has even encouraged the despoliation of White Clay Valley by letting contractors strip topsoil from the land DuPont expects to be flooded. By the time the public is finally (if ever) allowed to determine the proper use for the eroded, junk-strewn valley, the choices may be severely limited.

### THE VANISHING CITY

Like the White Clay Creek Dam, metropolitan government—the proposed merger of the governments of Wilmington and New Castle County above the Chesapeake and Delaware Canal—will be a major question facing county officials in the near future. At the present time, blacks comprise nearly 50% of Wilmington's population, and the chances that a black mayor will soon be elected increase. There are several possible black candidates available for 1972. For the city's blacks, a black mayor would probably be a welcome event. After years of segregation in Delaware, blacks might see such a mayor as a symbol of new hope and opportunity. The proposed merger of city and county governments might deny blacks the very opportunity that is so near. The corporate establishment worries that a black mayor would more likely respond to the interests of the city's poor—white, black, and brown—than to business interests. If the corporate community can get the city and county to merge, it can ensure its continued dominance.

One key policy that DuPont, a major holder of assessed land in Wilmington, might fear from a black mayor is a drastic increase in taxes. As the black community becomes more influential, it will continue to demand a higher level of services from the city. To meet these needs, Wilmington will likely have to increase its tax rate or raise its tax base by developing Cherry Island as an industrial complex, an approach the corporate leaders do not support. The only real increase in the city's tax base in recent years has come from the construction of office buildings for white-collar workers, which will probably continue at a steady pace. But this construction has been offset by deterioration or demolition of houses, churches, and other buildings for projects like the shopping mall. To keep Wilmington a white-collar city, without tax revenue that industry on Cherry Island would bring, the needs of city residents will have to be met by increased taxes on the corporations.

The corporate establishment is without allies in its fight for metropolitan government. Like black urbanites, white suburbanites oppose metropolitan government, though for different reasons. County residents do not want to help finance Wilmington. Moreover, many county residents fear that merger would result in a large influx of blacks into the suburbs.

Members of the corporate elite have couched the argument for metropolitan government in terms of efficiency. A merger of governments may eliminate the price of duplicated facilities, but the creation of huge governmental districts imposes a great increase in the cost of coordinating services. New officials must be hired and new departments created just to administer such a large organization. Similarly, a large metropolitan government would probably be less responsive to the needs of its constituents. Already one of the main complaints of urban residents is the slow reaction time of their governmental agencies.

Since the corporate elite knows it cannot gain political

support for metropolitan government from city blacks or county whites, nor muster a strong efficiency argument, it has steadfastly kept the metropolitan government issue from the public. Only once, when the county charter was revised in the early 1960s, did the elite tip its hand. H. B. du Pont, a member of the reorganization committee, stood up at the first meeting and said that metropolitan government was what the county needed. Then he offered to fund the work of the committee out of his own pocket. In fact, the committee report was funded by the Delaware School Auxiliary, a DuPont-run nonprofit group. However, the majority of the committee members were against metropolitan government and recommended a county council instead, with a provision that it could make agreements with the city to merge certain functions.

Because H.B.'s power play came to naught, the corporate elite, led by the Greater Wilmington Development Council and the *News-Journal,* began to push for metropolitan government by more clandestine methods. As Peter A. Larsen, the new executive head of GWDC, said in an interview with the Delaware Study Group in the summer of 1970:

> We are working toward the day when we will have shifted so many functions out of the hands of the city that Wilmington will cease to exist. When the city council comes to meet one Thursday night and finds they have nothing to do, there will be no more city of Wilmington.

Not surprisingly, the *News-Journal,* which has continuously supported metropolitan government, editorialized in October, 1970, "It may not be too many years before Wilmington City Council meets some Thursday night and finds it has no business to discuss." [22] And in the summer of 1971, the DuPont Company listed consolidating city and county services as one of the three major problems of Wilmington to which the company would directly contribute substantial manpower and money.

So far, the "creeping merger" policy of the corporate establishment has been very successful. Little by little, the GWDC and the newspapers have used consultant reports, efficiency arguments, or donations to convince the city to give up one or another function. The county has taken over assessing property. The county and the city now share facilities for some sewage treatment and landfill. As the county-city building in Wilmington has come under one head, a consultant has recommended that the county sell its office buildings and move into a jointly built office building in the proposed new civic center. Mayor Haskell and County Executive Conner have established 11 joint committees to plan for merger. The committees are seriously discussing merger of police, fire and urban-planning operations. Meanwhile, the state has taken over welfare for both city and county, and there are similar plans for public health. The *News-Journal* says the city should give the port to the state, and a commission has suggested a regional housing authority. Education has never been in the city's hands; it is run by an independent school district which levies its own property taxes and receives funding directly from the state.

Operation of the parks is now one of the last tasks left for the city government. Ironically, several city-owned parks are actually in the county, and are used mainly by county residents. Groups in the corporate establishment, like the *News-Journal,* argued that the city should *give* these parks to the county so urban residents would no longer have to pay for park maintenance. The argument is incredibly shortsighted. If the parks are not being used by the city residents, then the city should sell them—to the county or to the highest bidder—and use the money to buy parks for city residents. Since the land is quite valuable, the city could then provide for the sorely neglected recreational needs of its residents. The city should not have to subsidize county residents by giving the county free parks, yet the giveaway proposal almost passed the Wilmington City Council in 1969. In the end, the city gave long-term leases to the county for the land (which would have cost the county millions to purchase) and the county agreed to maintain it. In 1970 city and county agreed to turn over maintenance of the rest of the city's parks to the county. The city council, fearful that county operation of the parks might not benefit city residents, reserved the right to cancel the agreement within four years. Otherwise, the merger becomes permanent. Again, the county paid nothing for the parkland. Such a policy can be understood only within the context of a strategy for metropolitan government. Otherwise, it makes no sense for the city to forego millions of dollars from sale of the land to loan its parks free or even lease them out to the county on a long-term basis, particularly since Mayor Haskell now claims the county has failed to maintain the parks properly.

In the summer of 1971, the *News-Journal* appeared to reverse its position on metropolitan government. Instead of a merger of city and county governments, the *News-Journal* now proposed a step-by-step assimilation of county residents (above the Chesapeake and Delaware Canal) into the city government with the transfer of some local functions to the state government. But as one community leader explained to the study group:

> The *News-Journal*'s recent change is really no change at all. In the short run, the business community is now handing out a carrot to both city and county residents so they will agree to the merger. City blacks can think they will maintain power as they take over the county little by little; and county residents will feel that only small parts of the county are being opened to an influx of blacks. In the long run, the merged city government will be the same as the merged county government. While the part of the county beneath the canal is now dropped out, the most populous parts of the county are in the north anyway. So the blacks will lose political power to the whites through simple numbers. Similarly, white residents will find themselves living in a county with all Wilmington blacks who will want to invade their suburban enclave. The only group that wins, as before, is the business community, which prevents the election of a black mayor after the initial transition period, and spreads the tax burden from their downtown office buildings to property throughout the county.

There are several possible alternatives to a complete city-county merger. One would be to levy a county-wide surtax to provide Wilmington residents with sufficient funds to run the city properly, while promoting integration of the county through carefully planned construction of subsidized public housing units.* Such a proposal would retain for city residents political control over the city while redistributing resources within the entire county toward the city.

* See Chapter 10.

CHAPTER 12

# *Windfall to the Squirearchy: Property Taxes*

Property taxes are the major source of revenue for the city and county government in Delaware—about 55% for both Wilmington and New Castle County. Property tax rates for city, county, and school district budgets are based on the assessed value of land, buildings, and other tangible improvements made on the land—"real" property. The inequities of property assessments* in Wilmington and New Castle County have had a major impact on local revenues, compounding the problems of city and county government.

Delaware laws establish standards for real property taxes and assessments. The Delaware constitution requires that taxes be uniform for all real property within a taxing unit.[1]

* The Delaware Study Group focused its research and analysis on the assessment of land only, since our limited resources precluded an independent analysis of assessments on buildings and improvements. Though we are not analyzing the assessments of buildings and improvements, we do take into account that buildings and improvements affect the assessed and fair market values of land, and we realize that corporate property owners generally inflate the value of buildings to take advantage of tax savings through depreciation, and deflate the value of land. Assessors often cooperate in this practice, and we are assuming that inflation-deflation is done for all property owners.

Classifications of real property can be based on differences in the "use, nature, or character" of the land, but not solely on location.[2] Delaware law tells local boards of assessment to distinguish between "improved" and "unimproved" land,[3] but all assessments must be made at the fair market value (fmv) of the land.[4] Fair market value has been defined by a Delaware court as "the price which would be agreed upon by a willing seller and willing buyer . . . assuming the highest, best, and most valuable use for which the property is reasonable, adaptable, and available."[5] Assessments must be kept current each year[6] to reflect the fmv. Delaware courts have said that, while assessments should reflect the fmv to the greatest extent possible, "equality and uniformity are the cardinal principles to be observed in the levying of taxes."[7]

City and county assessment officials have not enforced the two basic requirements of real property law in Delaware—that assessments be equitable and uniform, and reflect the fmv of the property. Large landowners—residential, commercial, and industrial—benefit from relatively low assessments per unit of size (a/u)*on their land in comparison to smaller landholdings. Smaller landowners tend to bear a disproportionately greater tax burden than the large landowners, even though all property owners pay the same tax *rates* in each taxing unit. Nor is current fair market value reflected in the assessment of land, because comprehensive reassessments are not made annually; New Castle County and Wilmington have not conducted a general reassessment since 1955. Assessments relative to market prices are not uniform as required by state law.** The lack of reappraisal has benefited those landowners whose property has risen in value and hurt those whose property has depreciated. With the most valuable

* As used in this chapter, *assessment per unit of size* (a/u) means units of assessed value (dollars, cents) per unit of size (acre, square foot). The a/u is used as the prime measure for uniformity of assessments in this analysis. While the analysis of relative assessment per unit of size is novel to this book, the analysis is a valid basis for judging whether assessments are equitable under Delaware statutes, and furthermore, whether inequality of assessments per unit of size constitutes a violation of equal protection of the law under the United States Constitution.

** The analysis of the uniformity of assessment ratios is a traditional analysis used to judge the equity and legality of assessments. This analysis is separate and distinct from the first analysis in this chapter.

land being grossly underassessed, city and county revenues have been consistently shortchanged.

The DuPont family and company are the biggest landowners in northern Delaware, and have benefited more than most from inequitable assessments.* Their holdings are concentrated in northern New Castle County, where 70% of the Delaware population lives (see Map 1). About 70 DuPonts own nearly 13,000 acres—double the size of Wilmington—in New Castle County (see Appendix 6), as well as many large plots in Wilmington's most expensive residential sections. The family's city and county landholdings have a present market value between $200 and $300 million. Their assessments total only $22 million—less than 10% of the market value. The DuPont Company also owns a large amount of land in Delaware—4081 acres in New Castle County (see Appendix 7), 727 acres in Sussex County (southern Delaware), plus seven full downtown blocks and another 139 acres in the city of Wilmington.

### *County Residential Assessments*

Over 75% of the DuPont family and company lands are in large lots—20 acres and over. As the predominant owners of large pieces of land in New Castle County, the DuPont family and DuPont Company benefit more than other property owners from the county's lower a/u made on large holdings than on small properties, a practice of questionable legality under Delaware law. Appendix 8 gives assessment data for some representative DuPont family landholdings in New Castle County. Assessments for DuPont family land range from $33 per acre for 27 unimproved acres owned by Robert N. Downs III in Mill Creek Hundred to $4781 per acre for the small mansion site of Anne T. du Pont on the Kennett Pike in Christiana Hundred. Most "mansion sites," meaning those manicured grounds and gardens on which DuPont chateaux stand, are assessed at $700 per acre. But many mansion sites are

* Documentation is from the New Castle County assessor's office unless otherwise specified. Some of the information on company-owned land was provided by the DuPont Company in response to questions submitted by the study group.

assessed below this figure. A 29-acre homesite owned by Alfred du Pont Dent is assessed at $445 per acre, while Lammot du Pont Copeland, Sr.'s 20-acre mansion site in Mill Creek Hundred is assessed at $105 per acre. Almost 45% of the DuPonts' land is in Christiana Hundred, where their assessments average $400 to $500 per acre. The highest assessments on DuPont family land are in Brandywine Hundred, where the average a/u for family land is $700 to $800 per acre. But only 10% of the family's land is in Brandywine Hundred. Assessments on the 45% of family land in Mill Creek, White Clay Creek, New Castle, and St. Georges hundreds average under $100 per acre.

One way to understand the underassessment of this family land is to compare the a/u of the DuPont mansions and grounds to smaller residential lots in the county. The 277-acre estate of the late William du Pont, Jr., in Brandywine Hundred has an a/u varying from $317 per acre to $2114 per acre. On the land are several dwellings, a gatehouse, a ham house, swimming pools, greenhouses, and numerous other buildings, in addition to the mansion, which increase the value of the land. A few blocks from William's property stand the first four residences listed in Appendix 9. Each site is less than one-half acre. As Table 12-1 shows, even the highest du Pont assessment, $2114 per acre, which applies only to 3½ acres of the 277-acre estate, is well below the assessments on the small homeowners' lots, and the other two assessments on du Pont's estate, $317 per acre and $840 per acre, are grossly lower than those for nearby residences. While portions of the estate may in fact be worth less than small suburban plots, the vast difference is certainly unwarranted under both the uniformity and fair market value requirements of Delaware law. A typical homesite in Alapocus, a relatively old

TABLE 12-1.
*Assessments per Acre of Some Estates in Brandywine Hundred*

| *William du Pont, Jr.* | *Four Adjacent Homeowners* |
|---|---|
| $2114 (3.5 acres) | $4809 |
| 840 (257 acres) | 5227 |
| 317 (17 acres) | 4800 |
| | 3223 |

suburban area in Brandywine Hundred, is assessed at approximately $8600 per acre (see Appendix 9). But the 41-acre mansion site of the late Jessie Ball du Pont is assessed at $2099 per acre (see Appendix 8), less than one-quarter of the suburban homeowners's a/u.

Similar examples abound. In Christiana Hundred, where most of the DuPont estates are located, a few exclusive areas have been developed. The assessments on residential sites built on land formerly owned by DuPonts are increased after family members sell them. One such development is Owl's Nest, built on the former estate of Eugene du Pont. The unimproved land was reassessed after subdivision into residential lots; these lots are now assessed at figures ranging from $1820 to $6599 per acre. The 18-acre mansion site of Eugene's estate, on the other hand, was sold to the exclusive Greenville Country Club and retained the assessment of $770 per acre. The Meadows, a development west of several DuPont estates, has three and one-half acre homesites assessed at $1555 and $1816 per acre. Compare these to the assessment on the most highly valued section of the estate of Irenee du Pont, Jr.—$700 per acre for the site of the mansion itself.

### *County Industrial Assessments*

Land owned by the DuPont Company in New Castle County is likewise assessed at extremely low a/u compared to other industrial, commercial, and residential properties. Under Delaware law, industrial properties are classified with commercial and residential for assessment purposes. Assessments of DuPont industrial and research sites hardly reflect the utilities, buildings, and other improvements that greatly enhance their value. Industrial assessments are generally far below those on suburban homesites, often below those on DuPont mansion sites, and sometimes lower than those on open fields (see Appendix 10).

A conspicuous case of underassessment is that of the DuPont Experimental Station in Brandywine Hundred, a campuslike complex of about 30 buildings—laboratories, storage buildings, shops, offices, and a cafeteria. The *News-Journal* called the Experimental Station "probably the single most valuable piece of real estate in the state."[8] But according to figures supplied by the DuPont Company to the study group, the 45 acres of land at the Experimental Station are assessed at $699 per acre, the same as the adjacent DuPont Country Club golf course. Meanwhile, the 35.59 acres of land where Columbia Gas System's headquarters stand, a mile or so away from the Experimental Station, is assessed at $1492 per acre—itself an underassessment. The 76-acre office and laboratory complex of Atlas Chemical Industries, located a few miles from the DuPont Experimental Station, is assessed at $2102 per acre—three times that of the Experimental Station, even though the location, uses, and size of the two pieces of land are comparable. And other properties in the area have been assessed even higher: Independence Mall Shopping Center, $6244 per acre; a home in Augustine Hills, $5808 per acre; a home in Alapocus, $8672 per acre; Friends School in Alapocus, $7000 per acre; a home in Woodbrook (near DuPont Country Club), $5562 per acre; a home in Sharpley (near DuPont Country Club), $7389 per acre.

Every other piece of DuPont Company land in New Castle County is similarly underassessed. Except for an unusual assessment of $3348 per acre on 2.3 acres in the Germay Industrial Park, no company land in the county is assessed above $1867 per acre. The Louviers Laboratory site is assessed at $127 per acre, only slightly higher than the $93-per-acre assessment on the company's totally "unimproved" White Clay Creek land, which has no buildings, roads, or other additions to increase its value. The land supporting other multimillion-dollar DuPont industrial and research complexes is assessed from $376 per acre at Centre Road Laboratory to $500 per acre for Chestnut Run Laboratory and the Newport paint pigments plant. The thousands of nearby middle-class and lower-middle-class homeowners, on the other hand, pay property taxes on land with a/u's five or ten times those of the DuPont Company.

### *County Assessments and Market Value*

Clearly, the assessments per unit of size on the property of the DuPont family and company are consistently low relative to smaller properties with similar uses. But the state constitution and property tax laws not only require uniform and equitable assessing; they stipulate that all assessments be made at fair market value (usually the same as sales price). The fmv of property in Delaware is not reflected in assessments largely because New Castle County and Wilmington have not made a general reassessment of property since 1955. The failure to reassess the land at full value violates Delaware law twice: first, that assessments be made on the "estimated full value" (present fmv) of the property, and second, that assessments be kept current each year. City and county assessment officials agree that infrequent reappraisal undercuts these requirements. They do not agree, however, that the city and county have violated state law for the lack of a general reappraisal and reassessment. Pleading lack of money and political support, assessment officers claim that the retention of the below-market-value 1955 assessments has affected every property owner equally: when property is sold for more than the assessed value, the assessment is not changed to reflect any increase in market value; and when new buildings are added to the assessment roles, they are assessed at the same values used in the 1955 reassessment. So the argument offered by the county and city officials is that all properties are equally unaffected by the increases in market value because, first, the value of all new buildings revert back to the 1955 values; second, newly developed residential land is assessed at values comparable to the 1955 assessment; and third, assessments remain the same despite increased sales prices.

But in fact the lack of reappraisal works to the advantage of wealthy landowners, whose land has generally risen rapidly in value, and to the disadvantage of poor and middle-class landowners in the city and county, whose property has risen in value more slowly, if at all, or even decreased in value. Assessment officials lower the assessment of properties that have dropped in value only if the owners petition the assessment board; but the assessors have not notified all property owners of their right to seek a decreased assessment. Most small landowners whose property has decreased in value are not aware that the assessment can be changed or cannot afford to hire a lawyer to do it for them.

Those whose property value has increased least since 1955 pay the heaviest tax burden; property with the highest increase bears the lowest tax relative to market value. Consider three homeowners, each owning property worth $15,000 in 1955 and assessed at $15,000. The market value of one property located in chateau country has risen greatly and in 1971 was worth $40,000. A second land parcel, in a lower-middle-class area, increased to only $25,000 during the same period. The third property, located in a deteriorating all-black suburb south of Wilmington, declined in value to $10,000. But in 1971 all three landowners were still taxed as if they owned a $15,000 piece of land. The latter two owners are paying higher proportional taxes on the market value of their properties than is the first. If assessments equaled market value, the first property owner would be paying just over one-half of the total taxes; but he is actually paying the same one-third as the other two owners without a reassessment.*

In New Castle County, the DuPont family and company benefit from the lack of frequent reappraisal more than most other landowners because their large landholdings have increased tremendously in market value. DuPont family land is worth a great deal because the development of expensive residential areas, much in demand in northern

* If market value equaled assessed value as required by law, the proportional tax loads would be:

$$\text{Owner A } \frac{40}{10+25+40} = 53\tfrac{1}{3}\%$$

$$\text{Owner B } \frac{25}{10+25+40} = 33\tfrac{1}{3}\%$$

$$\text{Owner C } \frac{10}{10+25+40} = 13\tfrac{1}{3}\%$$

As the practice now is, however, owner C would pay a disproportionately high tax *even if he took advantage of his right to have his property reassessed to reflect its lower value,* since the other two properties would not be reassessed to reflect their increased value. He would, in this case, pay $\frac{10}{10+15+15} = 25\%$ of the total burden, nearly twice the $13\tfrac{1}{3}\%$ he should pay.

Delaware, depends upon the release of large plots of DuPont family land; other than Woodlawn Trustees, there is no other source of attractive undeveloped residential land in New Castle County. The fair market value of DuPont land should be based on the value of nearby land being developed for residential purposes, since this is the "highest, best, and most valuable use" for the property, the standard used to determine fair market value.

The mansion of Eugene du Pont and its 18-acre site were sold in 1961; the land alone brought in \$4000 per acre. This property, now the Greenville Country Club, is still assessed at \$770 per acre. In the same year the heirs of Eugene sold approximately 220 acres of undeveloped estate land, assessed at a figure well below \$770 per acre, which, according to Carroll W. Griffith, a Wilmington realtor and developer who bought the land, cost around \$4550 per acre. Griffith in turn has been selling improved two-acre lots in the Owl's Nest development for \$15,000 (in 1961) to \$27,500 (in 1971). The 200 or so acres of the Griffith development could conceivably bring in nearly \$5 million for the developer. Based on this use of the land and the selling prices before improvement, the fair market value of the DuPont land is over \$4000 per acre. The unimproved parts of other DuPont estates are still assessed at \$100 per acre, but have a similar fmv. A piece of land in Mill Creek Hundred, owned by the heirs of Henry B. du Pont, is similar to the 220 acres of Eugene du Pont's estate before they were improved. The land is now assessed at \$338 per acre, far below the fair market value of the land.

Nearly all county property is assessed well below market value (see Appendix 11). But the assessment ratio * is hardly uniform. Middle-class suburban dwellers pay taxes on their homes and homesites at an assessed value roughly one-half (.50) the actual value of their property. William Henry du Pont purchased properties near the Owl's Nest area, with assessment ratios of .29, .19, and .10. The market value of the properties, as indicated by the

* The relation of assessed value to actual market value. The ratio is derived by dividing assessed value by market value (see Appendix 11). An assessment ratio of one means the assessments equal market value; a ratio below one indicates underassessment.

sales price of the land (see Appendix 11) were 3.4, 5.2, and 10.0 times the assessed values. Du Pont's taxes on the 51-acre site are roughly one-tenth what they should be. Similarly, Reynolds du Pont bought 8.5 acres of land in chateau country from Delaware Governor Russell W. Peterson for 4.5 times the assessed value. And William V. Roth, U.S. Senator from Delaware, purchased an estate in chateau country for a price 5.5 times the assessed value. Owners of large plots, such as the DuPonts and Roth, pay taxes based on one-fifth or one-tenth the market value.

One specific example of ridiculously low assessment ratios on DuPont family land is the estate of Henry B. du Pont. H.B.'s land included his mansion and surrounding grounds—Ashland Tract—as well as several adjacent, relatively undeveloped tracts. When he died in 1970 the property was appraised for its fair market value for estate tax purposes.* As Appendix 12 indicates, the assessment ratios of du Pont's property ranged from .10 to .04; fair market value was 10–25 times the assessed value.

Henry B. du Pont's landholdings are not unlike those of many DuPonts: a relatively large mansion site of 5–25 acres, 10 to several hundred "unimproved" acres surrounding the estate, and farmland or hundreds of unimproved acres elsewhere in the county. For example, S. Hallock du Pont owns over 1500 acres of farmland in addition to his nonfarm landholdings, and William K. du Pont owns 255 acres of farmland. Each of these landlords benefits from the inequitable property assessments in the same way that H.B. did. Their properties are taxed at one-fifth to one-tenth the rate borne by other taxpayers, and one-tenth to one-twentieth the rate required by law.**

While the assessment ratios of family land in New Castle County are low, assessment ratios for industrial land are ridiculously low. Since little county land is zoned for industry, industrial land has a very high market value, as

* These fmv's must be considered the lowest possible estimates. For obvious reasons valuations made by the executors establishing the taxable value of the estate are seldom inflated or extravagant.

** These estimates of the relative degree of tax avoidance do not take into account that tax *rates* would probably be lowered if the assessment base were raised. But for purposes of comparing tax avoidance relative to other property owners, the estimates are valid because the higher tax rate is uniformly applied to all property owners.

recent sales data for commercial and industrial land indicate. The lowest assessment ratios (.01 to .04) shown in Appendix 11 are for industrial land. Columbia Gas System paid Dorcas Buck Farquhar, a du Pont, 32 times the assessed value of part of her estate to build a suburban office building. Since the nearby DuPont Experimental Station land is assessed at roughly one-half that of Columbia Gas, the actual fmv of the station must be more than 50 times the assessed value.* The state of Delaware paid the DuPont Company $6963 per acre for a 54-acre section of the company's undeveloped White Clay Creek site in 1970. The assessed value of the 748 acres at White Clay Creek is still only $92.78 per acre. The company paid $2880 per acre for a portion of this land less than 10 years ago. The fmv of the White Clay Creek land is between $2880 and $6963 per acre, 25–75 times the assessed value. When the Welfare Foundation purchased 590 acres in White Clay Creek Hundred between 1964 and 1967, it paid 22 times the land's present assessed value of $105,000; from 1967 to 1969, the land increased $365,000 in market value, while the assessment remained the same.

Mill Creek and White Clay Creek hundreds are among the few areas left in New Castle County where middle-class residential developments or new industrial and commercial plants and offices can be built. As a result, land prices in this area have increased greatly, and assessment ratios range from .01 to .04, meaning that asessments are one seventy-fifth to one twenty-fifth the fmv of the large, yet-to-be-developed parcels of land. Over 17% of this vacant land in Mill Creek and White Clay Creek hundreds is now owned by the DuPont Company and family.

On the other hand, a middle-class purchaser would have bought a house and small suburban lot with an assessment ratio of .40 to .50. The sales prices and assessed values for new houses purchased in 1970 in three developments near the DuPont Country Club and Experimental Station are shown in Table 12-2.

* The calculations on this and following pages are the only indicators we have to measure the fmv of the Experimental Station (and all the DuPont property), since the company refused to disclose this information to the study group.

TABLE 12-2.
*Assessment Ratio of New Houses in New Castle County*

| *Location of Homes* | *Assessed Value* | *Sales Price* | *Assessment Ratio* |
|---|---|---|---|
| Sharpley Development | $18,600 | $49,900 | .37 |
| Woodbrook Development | 23,500 | 60,000 | .39 |
| Tavistock Development | 28,200 | 55,800 | .50 |

Compared to the assessment ratios and taxes paid on DuPont Company and family lands, these home purchasers have to pay taxes many times as high per unit of market value. The DuPont Company's county tax bill on land is roughly one seventy-fifth what it would be at the present tax rate if increases in the market value of the company's land were reflected in increased assessments on that land,* while the average homeowner's county tax bill is roughly only one-half what it would be after such a reassessment.

## *Property Assessments in Wilmington*

The assessment situation in Wilmington is like that in New Castle County. As in the county, there has been no general reassessment since 1955. Although large landholdings are not as grossly underassessed as in the county, there are some significant inequities in a/u, as well as disparities between assessment ratios.

Smaller DuPont family properties have an a/u similar to those of nonfamily residential property owners in the city. However, the relatively large city estate grounds of family members, located mostly in the northwest corner of the city, are assessed at significantly lower a/u than the nonfamily plots listed in Table 12-3. For example, two properties of the H. Rodney Sharp estate are assessed at 16.7 cents per square foot for a 317,000-square-foot site and 19.7 cents per square foot for a 143,900-square-foot site. The 58,000-square-foot residence and grounds of Natalie R. Weymouth are assessed at 21 cents per square foot, and Margaret Lewis du Pont's 62,000-square-foot resi-

* Based on available sales data, industrial land in New Castle County is presently selling for around $30,000 an acre. This figure was confirmed in interviews with Wilmington realtors who sell commercial and industrial properties. The average assessment on land at DuPont Company industrial sites in the county is $400 per acre, one seventy-fifth the fair market value.

TABLE 12-3.
*Non–DuPont Family Residential Sites in Wilmington*

| *Location* | *Size (Sq Ft)* | *Land Assmt ($)* | *Land Assmt/ Sq Ft ($)* | *Improvement Assmt ($)* |
|---|---|---|---|---|
| Pine St | 1,465 | 500 | .34 | 4,300 |
| N Broom St | 13,000 | 6,500 | .50 | 29,900 |
| W 19 St | 1,378 | 800 | .58 | 5,700 |
| Riverview Rd | 4,485 | 1,700 | .38 | 7,800 |
| Blackshire Rd | 13,300 | 6,800 | .51 | 31,800 |

dence on West 11th Street is assessed at 21.6 cents per square foot.

The market value of family properties in the city is difficult to determine, as there have been relatively few sales transactions recently. However, evidence exists to indicate that the property has risen in value. Sales prices for city residential properties near family holdings are from 1.6 to 4.0 times the assessed values, while sales prices are going down in other residential areas.

Rising land values in the city are concentrated around the DuPont Company office buildings in downtown Wilmington. The sales prices in 1956–57 for the land where Wilmington Trust erected its new office building was four times the assessed value. The site for DuPont's new Brandywine Building was bought between 1965 and 1967 for over seven times its assessed value. In contrast, neither commercial properties farther down Market and adjacent streets nor downtown residential properties have appreciated as much in value. In some cases their value has actually declined. The market value of land adjacent to the north of DuPont's buildings is notably higher than its assessed value. Here the company owns several residential lots and commercial properties now leased as parking lots. All its latest downtown purchases have been in this northerly direction, indicating future expansion there.

Small shopkeepers and homeowners in areas not lying in the direction of DuPont's future expansion bear a greater tax burden relative to the fair market value of the property than does the DuPont Company. If assessment were at current fair market value, the DuPont Company properties would be assessed at three to seven times their present levels, yielding substantially more tax revenue for the city and shifting the burden of taxation away from residential and commercial property owners in deteriorating parts of town.

The assessments of DuPont property in downtown Wilmington are below those of land under other office buildings there (see Appendices 14 * and 15). The two major DuPont office buildings sit on land assessed at $17.93 per square foot (DuPont Building) and $12.98 and $7.325 per square foot (Nemours Building). Under two buildings within one block of the DuPont Building—Market Tower and Farmers Bank buildings—land is assessed at $33.11 and $31.79 per square foot respectively. The most striking comparison to the minuscule DuPont assessment is the valuation of Rodney Square, parkland assessed at $22.63 per square foot—$5 per square foot more than the land under DuPont's major office building, directly across Market Street.

DuPont Company industrial land in the city is assessed extremely low. One of the most egregious examples of the inherent bias in the city assessments favoring large landholdings is DuPont's Christiana Laboratory on Christiana Avenue. The 22.69 acres of laboratory land inside the city are assessed slightly below 4 cents per square foot, while close-by residential properties are assessed from 20 cents to $1.50 per square foot in Wilmington and up to 23 cents per square foot in the county. The homeowner loses again.

## *Refund and Reform*

The DuPont Company and family have saved millions of dollars in local property taxes over the last 15 years. In 1970 alone, if DuPont family land had been assessed at the same level per unit of size as that of most residential lots in New Castle County, the family would have paid over one million dollars more in property and school taxes to the county at present rates. Also, if the DuPont

* As the last column of Appendix 14 indicates, much of DuPont's land downtown is devoted to parking lots. The a/u of the lots range from $.667 to $4 per sq ft, most of them being around $2 per sq ft. Though DuPont is leasing these parking facilities only on an interim basis, Wilmington's tax base is still lowered considerably. The lack of mass transit and the existence of superhighways to the outlying suburbs insure that the pressure to convert more land to parking lots will continue.

Company's industrial and research sites had a/u's similar to those of most small homeowners, the company would have paid $320,000 more in property taxes to the county, *just for the land.*

The owners of property with an a/u below a certain point should pay the city and county the property taxes not paid on their landholdings since the 1955 reassessment —with 6% interest. Because of the bias in the assessments favoring large landholdings over smaller ones, the DuPonts would bear the brunt of the refund. The amount due from the family to New Castle County is about $12,600,000 plus $756,000 interest; due from DuPont Company to the county, $3,500,000 plus $210,000 interest; and company to Wilmington, $1,050,000 plus $60,000. These are the amounts of taxes that would have been paid between 1955 and 1970, at the same tax rate as was in effect each year, if family and company lands in the county had been assessed at the same a/u as small residences and if land under the two company office buildings in Wilmington had been assessed at the same a/u as the sites of nearby office buildings with the highest a/u. These figures *do not include* taxes for any underassessed buildings and improvements or underassessments on other company-owned land in Wilmington.

Similarly, property owners with assessment ratios less than 40% of market value should voluntarily refund the taxes properly due to local governments under State law. Such a refund would fall mainly on the corporate elite. For instance, in 1970 alone, the DuPont Company would have paid an additional $2 million in county property taxes just on its land if assessments equalled market value.

The city and county should also take immediate steps to remedy the inequities of assessment and taxation of real property within their jurisdiction. A perfect opportunity exists for changes to be made in the assessment system before the reappraisal due for completion in 1972 takes effect. The structural deficiencies of the assessment system, which allow large landholdings with greatly increasing market values to be underassessed relative to smaller ones with decreasing or slowly increasing values, can be corrected and reflected in the new assessments.

# *Part* V

# State Government

CHAPTER 13

# *All the King's Men: DuPont in State Government*

According to the pluralist concept of political democracy, society is composed of many groups which put different priorities on various services. Through democratic processes, through logrolling and compromise, each group obtains a roughly equal share of its objectives. But this model is not applicable to Delaware, where the DuPont Company and the DuPont family are so overwhelmingly powerful that the balancing process simply does not work. At times, the interests of the corporate elite correspond to or overlap with the interests of others. More often they do not. As a result, in the words of the Delaware Chamber of Commerce,

> in no other place in the country does government maintain such an attitude of dynamic cooperation with industry.[1]

Three major statewide elections in 1970 brought DuPont political power to a new high: Pierre S. du Pont IV was elected Delaware's sole U.S. congressman; another family member, W. Laird Stabler, was elected attorney general; and William Roth, firmly entrenched in the corporate establishment, became U.S. senator. In the state legislature, the Republicans retained lopsided majorities in both houses, a result widely viewed as a sweeping vote of confidence in Republican governor and former DuPont researcher Russell W. Peterson.

A major cause of the DuPont landslide of 1970 was the corporate establishment's near monopoly over important political resources: people, time, expertise, money, and media.* Some of these belong to the company, some to the family.

## *Political Resources*

The DuPont Company's most basic political resource is its employees, 11% of the state's work force, most of whom are middle-level and managerial white collar employees—reflecting DuPont's white-collar headquarters. Their votes usually reflect their higher status and relative affluence; their political homogeneity is solidified by exposure to company publications and political pressures (see Chapter 3). This white-collar, middle-class bloc provides a big share of the precinct workers and votes needed to elect DuPont-related candidates to public office. With the reapportionment of the state legislature ordered by the court in the mid-1960's, the professionals from the chemical companies have become the strongest political force in Delaware. Before reapportionment, Kent and Sussex counties dominated the legislature; now the suburban residents of New Castle County dominate, and GOP candidates ride to victory on the ballots cast in DuPont bedroom suburbs.

To encourage political activities by certain employees, DuPont gives workers who hold public office 20% of their time off with full pay. In a state with a part-time legislature, the 20% rule gives DuPont white-collar workers a great advantage. While citizens working for other firms may have to quit the legislature after a term or so and return to work, DuPont employees have maintained legislative positions for years, thereby gaining experience and impor-

* See Chapter 9 for a discussion of DuPont control of news media in Delaware and Chapter 3 for DuPont Company's political propaganda.

tant seniority. Significantly, the 20% rule seems not to apply to blue-collar workers.* One of the few blue-collar workers elected to a local post told the study group that his supervisor actually harassed him instead of giving him 20% time off. He had never heard about the policy.

Another DuPont resource is expertise. It is just one example of company employees using their skills for political ends that Harlan Wendell, DuPont's assistant director of public relations, was described by the Wilmington papers as a "Longtime Haskell confidant [who] advises on [the mayor's] image problems." [2] Similarly, Peterson's carefully planned campaign began with the formation of a People for Peterson Committee in November, 1967, headed by DuPont research supervisor Andrew G. Knox. *News-Journal* reporter Jerry Sapienza was immediately hired as administrative assistant. In 1970 other committees were established to support the campaign of Pierre S. du Pont IV for U.S. congressman. The committees were headed by a DuPont family member, a corporate lawyer, and Pierre's campaign manager.

While federal law prevents the DuPont Company from contributing directly to political campaigns, DuPont executives and family members can legally donate large sums to their political friends. In 1966, for instance, 21 Delawareans were listed as donors of $1000 or more to the Republican Congressional Boosters Club; all but one were connected with the DuPont family or the company, and the one was with the Wilmington Trust.[3]

DuPonts are almost the only big givers in Delaware politics, and the GOP is almost always the recipient. The best available data, compiled by the Citizens' Research Foundation, show that in 1968, 36 of 42 recorded donors of more than $500 in Delaware were either DuPont family members, employees of the DuPont Company, or officers of DuPont-related banks. In 1969, 22 of 26 donors of $500 or more were family members or DuPont employees (another was a Wilmington Trust officer). In 1968, 34 of the 36 DuPonts gave their money to the GOP, and all 23 did so in 1969. Those donating more than $1000 to the GOP in both

* DuPont refused to release the text of the 20% rule to the Delaware Study Group, claiming that it was "confidential information."

years included Edmund N. Carpenter II, Lammot du Pont Copeland, Robert N. Downs III, Reynolds du Pont, George P. Edmonds, Crawford H. Greenewalt, C. J. Harrington, C. B. McCoy, and Hugh Sharp, Jr.[4]

With the corporate elite's support, the GOP usually has two to three times as much campaign money as the Democrats. Governor Peterson's 1968 campaign reportedly cost over $500,000; * the Delaware Study Group was told his Democratic rival spent less than $100,000. In the 1970 Congressional race, Pierre S. du Pont IV intentionally remained ignorant of the exact amount raised by his campaign committees to take advantage of a loophole in the federal law.** But Pierre admits that many DuPont family members, as well as from 6 to 12 top-level DuPont executives, made substantial contributions, and while his opponent struggled to finance countywide mailings, Pierre could afford to pay professional pollsters.

A key GOP money man is Harry Haskell, whose mayoral campaign was hugely expensive (see Chapter 10). As a former U.S. congressman and GOP national committeeman, Haskell has influence that extends far beyond Wilmington. According to many local politicians, Haskell made liberal use of his personal fortune, estimated conservatively at $50–75 million,[5] in both his and Peterson's campaigns in 1968. In 1970, according to a former top Republican official, Haskell spent about $60,000 on local legislative primaries to promote his favorites within the GOP.

Like Haskell, state senator Reynolds du Pont, uncle of U.S. Representative Pierre S. du Pont IV, is a key financier of GOP campaigns. In a small state like Delaware, where campaigns are generally run on shoestrings, Reynolds can profoundly influence elections by contributions of $1000 or so. Reynolds estimates he donated $10,000 to Peterson's campaign in 1968. Every year, he gives at least $3000

* Peterson claims this figure is too high, but refused to tell the study group how much the campaign did cost.

** A candidate need only report monies raised directly for him, or funds which he knew about. Therefore, a candidate can purposely remain ignorant of money raised for him by committees and none of that money need be reported anywhere.

each to the state, county, and Wilmington GOP committees. To help individual legislative candidates, Reynolds will give the chosen between $500 and $2000 each. By his own account, when Senator du Pont does not like a candidate, he will spend even more to defeat him. Reynolds provided Michael Castle with $5000 to beat the incumbent Democratic state senator, Russell Dineen, whom Reynolds disliked.

Even in primaries, Reynolds du Pont will cough up to punish an enemy. One such instance involved John Billingsley, a Republican state representative from Newark and a DuPont supervisor. Billingsley, a strong critic of the state liquor industry, much displeased Senator du Pont, who holds stock in Delaware Importers, a large wholesale liquor company. Before the 1970 primary, Reynolds du Pont and a group of Newark businessmen who opposed Billingsley for local reasons, promised financial aid to a Newark high school principal if he would run against Billingsley. The educator declined at the last minute, so William Warwick, one of the businessmen, ran. Warwick, a former legislative page for Senator du Pont whom du Pont has since aided in business, was indicted for embezzlement of public funds in 1954 while he was Prothonotary of New Castle County. (The indictment was dismissed because of a technical error in the complaint; there was no adjudication on the merits.) Later Warwick was elected coroner, and has since been charged by the state medical examiner with doubling his income as a funeral director while serving as coroner.

Warwick's handsomely financed campaign included advertisements in the *News-Journal* and on radio, paid telephone canvassers, extensive mailings, and a Main Street campaign headquarters. A campaign committee spent about $3000; receipts included a $1000 treasurer's check which the committee's leader indicated was from Reynolds du Pont. Warwick himself paid for all the advertising, again with aid from Senator du Pont.

Despite the cash, the Warwick campaign flopped. But its significance lies in the attempt, not the failure. Potentially independent legislators realize that failure in this instance does not mean such efforts always fail. As one Delaware political observer said: "Money is the blood of politics, and the DuPonts run the bloodbank in Delaware." *

Healthy injections of DuPont money have helped the GOP remain dominant in Delaware over the past 70 years. In fact, in this century, only three Democrats have been elected governor in Delaware. Of the DuPont family members and company employees in the 1970 Delaware legislature, all but one were Republicans. So complete is DuPont dominance over the GOP that even a reportedly anti-DuPont Republican, David Buckson (attorney general, 1967–71) told a journalist:

> I'm from DuPont country and I'm glad of it. . . . A family different from the DuPont family would have controlled the state. If they did, would I have been nominated?

DuPont domination of the Republican Party is taken for granted in Delaware, but few know that the Democrats are also permeated with corporate influence. As a Delaware politician put it, "There are two political parties in Delaware: the DuPonts and the Anti-DuPonts, with the proviso that many DuPonts are members of the Anti-DuPont Party." The Democrats are the "Anti-DuPonts." Traditionally, Delaware's gentry class has provided the key link between DuPonts and the Democratic party. As *News-Journal* reporter Jack Nolan pointed out:

> Both parties had their "respectably rich" old-line leaders in the early 1960's.
>
> In the Democratic party, these men had access to money, gave the party a pleasant image, and acted as a moderating force among party factions.[6]

Most prominent of the gentry is the Bayard family, which has produced five United States senators. Alexis du Pont Bayard—son of Senator Thomas A. Bayard and Elizabeth Bradford du Pont, ex–lieutenant governor, Democratic candidate for the U.S. Senate, and State Democratic chairman from 1967 to 1969—once said: "DuPont has people on both sides of the fence; often they are diametrically opposed. Nevertheless, all those individuals are sympathetic to DuPont."

* Keeper of the GOP bloodbank is state Republican treasurer Edward du Pont, son of the late Henry B. du Pont.

Other prominent members of the Democratic gentry, such as the Tunnell family and William Potter, are also closely tied to the DuPonts. James Tunnell, son of a U.S. senator and Democratic candidate for the Senate in 1966, is a senior partner in Morris, Nichols, Arsht & Tunnell, a DuPont Company law firm. Tunnell also is a trustee of the University of Delaware and a board member of the Wilmington Trust, and mingles with his peers at the Wilmington and Greenville country clubs. William Potter, of Potter, Anderson & Corroon, is married to a DuPont, is active in DuPont family affairs, and represents several family members in his law practice. He was also Democratic chairman from 1942 to 1944 and has been Democratic national committeeman since 1955.

Nongentry Democrats are often just as closely tied to DuPont interests. J. Allen Frear was a small-town banker prior to his two terms (1949–61) in the U.S. Senate, but fervently supported DuPont while in office. It was Frear who asked Congress to vote special tax concessions for the DuPont divestiture of General Motors stock. After his defeat in 1960, Frear joined the Wilmington Trust Company, and his administrative aide, Robert Kelly, became DuPont's chief Washington lobbyist.

Even Elbert Carvel, reportedly one of the most anti-DuPont Democrats since World War II, reached an accommodation with the corporate elite. In his first term as governor, (1949–53), Carvel flaunted his anti-DuPont opinions. He even removed Francis V. du Pont from the highway commission. About his second term (1961–65), Carvel reminisced to the Delaware Study Group: "I had become mellowed, more mature, determined to appoint the best man regardless of any DuPont tie." The "best man" was named DuPont surprisingly often: Carvel named H. B. du Pont to the planning council, R. R. M. Carpenter, Jr., to the racing commission, Mrs. A. Felix du Pont to the ad hoc goals committee, *News-Journal* editor Charles Reese to the Council on the Administration of Justice, and a DuPont employee, Frank Mackie, to the highway commission.

Probably the best recent example of DuPont influence in Democratic circles was Governor Charles L. Terry (1965–

69), a close friend of H. B. du Pont. In 1965, Terry said: "I could not sponsor or approve any shortsighted tax measure which could possibly change the corporate atmosphere we now enjoy." [7] In 1967 he took Lammot du Pont Copeland, Sr., DuPont's board chairman, to the National Governor's Conference so Copeland could lobby for trade restrictions on textile imports.[8] The same year, Terry pushed a resolution through the Southern Governors' Conference opposing the implementation of agreements related to the chemical industry made at the Kennedy round of tariff negotiations in Geneva, Switzerland.[9]

Yet in the end Terry fell out of favor with the DuPonts when his politics proved embarrassingly reactionary to the corporate elite. It was Terry who sent the National Guard into Wilmington for nine months after a small civil disturbance in the wake of Martin Luther King's assassination. As the military occupation was prolonged and Wilmington's image became increasingly tarnished, the DuPonts tried to persuade Terry to pull the Guard out. By that time Terry had become bent on making his anti-black stance the key to his 1968 campaign and would not relent. Those in the elite who favored a softer line embraced the candidacy of Russell Peterson, who was more liberal than the heavy-handed Terry.

Terry's running mate for lieutenant governor in 1968 was Sherman W. Tribbitt, then speaker of the Delaware House of Representatives. Tribbitt, now minority leader in the House, is the Democrat most often mentioned for the 1972 gubernatorial nomination. His prominence in the party is evidence that while the control of the gentry over the party is waning,[10] DuPont influence is not. Tribbitt is the man who introduced the legislation in the Delaware General Assembly which granted special tax treatment to DuPont's General Motors divestiture.

## *DuPont Grip on Public Office*

As a result of large numbers, superior expertise, control over both political parties, and inexhaustible money sources, many DuPont family members, company employees, and employees of corporate agents hold important state offices.

Governor Peterson and Attorney General Stabler are both members of the elite. Other state officials have corporate ties, such as former state treasurer Daniel J. Ross, an ex-DuPont employee who still serves in Peterson's administration. Governor Peterson's personal staff during 1970 included Christopher Perry, son of a former director of DuPont's public relations department; G. Daniel Enterline, Jr., who previously worked for the DuPont family's Wilmington Trust Company; Jerry Sapienza, former reporter for the *News-Journal;* and Arva Jackson, a former staff member of the Greater Wilmington Development Council.

The governor's cabinet is similarly flooded with DuPont employees and family members. Three cabinet officers are DuPont-connected: Robert Halbrook, former DuPont attorney, now secretary of community affairs and economic development; Kirk Mearns, secretary of highways and transportation, who worked for DuPont from 1948 to 1950 and served as vice president and treasurer of the DuPont-owned Delaware Trust Company, until he was appointed to his state post; and William Bradford, the secretary of finance, who was a former corporate executive. DuPont employees chair the two most important state commissions, for education and transportation, and were members of six other state commissions as of 1970. Family members, too, abound in such posts: George B. Pearson is on the Bank Advisory Board; C. Douglass Buck, Jr., on the Human Relations Commission; Samuel Homsey on the State Planning Council; and R. R. M. Carpenter, Jr., on the Delaware Racing Commission.

DuPont influence is also strong in state legislative bodies. In the 1970 state senate, 2 of the 19 senators were DuPont company employees, together with Reynolds du Pont, Louise Conner (wife of county executive and ex-DuPont attorney William Conner) and a corporate lawyer. In the same year, the 39 members of the House of Representatives included 7 company employees and the wife of another, 2 family members, and an employee of the Wilmington Trust. Moreover, DuPont-related representatives held many of the most important positions in the state legislature. In 1970 Reynolds du Pont was the president pro tempore of the Senate, another family member was majority leader of the House. DuPont-related legislators chaired 5 of the 17 committees in the Senate and 4 of 14 in the House, and one DuPont employee, Herbert A. Lesher, headed the most important body in the legislature, the Joint Finance Committee, composed of the members of the House Appropriations Committee and the Senate Finance Committee. The latter committee was chaired by Dean Steele, another DuPont employee. Of the 12 members of the Joint Finance Committee, 5 were employed by DuPont and 1 by the Wilmington Trust.

DuPont political dominance is facilitated by certain governmental procedures, for Delaware discourages public participation in important political decisions. First, a new state constitution, presently under consideration, will never be voted on directly by the electorate. It need only be approved by two successive general assemblies. Second, until 1970 there were no primaries for state races, and even now a candidate can force a primary only if he has 35% of his party's state convention vote. Until 1970 Delaware was the only state that did not allow write-in votes. Edward S. Stansky, a state legislator who apparently thought elections were for politicians rather than citizens, argued that it would not "be fair if a party-backed candidate who had spent a lot of campaign money and time were beaten by a write-in candidate." [11] One legislator who voted against allowing write-ins was Pierre S. du Pont IV, who explained his position to the study group by saying that in 1964 thousands of Southern blacks had been misled into voting for Martin Luther King via write-ins, thus aiding Goldwater.

When citizens do get to vote on political issues, Delaware law weights the scales heavily on the DuPont side. Delaware is one of seven states with no campaign expenditure reporting provisions of any kind; [12] the state neither limits the amount a candidate may spend nor requires a candidate to disclose the sources of his funds or the amount he spends. In 1970, legislation was introduced in both houses of the state legislature which would have required campaign contributions to be reported to the commissioner of elections. Neither chamber of the legislature deigned to bring the proposal to a vote. Curiously, Delaware at one time had a law on disclosure of campaign expenditures,* but it was "lost" at the printer when the *Delaware Code* was revised in 1953 by attorney S. Samuel Arsht. Arsht claims that when he discovered that the disclosure law and several other laws had been left out of the new code, he wrote a corrections bill containing the missing laws, and the legislature agreed to reenact all the missing laws except the disclosure law. Arsht maintains that the deletion made no real difference because the state had never bothered to enforce it anyway. The absence of legislation on political contributions penalizes voters, who cannot find out the financial ties of persons running for public office, and benefits those candidates who have lavish amounts of money to spend.

Once DuPont-related individuals get into public office through well-financed campaigns, Article II, Section 20, of the state constitution requires them to watch out for potential conflicts of interest:

> Any member of the General Assembly who has a personal interest in any measure or bill pending in the General Assembly shall disclose the fact to the House of which he is a member and shall not vote thereon.

The provision is honored only in the breach. When the new state constitution was being considered, some members of the Constitution Revision Commission even "suggested deleting this provision because it is not followed. The majority felt it should remain because of the protection it offers." [13] The protection is minimal. In 1962 Representative Lee Bartleson, a DuPont employee and stockholder, asked Attorney General Bove, now a partner in a firm which does patent work for the DuPont Company, whether his vote on the GM divestiture bill might be considered putting money into his own pocket as a shareholder and and as an employee. Bartleson need not have worried. Bove interpreted "personal interest" to mean one "of a

* Article 6, Revised Code of Delaware, 1935, §155: "Every candidate . . . and every treasurer of a political committee . . . shall, within thirty days after every election at which such candidate was voted for, . . . if the amount received or expended shall exceed the sum of fifty dollars—file . . . a full, true and detailed account . . . of money contributed, received or disbursed by him for election expenses."

purely personal or private nature, separate and distinct from any interest such member may have with other citizens affected by the contemplated legislative enactment." This bill did not present such a personal interest because it "applies generally to all forced corporate distributions." If a DuPont-related representative can vote on the divestiture bill, he can vote on anything that comes up in the legislature, unless it actually names the DuPont Company as its beneficiary, according to Bove's interpretation.

Bartleson was more sensitive than most legislators to conflict-of-interest problems. A more typical attitude was expressed by Senator Reynolds du Pont, owner of shares of DuPont, Texaco, Standard of New Jersey, and other stocks. Reynolds said that he would have to stay home if he could not vote on issues affecting companies in which he has stock. Senator du Pont takes an active interest in promoting the liquor industry in the state while holding stock in Delaware Importers, the biggest liquor company in Delaware. By his own account, he has never disqualified himself from any vote affecting the liquor industry.

Nor can the public closely scrutinize the activities of the DuPont-dominated government, because the state lacks a public information law. Citizens have no legal right to demand and obtain any data on governmental operations and administrative decision-making—an insulation that encourages clandestine deals and augments the power of those with close contacts to insiders. A public information act offered in the 1970 legislature died in a house committee.

The overwhelming DuPont presence in state offices and the absence of procedural checks on abuse of political power means that the corporate establishment rarely needs to exercise overt political pressure. The president of DuPont does not need to browbeat a legislator; nor does a family member need to bribe an administrator. As John Kenneth Galbraith points out, crass, overt corruption is only rarely the mark of relations between the modern corporation and the state:

> It may well be to the advantage of the industrial system that simple men should continue to suppose that influence is exerted on the state principally by such means [bribery

and the like], because the true nature of corporate power is then obscured.[14]

## *The Legislature and Special Interests*

A good example of the methods by which the business community can manipulate the legislature when necessary and of the manner in which legislation often gets passed in Delaware is the 1967 revision of the General Corporation Law (GCL). The legislature farmed out the drafting of the GCL to a committee appointed by the secretary of state. Four of the nine members of the commission were associated with major corporate law firms; two were executives of companies that performed various services for corporations chartered in Delaware; and one headed the state's corporation department, though he has since become executive vice president of the Corporation Service Company. The committee also solicited written advice and comments on the law, primarily from corporations and large corporate law firms. The solicitation was intended to be as much an advertisement to corporations that Delaware was trying to attract them as it was an attempt to get more ideas. David H. Jackman, president of the United States Corporation Company of New York and a member of the commission, said that he thought the solicitation letter could be used "to publicize the serious effort being made to attract corporations."[15]

The commission obtained more promanagement views through personal discussions with such business-related groups as the Corporate Committee of the Association of the Bar of the City of New York. The general counsel and several other attorneys from the DuPont legal department appeared before the commission to discuss directors' liability. The commission hired Ernest L. Folk III, a professor of law at the University of North Carolina, as its major consultant. Folk, who had rewritten the corporate laws for South Carolina, had described himself as being "promanagement" and once wrote that "inevitably the drafting of the corporation law is aimed at the interests of the corporations themselves." But even Folk, many of whose suggestions were not followed, wrote of the law:

> Indeed the new statutes seem to be exclusively concerned with only one constituent of the corporate community—management—and have disregarded the interests of shareholders and creditors, let alone more tangentially interested parties, such as employees, customers, and the general public. Clearly the Delaware statute does not represent a balancing of interests.[16]

Next, the commission quickly pushed the new GCL through the Delaware Bar Association. The bar's own committee on corporation law, which normally considered legislative revisions, played almost no role in the 1967 law revision. Richard F. Corroon, chairman of the bar's corporation committee and vice-chairman of the GCL commission, was a perfect middleman. He called only one meeting of the bar's corporation committee—to obtain approval for a draft of the commission's bill, which the bar committee's members had not been given an opportunity to read. After objection by a member of the bar committee, the meeting was postponed to allow the committee to read the draft, after which the bar committee almost unanimously voted its approval.

The small group of corporate lawyers on the commission also made sure to retain a substantial influence over the GCL in the future by assuring the absence of a legislative history. In the absence of official documents explaining the statute's provisions, records of committee hearings, and publications by the commission, the commission members are the only ones who can authoritatively say why a certain provision was included or omitted. Courts frequently consider records of a law's genesis to ferret out the law's intent—often a crucial factor in litigation. Without a generally available history of the 1967 GCL, commission members have a very special position in the courtroom, for they alone can produce evidence of legislative intent. As a law review article said: "Thus, the participants are left free to write their own 'legislative history,' an invaluable opportunity for a lawyer. This can be done through writing books and articles 'explaining' the law, or through argument in litigation."[17] Arsht and Canby have written such articles, and according to Irving Morris, a member of the commission, another member has used his commission position advantageously in court.[18]

The state legislature's input into the new GCL was as minute as that of the bar association. The legislators did no independent research to check up on the commission's work. As a law review study put it:

> Simply stated, the commission never expected the legislature to do anything with this law except pass it. One member of the commission referred to the legislature as 'just a bunch of farmers.' Corroon did attend a caucus of Democratic Senators, and Canby did attend a caucus of Republican Senators. But Corroon was out in fifteen minutes, Canby in three and neither was asked any questions about the law.[19]

The legislators' only input was a change in the filing procedures for the proposed law, a change designed to retain jobs for county registrars as political patronage. On the floor of the legislature, according to GOP Representative Everett Hale, discussion of the GCL revision took only three minutes. In sum, as the law review article commented on the GCL revision:

> State legislatures may not be noted for thorough-going consideration of proposed bills, but the Delaware legislature's lack of concern seems extraordinary. The legislature simply abdicated its responsibility to consider the merits of its corporation law. It made no attempt to go outside the Commission and determine whether the statute served that 'public interest' a legislature is supposed to represent.[20]

In like fashion, Delaware legislators approved subsequent amendments to the new GCL which were written by corporate lawyers from a state bar committee. Pierre S. du Pont IV introduced most of the bar's proposed amendments in 1969. In a 1971 interview, du Pont said: "I honestly don't remember what was in the bill." Neither du Pont nor other legislators did any independent research on the amendments; nor did they compare the proposed changes to laws in other states. The Delaware Bar Association sent two representatives to explain the proposed changes to the docile legislators who rubber-stamped the proposals. Du Pont said later, "I'm certainly not an expert on corporate law . . . so we had to take the [bar] committee's word on it."

Just as it turned to private lawyers to write the GCL, so has the legislature sought and received assistance from the DuPont Company for other laws concerning corporations.* When James Snowden, a company employee and state representative, needed legal help drafting a corporate income tax proposal for Delaware, he asked the legal departments of DuPont and Hercules for aid. Asked by the Delaware Study Group why he sought advice from the corporations who were slated to be taxed, Snowden replied: "There were no other qualified legal personnel to turn to for help."

Recently, the state relied on corporate personnel and financing to study the government's efficiency. The state legislature had no input into the study, which began in early 1969 when Governor Peterson met with business leaders to solicit their aid in "streamlining" state government. Contributors included the DuPont Company, other large corporations, corporate law firms, and DuPont family foundations. The Welfare Foundation alone gave $20,000, the businesses $1000 to $2000 each. To staff the Economy Committee, corporate officials loaned 34 executives on a full-time basis and 18 others part-time.

The Economy Study Committee investigated every state agency and made 515 recommendations. According to Chairman Eugene R. Perry, there was no policy content in the study; it took a "purely fiscal approach," so that only people with business experience were needed. But several state agency heads felt that the committee's evalu-

* The DuPont Company does not always wait for legislators to come to it, but maintains a large Legislative Affairs Department whose lawyers scan thousands of proposed state and federal bills. If a bill could affect the company, the DuPont lawyers send it to the relevant corporate department. For instance, a tax bill would go to the Finance Department. Instead of publicly opposing bills that might harm the company, DuPont first tries to obtain an amendment, according to company lawyer Charles Welch. By skillful draftsmanship, DuPont can slip in a favorable twist without appearing to be blatantly seeking its parochial interests. Since many legislators have neither the time to draft their own bills nor the willingness to oppose DuPont, the amendment approach is very successful—according to Welch, by offering amendments, the company has to fight openly only about 10% of the bills it initially opposed.

ation was biased toward business interests. For instance, the study recommended placing the clerks from the Water Pollution Control Division under an administrative services office to save a few thousand dollars; John Bryson of the Water and Air Resources Commission said that an administrative services office would have "no idea what water pollution control is." Perry explains that the committee "used its best judgment" in balancing the dollar saving against possible inefficiencies in the fight against pollution. But a group composed only of businessmen from major corporate polluters may put less value on environmental cleanliness and more weight on efficiency than other Delaware citizens. The committee also recommended abolishing the posts of antidiscrimination inspector in the Labor Department and full-time director for the state Human Relations Commission. In both cases, the rationale was that too few complaints had been processed. The committee did not consider the obvious possibility that few complaints were processed precisely because the agencies were understaffed.

In addition, the Economy Committee asked that the elective offices of state treasurer, auditor, attorney general, and insurance commissioner become appointive, and that the governor and lieutenant governor be elected jointly from the same party. Since both proposals involve major changes in the structure of political accountability in Delaware, they should be made by representatives of all state citizens, not by a homogeneous business group.

In many cases, special-interest legislation for the DuPonts is passed almost unnoticed. For instance, in 1963, at the request of a private person, state representative Everett Hale introduced a bill authorizing the county government to build the White Clay Creek dam. Hale gave the bill to DuPont, his employer, for comment; the company recommended its passage. The White Clay project has become one of the most important planning issues in New Castle County. Yet according to Hale, the bill received scant legislative attention and passed quickly by a 42–1 combined vote of both houses.

Similarly, special legislation for the DuPont family may be passed without much discussion. In 1969 a rider to the

School Capital Improvement Act ordered the Delaware Board of Education to give preference in school inspection to nonprofit organizations. Since there were only two bidders for the school inspection contract—a private firm named Daniel Koffler and Associates and a nonprofit group called the Delaware School Auxiliary (DSA)—the rider in effect directed the state to award school inspection contracts to the DSA rather than the lowest bidder. The DSA is a DuPont-run group, founded by Pierre S. du Pont in 1927. In addition to state contracts, DSA is funded by H. B. du Pont's Welfare Foundation, which gave DSA $183,000 in 1967 and $121,000 in 1968. For years, DSA had had exclusive rights to the school inspection contract for Delaware. But in 1965, the state opened school inspection to competitive bidding. On the basis of the lowest bid the school inspection contract was awarded to Koffler's private firm in 1967 and 1969. In response, Senator Dean Steele, a DuPont employee and friend of DSA's executive head, introduced the special interest legislation. Reynolds du Pont and W. Laird Stabler, both members of the DSA board, voted for this bill, which passed the state legislature.

While usually exercising their influence in the state legislature quietly and subtly, from time to time the DuPont Company and family boldly assert their immense power over legislators. After the Supreme Court ordered DuPont to divest itself of its General Motors stock because of antitrust violations, the DuPont legal department drew up legislation to provide special capital-gains treatment for the required sale. While the company said the law was necessary to protect all the widows and orphans holding DuPont stock from a decline in market value, the bill was more directly aimed at tax concessions for the DuPont family, taking away about $48 million from the state treasury. Attorney William S. Potter handled the bill in Dover with the assistance of Robert H. Richards, Jr., Alexander Nichols, William Poole, and Daniel Herrman. Potter took DuPont Company general counsel Charles A. Rittenhouse to see House speaker Sherman Tribbitt, who eventually introduced the DuPont-written legislation. According to a newspaper account: "Proponents of HB 513 did not debate; they had the votes. Support for the bill had been lined up by William S. Potter, Democratic national committeeman, and others." [21] The vote in the house was 31–2 and in the senate 15–1. The dissenting votes were all cast by downstate Democrats.

An even more blatant show of DuPont political power occurred on the university audit bill. In 1964 state budget director Earl McGinness decided, and the attorney general agreed, that his functions included examining the expenditures of the University of Delaware, since it received 80% of its funding from public sources. But the other 20% came mainly from the DuPonts, who wanted immunity from state audit. DuPont representatives drew up a bill that provided that the budget director could examine only the expenditure of funds supplied by the state, despite the obvious intermingling of private and public monies. To lobby for the bill, the university trustees arrived en masse on what is now known in Delaware legislative history as "Rolls Royce Day." According to several legislators, university trustee notables like James Tunnell and H. B. du Pont actually trod to the floor of the state legislature to buttonhole representatives. The bill passed quickly with only a few negative votes.

## *Environmental Politics*

The environment has become a major political issue in Delaware, as elsewhere in the country, within the last 10 years. Part of the DuPont Company's environmental philosophy is that a community has to compromise its ideals:

> Highly industrialized communities may have to balance benefits of industrial expansion against less than ideal conditions. . . . There may well be cases where a community has to decide which is more important for the time being: water as clean as it would like, or industry producing products and providing jobs. It can't always have it both ways.[22]

In Delaware neither is possible. DuPont has fought to weaken environmental laws against existing industries which are polluting the state's air and water. At the same time, members of the corporate elite have kept out new industries which, if the state had proper environmental protection laws, could have provided more jobs and tax revenues without ecological destruction.

All over the nation, DuPont has been involved in environmental issues: testifying at hearings, writing legislation, and supplying technical personnel. Asked why DuPont has been so active, Charles E. Welch, one of the company's leading spokesmen on pollution matters, said:

> DuPont has the greatest force of engineering specialists in this area. We have the greatest talent of any corporation. And, therefore, if you have those kind of forces and if you have the commitment to improve the environment, this company has taken the position that you ought to speak up and be constructive and do what you can.[23]

In the same vein, William J. Conner, New Castle County Executive and formerly chief environmental lobbyist in the DuPont legal department, noted three reasons why DuPont "exercised industrial statesmanship" on behalf of the chemical industry: the company's "missionary zeal," its previous expenditures in controlling pollution, and its desire to forestall onerous environmental regulations.

A good example of DuPont's "leadership" was its role in formulating Delaware's Water and Air Resources Act of 1966, which reorganized all the environmental statutes. DuPont supported the bill to obtain "good, effective state laws and agencies so that we don't get bad federal laws." [24] On behalf of DuPont, William Conner inserted Section 6203(b) into the bill; John C. Bryson, head of the Water Pollution Commission at the time, told the study group he had to accept the section to get the bill passed. The section expressed DuPont's basic line that there should be different environmental standards for different neighborhoods, despite the proximity of residential and industrial areas in Delaware: the commission must give "due recognition to . . . existing physical conditions, zoning classifications, topography and prevailing wind direction and speeds, and also the fact that a rule or regulation and the degree of conformance therewith which may be proper as to an essentially residential area of the State may not be proper as to a highly developed industrial area of the State."

Under the guise of consolidating procedural provisions, Conner greatly increased the delays in enforcement of the act. Section 6006 reads in part:

> Whenever the Commission determines that a person has violated any of the provisions of this Part, or any rule or regulation duly promulgated thereunder, or any order of the Commission, it *shall endeavor by conference, conciliation* or *persuasion* to obtain compliance with all requirements. [Emphasis added.]

In addition, Conner persuaded the legislators to require the commission to send a written warning to a polluter who did not agree to conciliation, then request him to appear before the commission, and finally allow an appeal of any commission ruling—each step giving the polluter at least 20 days notice. The act allows the commission to seek injunctive relief in courts only after it has run the gamut of conciliation, warning, appearance, and appeal.

The act's enforcement provisions permit special concessions and secrecy Section 6007 allows polluters to obtain variances * from any regulations promulgated under the act. The public hearings which the section calls for may be waived by an applicant for a variance or by the commission at its discretion. When public hearings are waived, Delaware citizens have no means of knowing who is seeking a variance or why. On the other hand, the act penalizes state employees who reveal pollution data to the public. Section 6014 says:

> It shall be a misdemeanor for any member of the Commission, any officer or employee thereof, or any person performing any function or work assigned to him by the Commission, to disclose any confidential information obtained pursuant to this Part or to use any information obtained pursuant to this Part for purposes other than the administration of the functions, responsibilities, and duties vested in the Commission by law.

* A variance, when granted to a polluter, allows a particular source of pollution to exceed the limits set by law. The DuPont Company applied for the first two variances under this provision, according to state officials. The DuPont Company had lobbied for an even more open-ended, permissive variance section, but state officials succeeded in having it removed from the bill.

Worse, Delaware residents have no way to force the commission to reveal data, since the state has no public information law.

The least used section of the act is 6013, which provides for a fine of "not more than $500 for each violation, failure or refusal [to obey a regulation]." A fine has never been levied under this section, and in any case the fines are too low to deter a corporate polluter. One of the few additional powers given the commission under the act was Section 6306, which allows *but does not require* that the polluter be ordered immediately to cease the discharges of harmful pollutants into waters when conditions are threatening to the public health. The commission has never used this power.

To administer this legislation, the Water and Air Resources Commission (WARC) was established. WARC was composed of two types of members—men with no expertise on environmental matters and industrial representatives. The first chairman of WARC was Loren H. Frye, vice president of the DuPont-controlled Wilmington Trust Company, who told the study group he knew nothing about air pollution at the time of his appointment. But Frye's vice-chairman was an expert: he was Harold L. Jacobs, a DuPont engineer from 1938 to 1967. Jacobs worked mainly on solid and liquid waste disposal for the company and had served as chairman of the Delaware Water Pollution Commission, one of WARC's ancestors.

Jacobs believed and defended DuPont's position on environmental matters. At a public hearing in Wilmington while Jacobs was vice-chairman of WARC, a speaker mentioned that a federal task force which included a DuPont vice president had recommended a greater reduction in industrial stack emissions than the proposed Delaware law would effect. Jacobs then explained that the company's position was not the same as that of the task force, even though the DuPont executive had signed the task force report. If Jacobs felt compelled to explain DuPont's position at a public hearing, there can be little doubt that he acted as a company propagandist in the closed sessions when the regulations for WARC were being formulated.

Furthermore, Jacobs tried to indoctrinate Chairman Frye into the DuPont viewpoint on pollution control. According to Chairman Frye, Jacobs would frequently introduce him to DuPont employees working on the company's environmental problems, who would sometimes lunch with Frye and Jacobs in the dining room or snack bar of the DuPont Building to discuss environmental control. These meetings must have made a large impact on Frye, since he was a novice in the pollution field. On the other hand, Frye seldom met with groups like the Delaware Citizens for Clean Air, which had other viewpoints on pollution.

Because most WARC board members lacked technical expertise, the state formed an air pollution advisory board, headed by Jacobs. DuPont also had on the advisory board William Chalker, one of its environmental experts and a member of the Dover Pollution Commission. Other members included George J. Pinto of Delmarva Power and Light, a major polluter, and Richard W. Ladd, environmental expert for Getty Oil Company, whose Delaware refinery is the worst air pollution source in the state.

With a weak environmental law and a commission beholden to the corporate establishment, enforcement of pollution control laws in Delaware was ineffective for years. From the early 1950s to 1969, WARC and its predecessors held fewer than 25 hearings on air and water pollution violations. Instead of prosecuting corporate violations of the law, the commission met periodically with industry to "anticipate their needs," according to a high WARC official. Not a single corporate air polluter has been fined under the 1966 Water and Air Resources Act, nor have air quality standards been enacted under it, though companies like Getty Oil and Delmarva Power and Light have had emissions which would probably be in violation of air quality regulations if sufficient data were available for a prosecution.* The commission has not sought a court

* In 1972, the state finally brought suit to enjoin Getty Oil from violating air quality standards.

injunction against a major air pollution source, even during air pollution alerts. Similarly, the commission has never prosecuted any corporate water polluter, though the DuPont Company has been dumping millions of gallons of poorly treated sulfuric acid waste into the Delaware River. Before 1971 the commission's only enforcement action in court was against three individuals with overflowing septic tanks. All three suits were dismissed on technical errors made by the commission, unaccustomed to enforcing its own laws.

In 1969 the revision of the Ambient Air Quality Standards, required by the federal government, marked the first victory for the environmental forces over DuPont and its corporate cohorts. Delaware's Air Pollution Advisory Board (APAB) proposed new standards in July, 1969, and hearings were held in September. APAB, dominated by industry, proposed standards following the DuPont-promoted concept of different standards for rural, residential, commercial, and industrial areas. But as many environmental groups pointed out at the hearings, every industrial and commercial area in the state is so close to residential areas that industrial pollution necessarily contaminates residential areas. At the September public hearings, the federal regional air pollution control director for Delaware explained that APAB's proposed standard for sulfur dioxide in industrial areas, including DuPont's Edgemoor plant, was far too high for public health. At the level proposed for a 24-hour concentration, plant life is damaged, visibility is reduced to less than five miles by sulfuric acid mist, absenteeism and hospital admissions increase, and deaths from bronchitis and lung cancer may be precipitated.

The proposed standards for *suspended particulates* were even more outrageous. The proposals were 75 $ug/m^3$ for residential neighborhoods, 90 $ug/m^3$ for commercial areas, and 110 $ug/m^3$ for industrial districts. According to the air quality criteria, any concentration of suspended particulates above 80 $ug/m^3$ results in an increased death rate and an accelerated corrosion rate for steel and zinc. Nevertheless, Dr. Frank Bodurtha, senior consultant on environmental control for the DuPont Company, said at the hearings:

> Our Company is committed to a policy of air pollution control which insures that DuPont's air emissions in this state will be controlled to a very high degree. This is, after all, our corporate home. . . . It is our considered opinion that the proposed revised air quality standards for these two contaminants will not only protect the public health and welfare but will also provide the citizens of Delaware with a substantial margin of safety.[25]

Bodurtha even claimed that "from 50 to as much as 90% of the concentrations of dirt and $SO_2$ where people live and breathe" is caused by sources other than industries and utilities.[26] But according to data collected by Delaware's Division of Environmental Control, industrial polluters emit 80% of the sulfur dioxide in northern New Castle County.

Because the public pressed and the federal government refused to approve the proposed regulations, WARC adopted tougher ambient air quality standards and abolished the four-area classification system for ambient air standards. The new regulations, including limits on carbon monoxide, photochemical oxidants, and hydrocarbons, were approved by the federal government.

The state also appointed a new chairman for WARC who is not so closely wedded to DuPont and a representative from the environmental health commitee of the Delaware Medical Society; less encouragingly, Jacobs was succeeded by an employee of Hercules. State government has taken a somewhat tougher stance against some polluters, but only after constant public and federal pressure. The commission has issued several letters and orders, preliminary to court action, to obtain compliance with various regulations; succeeded in getting several major air pollution sources to use low sulfur content fuel; and banned open-air burning in New Castle County.

The government framework for environmental enforcement in Delaware still leaves much to be desired. WARC was one of the few commissions which was not abolished by the executive reorganization of state government; instead, it retained commission status within the new Department of Natural Resources and Environmental Control. Most of the commission's powers were shifted to the new Division of Environmental Control, but no new state power was included in the transfer.

In 1970 and 1971, legislation was introduced to transfer the rest of the commission's power to the department and to strengthen many provisions of the weak state law. In an interview with the Delaware Study Group, Austin N. Heller, new secretary of the department, stated that one of the major reasons for introducing the bill was that sulfur dioxide levels in the state had not been lowered sufficiently after four years of government-industry co-operation. Businessmen successfully opposed the bill, claiming that complete transfer of WARC authority to the department would have given the department head almost dictatorial power. (Interestingly, corporate executives did not raise this argument against the reorganization of any other state agency.) Those parts of the bill strengthening the state's pollution control laws were also defeated.

While efforts to strengthen the state's pollution control laws have failed, the state has not staffed the new department with aggressive law enforcers. The secretary of the department, Austin N. Heller, came to Delaware from New York City, where he did not have a reputation for being an advocate of strong environmental enforcement despite his many years of experience in the environmental field. In an interview with the Delaware Study Group, Heller said his position is that government should do all it can to work in cooperative ways with industry, staying out of court as much as possible. Heller later said in a newspaper interview: "I feel that we can work with industry in this state to get them to set an example." [27]

In addition, Attorney General Laird Stabler, a DuPont family member, still believes that "the old things of conference, conciliation, and persuasion should be a part of" the state's efforts to stop pollution.[28] Neither the commission nor the department has its own attorney, and Stabler has assigned only one lawyer one day per week to work with them.

The need for strong regulations and strict enforcement of environmental laws are still very real in Delaware. As a recent newspaper article said:

> An analysis of a typical milk bottle full of river water from near the Delaware Memorial Bridge at the mouth of the Christiana River shows dissolved oxygen levels too little to support fish and certain bacteria counts four times the permissible drinking water standards.[29]

Delaware, New Jersey, and Philadelphia industries have contributed to this high level of water pollution. Significant amounts of oxygen-demanding wastes are pouring into the Delaware River from DuPont's Chambers Works, DuPont's Edgemoor plant, the Allied Chemical Corporation, and Wilmington's sewage treatment plant (see Chapter 2). Philadelphia firms contribute nearly 60% of the oxygen-demanding waste in the Delaware River. Yet when the Delaware River Basin Commission proposed water quality standards to limit discharges into the Delaware River, several large industries, including DuPont, spoke against them.

The level of air pollution in Delaware is often critical. According to figures from Delaware's Division of Environmental Control, the 350,000 people of New Castle County, and the industries located there, emit 200,000 tons of sulfur dioxide every year; the 10,000,000 residents of metropolitan New York, and industries there, put out 400,000 tons. In July, 1970, the whole Wilmington area was gripped in a week-long air pollution alert, intensified by atmospheric inversion and high temperatures. During this time, sulfur dioxide levels rose to as high as .4 parts per million, far above the .1 ppm which is the maximum level considered safe for personal health. The .4 ppm reading was recorded on the morning of July 28, 1970, by the state's Marine Terminal station, which monitors air pollution near DuPont's Edgemoor and Chambers Works plants and the Delmarva Power and Light plant at Cherry Island. The state invoked a 24-hour pollution watch which merely limited open burning and incinerator operations from 10 AM until 3 PM daily. But under existing Delaware law, the state could not have forced industrial plants to shut down, even if sulfur dioxide levels had been twice as high as they were.

### *The Power Elite's Opposition to New Industry*

At the same time that Delaware industry has fought strong pollution control, it has sought to keep out companies that would have brought increased employment and a broadened tax base. For years, members of the corporate elite have kept firms out of Delaware—except for corporate offices and chemical industry plants. According to a 1935 *Fortune* article, the DuPonts would not allow the Ford Motor Company to start a factory in Delaware because the Fords represented a threat to the DuPonts' political control of the state. Whenever a new firm planned to come to Wilmington, the Chamber of Commerce would consult Robert H. Richards (a director of Christiana Securities and a DuPont family lawyer and adviser) before deciding whether to encourage the move.[30] While some manufacturing plants came to Delaware after World War II, currently members of the corporate elite, often through GWDC, encourage white-collar offices instead of blue-collar factories which would undercut the power of the corporate class.

On the state level, the DuPont drive to maintain Delaware as a corporate headquarters state has resulted in the lowest expenditures of any state in the country on industrial development. In 1966 Delaware spent only $22,316 expressly for industrial development.[31] Both the Delaware Development Department (DDD) and the Delaware Industrial Building Commission (DIBC) have attempted to recruit new firms, but the state has not supported either group. Both agencies were initiated by downstate Democrats rather than Republicans (though nationwide the GOP is the traditional supporter of industrial recruitment). At the urging of Governor Carvel, a liberal Democrat from Sussex County, the state created the Development Department in 1949. In the first few years, Delaware appropriated very little money to the agency. Even by 1964 the department's budget was less than $100,000 and most of its activity involved the promotion of tourism. While the Development Department's budget increased to over

$700,000 by 1969, department officials still spent very little in bringing new businesses to the state.

The DIBC was designed to guarantee bank credit for new firms. A group of businessmen from Kent County, with the support of Governor Carvel, had the bill introduced in the General Assembly during 1961. It passed despite the opposition of the *News-Journal*.[32] The bill authorized the new agency to guarantee bonds up to $10 million to new businesses, with a maximum of $2 million to any single firm. In 1962 Attorney General Bove unsuccessfully attacked the DIBC as unconstitutional. While several concerns backed by the DIBC have closed, by 1968 DIBC officials could rightly claim that the commission had cost the state no money. The firms that folded eventually repaid the state; the successful firms provide 3294 new jobs, a payroll of over $17 million, and $318,000 in taxes. Nevertheless, the DIBC has been subjected to a continuous barrage of criticism from powerful politicians like State Senator Reynolds du Pont, and has not been able to obtain a $10 million increase in its bond authorization after exhausting the original appropriation.

Similarly, the state has not used its financial control over Farmers Bank to promote development. The state owns 49% of the common stock in Farmers Bank, one of Delaware's four biggest commercial banks. University of Delaware economists have recommended that the bank use its loans to promote business development. However, public officials have not acted to encourage the bank to do so. The bank has made little effort to attract new firms to Delaware and even refused to participate in the loan program of the Small Business Administration.

At the same time, DuPont-related individuals have succeeded in imposing their white-collar bias upon state planning efforts. H. B. du Pont was the key man in establishing the State Planning Office in the early 1960s. The initial State Planning Council included DuPont family member Samuel Homsey; H. B.; Charles Hackett of the family's News-Journal Company; and J. Allen Frear, Jr., an avid DuPont supporter while in the U.S. Senate. Both H. B. du Pont and Samuel Homsey were long-time advocates of land-use planning in Delaware, but their particular brand of planning is protecting family land from residential, commercial, and alien industrial incursions while leaving alone expansion of chemical industry office, research, and production facilities.

According to state officials, the planning council was dedicated to keeping heavy industry out of Delaware. Its land-use plans downplayed the role of blue-collar firms in developing the state. In early 1969, the council adopted a resolution opposing "obnoxious heavy industry"; but council members like H. B. du Pont did not move against corporate sources of pollution, like the DuPont company, already in the state. Nor did the council sort out firms by types and allocate sites by advanced planning techniques or strict environmental control standards. As Edward F. Spear of the Delaware Chamber of Commerce said, the council took an essentially "negative approach." [33]

Public concern for the environment has inadvertently added impetus to the corporate elite's efforts to maintain Delaware as a corporate headquarters state. Governor Russell W. Peterson, who told us he wanted Delaware to attract office complexes and keep out heavy industry, successfully utilized the support of environmental groups in gaining passage of a 1971 coastal zoning bill, over the opposition of local chemical firms. The bill bars certain types of heavy industry from Delaware's undeveloped coastline.

While the coastline bill is a laudable step toward ensuring a decent environment, it indirectly benefits the corporate elite. The law is fully consonant with land-planning concepts long urged by DuPont family members, who want to preserve their aristocratic playland. Nor will the bill hurt the DuPont Company very much, since the company's recent growth in Delaware has been concentrated in office, research, and light production facilities. Moreover, by barring industry from downstream sites, the law gives the upstream chemical plants a monopoly over available industrial land and use of the Delaware River for waste disposal purposes.

On the other hand, the coastline bill may have grave implications for public policy in Delaware. According to Peterson, the law in the short run will keep two major industrial complexes out of Delaware; in the long run, it will promote an atmosphere supportive of white-collar firms.[34] Thus, the law deprives Delaware of a significant increase in tax revenues at a time of urgent need for more public funds. And by limiting the growth of a blue-collar movement, the law reinforces the political strength of the corporate middle classes who continue to support the DuPont-dominated Republican party. A better strategy for Delaware would have been to ensure rational industrial growth throughout the state while stringently enforcing antipollution controls, together with increasing public expenditures on recreation facilities. Such a strategy would have improved the environment without taking away needed tax revenues or undercutting a viable two-party political system in Delaware.

CHAPTER 14

# Unequal Opportunity: State Finances

Delaware's corporate elite is so influential it determines government policy whether or not it actively exercises power. For years the DuPonts curtailed state government by not exercising power publicly and by providing various social services, such as hospitals, privately. As a result, the state treasury was small and state services were few. In the last decade, many corporate liberals have found that they must depend on state assistance to carry out many projects. These power brokers streamlined state government in the name of efficiency, facilitating their control. Taxes have been increased to pay for the additional services being provided by the state, at a higher cost to middle-income families. The upper-class and corporate executives have oriented many of these services toward their own interests, while ignoring the needs of lower-income residents. Partly as a result, Delaware was one of three states in the country where the number of people with income below the poverty level *increased* in the 1960s.[1] Today, Delaware combines an unusually high incidence of poverty with an unusually high incidence of great wealth. Despite slowly increasing revenues and a major reorganization of state government, Delaware endured a gigantic fiscal crisis in 1971.

## *Reorganization without Taxation: Delaware's Efficiency Crisis*

Shortly after his 1968 victory, Governor Russell W. Peterson reorganized state government along the lines of a corporate hierarchy. Peterson replaced the more than 100 semiautonomous state commissions with 10 cabinet-style departments. The key men in the reorganization, besides Peterson, were the chairman of the reorganization committee, E. Norman Veasey, a corporate lawyer whose best known client is the bankrupt Lammot du Pont Copeland, Jr., and the director of the task force on reorganization, Robert Halbrook, who resigned from DuPont just before taking the reorganization job.

The need for reorganization had been discussed as far back as 1918.[2] A plan like Peterson's was developed during Governor Elbert N. Carvel's first term, and in 1960 Governor Caleb Boggs proposed a "New Day for Delaware." Unlike these previous plans, Peterson's sailed through the state legislature, surprising even Robert Halbrook, who feared that this reorganization attempt would meet the fate of the earlier ones. The difference, of course, was the elite's involvement, which changed inertia to swift action. In the spring of 1970, the legislature passed the reorganization plan, which centralized power in the governor's hands. As Peterson claimed, he became the man responsible for the success or failure of state government. A proposed new state constitution will further increase the power of the executive by giving the governor the right to make certain statutory changes by executive order (subject to legislative veto) and providing that the governor's proposed budget becomes law if not approved by May 1.

While the reorganization and the new constitution may provide certain efficiency gains, they may also reduce the political accountability of state officials. As Senator J. William Fulbright has pointed out, certain slow-moving government procedures act as checks on abuses of power.[3] The plight of Emily Womach portends the inherent problems of centralized power. In November, 1970, Womach, the only Democrat elected in a statewide race, ousted the incumbent state treasurer, an ex-DuPont employee named Daniel J. Ross. Immediately after her victory, Womach and the voters learned that Governor Peterson's reorganization had transferred most of the treasurer's functions to a new appointive official, the director of the Division of the Treasury. The new appointee was Daniel J. Ross. The public's outrage forced the governor to restore some of the treasurer's powers, but the added authority was just a gift, unprotected by law.

Whether the reorganization was efficient or whether it worsened the state's fiscal situation came into serious question on June 28, 1971. On that date, Governor Peterson told an emergency session of the legislature that Delaware faced a $30-million deficit for the year, largely as a result of a colossal miscalculation of revenues from the corporate franchise tax. The official franchise tax revenue estimate was $62 million, but at the end of the fiscal year state officials discovered that only $52 million had been received. Administration officials blamed the error on understandable miscalculations; others say it resulted from a juggling of accounts the year before. Whatever the cause, the main question is how the error went unchecked.

Many factors contributed to the crisis. The reorganization centralized fiscal policy in the governor, further insulating him from citizens and officials who might have found something amiss.* A key factor was administration control of the supposedly independent, bipartisan Governor's Economic Advisory Council. Several members of the council told the study group that Secretary of Finance Joseph Cashman dominated the council, headed during the crucial period by Eugene R. Perry, a close Peterson associate. Cashman reportedly pressed the council to make more and more optimistic predictions of the state's financial future. Further, the weakened treasurer's office did not dare scrutinize state finances closely for fear that Governor

* Governor Peterson, asked "how could the experts make such a huge error?" could only reply, "It was done." [4]

Peterson would remove the authority he had informally given it.

The lack of a public information law and the characteristic somnolence of the state legislature further lessened control over Peterson's actions. As a *News-Journal* reporter explained:

> For the most part, the legislature's knowledge of how badly and why the state was in debt came solely from the governor—the chief of the executive branch. . . .
>
> [The legislature's] professional staff in charge of looking at finances consists of one man, whose main duty is to work with the coming year's budget.[5]

Delaware's long-established slavish reliance on and coddling of corporations contributed to the crisis, too. The corporate franchise tax is an inherently inconsistent revenue producer, due to business fluctuations, but it provides 13% of Delaware's budget, more than double the percentage in any other state. Compounding the inherent problems of depending on an undependable tax is the permissiveness caused by fear of losing the state's corporate benefactors. In Delaware, corporations can pay the franchise tax on the lower of two bases, the company's authorized shares of stock or its gross assets. If a firm has filed an annual report, it is billed on the lower of the two; if it has not filed a report it is billed on authorized shares. Between one-half and one-quarter of the firms incorporated in Delaware chose not to file a report, according to the corporation division, and these firms were consequently billed on authorized stock. However, many of these firms, particularly new ones, chose to base their payment on gross assets. Peterson himself mentioned one firm billed $50,000 based on stock which paid $181 based on assets.

Cashman feels that this failure to file was the main cause of the crisis.[6] By law, all firms are required to file; if they do not, they used to face a whopping $25 fine and an investigation. Secretary of State Eugene Bunting never carried out a single investigation as required by law, claiming that his office was understaffed. And for many firms, it was easier to pay the fine than to file. When the lack of filings became an issue *before the fiscal crisis was an-*

*nounced,* Peterson did not try to tighten up the law. Instead, he signed into law a bill suggested by the Delaware Bar Association, eliminating the required investigation of nonreporting firms.

## A HISTORY OF INEFFICIENCY AND UNDERFINANCING

The 1971 financial crisis is rooted in a long history of underfinanced state government. For decades Delaware taxes were low while both its average personal income levels and its levels of poverty were among the highest in the nation. The historic pattern of undertaxation is shown in Table 14-1.

TABLE 14-1.
*Comparison of Delaware Tax Revenue with National Average*

| | *Per Capita Revenue ($)* | | *Revenue per $1000 of Personal Income ($)* | |
|---|---|---|---|---|
| *Year* | *Delaware* | *US Average* | *Delaware* | *US Average* |
| 1957 | 206.68* | 224.11 | 73.77 | 109.69 |
| 1953 | 161.28 | 172.49 | 65.35 | 96.44 |
| 1942 | 69.17 | 77.79 | 54.21 | 85.10 |

SOURCE: "State and Local Government Finances in 1942 and 1957," p. 16; *State and Local Government Study* #43, 1959, Dept of Commerce.
* Figures are for state and local revenue combined.

To make up for undertaxation, state and local governments raised the tax rate—170% between 1957 and 1969, the highest increase in the nation.[7] But Delaware had the nation's twenty-ninth lowest dollar amount of taxes per person in 1969, compared to twelfth lowest in 1957. In 1968–1969 the average state collected $167.54 per $1000 of personal income; Delaware collected only $158.53.[8] As a University of Delaware study reported: "By national standards Delaware state and local governments have very high relative fiscal ability but have made average or below-average fiscal efforts."[9]

Delaware also has a long history of tax maladministration. In 1925 Pierre S. du Pont, concerned with the tax commission's failure to collect taxes, was appointed tax commissioner. He made a list of all tax delinquents, and pursued them relentlessly; tax revenues increased greatly. But after Pierre quit, the tax department sank to its old level. A 1965 report by the governor's Revenue Study Committee said: "Based upon a limited study of the State Tax Department, there is evidence of serious weaknesses in tax administration programs."[10] State legislator John Billingsley, not the tax department, uncovered a $2-million manufacturers' license tax deficiency on the part of the General Motors assembly plant * in Delaware.[11]

With a relatively low tax level and an inept tax administration, state government in Delaware has built up an impressive record of debt. Debt service—the principal, interest, and administration costs of state bonded indebtedness—rose from 12.9% of total general state expenditures in 1954 to 18.6% in 1964. In 1963 Delaware's long-term state and local debt outstanding was $796 per capita, an amount exceeded only by the state of Washington. The debt situation had worsened by 1967. Delaware had more than twice the debt of the average state.[12]

Nor has Delaware aggressively sought assistance from the federal government to supplement state revenues, as a result of Delaware's traditional distaste for federal intervention. A federal study of intergovernmental revenues in three representative years (1942, 1953, and 1957) showed Delaware receiving less federal money than any other state in each year, even though its population was not the smallest.[13] In 1967 Delaware got only $72.87 in federal money per capita, while the national average was $77.68 per capita. In 1969 Delaware was even further behind, with only $78 per capita from the federal government, compared with a national average of $100 per capita.[14] The gap continued to widen in 1970, when per capita federal grants to Delaware were $93, while the national average had risen to $119.[15]

## *Response to the Crisis: Too Little, Too Late*

The state met the 1971 fiscal crisis with a $9.2-million budget cut and tax increases of $19.35 million. Across-the-board budget cuts were made, with emphasis on cutting back new programs, such as reform of the family court and a new drug abuse program. Taxes were imposed or

* General Motors has now paid $1.2 million of the tax under protest.

raised in 12 areas, from gasoline and cigarettes to corporate and personal income. The changes were in the right direction, but not far enough. In the past, Delaware has managed to avoid the sharply regressive state sales tax,* while, however, making tax concessions to wealthy individuals and corporations. The changes modified some of the concessions, but none were abolished, and the new taxes fall mainly upon consumers. The rise in taxes on corporations and the wealthy will yield only $4.4 million, but new consumer taxes will yield $14 million or more.

### TAX CONCESSIONS FOR THE RICH

The state's largest source of revenue is the personal income tax, in theory one of the more progressive state income taxes in the country. But at least until the 1971 tax reforms, progressivity in practice ended around $30,000, as shown by Table 14-2.

The 1971 tax changes created new tax rates above $20,000. The highest rate, as Table 14-3 shows, is now 18% on income above $100,000, with rates between $20,000 and $100,000 more steeply graduated.

Other tax concessions to the rich have been slightly changed as a result of the legislature's response to Delaware's fiscal crisis in 1971. Traditionally, Delaware has levied extremely low death and inheritance tax rates; as of 1969, these rates had not been raised since 1937. Nearly every state with such taxes had higher tax rates. Even the new death tax rates are lower than those of most other states, and the maximum rate on bequests to a spouse was not raised; it is still lower than in 27 of the 36 other states with inheritance taxes. The maximum rate on bequests to children was raised only two points to 6%, still lower than in 31 other states.[16] Since 90% or more of bequests are made to either spouse, or children, the increased inheritance tax rates enacted by the Delaware legislature have little effect.

A major concession to the wealthy in Delaware has been the lack of a state gift tax. Under the pressure of

* There is one exception—a "hidden sales tax" in the form of a ¾% mercantile tax instituted by the Peterson administration in 1969.

TABLE 14-2.
*Effective Delaware Personal Income Taxation, 1967*

| *Gross Income Brackets ($)* | *Average Effective Rate (%)* | *Posted Rate* |
|---|---|---|
| 0–3,999 | 1.0 | 1½% to $1,000<br>2% for $1,001–2,000<br>3% for $2,001–3,000 |
| 4,000–5,999 | 1.6 | 4% for $3,001–4,000<br>5% for $4,001–5,000<br>6% for $5,001–6,000 |
| 6,000–8,999 | 2.0 | 7% for $6,001–8,000 |
| 9,000–11,999 | 3.0 | 8% for $8,001–30,000 |
| 12,000–14,999 | 3.6 | |
| 15,000–17,999 | 4.3 | |
| 18,000–20,999 | 4.2 | |
| 21,000–25,999 | 5.2 | |
| 26,000–30,999 | 5.6 | |
| 31,000–40,999 | 6.4 | 9% for $30,001–50,000 |
| 41,000–49,999 | 6.8 | |
| 51,000–60,999 | 6.3 | |
| 61,000–70,999 | 6.7 | 10% for $50,001–100,000 |
| 71,000–79,999 | 6.9 | |
| 81,000–99,999 | 5.6 | |
| 200,000–225,000* | 6.8 | 11% above $100,001 |

* Data for incomes above $225,000 were not available.
SOURCE: *Public Choice in the Delaware Economy,* U. of Delaware, 1969, p. 10.

TABLE 14-3.
*Results of 1971 Tax Changes*

| *Previous Posted Tax Rate* | *New Tax Rate* |
|---|---|
| 8% for $8,000–30,000 | 8% for $8,001–20,000<br>8.5% for $20,001–25,000<br>9% for $25,001–30,000 |
| 9% for $30,001–50,000 | 11% for $30,001–40,000<br>12% for $40,001–50,000 |
| 10% for $50,001–100,000 | 14% for $50,001–75,000<br>15% for $75,001–100,000 |
| 11% for $100,001 and up | 18% for $100,001 and up |

* SOURCE: "Special Report," *Delaware Tax Reports* (Commerce Clearing House, August 4, 1971).

financial breakdown in 1971, a gift tax was enacted. The new rates are shown in Table 14-4. While a gift tax is not ordinarily a large revenue producer, there is strong evidence that the gift tax in Delaware will yield substantial sums.

TABLE 14-4
*Delaware Gift Tax*

| *Taxable Amount** ($) | *Tax Rates* (%) |
|---|---|
| 1–25,000 | 1 |
| 25,001–50,000 | 2 |
| 50,001–75,000 | 3 |
| 75,001–100,000 | 4 |
| 100,001–200,000 | 5 |
| 200,001 and up | 6 |

* Based on amount taxable under federal rates, except $30,000 lifetime exclusion is not allowed.
SOURCE: "Special Report," *Delaware Tax Reports* (Commerce Clearing House, August 4, 1971).

According to a 1969 study done by a university of Delaware economist, in Delaware one dollar in federal gift tax is paid for two dollars in federal estate tax, while the national average was one to eight. This ratio suggests that the DuPonts and other rich Delawareans avoid federal and state death taxes by giving their money away before they die. Furthermore, Delaware law requires that a donor need live only six months after his gift is made to preclude taxation on the estate, rather than the two years required by many states or the three years stipulated for federal exclusion. The tax reform did not affect this. Thus, it is easy for wealthy individuals to make substantial gifts and not pay state taxes on the transfers.

Changes in death and gift taxes have been advocated for several years by local economists and government advisers. In *Public Choice in the Delaware Economy,* a 1969 University of Delaware study, economists maintained that doubling inheritance taxes would produce $1 million in income and "still leave Delaware in the category of low death-tax states." [17] The authors also suggested ending Delaware's exemption of life insurance policies, which are taxed in 20 states, from death taxes, arguing: "Exclusion favors one form of investment over another and ending this discrimination would produce between $230,000 and $1.1 million in additional revenue."[18] Along the same lines, the 1965 Revenue Study Committee recommended a gift tax, which the committee felt would yield $500,000 if set at the same level as the inheritance tax, and would reduce the incentive for wealthy individuals to avoid death taxes by making huge gifts.

According to many state legislators, economists, and others, the main reason for past inaction on tax reform has been the fear that the DuPonts would leave the state if higher rates were imposed. The spectre of wealthy DuPonts choosing to die elsewhere has had an extremely chilling effect on tax legislation in Delaware. In fact, the fear is a chimera. In an interview with the study group, Congressman Pierre S. du Pont IV said that tax rates are only one of a multitude of factors determining where family members live. DuPont's opinion is shared by the authors of *Public Choice:*

> The fear that an increased inheritance tax will cause some persons to relocate in other states can be over-emphasized by lack of perspective. Relocation is not a certain result. Many factors influence the decision to reside in Delaware and death taxes do not have the same relative importance for all persons. With increasing age and wealth, some persons might seriously consider relocating in other states. For estates large enough to benefit from the federal estate tax credit, a higher Delaware inheritance tax would be offset by a larger credit against federal estate tax liability and a reduced pickup tax.* The combined state and federal tax would stay the same.
>
> For persons not wealthy enough to benefit from the federal estate tax credit, it might pay to relocate in another state. But this choice is open to them now. The factors governing their choice to reside in Delaware will likely prevail even if the inheritance tax is increased. Even if some persons do relocate, the loss of their inheritance taxes would be offset by an increased tax paid by other estates.[19]

One of the few Delaware tax provisions which did not favor the rich was eliminated in 1970. For years Delaware

* Tax imposed by a state that amounts to the difference between the maximum federal estate tax allowable and the amount of federal estate tax actually levied.

had taxed capital gains—income from the sale of stocks and bonds—on the same scale as other income; federal law allows a lower tax rate for capital gains. Because the wealthy derive most of their income from investments, not salary, the corporate elite tried for many years to get Delaware to follow the federal setup. But it was not until Peterson put his weight behind a bill treating capital gains more leniently that legislators adopted the federal formula.

The immediate outcome of the new capital gains law, achieved through subterfuge * with the overwhelming support of DuPont-related legislators, will be a great loss of income to the state government. The new bill further distributes wealth toward the very rich and rewards those who derive their income by selling stocks instead of those who earn their livelihood by working each day for a salary. Because of its expected adverse impact on state revenues, the law provided that it would not be effective until January, 1972. Therefore, the new law had not gone into operation when the state fiscal crisis arose. Allen Cook, the Democratic Senate leader, proposed repealing the new treatment of capital gains in light of the fiscal crisis; his suggestion was brushed aside, as was a bill postponing the effective date of the new law.

A final tax advantage to the very wealthy in Delaware is the total absence of a personal property tax. Personal property consists of movable, tangible objects such as jewelry and furniture, and intangible objects, such as stocks and bonds. Only 6 states, including Delaware, tax no personal property. According to the *State Tax Guide, All States,* 25 states tax either household goods, personal effects, jewelry, vehicles, stocks and bonds, or all personal property, with exemptions and deductions ranging from $5000 for all types of personal property in Massachusetts to $100 exemption for jewelry and a total exemption of household goods and personal effects in Mississippi. Montana, Ne-

* In 1967 Delaware legislator George Hering convened a meeting of Wilmington tax lawyers to discuss the state's capital gains law. As a result of this meeting, corporate tax attorney Johannes Krahmer was assigned to rewrite the Delaware personal income tax law. Krahmer's revision was presented and sold to the public as a "simplification" because it based state tax payments on federally determined gross adjusted income. Sponsors of the bill seldom mentioned that the new approach meant a reduction in capital gains taxes.

braska, Nevada, and 6 other states exempt no personal property. Maryland taxes only jewelry, while Arkansas, Indiana, Florida, Louisiana, Missouri, and others tax intangible property. The lack of personal property tax in Delaware works to the particular advantage of the corporate elite. For a typical Delaware resident, personal property is relatively small, his major investments are his house and land, both of which are taxed as property. In contrast, the wealth of most DuPonts is concentrated in stocks, bonds, jewelry, and other property not subject to taxes. For instance, Crawford Greenewalt and his wife own property worth $20–30 million, yet pay property taxes on only 1–2% of their holdings.

Just as Delaware's personal income tax is fairly equitable *compared to other states,* so is the corporate income tax. However, Delaware's corporate taxation favors firms like DuPont that have high profit levels, large investments in business equipment, and a high number of shares. As a Delaware Chamber of Commerce publication said: "The tax structure of the state is equitable and business-oriented."[20] One-half of this curious balance is the corporate income tax, plus a surcharge added during the fiscal crisis. The other half is that many types of business property are not taxed, as the local chamber of commerce says:

> Delaware has a tax structure, a governmental and judicial attitude toward business, which has found a happy combination between business-orientation and people-orientation. The state has no tax on securities or personal property. There is no stock transfer tax, no state real estate tax, no tax on goods in process, machinery, equipment, or raw materials. . . . Compared to the strangulating tax structure of many other states, Delaware's tax laws are not restrictive and are eminently fair to industry.[21]

One key benefit to Delaware corporations is the absence of a business personal property tax; this legal gap is especially advantageous to the DuPont Company and the capital-intensive chemical industry in general. In firms like DuPont, a significant portion of capital investment goes into machinery, process equipment, and research laboratory facilities; none of these items are taxed in Delaware.

Delaware companies also benefit from the low price they pay to incorporate in the state, compared to the advantages they reap from Delaware's favorable corporation law and friendly courts. As one tax authority put it, "If the franchise tax is viewed as the price paid for the benefits of incorporating under Delaware law, benefits have increased substantially, especially from the 1967 revisions, while the real price has decreased." [22] The franchise tax was not raised for many years because legislators believed corporations would incorporate elsewhere rather than pay a higher tax. But as the governor's fiscal study committee of 1969 concluded:

> The established body of corporation laws and court decisions in Delaware—not the corporation franchise tax—is the controlling factor in explaining why . . . approximately one-half of the nation's 100 largest industrial enterprises [are incorporated in Delaware].[23]

The committee recommended raising the maximum tax from $100,000 to $200,000, especially since half the increase would be offset by a federal tax reduction. The legislature merely raised the maximum to $110,000. During the 1971 crisis, the legislature considered and rejected the recommended increase to $200,000, which would have applied to 30 large companies, including DuPont, and produced about $2.7 million in revenue. One legislator told the study group that legislators did not pass a maximum rate of $200,000 because they "did not want to kill the goose that laid the golden egg": this fear of a corporate pullout is much like the dread that the DuPont family would move if personal death taxes were raised. With fear uppermost in their minds, legislators could not rationally consider the Brams report which argued: "It is reasonable to conclude that an increased franchise tax will impose minimum restraints on the economic growth of Delaware while maximizing revenue." [24]

In addition to these long-standing corporate tax concessions, Delaware recently passed two new ones. In 1970, House Bill 680 reduced taxes on flat racing by cutting the state's share of revenues from pari-mutuel betting because the only flat-racing track of any significance in

Delaware, Delaware Park, was running at a loss. Delaware Park is owned by the Delaware Racing Association—a nonprofit group formed and run by the DuPont family; family members use the track to race their horses. Any profits from the track are given to Delaware hospitals. W. Laird Stabler, Jr.—an old friend of Baird Brittingham, a director of the Delaware Racing Association—introduced HB 680. The bill passed unanimously. Most legislators voted for it because Delaware Park profits go to hospitals. But they did not consider the fact that operation of the track is a subsidy to race horse owners, that horse racing provides tax losses and deductions for wealthy horse owners like the DuPonts, or that Delaware hospitals might be better served with public funds. To the legislators' credit, after the fiscal crisis, the tax reduction for Delaware Park was cut in half and delayed one year.

Even during the fiscal crisis, the legislature did not repeal the other tax concession, made to encourage paternalistic giving in Delaware. In 1968 state legislator George Hering introduced a bill to encourage corporate giving to private groups. As one politico said, corporate executives may not have asked Hering to submit the legislation, but they were quite happy when he did. Hering's bill, the Neighborhood Assistance Act, allows firms paying Delaware corporate income tax to deduct up to $50,000 a year from their tax bills if the money is donated to certified nonprofit community organizations (see Chapter 8). Any unused tax credit can be carried into subsequent years until the entire credit is used. State Tax Commisioner James Kennedy told the Delaware Study Group that mainly the big firms —DuPont, Atlas, Hercules, and Diamond State Telephone —take advantage of the act. But exact information is not available to the public since the attorney general has ruled that data on corporate use of the Neighborhood Assistance Act are confidential. The citizens of Delaware have no way of finding out how much money the big companies are channelling at public expense to nonprofit groups, like the Greater Wilmington Development Council, run by corporate executives.

In short, while the *general* structure of Delaware personal and corporate taxes has been equitable relative to other states, Delaware state government consistently has collected low taxes and has been chronically in great debt. The state's tax laws have been riddled with special concessions to wealthy individuals and large firms like DuPont. Even under the pressure of the 1971 fiscal crisis, legislators eliminated some of the flagrant tax concessions to the corporate elite. After several years of upper-class resistance to progressive tax proposals, the legislature finally increased taxes on personal income above $20,000, enacted a gift tax, and increased the inheritance tax. However, major concessions remained intact, and the new capital gains rates add to them. The legislature did not raise the maximum franchise tax, the new death taxes are still below those of other states, and the 1971 changes placed a much greater burden on consumers than on corporations or wealthy individuals. And Delaware still has no tax on personal property for individuals or corporations, a legal gap especially beneficial to the corporate elite.

### *State Expenditures: Cars or People?*

Even before the 1971 fiscal crisis, the inequities in Delaware's tax structure deprived the state of enough money to meet the needs of all its citizens. The cash shortage means that the state must choose among a vast array of competing political bidders—and the corporate establishment has usually come out the winner.

The most important administrative agency in Delaware is the Department of Highways and Transportation, formerly the Highway Department. Despite Delaware's small size, its "highway spending is more than twice as much as in neighboring states, and higher than the median for all states." [25] In 1969 the Engineering and Controller divisions alone spent nearly 10% of the state budget. The highway department is so strong that it was one of the few agencies successfully to resist Governor Peterson's administrative reorganization.

The DuPont family and company have been closely tied to the highway department since its beginning. In 1912 T. Coleman du Pont decided to build a highway from

Wilmington to Delaware's southern border.* After spending $5 million of his own money, Coleman cajoled the state into creating a highway department to finish the job and became the first commissioner of the department. Coleman was succeeded by his son, Francis V. du Pont, who served as chairman for much of the time between 1922 and 1949. During this period, C. Douglass Buck, Francis's brother-in-law, was the highway department's chief engineer before becoming governor in the early 1930s. Four years after Francis retired, family member Hugh R. Sharp, Jr., took over the reins of the Highway Commission, serving until 1961 and as chairman from 1953 to 1955. In the 1960s, family member J. H. Tyler McConnell and employee Frank Mackie continued the line. The present chairman is DuPont employee Charles S. Eller, who joined the council with Frances DeDominicis, wife of a DuPont scientist. The head of the new Department of Highways and Transportation is A. Kirk Mearns, Jr., on leave of absence from the DuPont-owned Delaware Trust Company.

The programs of the highway department have reflected its leadership. Hugh Sharp was the key man in rallying prohighway forces in the mid-1950s, after an initial route for I-95 was rejected. The route, through the center of Wilmington, destroyed a large working-class neighborhood to serve corporate commuters. The highway department could have planned a route circumventing Wilmington that would have been a catalyst to developing the port area.

Like I-95, the currently proposed Route 141 is meant to serve mainly the employees of DuPont and other large chemical firms, according to Ernest Davidson, the department's chief engineer. As Map 5 shows, large facilities of DuPont, Atlas, and Hercules are located on Route 141. By making 141 into a superhighway, the state will reduce travel time for employees. It will also facilitate transportation of employees and materials between various DuPont

* Coleman's philanthropy was not fully appreciated; in fact, it had to be forced down the throats of Kent and Sussex citizens who feared maintenance of the road would greatly increase their taxes. When farmers refused rights-of-way to Coleman, he triumphed by threatening to obtain court injunctions.

installations along the route. Only 3% of 141 traffic will be interstate.

On the other hand, the building of 141 will significantly increase air pollution, dislocate hundreds of families and businesses, and run smack through the residential and commercial center of the small town of Newport. The highway may also destroy the residential and commercial districts along Concord Pike, the planned route for extension of 141 from north of Wilmington into Pennsylvania. After the residents and merchants vehemently protested the Concord Pike Route at a public hearing, the department undertook a $50,000 study of alternative route A (see map 5) through the DuPont Country Club. But according to Davidson, the department will never consider alternative A seriously, so the survey wasted $50,000 of the taxpayers' money.

In contrast, members of the corporate elite have been very effective in rerouting or stopping highways planned near their homes. An alternate route for 141 through chateau country (B) was found "infeasible." The approved 141 plan originally had a four-leaf-clover intersection near the house of Tyler McConnell. After much pressure from McConnell, the highway department changed the plan: the intersection near McConnell's house will be one of the few three-leaf clovers in highway history. Instead of a fourth ramp into an underpass, there will be a stoplight in the middle of Kennett Pike for left turns to 141 eastbound traffic. The highway department estimates each traveler will sacrifice one minute a day to Tyler McConnell; multiplied by 20,000 cars per day, the tribute equals over 110,000 hours per year. Once the highway officials changed their plan, McConnell gallantly donated some land to the department.

The routing of I-95 and 141 exemplified the power of the upper class to prevent intrusions into chateau country. The upper class even was able to stop one highway altogether—a scenic road along the Brandywine River, the eastern border of chateau country, proposed by Mrs. Lyndon Johnson in the mid-1960s. According to Pierre S. du Pont IV, residents of the area, working through the Brandywine Valley Conservation Association and the

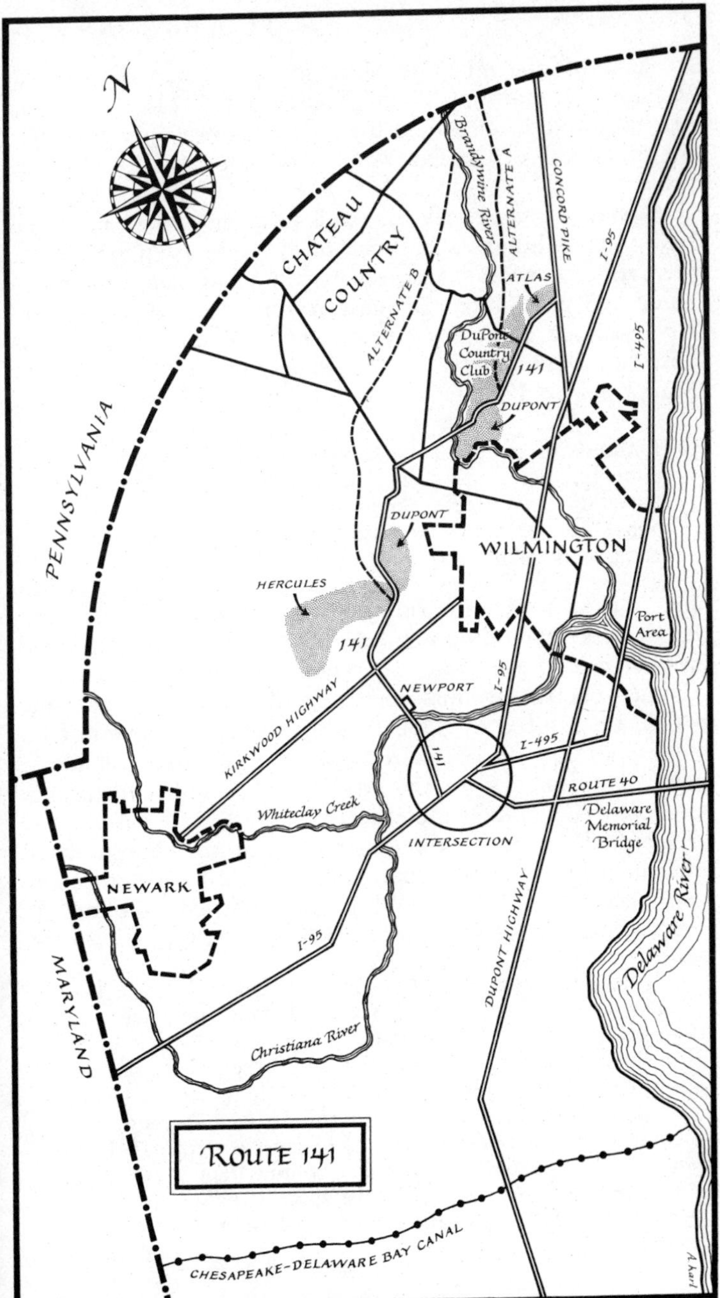
N
PENNSYLVANIA
CHATEAU
COUNTRY
ALTERNATE B
Brandywine River
ALTERNATE A
CONCORD PIKE
I-95
ATLAS
DuPont
Country
Club
141
DUPONT
I-495
DUPONT
WILMINGTON
HERCULES
141
Port
Area
KIRKWOOD HIGHWAY
NEWPORT
I-95
141
I-495
ROUTE 40
Delaware
Memorial
Bridge
Whiteclay Creek
INTERSECTION
NEWARK
I-95
DUPONT HIGHWAY
Delaware River
MARYLAND
Christiana River
ROUTE 141
CHESAPEAKE-DELAWARE BAY CANAL
A. Karl

trustees of the Hagley Museum, persuaded Governor William Scranton of Pennsylvania to tell Mrs. Johnson his state would not extend the scenic highway one inch on the other side of the Delaware; Mrs. Johnson dropped the project.

As state residents pay for roads to carry traffic to corporate office buildings and choke on the exhaust fumes from the cars of corporate researchers, they may begin to think about the possibilities of mass transit. The autoless poor have suffered especially great losses because of Delaware's obsession with highways. The state's own Comprehensive Manpower Study points out:

> Hundreds of potential workers in center city Wilmington residential areas are denied job opportunities simply because they cannot get to and from work. Others are forced to give up jobs when the persons they ride with quit or are fired from jobs in the same firm or area.[26]

In 1964, 68% of those riding buses in Wilmington did not have access to an automobile.[27] If an adequate mass transit system were developed for Wilmington and New Castle County, planners estimate the demand for off-street parking would be reduced by 2500 to 3000 spaces; congestion and auto pollution would be reduced; and suburban employment opportunities for the poor, young, handicapped, and unemployed would be increased.[28]

Despite the poor prospects for a future without mass transit, transportation department officials have not begun one mass transit project. Without a "total commitment to mass transit" in Wilmington, matters will only get worse:

> [There will be] more congestion and delay than we have today . . . a higher level of air pollution (the magnitude of vehicle trips will more than double by 1985), a dilemma in downtown Wilmington that would necessitate constructing over 7000 additional off-street parking spaces (this is in addition to 4000 new spaces for the new shopping mall and governmental complex) at an average cost of $4000 per space ($28 million), and a continuation of the land-consuming, auto-oriented development pattern that has been in evidence since the end of World War II.[29]

The state has ignored not only mass transit: it provides a very low level of all social services for low-income residents. The 1970 budget for the highway department was over $30 million; the cost of all programs carried out in 1970 by those agencies now included in the new Department of Community Affairs and Economic Development (CAED) was only $1 million. Yet CAED, according to the Governor's Reorganization Task Force, is supposed to direct all "programs that bear upon unmet needs—poverty, inadequate housing, unemployment, discrimination, consumer." Nor has Delaware taken full advantage of federal programs to serve the needy. For instance, although the food commodities program to give out surplus farm products began during the 1930s, Delaware was one of only four states without the program in 1958. Delaware is one of four nonparticipating states in the federal government's food stamp program.

One of the reasons for the low level of state social services is DuPont paternalism, substituting private charity for public effort, which has produced several debilitating effects on Delaware society. First, a small group of rich people make all the important decisions in relation to important community functions. Second, the sporadic, irrational nature of private charity denies poor families the planned, long-term commitment to social improvement they need. And third, reliance on private groups insulated from public control forestalls development of a lobby to press for adequate public services. As political scientist Paul Dolan, a University of Delaware professor sympathetic to the DuPonts, wrote:

> As a result of private largess, apathy on the part of the general public may result. The average citizen is apt to forego his duty in seeing to it that public welfare needs are met by public funds when he has the feeling that private charity may be doing part of the job. If private citizens continue to bear a disproportionate share of the cost of maintaining welfare services, some of the basic assumptions respecting administrative responsibility in a democracy will be challenged. . . . There are steady indications, however, that private support cannot meet the challenge

posed by the changing social and economic picture in the state.[30]

The problems of noblesse oblige are not just theoretical. In 1969, 18% of all housing units in Delaware were substandard. Despite the construction of large numbers of new homes, shelter conditions are improving very slowly. Between 1960 and 1970, there was only a 2% decrease in substandard houses in Delaware. The housing shortage is especially acute in the two southern counties—21% substandard in Kent and 34% in Sussex.

Recently, the state established a 10-year plan calling for 20,000 units to be replaced by the end of the decade. To finance this timetable, the state set up a $5-million development fund. But Robert Moyer, director of the state Division of Housing said: "A little arithmetic will prove that the $5-million development fund won't come close to meeting the 10-year timetable." [31] Moyer estimated that the development fund could support the construction of fewer than 2000 homes in the next decade. To make matters worse, the Division of Housing has concentrated 90% of its aid in the two cities in which DuPont is centered, Wilmington and Seaford. The largest single recipient of the division's funds is the Greater Wilmington Housing Corporation, would could raise private money more easily than any other housing sponsor in Delaware. Yet GWHC received the public funds sorely needed by others.

Like housing, state medical care is grossly inadequate. Delaware and Vermont are the only states in the country without state-funded public general hospitals. The state has "a very weak Medicaid program" and "practically no mechanism" for providing care for those individuals who do not meet the eligibility requirements of Title XIX of the Social Security Act.[32] Medical care in Wilmington is particularly insufficient for low-income residents. At a meeting on August 27, 1970, chaired by State Senator Herman Holloway, community residents brought charges of racism against the Wilmington Medical Center. Investigating these charges at the request of community groups, Sociometrics, Inc., found vestiges of racism from the pre-

1960 era. At that time, "the Medical Center did function pretty much as a 'plantation,' maintaining up until 1957–58 separate facilities for its Caucasian, black, and other minority patients." [33] The major problem now, according to the consultant group, is that the poor are forced to use the emergency room doctor as their primary physician. Neither the city nor the state has constructed medical facilities for Wilmington residents; on the other hand, "providing adequate health services, emergency and comprehensive, from all indications are [sic] beyond the capability of the Wilmington Medical Center." [34]

State care of the mentally ill is no better. Dr. Albert Ingram, head of health services for Delaware, said that the conditions in Delaware State Hospital, the major public institution for the mentally ill, were "appalling." [35] Dr. Kurt Anstreicher, superintendent of that hospital, was more explicit:

> We have reached a point where the remaining members of the staff are tempted, if not forced, to leave because of increasing frustration and overwork. Our patients continue to be adversely affected by the existing weaknesses in the services offered and by the absence of additional needed programs. The staffing situation in many divisions and services of the hospital is critical.[36]

The results of DuPont paternalism and public apathy are writ large on the map of New Castle County.[37] By far the highest infant mortality rates are in the census tracts for blacks and lower-class whites who must depend on the emergency facilities of private hospitals for medical care. In contrast, the residents of Brandywine, Christiana, and Mill Creek hundreds, who can afford private doctor fees, have extremely low infant death rates. Similarly, the highest incidence of mental illness is in the census tracts of poor whites and blacks.

While Delaware has always had a high per capita income, it has traditionally failed to provide even subsistence to needy families. Between 1960 and 1970, despite some increases in welfare expenditures, Delaware lagged far behind the national average (see Table 14-5).

TABLE 14-5.
*Welfare Expenditures Per Recipient (June, 1970)*

| *Type of Welfare* | *Delaware* (*$*) | *US Average* (*$*) |
|---|---|---|
| Old age assistance | 73.80 | 74.95 |
| Aid to families with unemployed parents | 32.52 | 45.50 |
| Aid to families with dependent children | 34.50 | 45.85 |
| General assistance | 29.48 | 50.95 |

SOURCE: Delaware Division of Special Services (June, 1970, Bulletin).

At the same time that it was making below-average welfare payments, Delaware had one of the lowest decreases in poverty rate in the country, dropping from 16.8% of the state's population in 1959 to 15.7% in 1969. The number of poor Delawareans rose from 73,000 to 85,000 in the 10-year period. The national rate dropped from 22.1% to 12.3% of the population in the same period.[38] Federal officials recently found Delaware's legal ceiling on welfare benefits to be too low to meet federal standards and threatened Delaware with a court suit to cut off all welfare payments. State officials therefore pressed the legislature to raise the legal ceiling, but the legislators would not act until they were assured that not one additional dollar would actually go to any welfare recipient. The bill passed in 1970, after the top welfare official

> promised that his department was only interested in raising the ceiling because of the federal threat, that his department neither had the financial resources nor the intent of paying out any more money than the present schedule stipulated.[39]

Despite the high incidence of poverty in the state, Delaware can easily afford to spend more for welfare. The state ranks ninth in per capita income; but Delaware spends only 5.1% of its state budget on welfare, compared to a national average of 8.4%.

Like the welfare department, the state agency concerned with industrial safety had to be prodded into action by the federal government. Up to 1971 the state had only one man to inspect 15,000 businesses in Delaware for violations of safety regulations. The results were well described by

Willard Wirtz, Secretary of Labor: "Delaware was one of two states without any identifiable program to protect the health and safety of its working people."[40] State officials seemed willing to rely on the efforts of private industry to police their own safety equipment. Local companies supported the Delaware Safety Council, a private group whose board of directors included DuPont's Experimental Station site manager. The inadequacy of private policing was indicated by the initial findings of the state's new industrial hygienist, just retired from the DuPont Company. He found that the first 20 businesses he inspected had safety violations. With the passage of the 1970 federal Occupational Safety and Health Act, the state government was pushed into action. In 1971 two more inspectors were added, an improvement which leaves Delaware just ahead of the two inspectors working for the Chrysler plant in Newark, Delaware, and far behind another small state, Rhode Island, which has 20 inspectors.[41]

Because Delaware has such a poor safety program, the state benefits paid under the Workmen's Compensation Law for industrial accidents are very important. Delaware has the lowest ratio of maximum weekly benefits to average weekly wages in the country: the Delaware median ratio is 36.7% compared to a national average of 51%.[42] According to Bruce Ralston, a Delaware Chamber of Commerce representative, Delaware meets only 14 of 23 standards set by the International Association of Industrial Accident Boards and Commissions.

While Delaware has refused to provide enough money for housing, health, welfare, or safety programs, Governor Peterson gave crime control first priority in his "Future of the State" message of January, 1970. Peterson spoke glowingly of the renaming and revitalization of the Law Enforcement Planning Agency to the Agency to Reduce Crime. He said the agency was slated for a $528,000 grant from Washington under the Safe Streets Act. While the agency got the money, the governor's high hopes for cutting crime were dashed by a federal report saying the agency's plan to reduce crime "showed little creativity," and lacked adequate statistics.[43]

Instead of "Crime in the Streets," Governor Peterson was forced by public pressure to deal with "Crime within State Institutions." In December, 1968, Howard James, a distinguished newspaperman, studied Delaware's Ferris School for Boys as part of a national study. According to James, "Ferris was the worst institution I had seen. Yet those who ran it were selling it as the best in the nation." [44] There was little educational equipment at the reform school. Three thousand dollars worth of library books was kept in unopened boxes. James found boys "with punctured eardrums, others who had been hit in the face with a belt." [45] Yet "local officials [were] more concerned with staff morale than boys with punctured eardrums." [46] After James was given a six-hour grilling by members of the Delaware Youth Services Commission trying to discredit his research, the Youth Commission, faced with massive adverse publicity, finally suspended the policy of hitting children on the face until it could make a study of corporal punishment. Governor Peterson said immediate action would be taken on James's other recommendations, but James charged that the governor quickly changed his mind:

> In a press conference, however, it appeared that Governor Peterson had, in part, backed down—something certain members of his staff had encouraged—on my other complaints.[47]

Only after the Delaware Correctional Council (a group supported by DuPont family members) issued a scathing report on the juvenile treatment program did the governor ask the members of the Youth Services Commission to resign, in 1969.

Whether conditions have improved much since is doubtful. The *Evening Journal* recently reported that, instead of getting beaten, "inmates at Ferris School for Boys . . . are now locked up in their cottages for most of the long hours they must remain there." [48] Boys in the "jug," a high security unit, sleep on concrete slabs and have been handcuffed to a steel overhead beam for as long as seven hours.[49] While Delaware established an experimental youth center for juveniles in 1970, the center has yet to produce results; John J. Moran, director of the Division of Adult

Corrections, admits that the new center "is not fully meeting the needs of the age group from 16 to 18." [50]

The jails for adults are no better. Through the 1950s the state continued to use its whipping post, and Delaware law still allows flogging as punishment for criminal offenses.* In 1963 the Delaware Supreme Court, reviewing the sentence of 20 lashes imposed on a convicted robber, held the law to be constitutional and *not* a cruel and unusual punishment.[51] While convicts have not been officially whipped in the last decade, they still must suffer the abysmal conditions of state jails. In 1962 a series of articles in the *News-Journal* pointed up the neglect of prisoners, decay of buildings, and general lack of funds in the Delaware penal system. Today, Delaware jails are still aimed at retribution instead of rehabilitation. In 1970 a 17-year-old was chained to a cot in a solitary cell for five days by New Castle Correctional Institution officials.[52]

Although the state has recently completed a new prison downstate in Smyrna, it is tiny and ill-equipped. In protest against the inadequate facilities, 65 prison inmates held three guards hostage for three hours in September, 1971.[53] The following day, Governor Peterson announced that 17 additional persons would be hired to "help solve some of the problems at the prison by offering a more complete rehabilitation program." [54] John J. Moran, the corrections director, was quoted as saying that "Delaware's prison system isn't equipped to do the job it's supposed to do and it won't be until a lot more money is put into it." [55] Moran indicated that it will take several million dollars and more personnel to improve the "rehabilitation programs, educational projects, and basic daily life in the prison [which] are not ideal because the prison is not suited for the intended purpose, helping prisoners." [56]

## *Equal Opportunity for Some*

The state provides over 70% of all public primary and secondary school revenues in Delaware,[57] with school districts receiving different levels of funding depending on

* Another state law makes it a crime to have a camera near the whipping post.

need. But the state's effort to equalize educational opportunity has been poor. In 1970 Delaware ranked ninth in the nation in per capita income, but ranked only nineteenth in per-pupil expenditures.[58]

Members of the corporate elite have substantial influence over how these funds are spent. Appointments to the Wilmington school board are made by Governor Peterson and Mayor Haskell. H. B. du Pont was school board president of the Alexis I. du Pont Special School District for 30 years and a board member for 40 years. The head of the state board of education is Robert McBride, a full-time DuPont employee. McBride's job within the DuPont Company directly conflicts with his public responsibilities; he has the task of developing proposals for DuPont in aiding secondary education. Even McBride had reservations about taking on this corporate duty because of possible conflicts of interest, but, according to McBride, the company felt that he would not let his public obligations interfere with his corporate commitments.

When the Delaware Study Group called McBride on August 10, 1970, to schedule an interview, he said he would have to check with the company first. We insisted we did not want to talk about the DuPont Company, but only about the Delaware educational system. McBride replied that the company had been nice enough to let him serve on the state board of education so he felt he had to check back with them before discussing even purely public matters with us. Presumably, if the DuPont Company had not cleared our interview, we would have been denied access to information about Delaware public education for entirely private reasons.

McBride administers a system of primary and secondary education that reinforces rather than overcomes the unequal opportunity created by disparities of wealth and status in the state. The basic revenue source for individual school districts is the property tax, supplemented by state funds, so that school districts encompassing higher-income residential areas or including substantial amounts of industrial-commercial properties have a larger tax base and have taxpayers who can afford to pay a higher tax rate than poorer school districts.* The Alexis I. du Pont School District in Brandywine Hundred, where numerous DuPont employees live and the DuPont Experimental Station is located, has $55,691 of real estate value per child, the highest in the state. De La Warr district has the lowest, $13,377 per child.[59] Despite state efforts to reduce the most blatant inequalities, subsidies designed to equalize expenditures between districts have not succeeded. Even with subsidies, a school district in a low-income area like Richardson Park, just outside Wilmington, spent a total of only $535 per pupil; the Alfred I. du Pont Special School District spent $915 per pupil. If state equalization payments were to eliminate revenue differences between rich and poor school districts, De La Warr would receive $386 per pupil from the state and Alexis I. district would receive nothing; [60] however, equalization payments to De La Warr in 1970 were only $40 per pupil. In the De La Warr School District, serving mainly low-income blacks, Dr. Harry O. Eisenberg, the school superintendent, said that "with the low tax base, much that needs to be done is financially impossible.[61]

Indeed, educational achievement in poor schools is significantly lower than in well-funded ones. De La Warr district, with only one-third as many students as Alexis I., had three times as many high school dropouts as Alexis I. in 1968.[62] Schools in Brandywine Hundred, where most DuPont researchers live, have excellent science and language programs that are not available in the predominantly-black Wilmington schools and other lower-income districts.

The educational disparity is heightened by racial cleavages. Delaware was one of the losing defendants in *Brown* v. *Board of Education*, the 1954 Supreme Court case declaring school segregation unconstitutional. For years, Delaware had only one black high school. Today, Delaware schools suffer from de facto rather than de jure segregation. The school population in the northern suburbs of Brandy-

* Disparities in revenues of different school districts because of different ability to raise money from property taxes were ruled unconstitutional as a denial of equal protection of the law as guaranteed by both the California and United States constitutions in a recent California Supreme Court decision: *Serrano* v. *Priest*, filed August 30, 1971.

wine and Christiana Hundred is almost 100% white, while in Wilmington schools and certain districts to the south of the city, it is mostly black. In 1970 the American Civil Liberties Union announced plans to bring a lawsuit attacking the de facto pattern of racial segregation in Wilmington and its northern suburbs.[63]

The disparity in the public educational system has not hurt the DuPont Company. It can promise scientists and engineers a quality education for their children in Wilmington suburbs. Lammot du Pont Copeland once said, in reference to choosing plant locations:

> We are especially interested in the school system, because the kind of people we are seeking will insist upon good educational facilities for their children.[64]

A DuPont public relations brochure proudly touts the quality of schools in New Castle County—"Most schools are grade A, some are A+."[65] But the company is speaking only of the schools attended by the children of its white-collar employees, not those educational institutions serving poor whites or blacks.

Like most state services, Delaware higher education has always been underfinanced. The Carnegie Commission on Higher Education reported in April, 1971, that Delaware failed to give even .6% of per capita income through state and local taxes to institutions for higher learning, thus creating a need for "emergency" public efforts.[66] The commission added that Delaware ranked 44th in the nation in aid to higher education in relation to per capita income, down from 31st in 1953–54.[67] Other data assembled by the Carnegie Commission show Delaware to be one of two states without any coordinating agency or consolidated governing board for higher education and reveal that Delaware has the third smallest percentage of 18–21-year-old residents attending in-state institutions of higher education in the country.[68]

This underfinancing is even more shocking because, just as in primary and secondary education, funds which *are* spent on higher education are spent mainly for the benefit of upper-middle-class whites. Delaware State College (undergraduate enrollment: 1355 in 1970) and the University of Delaware (9270) are the two main public institutions of higher education in the state. Both are supported by the state government together with private monies. There the similarity ends. Delaware State has no DuPonts on its board; the 1970 University of Delaware board contained 8 DuPont family members, 2 company directors, 2 board members of the Wilmington Trust Company, and several corporate lawyers. Six of 14 members of the powerful Executive Committee were family members. Of the 7 Finance Committee men, 4 were family members and one a DuPont executive.

The key to this disparity in DuPont influence is simple: Delaware State began as a black college; the University of Delaware was traditionally white and has a long history of racism. In 1956 the university president refused to allow one of the few black students, a football star, to have a white roommate. In 1968, twice as high a percentage of blacks was enrolled at the University of Mississippi (1.4%) as at the University of Delaware (0.7%). By the fall of 1970, Delaware had caught up with Ole Miss—both had a 2.6% black enrollment.[69] In contrast, Delaware State was about 20% white in 1969–70. (Delaware's population is 14.5% black.)

As a result of these differences in DuPont influence, Delaware State has had to fight for survival while the University of Delaware has thrived. Delaware State has no endowment; the University of Delaware has the fourth largest endowment of any public-related university in the country. Forty percent of the endowment comes from the H. Rodney and Isabella du Pont Sharp Trust.* H. Fletcher Brown, R. R. M. Carpenter, Jr., and Walter S. Carpenter, Jr., also had all made "substantial contributions" for capital improvements. The DuPont-related Longwood Foundation gave $875,000 to help build P. S. du Pont Hall for civil and electrical engineering. In 1964–65, the Uni-

* H. Rodney Sharp was a university trustee for 53 years. When he died in 1968, the university said, "Mr. Sharp, more than any other single individual, has been responsible for the dramatic growth and development that has characterized this University in the second and third quarters of this century. His gifts of buildings and land . . . and the income from the munificent trust established in behalf of his alma mater, which has swelled the University endowment, have all been major factors in this University's endowment."

versity of Delaware undertook construction valued at $27 million, of which $9.45 million came from private gifts. Meanwhile, Delaware State has been struggling to get $2 million to expand its library so it will not lose its accreditation.

With so few resources, Delaware State has serious difficulties in attracting and retaining Ph.D.'s on its faculty; college president Luna I. Mishoe's 1968–69 report says, "Salaries are about $4000 less than what is needed to make proper headway in attracting new Ph.D.'s." The salaries at the University of Delaware are competitive with most major universities in the East. The university has 25 endowed chairs, 23 established by DuPonts. Delaware State received only $6542 in private gifts for scholarship aid to both undergraduates and graduate students in 1968–69; the University of Delaware offered over 100 full fellowships just for graduate students and many more for undergraduates.

The DuPont Company has aggravated the disparity between the two schools. From 1966 through 1970, the company gave only $43,100 to Delaware State, while providing $964,000 to the University of Delaware. In 1969, for instance, DuPont made contributions of $7500 to Delaware State and $264,000 to the University of Delaware. Moreover, DuPont's Delaware facilities now employ as salaried workers 56 times as many graduates from the University of Delaware as from Delaware State—616 as opposed to 11.[70]

State government has reinforced the inequality of educational opportunity in the two schools. For years, Delaware gave Delaware State a shoestring budget. Although state contributions to Delaware State have recently increased significantly, one prominent state official says the college "is still in constant danger financially." In contrast, the University of Delaware always receives substantial funds from the state, even though the university at the same time receives large private gifts.

Within the University of Delaware, the basic problems stem from DuPont's *private* control over an institution which derives 80% of its budget from *public* contributions—state and federal governments and tuition. The dual nature of the University of Delaware is reflected in the board. The governor appoints 8 board members, but the DuPont-dominated board itself elects 20 more. Also, this quasi-public board is dependent on the discretion of private individuals for substantial contributions. For instance, one of the largest private sources of university capital is the Unidel Foundation, established by Amy du Pont.

The DuPont influence and money have biased this quasi-public university toward the sciences. Only the chemistry and chemical engineering departments rate high nationally. In 1969–70, for instance, the University of Delaware Research Foundation, run by Samuel H. Lenher, a DuPont Company board member, gave a large number of grants mainly to chemistry, mathematics, physics, statistics, and computer sciences, as well as mechanical and aerospace engineering; the DuPont Company has concentrated its university grants in the areas of chemistry and engineering. While some nonscientific departments have thrived, they have almost all been related to some personal concern of a DuPont family member. University President Arthur Trabant pointed out in an interview that the art history, history, and horticulture departments were making the greatest strides forward. The art history department is closely connected with the Henry Francis du Pont Winterthur Museum. The history department has concentrated on American industrial and technological history, drawing heavily on the resources of the DuPont-owned Eleutherian Mills–Hagley Museum. A program in ornamental horticulture was recently instituted in cooperation with the DuPont family's Longwood Gardens. All three programs offer very attractive graduate fellowships, and joint appointments in the university department and the DuPont-related institutions.

Sometimes university research projects are carried out because of the personal interest of DuPont family members, such as the canal study done in 1967 by the university's Water Resources Center for H. B. du Pont. Robert R .M. Carpenter, Jr., a du Pont who owns the Philadelphia Phillies, gave a substantial sum to the university for "scientific research" into methods of electronically monitoring baseball swings. Carpenter apparently hoped to provide

Phillies scouts with better tools for analyzing prospective team members.

As a result of DuPont influence, the university's priorities are not those of a broad cross section of Delaware citizens who pay a substantial portion of its annual budget, or university students and faculty. Delaware is one of the few states without a medical or law school. The school is oriented toward the chemical industry, and nonscience programs depend on DuPont family money and museums to make above-average efforts. As the university president's report in 1964–65 said:

> Paradoxically, those disciplines where enrollments are disappointing represent some of this University's strongest academic programs with the best and newest facilities.
>
> Those who enroll in humanities, social sciences, business, and education . . . are overlooking the basic scientific nature of contemporary civilization and the substantially greater remuneration paid those with quantitative skills.

Despite the extent of private influence, the university has often used its semipublic nature to rationalize questionable policies. The state has given the university the power of eminent domain, which has caused serious land-use problems for its host city, Newark. A city document states, "There has been little, if any, mutual cooperation." According to a high-ranking city official, W. W. Laird, Jr., bought 200 acres of land on New London Road near the university to develop as a housing project. After Laird ran into problems implementing his original scheme, he gave the land to the university for tax benefits. There the university plans to build a dormitory, which would violate the city's zoning plan. University officials argue that the school's power of eminent domain lets them do what they please with the land.

In addition to its domineering relationship to the city, the university infringes upon constitutional rights of free speech and freedom of assembly of its own staff. The *1969 Handbook for Faculty* says:

> The position of the University of Delaware as a state-assisted but non-political institution imposes on faculty members special responsibilities for the use of good judg-

ment in political matters. . . . Faculty members proposing to engage in political activity are expected to notify the President of the University *in advance*. [Emphasis added.]

The handbook's warnings are not idle threats. In three recent cases, the university did not renew the contracts of professors participating in antiwar rallies despite good teaching records, widespread student support, and, in one instance, the favorable recommendation of the professor's department. While university officials insist they judged all three cases on purely academic criteria, each of the men quickly obtained a new teaching post at a university of comparable standing. One of the three, Edward Kaplan, crew-cut professor of Chinese history and a self-described Stevenson Democrat, explained:

There really is an Oligarchy . . . and it really does control this state, though its control has been slipping in recent years. At the top, of course, are the DuPonts.[71]

When asked how the university administration fits into the picture, he said:

That's simple enough. Their job is to keep things quiet on campus. Whenever they are in doubt they ask the Oligarchs what to do.[72]

CHAPTER 15

# Conclusion: Toward a Strategy for Corporate Responsibility

The Delaware Study Group has asked two basic questions about corporate responsibility, one concerning the process of decision making (*who makes the important decisions affecting the lives of Delaware citizens?*), the second about the outcome of decisions (*whose interests are served by private and public policies?*). The answers to these questions break down into three parts—the private market, public government, and special responsibility.

## *Decision Making in the Private Market*

Residents of Delaware consume a wide range of goods and services provided by the private market. While many consumer products are supplied by national firms, Delaware consumers must look to local companies for jobs, land, and capital, as well as services like newspapers, legal help, and health care. Consumers may have a voice in decisions about these localized goods and services in one of two ways: (1) externally through the threat of patronizing competing organizations; or (2) internally through a supplier's decision-making processes.

External market controls assume the existence of many vigorously competing producers. In such a market, consumers are sovereign; through their purchases they hold private producers accountable. For many localized goods and services, however, the Delaware market is uncompetitive, and Delaware consumers must accept the goods and services of one or a small group of suppliers.

Delaware consumers face a tightly knit corporate establishment with a very strong and sometimes exclusive position in the local market. Since the DuPont Company alone controls 13% of the state's work force and sets the employment pace for the large chemical firms in the area, the company determines the Delaware job market to a large degree. The DuPont family, together with allied groups like Woodlawn Trustees, control another important local commodity—vacant land in northern New Castle County. Of the four major commercial banks in the state, two are owned outright by DuPonts, while the others are closely linked to the corporate establishment. The DuPont family owns the News-Journal Company, which puts out the only two large dailies in Delaware. The best lawyers are in Wilmington corporate law firms institutionally dependent on the DuPont family and company. DuPonts even dominate the major medical center in Delaware.

Thus, the business community has merged previously independent or loosely tied units under the direct management of the corporate elite, thereby eliminating sources of competition. DuPont-related financial institutions have been aggressively buying up small banks in the state; the DuPont family's Wilmington Trust has purchased Delaware's largest home finance corporation. The Greater Wilmington Housing Corporation, headed by a DuPont Company executive, took over a nonprofit housing group called Block Blight. And the corporate elite brought the three major hospitals in New Castle County, each associated with a DuPont, under a central administration.

The corporate establishment has further maintained its market hegemony by keeping out alternative suppliers. DuPont kept a large Ford plant out of Delaware in 1935, according to *Fortune* magazine. While a few manufacturing units moved into Delaware soon after World War II, a DuPont family member then played the key role in the selection of a highway route which effectively stymied industrial development in Wilmington. Later the new firm recruitment committee of the GWDC, a corporate bastion, served more to discriminate against blue-collar firms than recruit them. In the name of environment, the corporate elite have recently closed off the prime industrial sites in New Castle County to any blue-collar factories by land purchases and consultant studies, though these aristocrats have not protested against environmental despoliation by local chemical firms. Similarly, the business community has fought hard against federal services. For example, banks in Delaware, especially Wilmington Trust, have traditionally refused to cooperate with the Small Business Administration or take advantage of the Small Business Investment Corporation program run by the Department of Commerce.

At times, businessmen have utilized both methods at once—merging local units and keeping out new suppliers. The DuPont family merged the major newspapers in Delaware into the *News-Journal,* which then tried to eliminate the *Delaware State News,* a small daily in southern Delaware. Conversely, the corporate elite has kept out alternative funding sources and then tucked an organization under DuPont's wing. Delaware's Opportunities Industrialization Center (OIC) was the only OIC in the country not started by local blacks and not funded federally. After several years of tutelage under the GWDC, OIC finally received federal funding, but only as the agent for a federal job training grant obtained by DuPont and other local chemical firms.

Although Delaware consumers cannot control local suppliers by *external* means through the market, they might influence the *internal* processes of corporate decision making. Delaware consumers could influence private producers through elections of directors, votes on policy resolutions, or as public-interest board members. Currently, however, most Delaware consumers have no say in the internal forums of the corporate establishment.

Decision making in the DuPont Company is closed to

consumers and to most employees. DuPont is a traditional, family-dominated company. The DuPont family controls both the finance committee of the board of directors and 35% of the company's common stock. Family patriarchs, like Pierre S. du Pont and Irenee du Pont, Sr., have traditionally ruled both family and company. Advancement within the rigid, male-dominated company is open only to persons acceptable to top management and family members. No women or blacks are directors or executives, and until very recently, no Jew has ever been a director or top executive. Since the shares of the DuPont family and the proxies held by corporate executives comprise a majority of the votes, it is futile for Delaware consumers to attend stockholders' meetings of DuPont or the two DuPont-related banks.

Even in quasi-public institutions controlled by the DuPonts, the election processes are severely biased. In the GWDC, the Wilmington Medical Center, and many other nonprofit, nonpartisan groups, elections merely rubber-stamp nominations which are carefully worked out to include only token representation for noncorporate groups.

Not surprisingly, the directors of various corporate boards constitute a very small sample of Delaware consumers. The DuPont Company board contains only one person who is not a company manager or family member; even this recent appointee was well known in the chemical industry prior to his nomination. No DuPont-controlled business institution has board members who explicitly represent consumers or the Delaware community; and no important DuPont-related quasi-public group has an array of directors roughly reflecting its clientele. In fact, the same men are the key decision makers in many institutions. Irenee du Pont, Jr., for example, is a director of the DuPont Company, Wilmington Trust, News Journal Company, Christiana Securities, Delmarva Power and Light, and the GWDC. The key decision makers belong to the same social clubs, where they mix discussions of corporate matters with lighter topics of conversation. At the exclusive Wilmington Club, these powerful men sit around one large, round table for lunch. After work, key members of the corporate community gather at the Wilmington Country

Club, Vicmead Hunt Club, or Bidermann Country Club to discuss business, play golf, or hunt foxes.

In most DuPont-related institutions, Delaware consumers cannot even obtain enough information on goods and services to *assess* internal policy making. The executives of Wilmington Trust were unwilling to release statistical data on loan and trust portfolios in any detail. While DuPont management floods Delaware consumers with propaganda, the company will not provide quantitative data on minority employment, pollution, or its Community Affairs Committee, even though this information is obviously relevant to Delaware consumers. Quasi-public groups related to DuPont likewise refuse to hand out accurate information. Soon after the head of the Wilmington Medical Center insisted that his hospitals were providing excellent health care to the urban poor, a consultant study unearthed statistics supporting the opposite conclusion.

## *The Results of a Defective Private Market*

While consumers in Delaware clearly cannot hold local suppliers accountable, corporate executives and family members argue that this makes no difference. The business community, the argument goes, uses its market control to meet the needs of all Delaware consumers, not just those of the corporate elite. In practice, the argument does not hold up. Although there is some overlap of interest, the private market is more oriented toward the corporate elite than toward the majority of Delaware citizens.

Since DuPont dominates the local job market, it can recruit top-notch workers while maintaining strict control over them. Workers do not have a significant role in corporate decision making either through representation on corporate boards at any level within the company or collective bargaining through well-organized unions. As a result, management can move workers around with great ease to meet the rapidly changing production and research needs of the chemical industry. Blue-collar workers have almost no bargaining power on wages or other contract issues, and must sometimes endure debilitating working conditions like the shift system at Seaford. The DuPont white-collar employee agreement lessens job mobility without providing job security.

The DuPont family's control over the land market has led to many abuses. The family's vast estates have artificially reduced the supply of vacant land, and the company has created a tremendous demand for land by building new facilities; so home sites in New Castle County have higher prices than equivalent sites in nearby states. Moreover, the corporate community's control over vacant land has allowed establishment institutions and individuals to discriminate against certain types of purchasers. In at least one large development constructed by Woodlawn Trustees, restrictive covenants prevented housing sales to blacks as late as 1968. In suburban developments built near the DuPont family estates, some would-be residents have had to obtain approval of neighbors at private tea parties before paying $25,000 for two acres of land.

The largest commercial banks in Delaware, controlled by the DuPonts, serve the interests of the corporate elite more often than the needs of the public. The biggest, Wilmington Trust, effectively protected a large part of the assets of Lammot du Pont Copeland, Jr., from his other creditors. On the other hand, the Wilmington Trust has a lower ratio of loans to deposits than the other major banks in the state. Banks with strong corporate links have been adamantly against handling "spot loans" for housing rehabilitation. Banks have cut off financing to developers because their projects were too near DuPont estates, and families have lost their credit ratings because they would not cooperate with local realtors who were also bank directors. In addition, by downplaying the federal SBA and FHA programs for loan assistance, commercial bankers have greatly reduced the amount of risk capital available for small businessmen and home loans earmarked for moderate-income families.

DuPont's near monopoly of local news in Delaware prevents consumers from obtaining a comprehensive, unbiased account of current events. The *News-Journal* has enjoyed a well-deserved reputation for watering down stories about the DuPont family or its pet institutions like the University of Delaware. It has mouthed the DuPont line on many important local issues like the General Motors divestiture bill or the White Clay Creek dam proposal. The major periodicals put out in the state by the DuPont Company are very distorted and manipulative. This public relations material gives the false impression that employees have an important role in corporate decision making while subtly conveying the company's political message.

The major advocates in Delaware are corporate law firms and the DuPont-dominated GWDC. Corporate lawyers, expert at helping wealthy individuals preserve their fortunes and insulating business executives from the public, have little experience in dealing with the pressing legal problems of the poor. The *pro bono* work of the DuPont Company and DuPont-related law firms are at token levels. Similarly, the published reports of the Greater Wilmington Development Council, often the only well-heeled advocate on urban issues, have misled Delaware residents by hidden assumptions. For instance, the Reeder report promulgated a high vacancy rate for housing, but the report's own figures indicate a negative vacancy rate if substandard units are considered uninhabitable. GWDC has sometimes covertly supported DuPont interests in projects; for example, the "major land assembly" adjacent to GWDC's proposed shopping mall was owned by a DuPont family member.

In the area of health services, the story is the same: the DuPont family and company have used their power to establish the only major suppliers of an essential service which is oriented toward the corporate establishment. Medical care is excellent in New Castle County if a consumer is wealthy enough to have a car, to pay the high fees of private doctors, and to afford a private or semiprivate hospital room; but medical care is inadequate for low-income families since they do not always have transportation to local hospitals, clinics are run at inconvenient times, and preventive medicine administered by private doctors is too expensive.

## Public Power and Government Bodies

According to traditional democratic theory, citizens hold public decision-makers accountable through public discussions and elections. Since public officials are open to electoral defeat, they must take their constituents' views seriously. The corporate establishment in Delaware is the complete opposite of the democratic model. In almost every DuPont-related institution, information on policy issues is reserved for insiders, and the principle of one man, one vote does not hold. Business executives and DuPont family members maintain that they act as merely one of a vast array of groups pressuring public organs. In fact, the corporate establishment is the dominant political force in Delaware.

DuPont's public power is based, first, on its stranglehold on the private market. DuPont has helped minimize unions as a political force. Since Delaware citizens depend upon DuPont-owned newspapers for Delaware news, they have received one-sided political information. There are no commercial television stations in the state to offset DuPont's news monopoly. Public officers may often need legal advice, and legal expertise locally is concentrated in the corporate elite. For this reason, a state legislator said he was forced to depend on DuPont's legal department to draft the state's corporate income tax law. Finally, since private groups like the Wilmington Medical Center have taken over programs traditionally run by public bodies, government officials must fit their programs into DuPont-controlled institutions.

With this private basis for public power together with other types of resources, the DuPonts have built a powerful political machine. One key DuPont resource has been money. DuPont forces can buy their way into public office, since the state legislature has not passed limitations or disclosure requirements for campaign spending. According to important political figures, the son of a former DuPont executive won the Wilmington mayoralty race in 1968 by spending over seven times what his opponent did. By contributing to campaigns, DuPont family members have built up control over the Republican party. Men like Reynolds du Pont will provide especially large amounts of money to defeat candidates they dislike even within their own party. In addition, over the years, the DuPont-related gentry have also dominated the Democratic party. Democratic legislators like Allen Frear have been so pro-DuPont that they were opposed by traditionally Democratic labor unions.

The other main political resource of the business community is its employees. After reapportionment in the middle 1960s, the corporate middle-class in New Castle County became the most important group of voters in Delaware. DuPont-related candidates ride to victory on the ballots of suburban white-collar workers from Brandywine Hundred. Since many elected offices in Delaware are part-time, the corporate community in effect subsidizes its own candidates: white-collar DuPont employees get 20% of their time off with full pay if they occupy public office. Moreover, corporations contribute experts to advise the government on crucial areas of public policy. DuPont and other large firms nominated men to the Air Pollution Advisory Board, which deals with environmental problems directly concerning these companies.

When countervailing sources of political power arose on the horizon, the corporate establishment either co-opted or kept out the potential challenger. Through the funding mechanisms of the DuPont-controlled GWDC, the United Fund, and private foundations, the business forces have been able to co-opt potential competitors for public power. For example, when the Wilmington Youth Emergency Action Council (WYEAC), a group of black militants, arose as a political factor on the Wilmington scene, it was quickly smothered to death with corporate largesse and red tape. The University of Delaware requires prior registration of political activities by faculty, and the university did not renew the contracts of three professors involved in unapproved political protests. The corporate elite refused to broaden the white bloc in the Urban Coalition to include liberal elements, and the business community rejected local chapters of other organizations with national political bases, like the Urban League. If a group could not be co-opted or kept out, its days were numbered. William Henry du Pont would not honor his funding pledge to Organization Interest (OI), a group of blacks serving ex-offenders until pressured by OI directors. OI still folded because it could not raise funds in the DuPont-dominated private sector. After explicitly raising the question of excessive corporate power during the nine-month military occupation of Wilmington, some professionals working for a DuPont-funded church group lost their jobs.

As the major political force in Delaware, the corporate elite has influenced public policy both covertly and overtly. Even its gifts can control government policy. The DuPont Company virtually preempted any fair public determination of a site for a county reservoir when it bought up large amounts of land near its Louviers site; the company would make land available to the county, it said, only if the land were used for a reservoir. H. B. du Pont's Welfare Foundation donated land for a hospital, although public planners, after public hearings, had designated the same plot as the county's prime industrial site. The public plan lost because of the gift. A DuPont eliminated one leaf of a four-leaf clover interchange of a state highway by a combination of political influence and a gift of free land if the highway were not put too close to his home.

The corporate elite has also made a substantial impact on public policy by monopolizing the information base. A small group of corporate lawyers wrote the new General Corporation Law (GCL) which was passed without independent analysis by the state legislature in less than 20 minutes. Members of the corporate elite insist that their advice is neutral. But the governor's Economy Study (done by businessmen) contained recommendations with far-reaching political implications, like making many elective posts appointive. Consultants have recommended projects to one client that will benefit another client, like the Whitman-Requardt studies of the White Clay Creek dam proposal. Experts have been hired specifically to develop an argument for wealthy families—for example, the Greenville study on planned unit development in New Castle County. And consultants have been replaced if their conclusions were not what the corporate establishment wanted. In one case, outside consultants were substituted for local professors who did not favor a grandiose shopping mall for Wilmington.

The corporate establishment has even pushed important bills through local legislative bodies, sometimes quietly. A DuPont employee introduced a bill authorizing New Castle County to build the White Clay Creek Dam, now a major planning controversy, which passed both houses without debate. A rider to an appropriations bill silently gave all school inspection contracts to a DuPont-financed group instead of being put out to public bid. At other times, the DuPonts have come out in full force. The DuPont Company financed a large lobbying effort to obtain special tax concessions for the court-ordered divestiture of General Motors stock. When the state budget director tried to audit the books of the University of Delaware, a pet DuPont family project, the corporate elite came to Dover on "Rolls Royce Day" to make sure elected representatives passed a special protective bill.

### *Corporate Orientation of Public Resources*

By undercutting democratic processes through disproportionate political power, the corporate establishment has substituted its own judgments of the public good for those of Delaware citizens. Although an oligarchy or dictatorship could in theory use its influence to serve all people equally, DuPont's political power has skewed public policies toward its narrow aims. In the Seaford, Wilmington, New Castle County, and state governments, the same pattern emerges: the DuPont family and company face low taxation relative to community needs, while limited public resources are oriented more to the corporate rich than to the needy.

In Seaford, DuPont pays no property taxes because its huge plant and country club lie conveniently outside the jagged eastern border of the town. Moreover, the company's school taxes are based on an average assessment of $4300 less per acre than the average assessment per acre of the town's property tax base, which includes streets, church land, and other large tracts of tax-exempt property. Contrary to Delaware law, in New Castle County the assessments on the 17,000 acres of company and family land are neither at the same assessment per unit of size as other land holdings nor at levels reflecting current market value. If the assessments of DuPont-related land met the criteria established by Delaware law, the county would have reaped over $1.25 million in property and school taxes during 1970 alone. Similarly, in Wilmington, the company's property is assessed at lower ratios than equivalent building sites and contemporary market trends. On the brink of financial ruin, the city government pushed through a regressive wage tax that falls most heavily on workers earning between $6000 and $10,000 per year, while exempting the income from stocks and bonds mainly held by the corporate rich.

The state government has a long history of incompetent tax administration, erratic tax receipts on a year-to-year basis, and a consistently low revenue yield relative to per capita income. From the viewpoint of Delaware firms, state law provides a trade-off on balance favorable to giant companies like DuPont with high profits, many shares of stock, huge investments in business equipment, and large legal staffs. Delaware corporations pay a flat percentage income tax regardless of profit level. Although the rates on the corporate franchise tax were raised in 1969 according to the recommendations of an independent study, the maximum franchise tax on stock shares is only $110,000—$90,000 short of the report's recommendation. In addition, Delaware imposes no tax on goods in process, raw materials, or business machinery, like DuPont's research or office equipment. Delaware firms further benefit from the country's most lenient incorporation law and most pro-business courts.

While Delaware taxes on individual incomes have been generally equitable in comparison to other states, Delaware tax laws still have been riddled with concessions to the rich. The personal income tax has in the past stopped being progressive after $30,000 per year.* Delaware does not assess personal property, like jewelry and expensive furnish-

* Because of the state's fiscal crisis in summer, 1971, Delaware passed a law which may increase the progressiveness of income taxes in the higher brackets.

ings, held in large amounts mainly by the corporate rich. The state fails to tax stock transfers for those who deal extensively in securities. Moreover, Delaware allows wealthy families to pass on wealth virtually undisturbed from generation to generation. Until very recently, the state imposed very low death taxes, which could be avoided entirely by donations to relatives since Delaware had no gift tax.

While the various governments of Delaware have all experienced serious financial problems, they have all allocated the scarce funds that have been available to projects serving the interests of the business community rather than the needs of most citizens. Wilmington has provided superhighways and enormous parking facilities to accommodate the needs of corporations with downtown office buildings. As a result of this highway program together with demolitions to prepare for the city's urban renewal projects, a severe housing crisis exists in Wilmington. The construction of I-95 alone necessitated tearing down about 800 living units of relatively high quality. Like the highways, the urban renewal program—mainly the civic center and the shopping mall—has shown a distinct corporate bias. These two projects will cost Delaware residents millions of dollars with a low return in tax income over the next decade. The real beneficiary will be the corporate establishment—a shiny downtown for visitors to the world's chemical capital. In contrast, the city government has failed to develop an industrial base at its port and on adjacent vacant land. Industrial development, which would provide tax revenue and jobs for the city, would not be in keeping with the white-collar atmosphere stressed by the corporate community. In poignant acts of public subservience to corporate interests, Wilmington sold the DuPont Company part of an important city street for well below its appraised value and established an elegant boulevard to glorify DuPont's new downtown office building.

In New Castle County, public policies have similarly supported DuPont influence in the private land market. The county zoning code reinforces existing land-use patterns that effectively immunize upper class areas from development, while providing the DuPont family and company with a firm grip on the land market. When the county passed an ordinance to encourage more land-use planning and low-income housing construction, it made special concessions to the Greenville area, where DuPont lands are centered. While public debate raged over the false battle of zoning for Columbia Gas's elegant office building near some DuPont homes, the county decided to retain its airport for corporate rather than public use, without even a public hearing. The DuPont orientation of county policies has severaly hurt low-income residents of both county and city. The county government has failed to provide adequate parkland. Since the county has not built even one unit of subsidized housing for county residents, Wilmington is prevented by federal law from constructing even one unit of public housing for city residents.

The most recent policy proposal for local government calls for the merger of the city council of Wilmington with the county council of New Castle County. This proposal is strongly opposed by Wilmington blacks, who are close to holding an electoral majority in the city. Suburban whites, too, reject the idea of merger, because they do not want to finance the renewal of Wilmington. One group that clearly benefits from the policy of metropolitan government is the corporate establishment. By merging the city's black population into the DuPont-dominated county council, the business community hopes to protect itself from progressive measures that might be promoted by a black mayor. Despite its obvious unpopularity, metropolitan government was supported in interviews with the Delaware Study Group by the president of the county council and the mayor of Wilmington. Both are DuPont-connected. The real moving forces behind metropolitan government, however, are the GWDC and the *News-Journal,* two corporate agents which have been pushing for this policy *sub rosa.*

Even the state government spends its limited resources mainly for projects supporting corporate interests. The largest allocations in the state budget have gone to the DuPont-influenced Department of Highways and Transportation, which continues to emphasize roads to corporate facilities rather than mass transit. State expenditures to help low-income groups have been exercises in tokenism. The housing department is so small that it could not begin to attack the serious shelter problems in southern Delaware, let alone the rest of the state. Delaware is one of only two states without state- or city-supported general hospitals and one of only four states not participating in the federal food stamp program. State institutions like the Delaware State Mental Hospital are grossly understaffed, and Delaware's juvenile reform schools have been among the most barbaric in the country. While the legislature recently raised the ceiling for welfare benefits under threat of court suit by the federal government, welfare officials made clear that a higher ceiling would not increase actual welfare payments. Nor has the state provided a progressive educational system for all its citizens. The school tax, based on property assessments by district, guarantees tremendous disparities in educational expenditures between neighborhoods. In terms of higher education, the state has no four-year medical school, full-time law school, or well-developed program in the social sciences and humanities. On the other hand, the University of Delaware has excellent chemistry and chemical engineering departments—and art history programs built around DuPont family homes and museums.

## *Implicit Power*

When one group gains so much influence over other institutions, its power becomes implicit. The dominant group no longer has to give directions; dominated citizens know what is expected of them and do it. In Delaware, the implicit power of the corporate establishment derives from the almost complete fusion of public office with private interests, private budget with public function.

In Delaware, several governmental offices are so dominated by the business community that they could almost be categorized as corporate agents. The governor and New Castle County executive are former DuPont executives.* The county council president is a DuPont family member. The father of the mayor of Wilmington was a key DuPont

* All public offices are given as of 1970, unless noted otherwise.

executive. There are seven DuPont employees, one family member, and one wife of a DuPont employee in the state House of Representatives. Two employees, one corporate lawyer, one family member, and one wife of a former DuPont executive serve in the state senate. While this group represents approximately 11% of the state's work force, it comprises 25% of the legislature. Key committee posts are held by DuPont employees. For example, two company employees chair the Joint Finance Committee. While the city councils of Wilmington and Seaford each include two DuPont employees, the New Castle County Council contains four DuPont employees. Four of the governor's key personal aides previously worked for corporate agents. Until 1971, the state treasurer was a retired DuPont employee; since then, a DuPont family member has become attorney general of the state. At least eight state commissions included DuPont employees and family members; even the state court system is studded with judges formerly connected with the corporate establishment.

With such a great overlap between public officers and corporate elite, conflicts of interest have become a way of life in Delaware. Full-time DuPont employees like the chairman of the Council on Highways are constantly confronted with decisions which have a bearing on the company's welfare. When we tried to interview the chairman of the state education board with explicit promises that questions would be asked only about education, he said he would have to clear the interview with the DuPont Company first. The state attorney general told a DuPont employee and stockholder he could cast a ballot for a bill providing tax concessions for DuPont's court-ordered divestiture of General Motors stock. Similarly, after voting for an unusual sale of an important city street to DuPont for its new office building, a city councilman—employed by DuPont—told us there was no conflict of interest because he did not work in the section of the company which made the purchase.

DuPont executives who have left the company upon taking office are also tainted with conflicts of interest. The pensions of retired DuPont employees are explicitly revocable for actions against the interests of the DuPont

Company. Governor Peterson is one of the few DuPont employees who has ever obtained an exception from this clause upon becoming a full-time government official. Attitudes and contacts an employee develops while with DuPont carry over to his term of public office. Harold Jacobs, retired DuPont employee and former vice-chairman of the Delaware Water and Air Resources Commission (WARC), protected the company's interests while presiding over public hearings and set up informal lunches with his former DuPont colleagues to educate the WARC chairman, a novice on pollution matters. Moreover, with a system of transfer between public and corporate personnel, a public officer may think twice before ruining a future job opportunity. Wilmington's chief city planner, Peter Larsen, received a substantial salary raise when he moved over to the DuPont-dominated GWDC, and Robert Kelly, the administrative assistant of Senator Frear from Delaware, became a DuPont lobbyist in Washington when the senator was not reelected.

Just as the business community has merged the public into the private, so it has transformed the private into the public. The corporate elite have taken huge business profits—money that would have gone into the public till—and redirected these funds toward nonprofit agents of the corporate establishment. The DuPont family is practically the only group of individuals in the state with enormous wealth, unnecessary for personal needs. If a DuPont family member puts this excess money into a private foundation, he receives a large exemption on both federal and state taxes. If the DuPont Company gives money to the GWDC or similar groups, it receives a federal tax exemption of up to 5% of taxable income and an outright tax credit of up to $50,000 from the state. At the same time, the corporate community has created its own informal taxing structure to raise money for approved projects. The GWDC, for example, assesses each company by its proportionate share of the relevant employment base—an assessment which is effectively enforced by peer group pressure. Moreover, the corporation coerces employees into contributing substantial sums to nonprofit groups over which the employees have almost no control. Many large businesses in

Delaware establish quotas for donations to the corporate-controlled United Fund and use strong pressure from management to force workers to meet their designated shares.

Through these various forms of tax exemption and self-taxation, the corporate establishment has created an annual budget that rivals the expenditures of regular governments. In 1968 DuPont foundations gave away $12–13 million; Wilmington spent about the same for general city operations in 1968–69. The 1969 United Fund distributed slightly less than $5 million, while the county government budgeted slightly over $5 million for public safety, health and welfare, recreation, education, the judiciary, and for legislative, executive, and staff agencies. The large expenditures of nonprofit agencies thus become a shadow government. Private groups related to DuPont have undertaken health, education, housing, recreation, and public works programs traditionally run by government bodies. In Wilmington, GWDC set up neighborhood centers which closely paralleled the city's OEO community offices. Downtown Wilmington, Inc., a nonprofit group run by a full-time DuPont employee, has the main responsibility of developing Wilmington's civic center and shopping mall. While the state has only one safety inspector for industrial plants, the Delaware Safety Council, financed by local business, runs a full-scale industrial safety program.

The really major difference between the public and the corporate regimes is control. The public government is theoretically controlled by all citizens through elections and public discussion. The private government is run by a small coterie which operates without publicly defined standards or public checks of any kind. In most foundations, DuPont-related directors give out millions of dollars based on personal interests or friendships; without a research staff these directors often spend less than 20 minutes on each grant application. When the United Fund cut off support of a black community newspaper in deference to a prominent corporate official, there was no hearing, no court appeal—and no other funding source.

On an institutional level, this fusion of public and private in Delaware has brought about a situation which might be called "community monopoly." DuPont has become both the "price leader" for private groups and the "floor leader" in public circles. The antitrust laws prohibit combinations of private companies that manufacture products for the same market, and the state constitution provides for separation of powers between branches of government to maintain some independence for each. But there are no "community antitrust" statutes which deal with combinations of private groups in the same political unit.

When the corporate establishment has supported a project, other public and private groups follow suit. For years, city planners and blacks decried the decaying condition of central Wilmington, but only when DuPont became interested in urban renewal did the city government respond. Although H. B. du Pont was able to raise close to a million dollars in 10 minutes for the Neighborhood Improvement Program, it could obtain no more funding after it fell from favor with the corporate elite. On the other hand, the corporate establishment can create a power vacuum by inaction. The best example is the demise of a plan to promote voluntary open housing in the early sixties, supported by the Delaware realtors until DuPont refused to support the plan publicly. Since members of the corporate elite want to maintain Delaware as a white-collar center, officials working on Wilmington port development have never received serious support from private or public bodies.

An individual in Delaware feels overwhelmed by the presence of DuPont-related institutions. Since DuPont-related institutions are so pervasive and powerful, they are both the sources of personal benefits and the causes of personal setbacks. The love-hate syndrome is encapsulated in DuPont's nickname in Delaware, "Uncle Dupie," which connotes both filial affection and a protest against paternalism. As a significant consequence of this dual relationship, individuals anticipate the wishes or reactions of the corporate elite—out of either gratefulness or fear. The tax exemptions for corporations in the Neighborhood Assistance Act were said to have been a form of kowtowing to the DuPont Company. Many public officials are reticent to raise death taxes for fear that rich DuPonts will leave the state to preserve their wealth for the next generation. Certain members of a liberal church group would not go along with the group's open housing efforts because they felt the DuPont Company, their employer, would not like such a policy. Or as a former Democratic boss of Wilmington said of the DuPonts: "I recognize that without their stamp of approval you're not going to get very far. It's a fact of life."

In fact, individuals are confronted with a constellation of private and public choices so dominated by DuPont that the corporate establishment may actually set the level of expectations in Delaware. State citizens may become so awed by the physical proximity of so much wealth that they become almost entirely dependent on handouts from the corporate establishment. A man who recently moved to Delaware described to the study group his amazement that local groups thought only of which DuPont to beg from instead of finding ways to raise funds independently. Even avowed enemies of the corporate establishment begin to believe they cannot hope to win. These feelings of futility and self-doubt are very evident in DuPont union and Democratic political circles in Delaware. Delaware residents may be confronted with so few alternative models of corporate behavior that they come to view the status quo as the only possible reality. After admitting that DuPont's Seaford plant does not pay any property taxes to the town, the Seaford city manager honestly declared to the study group that he could not think of one more thing that DuPont could do for the city.

## *Special Responsibility*

A special responsibility goes with the power of the corporate establishment over public and private institutions as well as individual expectations. Since DuPont-related groups have implicit control through their fusion of private and public processes, they must bear a large part of the blame for Delaware's failures and reap much of the praise for the state's successes. As C. B. McCoy, president of DuPont, made clear in an interview with the study group, a company has a greater social responsibility if it is a large firm in a small political unit than if it is a small firm in a large political unit.

DuPont executives and family members feel they have made a special commitment to Delaware by contributing land and money to private and public institutions in the state. But such charity does not fulfill the special responsibility of the corporate establishment to Delaware. First, DuPont family members and institutions primarily serve their own self-interest by making gifts to lower their taxable incomes. By setting up foundations, DuPont family members avoid high income and estate taxes while retaining control over the money. Gifts of up to 5% of the DuPont Company's gross income can be counted as tax deductions, and the company has never approached the limit. Second, members of the corporate community have often oriented their gifts so as to serve their own interests rather than the needs of all citizens. The DuPont Company leased a top executive to head the National Alliance of Businessmen, the corporate solution to the problems of hard-core unemployment which failed miserably in Delaware. But the company refused to lease an accountant to a community group of ghetto blacks who desperately needed help in setting up and auditing their finances. Third, the contributions of the corporate establishment are often token; they receive a lot of good publicity without aiding those who are supposedly being helped. In contributing to WBOEDC, for example, Wilmington banks said they were making financial sacrifices to help minority businessmen. In fact, the black community had to raise a large sum of money for loan insurance so the banks would make their normal profit; and there is no indication that WBOEDC is making loans that would not have been accepted by the banks directly. Finally, the DuPont Company and family have frequently distributed their largesse in ways which worsen rather than improve the existing inequalities in Delaware. For instance, the DuPont family has been the financial backbone of the elite private schools which have served as strong deterrents to reform of the public school system.

With the tremendous wealth and expertise of the DuPonts, Delaware in theory could be the vanguard of social progress and justice in the United States. Instead, Delaware constitutes the model of a rigidly divided society with wide inequities between social classes. While the state's wealthy families grow and prosper, Delaware is one of three states in the country where the number of persons with income below the poverty level increased between 1960 and 1970.

For the DuPont Company, Delaware is an ideal corporate headquarters. While many other large American firms located their main offices in New York City, DuPont has stayed in Wilmington. The president of DuPont said in an interview that the company saves almost eight hours per week per employee because its workers do not have to expend as much time and energy on commuting as employees do in New York City. While New York is a heterogeneous mass of millions of people, Wilmington is a small, provincial society in which numerous residents are directly or indirectly connected to the corporate establishment. The public relations department of DuPont points to one of the key reasons for DuPont's success: Wilmington's small homogeneous society fosters a strong sense of community among employees. Research facilities and innovative manufacturing processes like Seaford's nylon plant can be located close enough to Wilmington to be personally supervised by top management. There are no threatening strong unions in nearby firms nor, for that matter, any large companies opposed to DuPont's white-collar atmosphere. DuPont managed to water down the state antipollution law which was administered by an agency accustomed to cooperating with big business. Moreover, Delaware has built a national reputation for its probusiness legislature and developed a judicial system run mainly by former corporate lawyers.

For the DuPont family and the social class which revolves around it, Delaware is an aristocratic playland. The family lives on large estates set off from the rest of the county by natural and governmental boundaries. The estates provide the physical base for an upper-class culture tantamount to a landed aristocracy. Members of the corporate elite enjoy tennis, golf, and swimming on the exclusive grounds of the various country clubs, far away from industrial and suburban developments. A short ride from chateau country, Wilmington contains all the private agents needed by an aristocracy. Banks act as trustees, law firms help avoid taxes, and a newspaper keeps the DuPont family off the front pages. Between hunting foxes and arranging personal affairs, the DuPont family takes time to supervise pet charities—the University of Delaware and the Wilmington Medical Center. Moreover, the government has been very cooperative in protecting family lands and fortunes. The county does not put public utilities into chateau country which would be needed for development, and highways are always routed around the DuPont estates. In 1954 Pierre S. du Pont's estate of over $58 million paid out only about $580,000 in state death taxes. In 1967 Delaware residents with earnings of $200,000–$225,000 paid the same percentage for state income taxes as Delaware citizens with earnings in the $41,000–$49,999 range.

For the upper-middle class of researchers, middle-level management, and professionals, Delaware has both advantages and disadvantages. Their jobs are fairly interesting, they get time off for civic duties, and salaries are high enough to pay for membership in the company country club. On the other hand, the upper-middle class is somewhat insulted by the obvious distortions in the *News-Journal*. They are forced to pay excessively high prices for their suburban homes, which are now threatened by a county sewer crisis, and their usual cordial reception at the local bank may quickly turn sour if they inadvertently alienate one of the powers that be. Government provides upper-middle class families with good roads and secondary schools, but imposes high taxes. Because both DuPont family and company land is severely underassessed, the upper-middle class pays higher property taxes. While the very rich have hired accountants to take advantage of special loopholes in wage, income, and death taxes, the upper-middle class bear the full brunt of all these government levies. Most important, upper-middle class people in Delaware are dissatisfied because they realize that, despite their Ph.D.'s, they may be as bound to the corporate will as the janitor who sweeps DuPont's floors. They have signed away all rights to their creative ideas on or off company time, and they know they must follow certain unwritten guidelines if they want to break into the top ranks of the corporate hierarchy.

Like DuPont researchers, working-class families in Delaware must bear an extra property tax burden to make up for the underassessment of corporate and family land, as well as the nonassessment of corporate equipment and personal property. In addition to federal and state income taxes, blue-collar employees in Wilmington must pay a regressive city wage tax. But unlike the upper-middle class, blue-collar employees are not left with enough income to pay for essential goods and services. A working-class couple with two children, living in a Wilmington house assessed at $12,000 and earning $7000 per year (at $3.50 per hour), would pay about $1195 in local, state, and federal taxes each year—leaving the family with only $5805 to live on—$150 less than the Department of Labor estimated was necessary for an urban family of four to meet its basic needs. Nor are blue-collar workers organized well enough to improve their living and working conditions. DuPont unions are too weak to press for their own interest in higher wages or better processing of grievances. Since the corporate elite are so much more politically powerful than unions, the working man has also been neglected on the state level. The workmen's compensation law in Delaware is inadequate; the state-owned Farmers Bank does not provide small businessmen with a helping hand; there is no serious public effort to build moderate-income housing; and the state lacks an effective legal or medical aid program for working-class families.

For the poor white in Delaware, the state is a nightmare. In 1969, 15.7% of all Delaware families had incomes below the poverty line, and about 40% of the families on welfare were white. The white poor are concentrated in Kent and Sussex counties. Public and private groups have generally neglected them. Their schools do not provide training for highly skilled jobs or for college. Nor has the state built a system of mass transit to make jobs accessible to the many white families without cars. While a few large firms including DuPont have built plants in southern Delaware, the state's recent coastline bill together with

H. B. du Pont's water study have reduced prime industrial sites which would provide jobs near poor white areas. Yet despite this lack of opportunity for self-improvement, the lower class has been denied assistance in obtaining the minimal necessities of life. For instance, 40% of the housing units in one 1960 census tract of southern New Castle County had no plumbing facilities. Meanwhile, government agencies have been tearing down more houses than they have rebuilt for low-income families. With high rates of infant mortality and mental illness, the poor are condemned to use the emergency wards of a private hospital for primary medical care because Delaware has no public hospitals. There are only a few legal aid lawyers in the whole state. Moreover, the level of direct income assistance is minimal; until recently the state ceiling on welfare grants was so low that it violated minimum federal standards.

For blacks, Delaware has been a racist state. In 1959 DuPont rejected the Peterson Plan, which called for upgrading job assignments of only four black workers at a single plant; * even now, blacks are conspicuously absent from top management posts. Racial discrimination in housing has been even worse. In the Wilmington area, blacks are predominantly confined to inner-city and county ghettos. In parts of southern Delaware, blacks are forced to live in unannexed portions of towns without proper plumbing facilities. In the past, blacks have received a very low standard of health care; presently, the Wilmington Medical Center is moving the city's largest hospitals into areas which are virtually inaccessible to ghetto blacks. There are only three black lawyers in the state. After years of turning blacks down for loans, the banks have supported a token loan fund for minority groups which could have been three times as large under a federal program. Delaware continues to run almost a dual education system for blacks and whites. Blacks are concentrated in a handful of school districts and are channeled into Delaware State College instead of the University of Delaware. The state Human Relations Commission is drastically understaffed. And the state itself created racial strife by its nine-month

* The plan was accepted a year later after President Eisenhower requested DuPont support for integration in industry.

military occupation of Wilmington's black neighborhoods. Moreover, through metropolitan government, the corporate establishment would deprive Wilmington's blacks of the opportunity to elect the first black mayor; Seaford already has at-large elections to combat the increasing black vote.

## *Recommendations*

Despite the immense influence of DuPont in Delaware, pressures from local and national critics have brought about some changes. From the turn of the twentieth century until the middle of the Great Depression, DuPont overtly ran Delaware and exploited the federal government through its near monopoly of the munitions market. But the 1934 congressional hearings conducted by the Nye Committee into wartime profiteering—which gave the DuPonts the nickname "Merchants of Death"—and later Franklin D. Roosevelt's overwhelming defeat of the DuPont-backed American Liberty League and Alfred M. Landon, led to a new company attitude toward corporate responsibility. DuPont relinquished much of its overt control of Delaware politics and provided fewer armaments to the federal government during World War II than in World War I, at lower profits. In the 1960s, after years of hibernation, the rise of social consciousness among businessmen generally, together with local pressure to overcome urban decay and outmoded governmental structures, brought DuPonts back into the public sphere.

Delaware may currently be on the verge of another major change in the relationship between the corporate establishment and the state. The recent groundswell of public opinion on pollution issues and stronger federal laws have forced Delaware's pollution control agencies to eliminate some loopholes and concessions in the state's antipollution laws. The state adopted more stringent air quality standards. After a full-time DuPont employee in charge of Wilmington's proposed civic center refused to promise jobs to blacks because it was a private project, the blacks rose up against this publicly subsidized boondoggle, the shopping mall intended to make Wilmington a shinier "Chemical Capital of the World." Lawyers in the Delaware chapter of the American Civil Liberties Union have recently become more aggressive, as shown by their suit against de facto segregation in Wilmington and its suburbs. When Governor Peterson, a former DuPont executive, led the state into a deficit of over $30 million, the legislature responded by tightening some of the widest state tax loopholes. And, perhaps most significant in the long run, the staff of the *News-Journal* has begun to react strongly against the censorship imposed by the DuPont family and top editors under the family's wing. The recent critical articles on the shopping mall proposal, for example, are signs of change.

At the same time, executives in Delaware may be realizing that a new corporate approach to the community is needed. When the black ghettos of Wilmington erupted after Martin Luther King's murder, the elite may have sensed that DuPont's high return on investment was not being evenly spread throughout the community. On the other hand, in projects like the Neighborhood Improvement Program, run by Russell Peterson and H. B. du Pont, businessmen learned that they could not solve the state's social problems overnight by financing a few neighborhood centers. Within the last two years, business leaders have shown signs of recognizing the need for broader representation on their boards—for example, the recent appointment of one Jewish and one outside director in the DuPont Company. Corporate executives and family members are not morally or congenitally incapable of becoming more accountable or responsive to the citizens of Delaware. Some members of the corporate elite have never thought of alternative ways to relate to Delaware; many have taken the easiest road of pursuing their own interests; others still naively believe that the aims of DuPont are the needs of the state.

Moreover, since we released our preliminary report on DuPont in Delaware, certain changes have occurred in corporate and governmental spheres, though these changes carried out only a few of the recommendations made in the preliminary report. The DuPont family has announced that it will definitely sell off the *News-Journal*. The DuPont Company has greatly increased its donations to the local black college, Delaware State. And a DuPont executive reportedly has sought advice on establishing a *pro bono publico* program for company lawyers as a direct outgrowth of the preliminary report. In the public sphere, officials of New Castle County have finally held public hearings on the White Clay Creek Dam and have stayed this Dupont-promoted project for independent reevaluation. In the two southern counties of Delaware, full-time legal aid offices have been set up.

The most serious flaws in DuPont's relation to Delaware, like the problems of most large corporations in their local communities, do not derive from a well-planned conspiracy of businessmen. The key problems in corporate responsibility are more prosaic—the day-to-day institutional biases and personal conditioning which grow out of the complicated structural relations of a large corporation with other private and public groups. If the problem were only individual malevolence, there would be only one recommendation—replace the occupants of high private and public offices with good people. But new officials would soon be caught up in old dilemmas. To make corporations more responsible to local citizens, it is necessary to alter the shape of the private and public arena in Delaware as well as in other states. The implicit, unarticulated biases created by the overwhelming presence of the DuPont Company and family make Delaware the prototype of a company state. Likewise, the strategies for reforming the company state in Delaware may be applicable throughout the country.

While it would be impossible to lay out the exact process whereby DuPont or any large business could achieve true corporate responsibility, we can propose some general guidelines toward which all groups can aim. These guidelines are not panaceas for corporate evils; they only attempt to delineate some changes which would improve the relations between large corporations like DuPont and their communities. These guidelines basically aim at reasserting the state's control over its own legal creation and broadening the basis of representation in private government. They would help assure that private corporations serve rather than master their public incorporators and constituents. Ultimately the citizens and officials of Delaware, as well as other states, must make whatever changes they deem necessary to achieve this goal through democratic mechanisms.

### THE DECISION-MAKING PROCESS: SHIFTS IN POWER

To make corporations more accountable to state residents, corporate power needs to be controlled by structural checks in public bodies, the private market place, and the internal processes of corporate decision making. There are two basic premises behind the need for checks on the *process* of decision making in any political unit. First, corporate power must be subjected to institutionalized controls because informal discussions provide no guarantee that corporate executives will even consider seriously views and interests other than their own. Second, checks on corporate power must be both external and internal. While a perfectly democratic government and a perfectly functioning private market might provide the necessary checks on corporate power. such perfection is inherently impossible in such a small state with such a large company. Since there will always be some co-optation of public officials by private corporations and some concentration of economic power in certain market sectors, local residents should be given some internal checks on corporate power through participation in corporate government.

To give citizens a significant voice in the process of deciding the matters most important to their daily lives, we can suggest general guidelines together with specific subgoals in each of three categories of structural checks on corporate power—private competition, public surveillance, and corporate democracy.

*Private competition:* As a general guideline, private and public groups should promote competition between suppliers of local goods and services.

A. BREAKING UP MONOPOLIES. Private groups with monopolies should divest themselves of a substantial segment of their holdings, and governmental bodies should by statute require the division of monopolistic holdings. In Delaware, the DuPont family should voluntarily sell the *Morning News* and *Evening Journal* to different buyers, either private firms or a consortium of newspaper employees, to ensure the proper flow of information within the state. In either case, the methods of financing should effectively insulate the new owners from the control of the Delaware corporate establishment. To eliminate the DuPont family's stranglehold on the land market in New Castle County, the county government should rezone areas now immune from development because of large-lot requirements and carefully police real estate dealings to stop racial and social discrimination. Parts of DuPont chateau country should be converted to public parkland.

B. EXPANDING SUPPLIERS. To encourage competition between suppliers, all levels of government should seek to attract alternative sources of goods and services as well as encourage the expansion of potential suppliers already present. For example, to promote banking practices more oriented toward small businessmen and minority groups in Delaware, the state-controlled Farmers Bank should be reoriented toward the federal SBA and MESBIC programs. The state banking commissioner should devise methods to ensure that state-licensed banks are not withholding from the market, through restrictive lending or reserves practices, excessive amounts of capital that could rationally be channeled throughout the state for development and renewal. Along the same lines, to provide a wider range of job opportunities, Delaware must change its image as a corporate headquarters state. State government should encourage blue-collar industry, the county should rezone the Wilmington Medical Center's county site as originally planned for industry, and the city should develop the industrial potential of Cherry Island and the port. Of course, all development should take place only with proper environmental controls and according to a publicly evolved land use plan for the entire state.

C. EQUALIZING BARGAINING POWER: BLUE-COLLAR WORKERS. To create an effective competitive system for setting wages and work conditions, there must be a rough balance of power between management and blue-collar workers. In particular, DuPont labor unions should organize nationally, either through the Federation of Independent Unions–DuPont Systems or with an international union.

This is a prerequisite to building up the strike fund and administrative capacity necessary for DuPont labor unions to gain a rough balance of economic strength with the corporation. On the basis of nationwide representation, unions could then negotiate with DuPont on wages and work conditions, including the industrial relations plans, wage increases, agency shop, and many policies governing working conditions presently contained in the contract supplement or *Administrative Plans and Practices* at the various plants. If management still refuses to bargain over these and other legitimate subjects for collective bargaining, DuPont unions should promptly file complaints with the National Labor Relations Board.

D. EQUALIZING BARGAINING POWER: WHITE-COLLAR WORKERS. White-collar workers, too, should organize themselves to defend their interests. Organizations of white-collar workers should press for written employment contracts providing job security; after a probationary period, dismissal should be only for cause or skill obsolescence. To guard against skill obsolescence, such contracts should require on-the-job training programs, guaranteed retraining for redundant workers, plus some type of supplementary unemployment benefits if retraining is infeasible. To promote job mobility, white-collar organizations should ask for pension rights with automatic vesting after a certain number of years and transferability to other companies. Also for job mobility, white-collar workers should demand that bonuses be paid in full during the year in which they are earned, and that group insurance plans continue for a grace period of at least one year after termination of employment. Moreover, to bolster the bargaining powers of white-collar workers, the government should limit the trade secret doctrine by narrowly defining confidentiality while recognizing legitimate business interests; and it should outlaw contract clauses that take away the rights of employees to inventions discovered after working hours.

*Public Supervision.* As a general guideline, the state should create a competent government with equal say for all state citizens.

A. ELECTIONS. To increase public participation in government, the state should pass liberal laws for open primaries after party conventions. Limitations on and disclosure of campaign expenditures should be required. In Delaware particularly, the state's annexation law should be changed from the present one dollar, one vote system to one man, one vote. Similarly, the state should ban at-large voting within municipalities like Seaford because such voting arrangements can easily be used to deprive minorities of legitimate rights.

B. LEGISLATIVE OPERATIONS. All state representatives and senators should be given a full-time salary, and all elected officials should be supplied with an adequate research staff. Such a system would encourage comprehensive consideration of issues by legislators instead of automatic reliance on corporate expertise. It would also help eliminate conflict-of-interest problems, which should be clearly regulated by a strong statute forbidding any elected official to vote on decisions in which he has a personal stake. Full-time representatives and adequate research aid are especially necessary in Delaware, since the corporate establishment employs so great a percentage of the work force and controls so large a part of the legislative resources in the state.

C. GOVERNMENTAL STRUCTURE. While proposals for executive reorganizations and metropolitan government may bring about more efficient public bodies in a financial sense, both types of restructuring offer grave possibilities of streamlining corporate control over public processes. The organizational methods of big business, when applied to government, may reduce costs, but often at the expense of public procedures needed for a functioning democratic system. Metropolitan government may be a façade for taking away the nascent political power of urban blacks by suburban groups who have fled the center cities. In Delaware, the executive reorganization of state government should be reexamined with an eye to antidemocratic implications, and the question of metropolitan government for the Wilmington area should be put to a public vote.

D. INFORMATION AND POLICY MAKING. To increase

knowledge and discussion of governmental issues, the state should pass a freedom-of-information act which would make all public reports and nonpersonal files open to inspection by any citizen. On the other hand, all levels of government should undertake independent studies of public issues instead of allowing private groups to have the only input of information into major policy questions. In Delaware, specifically, the state legislature should repeal the law which forbids the state auditor to inquire into the private revenue and expenditures of the University of Delaware. To reduce public decision making based on private information sources, the urban renewal programs of northern Delaware, Downtown Wilmington, Inc., and the Greater Wilmington Development Council should be abolished.

*Corporate Democracy*. As a general guideline, DuPont and all large corporations should promote the systematic input of views besides those of top executives into its internal decision-making processes.

A. CORPORATE INFORMATION. To provide citizens with the knowledge necessary to make an independent evaluation of corporate policy toward the community, firms should have the burden of proof in showing substantial business detriment before denying any information requested by citizens, employees, or stockholders. At a minimum, DuPont should make available directly to local residents information collected by its Community Affairs Committee, corporate figures on minority employment, data obtained by monitoring its own pollution, and the result of its research on product safety.

B. FIDUCIARY DUTIES. To provide citizens and stockholders with a means of forcing corporate directors to perform their duties, the present Delaware general corporation law should be changed. This corporation law affects citizens and stockholders in all states, since numerous large firms are incorporated in Delaware. Instead of promoting indemnification of directors and encouraging management to write its own corporate law, the Delaware statute should impose certain standards of corporate behavior on all firms, enforced by nonindemnifiable fines and jail sentences. Such changes, however, might have to be brought about by federal legislation to prevent local corporations from moving to other states with lenient laws.

C. PUBLIC INTEREST REPRESENTATION. The boards of directors of large corporations like DuPont and large banks like Wilmington Trust should be expanded, by democratic elections or through appointment by the present board, to include representatives of consumers, the local community, and minority stockholders. While these public-interest representatives may be outvoted by management and majority stockholders, the new directors (backed up by an adequate staff and budget) can at least raise community issues for discussion, issue dissenting reports, and advocate the interests of minority coalitions within the corporation. Furthermore, since DuPont gives each plant manager a high degree of discretion over community affairs, there should be publicly elected or company-appointed advisory boards made up of a cross section of local interests in every community with a large corporate facility. These boards would have the power to make proposals for corporate policy toward the community, which management would have to answer in writing. The board would meet at least once a month, and management would have to provide information to the board, excluding trade secrets.

D. INDUSTRIAL DEMOCRACY. To give workers a direct voice in the business operations affecting their lives, large firms like DuPont should permit worker representation on corporate policy-making bodies. After studying the experience of various European countries, DuPont managers and union officials should devise some formal mechanism by which workers can have substantial participation in running the company. Of course, the models from European countries should not be followed slavishly, and worker representation should not replace unions, which must necessarily continue as an independent pressure group for workers within the company. At the minimum, workers should control their own pension funds, serve on plant safety committees, and help determine shift systems as well as changes in production processes that substantially alter the nature of their jobs.

### THE RESULTS OF DECISION MAKING: REALLOCATION OF RESOURCES

To make public and private bodies responsive more to the needs of all state citizens than to the parochial interests of the corporate elite, business and personal wealth has to be channeled by more equitable policies on taxation, public expenditures, and charitable giving. There are two premises behind the concept of redistributing private and public wealth. First, to carry out many of the recommendations proposed here, the state needs more revenue—to pay for full-time legislators and expert financial analysts, for example. Second, if the taxation system were perfectly equitable and the government always made the best decision on the allocation of resources, then the recommendation could only be to eliminate any form of private program for public purpose or charitable donation and to substitute government-run public programs. But since there will inevitably be tax loopholes and fraud as well as governmental red tape and misallocations, private contributions to community groups can play an important role in both decentralizing decision-making power and meeting the substantive needs of Delaware citizens.

To orient private and public resources more toward the needs of all citizens than the interests of the corporate elite in Delaware and other states, we can delineate general guidelines and specific subgoals in each of the three main resource categories—taxation, public expenditures, and private contributions.

*Taxation.* As a general guideline, the state should strive for a progressive tax system without special concession to the corporate elite.

A. CORPORATE FRANCHISE AND INCOME. The state should require that companies pay substantial fees for the privilege of incorporation as well as annual levies on business income. Of course, if a national incorporation statute were passed, then the federal government should impose a uniform franchise tax. Until that time, the maximum payment for the corporate franchise tax in Delaware should be raised to at least $200,000, and corporate income taxes should also be increased.

B. PERSONAL INCOME. The state should impose levies on personal income which are effectively progressive. While Delaware has recently raised tax rates in the upper brackets, the state should take action to remove other regressive features of its levies on personal income. Delaware should revert to its pre-1970 treatment of capital gains as ordinary income, previously one of the most progressive aspects of the state's tax structure. Similarly, the Wilmington wage tax should be abolished, since the tax is a flat rate with exemptions for income from stocks and bonds mainly held by the corporate rich. Instead, the state should impose a surtax on income for all residents of New Castle County who use Wilmington as an economic and social center.

C. DEATH TAXES. State laws should work against the perpetuation of great wealth from generation to generation. Inheritance and estate taxes should be high, while a gift tax is needed to prevent the circumvention of the other death levies. To eliminate the competition between states for elderly millionaires, the federal government may have to pass national rates for death taxes. Currently, Delaware should take vigorous action to undercut the continuation of family dynasties based on inherited riches. The legislature should increase gift, estate, and inheritance taxes. Delaware should drastically change its treatment of wealth held in local trusts. Income of out-of-state trusts in Delaware banks should be taxed at the same rate as income of in-state trusts. Property held in trust should be exempt from inheritance taxes for only three generations, as in most other states.

D. PERSONAL PROPERTY. The state should tax both types of personal property: tangible, such as research equipment and jewelry, and intangible, such as stocks and bonds. But the taxes should be structured to fall mainly on large holdings of personal property for reasons of administrative efficiency and distributional equity. In Delaware, legislation should be enacted allowing the cities and counties to tax business personal property of companies of a certain size. By this measure, the industrial and research equipment of the capital-intensive chemical industry will become a source of much needed public revenue, helping to redress the imbalance of benefits accruing to the chemical industry in

Delaware. Delaware also has a particular need for an individual personal-property tax because of the great disparities between the lavish furnishings and tremendous stock assets of the corporate elite and the personal holdings of the average family.

E. REAL PROPERTY. The state should by statute establish a real property assessment system based on true market value with uniform assessment ratios and assessments per unit of size. Such legal requirements should be enforced in a manner which would not favor one class of landholder over others. Annual reassessments based on actual market value should be made through the use of computers and modern statistical sampling techniques. Alternatively, or in the interim before annual reassessments can be made, a rotating system of reassessments could be instituted, by which a governmental unit would be divided into districts, each to be assessed every few years. The reappraisal and reassessment now underway in New Castle County offers an excellent opportunity for reforms to be instituted almost immediately. The state should also develop a statewide school tax levied at the same rate per $100 assessed property value for each school district, but distributed equally according to the number of pupils in each district. Such a statewide tax would eliminate the gross disparities in educational funds among school districts. In addition, special measures are needed in Delaware. DuPont should voluntarily begin to pay property taxes to Seaford on an assessed value equivalent to the full, fair market value of the property, and should seek annexation into the town. The DuPont family and company, and other persons similarly benefited by the inequitable assessment system in New Castle County, should refund the tax losses (plus interest) incurred by local governments through the illegally low assessments of land over the last 15 years.

*Public programs.* As a general guideline, the state should allocate its funds to provide equal opportunity and a decent standard of living for all citizens.

A. MINIMUM PROTECTION. The state should set a floor of material benefits to assure a minimum standard of living for all its citizens. Such minimum protection should be provided in the fields of housing, medical care, legal aid, work conditions, and welfare benefits. In Delaware, state and county governments should allocate enough money to meet the assessed need for standard housing units, as well as initiate a program to provide plumbing facilities to all Delaware residents immediately. To meet the medical requirements of its citizens, the state should construct a general hospital system that would provide ambulatory and in-patient care, and begin a state health insurance program for low and moderate income residents. To provide legal counsel for all Delaware citizens, the public defender and legal assistance programs should be greatly expanded. The state should modernize its workmen's compensation laws, hire at least 10 more safety inspectors, and give jurisdiction over work conditions in factories to the Department of Natural Resources and Environmental Control. To attack the problems of poverty, the state should combine a full-scale job training program with benefits above the subsistence level for sick, unemployable, and elderly persons, as well as dependent children.

B. PROGRAM REORIENTATION. All levels of government should reorient public programs away from the interests of the corporate elite and more toward the needs of the average citizen. Instead of spending millions on highways for corporate commuters, Delaware's new Department of Highways and Transportation should begin serious efforts to construct a comprehensive system of mass transit. To alter the racially divided and science-based system of higher education, the state should increase the funds given to Delaware State, while building up departments at the University of Delaware in social sciences and humanities. The Delaware Bar Association should develop active committees for law reform efforts for consumers, criminal defendants, racial minorities, and other groups which have not received the same legal attention as corporations. County officials should not quietly maintain the Greater Wilmington Airport as a private runway for the planes of corporate executives. At a public hearing, county officials should discuss the major alternatives: to develop the airport as a general aviation facility, concentrating on increasing use of the airport for the air freight industry, or to enlarge the airport to serve as a regional passenger terminal for the Greater Philadelphia area. Neither the state nor the city of Wilmington should expend funds on the GWDC's proposed shopping mall or accompanying parking facilities—projects geared more to giving the city an attractive façade for corporate visitors than meeting the needs of Wilmington residents.

C. DEVELOPMENTAL REGULATION. The state should promote rational industrial development together with proper land-use planning and strict environmental controls. Delaware should transform Farmers Bank into a financing agent for local development, and allocate more money to state agencies like the Delaware Industrial Building Commission. At the same time, Delaware should adopt state-of-the-art criteria requiring firms to install the best pollution abatement equipment available. Industries should be obliged by statute to update equipment continually and to undertake serious research to develop cleaner production processes. The Air Pollution Advisory Board should be abolished because its industrial representatives can too easily influence state regulatory efforts. Similarly, the Water and Air Resources Commission should be integrated into the Department of Natural Resources and Environmental Control. This department should have an adequate legal staff to bring antipollution cases, rather than depend on the part-time efforts of lawyers from the attorney general's office. The statutory requirement of conciliation in antipollution suits should be eliminated because it has been used by large corporations to avoid their environmental obligations. Fines for polluters should be increased, and private citizens should be allowed to file suits against violators of state environmental laws.

*Corporate statesmanship*. As a general guideline, large corporations like DuPont should provide the community with contributions in areas of relatively low political volatility and relatively high levels of technical problems. At the same time, decisions about allocation of charitable resources should be democratized.

A. CORPORATE GIVING. To make corporate donors accountable to the community and assure that corporate gifts go to projects desired by local residents, all organs of orporate giving must be split up, or made more demo-ratic, or both. To eliminate DuPont-run private founda-ons as an alternative government in Delaware, the capital ınds of these foundations should be distributed among everal Delaware community foundations run by directors lected at a yearly conference of community groups. Al-ernatively, the current boards of the private DuPont oundations should be broadened to include majority repre-entation of community groups not connected with the orporate establishment. The newly constituted boards or ommunity foundations should be assisted by a full-time esearch staff to help implement a system of comprehen-ive, competent comparison of grant applications. In the ong run, these community foundations should also replace he United Fund and Council (UFC). In the short run, the orporate elite should broaden the UFC's board to include ecipient group and employee representation, and com-anies should cease pressuring employees to make contri-utions to the UFC. Similarly, the DuPont corporation hould either give money only to community foundations r broaden the composition of its committee on corporate iving to include representatives of workers and local resi-lents. State and federal tax provisions should grant tax leductions to companies and individuals only for gifts iven to community foundations or allocated by a broadly epresentative board.

B. Corporate assistance programs. Corporations hould confine their social action projects in the community o areas of high technical requirements and low political ontent. Because DuPont has a high degree of expertise n developing new products and helping customers design ew operations, the company should help create com-nunity spin-offs, which would manufacture products like vork clothes or office supplies used by DuPont in large olumes. With a long-term contract from DuPont as a tart, community spin-offs should soon become independent irms competing on the open market and providing jobs o minority groups as well as unemployed persons. To romote the construction of low- and moderate-income ousing units, the Wilmington banks should set up a large revolving fund together with technical assistance for nonprofit housing sponsors. With funds raised from the corporate elite instead of scarce public capital, the Greater Wilmington Housing Corporation should concentrate on building low-income houses in New Castle County suburbs to provide the trade-off units needed to break the deadlock on public housing in Wilmington. Since the DuPont Company and corporate law firms in Wilmington control the best legal resources in the state, these institutions should encourage their employees to engage in *pro bono* work for poor citizens on company or firm time. Such *pro bono* work should be concentrated in areas like criminal appeals with low probabilities of conflicts of interest. In contrast the DuPont Company should not try to plan land and water allocations for New Castle County government. Since the DuPont Company has bought hundreds of acres for the White Clay Creek Dam in the name of the public interest, it should turn over all the land to public officials, either as a charitable donation or for not more than the price paid by DuPont. Then, through open hearings and perhaps referendum votes, the county government could choose the best use for this large plot.

C. INTERNAL CORPORATE OPERATIONS. In the day-to-day running of the corporation, large firms like DuPont should seek to implement the spirit as well as the letter of constitutional and statutory provisions. To improve its currently poor record on minority employment, DuPont should make serious efforts to recruit blacks and women, especially into high-level management positions. While DuPont should hire graduates of public training schools, the company also should run its own training programs without public subsidies. Instead of waiting to be prodded by federal action, DuPont should aggressively reassess the environmental impact of all its facilities. Rather than spend the time, money, and effort opposing strict pollution standards at state and federal hearings, DuPont should devote these resources to developing new ways to cope with its waste. The company should make serious efforts to put out public relations material that accurately describes events without subtly trying to push DuPont's political line.

Nor should the company punish or harass corporate employees who use their expertise in community projects, even if the employees oppose DuPont's interests after working hours.

Finally, in its business relations with subcontractors, the company should insist that subcontractors abide by standards of pollution control similar to those the company itself follows. It should also require subcontractors to use only racially balanced crews for any work done for DuPont.

In short, DuPont in Delaware is the prototype of the large corporation in an American community. Like most big companies, DuPont is not just one of many firms competing in the local market for short-term profits; nor is the corporation merely one private interest group participating in a pluralistic political process. Such large corporations may undercut the democratic processes and resource allocations of the political units; such domination carried to extremes brings about the company state. In Delaware, the mother state has virtually been replaced by the mother company; corporate power is no longer private, but has nearly preempted public power. The resources of the state are more oriented toward helping the corporate elite than providing equal opportunity for all citizens; Delaware is one of the best examples of "poverty amidst plenty."

Yet executives of DuPont, as well as other large firms, often say that there is no viable path toward corporate responsibility. If DuPont runs social action programs, then it is accused of usurping public functions; if DuPont does nothing, it is chastised for corporate apathy. This is a false contradiction. The question is not whether any mammoth firm will make an impact on its political unit; DuPont affects the community even by its inaction. The question is: in what ways and by which methods should large companies like DuPont relate to the local community? The criteria must be: a large corporation should act so as to provide the community with a maximum of benefits and a minimum of domination. By following the recommendations of the Delaware Study Group for corporate responsibility, DuPont would become more accountable to the citizens of Delaware, so the corporation could be more responsive to their needs. While carrying through the reforms suggested in this book, Delawareans may regain a sense of control over their lives and become determined to accomplish a thoroughgoing rebirth of democracy in their state.

# Notes

*Chapter 1*

1. Milton Friedman, *Capitalism and Freedom* (U. of Chicago Press, 1962).
2. Quoted in "Company and Community: the Responsibilities of Business in Society," *This Is DuPont* (DuPont, 1967), p. 3.
3. *A. P. Smith Mfg. Co.* v. *Barlow,* 13 NJ 145, 98 A.2d 581 (1953).
4. *DuPont Facts Book* (DuPont, Mar., 1960) p. 15-1.

*Chapter 2*

1. *US* v. *DuPont et al.*, 188 F.127 152 (Cir. Ct., D. Del, June 21, 1911).
2. Alfred P. Sloan, *My Years at General Motors* (Doubleday, 1964), p. 12.
3. *US* v. *DuPont et al.,* 353 US 586, 606 (1957).
4. "The Market Place: Forum or Arena," speech by Crawford H. Greenewalt at 47th Annual International Convention, National Association of Purchasing Agents, Chicago, May 7, 1962.
5. See Vance Packard, *The Hidden Persuaders* (McKay, 1957).
6. See K. William Kapp, *The Social Costs of Private Enterprise* (Schocken, 1971); Ezra J. Mishan, *The Cost of Economic Growth* (Praeger, 1967).
7. "Corporate Political Affairs Programs," 70 *Yale Law Journal* 821 (Apr., 1961).
8. *Morning News,* Sept. 15, 1971.
9. *Evening Journal,* Sept. 16, 1971.
10. *Morning News,* July 2, 1971.
11. Ralph J. Baker and William L. Carey, *Cases and Materials on Corporations,* 3d ed. (Foundation Press, 1959), p. 359.
12. *DuPont Facts Book* (Mar., 1960), p. 1-21.
13. "DuPont and the Environment in Delaware," transcript of a forum sponsored by DuPont, June 2, 1970, p. 7.
14. Robin A. Wallace, William Fulkerson, Wilbur D. Shults, William S. Lyon, *Mercury in the Environment: The Human Element* (Jan., 1971), p. 10.
15. Ibid., pp. 9–10.
16. Ibid., p. 10.
17. "Hazards of Mercury," *Environmental Research* 4, #1 (Mar., 1971), pp. 43–4.
18. John Esposito, *Vanishing Air* (Grossman, 1970), p. 67.
19. Ronald E. Engel, "Health Hazards of Environmental Lead: A Position Paper," Bureau of Air Pollution Sciences, Air Pollution

Control Office, Environmental Protection Agency (Apr. 29, 1971), p. 1.

20. DuPont Company response to the Preliminary Report of this book.
21. Ibid.
22. *Evening Journal,* July 29, 1971.
23. *Evening Journal,* Sept. 10, 1971.
24. Interview with C. A. D'Alonzo, Aug. 25, 1970.

*Chapter 3*

1. Final Report of the Industrial Commission created by Act of Congress, 1898 (1902), as quoted in Clyde W. Summers and Harry H. Wellington, *Cases and Materials on Labor Law* (Foundation Press, 1968), p. 12.
2. Minutes from negotiations between management and union at DuPont Niagara Falls plant, Sept. 11, 1970, pp. 10–11.
3. Ibid., p. 1.
4. "The Organization and the Individual," *This Is DuPont* (DuPont, 1964), p. 26.
5. Ibid., p. 29.
6. Ibid., p. 29.
7. Ibid., p. 25.
8. "Life in a Large Corporation," *This Is DuPont* (DuPont, 1957), p. 10.
9. "The Story of Taxes," *This Is DuPont* (DuPont, 1957), p. 20.
10. "The Organization and the Individual," p. 1.
11. Marlene Dixon, "But Are You Really a Professional?" *Engineer* (Jan.–Feb., 1968), p. 18.
12. Ernest Dale, *The Great Organizers* (McGraw-Hill, 1960), p. 45.
13. "The Engineers Are Redesigning Their Own Profession," *Fortune* (June, 1971), p. 75. The study, conducted by Gene Dalton and Paul Thompson, further stated, according to *Fortune:*

    When told the bad news in counseling sessions with their supervisors, some of the men froze and performed even less effectively. The high-rated men felt confident enough to leave for new jobs, while the less able men feared a move and stayed on. Some supervisors admitted that they took away performance points from older men and gave them to younger men to qualify them for promotions. Caught in situations like this, older engineers feel doubly vulnerable because their formal learning has become outmoded and yet their salaries are comparatively high owing to longevity. If they are laid off, their age counts heavily against them in finding new work. One man summed it up grimly: "This is the only business I know where gray hair is a badge of shame."

14. Joseph A. Dallas, quoted in *Better Living* (Nov.–Dec., 1968), p. 6.

15. "Life in a Large Corporation," p. 16.
16. *DuPont Facts Book,* Introduction.
17. Ibid., p. 17-1.
18. William H. Whyte, *Organization Man* (Simon & Schuster, 1956), p. 121.
19. Quoted in the *DuPont Facts Book,* p. 4-23.
20. Ibid.
21. *Inland Steel* v. *NLRB,* 170 F.2d 247 (7th Cir. 1949).
22. *NLRB* v. *GE,* 418 F.2d 736, 756 (1969), *cert. den.* 397 US 965 (1970).
23. Minutes from negotiation meeting, Sept. 11, 1970, p. 7.
24. 337 US 217, 225.
25. 337 US 217 (1949), at 224. See also *NLRB* v. *Katz,* 369 US 736 (1962); *NLRB* v. *Herman Sausage Co.,* 275 F.2d 229 (5th Cir. 1960).
26. See *Steelworkers* v. *Warner and Gulf,* 363 US 574 (1960); *NLRB* v. *American National Insurance,* 343 US 395 (1952).
27. See *Gulf Power Co.,* 156 NLRB 622 (1966), enforced 384 F.2d 822 (5th Cir. 1967).
28. *Bethlehem Steel,* 136 NLRB 135, enforced 320 F.2d 822 (5th Cir., 1963), *cert. den.* 375 US 984 (1964).
29. 418 F.2d 736, 756 (1969), *cert. den.* 397 US 965 (1970).
30. Robert Blauner, *Alienation and Freedom* (U. of Chicago Press, 1964), ch 6, 7.
31. DuPont has a turnover rate for blue- and white-collar employees well below other companies'; in the early 1960s it was 80% below the average rate for all US manufacturing.
32. Letter, May 4, 1961.

*Chapter 4*

1. E. Digby Baltzell, *The Protestant Establishment: Aristocracy and Caste in America* (Random House, 1964), p. 252.
2. John K. Winkler, *The DuPont Dynasty* (Reynal & Hitchcock, 1935), p. 41.
3. Baltzell, p. 250.
4. Marquis James, *Alfred I. du Pont: The Family Rebel* (Bobbs-Merrill, 1941), p. 269.
5. Winkler, p. 219.
6. James, p. 354.
7. Winkler, p. 299.
8. James, pp. 423–6.
9. Ibid., p. 299.
10. Baltzell, pp. 250–51.
11. William H. A. Carr, *The DuPonts of Delaware* (Dodd, Mead, 1964), p. 311.
12. Ibid., p. 312.
13. James, p. 401.
14. Baltzell, p. 250.
15. Philip Stern, *The Great Treasury Raid* (Random House, 1964), pp. 255–6.

16. Marvin Brams, *Delaware Inheritance and Estate Taxes* (U. of Delaware, 1969), p. 11.
17. *People's Pulse,* Dec., 1970.
18. *Evening Journal,* Nov. 5, 1970.
19. "Opinions on the Impact of Merger upon Wilmington Health Services," *Delaware Medical Journal* 41, #4 (Apr., 1969), pp. 113–17.
20. *Evening Journal,* Jan. 9, 1968.
21. *Evening Journal,* July 29, 1970.

*Chapter 5*

1. E. Digby Baltzell,`*The Protestant Establishment: Aristocracy and Caste in America* (Random House, 1964), p. 251.
2. Directory of the Wilmington Country Club (1968), p. 43.
3. *Evening Journal,* Oct. 31, 1963.
4. *Open Space Fact Sheet* (Dept. of Parks and Recreation, New Castle County, Mar., 1970).
5. *Evening Journal,* Nov. 28, 1970.
6. *Evening Journal,* Sept. 15, 1970.
7. *Morning News,* Sept. 8, 1971.
8. Statistics are from *Neighborhood Environmental Analysis: A Background Study* (Dept. of Planning, New Castle County, 1968).

*Chapter 6*

1. Advertisement in *Pennsylvania Gazette,* June, 1971.
2. *Wall Street Journal,* Nov. 12, 1970.
3. *Evening Journal,* Nov. 24, 1970.
4. *Wall Street Journal,* Nov. 12, 1970.
5. *Wall Street Journal,* Dec. 3, 1970.
6. 5 *Delaware Code,* §927.
7. 1969 *Annual Report,* Wilmington Trust Co., p. 11.
8. 5 *Delaware Code,* §907.
9. *Morning News,* June 30, 1967.

*Chapter 7*

1. "Law for Sale: A Study of the Delaware Corporation Law," *U. of Pennsylvania Law Review* 861, 891 (Apr., 1969).
2. Letter from Bomar to Greenewalt, June 21, 1963. Quoted in *Minority Report to the Heirs of Irenee du Pont* (hereinafter referred to as *MR,* published privately by Ernest N. May), p. 6.
3. 2 *US Code,* §308.
4. Letter from Bomar to Greenewalt, June 10, 1963. *MR,* pp. 7–8.
5. Ibid.
6. Ibid.
7. *MR Appendix,* pp. 155–6.
8. Congressional Record, 88th Congress, Senate page 2321.
9. Ibid.

10. Ibid.
11. *MR Appendix,* pp. 155–6.
12. Arsht letter to guardians, Apr. 19, 1963. *MR Appendix,* p. 34.
13. Arsht letter to guardians, Apr. 25, 1963. *MR Appendix,* pp. 41–2.
14. Arsht letter to guardians, Apr. 19, 1963. *MR Appendix,* p. 34.
15. Arsht legal memorandum, May 3, 1963. *MR Appendix,* pp. 53–8.
16. Ibid.
17. William H. A. Carr, *The DuPonts of Delaware* (Dodd, Mead, 1964), p. 210.
18. Ernest L. Folk III, *The New Delaware Corporation Law* (1967), p. 9.
19. Ernest L. Folk III, "Corporation Statutes: 1959–66." *Duke Law Journal* 875, 889 (1966).
20. *SEC* v. *Texas Gulf Sulphur,* 401 F.2d 833 (1970), *cert. den.* 394 US 976 (1971).
21. Ernest L. Folk III, *Review of the Delaware Corporation Law (1965–7),* p. 93.
22. Joseph Bishop, "New Curse for an Old Ailment: Insurance against Directors and Officers' Liability," 22 *Business Lawyer* 92, 94–5 (1966).
23. *New York Times,* Jan. 12, 1969.
24. 372 US 335, 344 (1963).
25. See discussion of the Delaware annexation law in Chapter 10 of this book and the cases cited in Note 4, Chapter 10.
26. *Goldberg* v. *Kelly,* 397 US 254 (1970); *New York City Housing Authority* v. *Escalera,* 400 US 853 (1971).

*Chapter 8*

1. *News-Journal,* Dec. 9, 1960.
2. *Morning News,* Feb. 22, 1971.
3. Ibid.
4. *Plan for Development of Midtown Wilmington,* Wallace, McHarg, Roberts and Todd, consultants (commissioned by Greater Wilmington Development Council, 1966), p. 7.
5. William G. Dean, *The Wilmington Parking Authority: A Preliminary Report Prepared for the Mayor's Fiscal Study Committee* (Division of Urban Affairs, U. of Delaware, 1967), p. 46.
6. Charles B. Reeder, *The Market For New Housing in Wilmington and New Castle County, 1967–75* (prepared for Greater Wilmington Housing Corporation June, 1968).
7. The "trade-off rule" is required under provisions of the following federal laws: Title 6, Civil Rights Act of 1964; Executive Order 11063; *HUD Handbook for Preconstruction,* 7410.1, Ch. 1, §1. The *Handbook* states: "Any proposal for locating low-income housing only in an impacted area will be *prima facie* unacceptable."
8. *Evening Journal,* July 7, 1971.
9. *Evening Journal,* July 15, 1971.
10. *Evening Journal,* July 12, 1971.

11. *Parking Needs and Recommended Development Program, Central Business District, Wilmington, Delaware* (Wilbur Smith and Associates, 1970), p. iii.
12. *Evening Journal,* May 6, 1971.
13. Wilbur Smith report, p. ix.
14. *Evening Journal,* July 14, 1971.
15. *Evening Journal,* July 12, 1971.
16. *Evening Journal,* July 10, 1971.
17. *Evening Journal,* July 13, 1971.
18. *Evening Journal,* July 22, 1971.
19. *Morning News,* July 22, 1971.
20. Ibid.
21. *Morning News,* Sept. 15, 1971.
22. *Morning News,* Aug. 2, 1971.

*Chapter 9*

1. "DuPont III: Power and Glory," *Fortune* (Jan., 1935), p. 134.
2. *Morning News,* Mar. 13, 1968.
3. Ben Bagdikian, "Wilmington's Independent Newspapers," *Columbia Journalism Review* (Summer, 1964), p. 16.
4. *Wall Street Journal,* Dec. 4, 1970.
5. *Philadelphia Bulletin,* Oct. 11, 1970.
6. "Union's Loan to Copeland Paper Probed," *Editor & Publisher* (June 29, 1970), p. 12.
7. *Evening Journal,* Nov. 13, 1970.
8. *Delaware State News,* July 3, 1970.
9. *Evening Journal,* Apr. 9, 1964.
10. *Heterodoxical Voice,* Newark, Del., May, 1968.
11. *Evening Journal,* September 28, 1970.
12. Lee Cansler, News-Journal Company, to Jack Smyth, editor *Delaware State News,* Nov. 23, 1960.
13. *News-Journal,* Dec. 4, 1954, editorial "No Conspiracy."
14. *News-Journal,* Dec. 4, 1954, editorial "All for What?"
15. *News Journal,* Feb. 5, 1955, editorial "Appealed—For What?"
16. *News-Journal,* Feb. 5, 1955, editorial "Why?"
17. *News-Journal,* June 4, 1957, editorial "Illegal Per Se?"
18. *US* v. *DuPont et al.,* 353 US 586, 605 (1957).
19. *Evening Journal,* Feb. 23, 1971.
20. *Evening Journal,* Mar. 16, 1971.
21. *Wall Street Journal,* Mar. 15, 1971.
22. *Evening Journal,* June 24, 1971.
23. *Morning News,* Nov. 25, 1957, editorial "Is Bigness Bad?"
24. *Ibid.*
25. *Morning News,* Feb. 26, 1964, editorial "Taxes Are Still Too High."
26. *Morning News,* May 26, 1966, editorial "Keep the Variances."
27. *Evening Journal,* Aug. 15, 1967.
28. *Evening Journal,* Oct. 25, 1969.
29. *Morning News,* Aug. 9, 1964, editorial "Do We Want Unpolluted Water?"

30. *Evening Journal,* Feb. 20, 1971.
31. *Evening Journal,* July 2, 1971, and July 29, 1971.
32. Bagdikian, p. 16.
33. Ibid.
34. Ibid.
35. Ibid.
36. *Delaware State News,* June 25, 1970.
37. *Morning News,* July 16, 1971.
38. *Evening Journal,* Mar. 31, 1962.
39. *Evening Journal,* Nov. 20, 1969.
40. *Evening Journal,* Nov. 4, 1963.
41. *Evening Journal,* Jan. 22, 1968, editorial "Build That White Clay Dam."
42. *Evening Journal,* Nov. 13, 1970, editorial "Don't Just Sit There."
43. *Morning News,* Dec. 2, 1970, editorial "It's Time to Get on with the Dam."
44. *Morning News,* Feb. 19, 1966, editorial "Good Idea; Will It Work?".
45. *Evening Journal,* Mar. 11, 1966, editorial "A Boulevard If You Please."
46. *Evening Journal,* June 11, 1969.
47. Bagdikian, p. 16.

*Chapter 10*

1. *Company and Community: The Responsibilities of Business in Society* (DuPont, 1967), p. 3.
2. *Community Economic Profile, Seaford, Delaware.*
3. Television advertisement script from "Cavalcade of America," Sept. 17, 1952.
4. *Reynolds* v. *Sims,* 377 US 533 (1964) (one man, one vote principle); *Carrington* v. *Rash,* 380 US 89 (1965) and *Harper* v. *Virginia Board of Elections,* 383 US 663 (1966) (both cases overruled local election rules); *Avery* v. *Midland County,* 390 US 474 (1968) one man, one vote applies to local government); *Cipriano* v. *City of Houma,* 394 US 701 (1969) (invalidated law allowing vote in bond election only to property owners); *Kramer* v. *Union Free School District,* 395 US 621 (1969) (invalidated law allowing vote in school board election only to persons with school-age children or persons who paid property taxes).
5. *Evening Journal,* Oct. 5, 1970.
6. See *Preliminary Report, A Comprehensive Plan for Seaford, Del., Part I: Development Patterns,* §C, "Existing Land Use" Kendree and Shepherd, Planning Consultants).
7. *Seaford Comprehensive Plan,* "Housing, M," §G, Table G-1, p. G-4.
8. *Shelley* v. *Kraemer,* 334 US 1 (1948).
9. *Better Living* (Spring, 1971), p. 3.
10. *Evening Journal,* Apr. 8, 1969.
11. *Evening Journal,* Sept. 20, 1971, editorial "Light at End of . . ."

12. *Parking Needs and Recommended Development Program: Central Business District, Wilmington, Del.* (Wilbur Smith and Associates, 1970) pp. 77, 83, 84, 89.
13. Ibid., p. iii.
14. *Future Development of the Port Terminal,* Vol. I, "Administrative Considerations (Cresap, McCormick & Paget, 1968), p. II-1.
15. "Estimated Housing Need, New Castle County, 1970–75," *Housing Needs in the Wilmington Area 1967–80* (Harold F. Wise/Robert Gladstone & Associates, Dec., 1966), pp. 19, 256. The 3400 figure is in addition to the 1800 new publicly assisted housing units needed between 1965 and 1970. The report estimated that 5200 new public housing units were needed through 1975, in addition to the 1100 units then planned.
16. *Evening Journal,* Mar. 29, 1971.

*Chapter 11*

1. *Shelley* v. *Kraemer,* 334 US 1 (1948).
2. *Evening Journal,* Nov. 3, 1970.
3. Ibid.
4. Ibid.
5. *Evening Journal,* Mar. 8, 1971.
6. *Morning News,* July 13, 1970.
7. Ibid.
8. *Evening Journal,* Sept. 24, 1970.
9. Ibid.
10. *1964 Home Interview Survey, New Castle County Program* (New Castle County Planning Dept.).
11. *Morning News,* July 13, 1970.
12. *Greater Wilmington Airport: Developmental Pressures* (Kendree and Shepherd Planning Consultants, Mar., 1967), p. 1.
13. Ibid., p. 11.
14. *Market Demands and Opportunities: The Future Role of Greater Wilmington Airport* (Arthur D. Little, 1969), p. 10.
15. Ibid.
16. From a pamphlet published by Columbia Gas System on its move to Wilmington.
17. *Morning News,* Mar. 24, 1971.
18. *A Study to Evaluate Potential Solutions to the Problem of Insuring an Adequate Supply of Water for New Castle County* (University City Science Institute, 1971), pp. 117–18.
19. Ibid., p. 112.
20. Ibid., pp. 114–117.
21. *Kennett News and Advertiser,* Dec. 24, 1970.
22. *Evening Journal,* Oct. 17, 1970.

*Chapter 12*

1. Article 8, §1, Delaware Constitution.
2. *Philadelphia, B&W R. Co.* v. *Mayor and Council of Wilmington,* 57 A.2d 759, 765 (1948).

3. 9 Delaware Statutes, §8304.
4. 9 Delaware Statutes, §8307.
5. *Fitzsimmons* v. *McCorkle,* 214 A.2d 334, 338 (1965).
6. 9 Delaware Statutes, §8301.
7. *Fitzsimmons* v. *McCorkle,* 214 A.2d 334, 339 (1965).
8. *Morning News,* June 18, 1971, editorial "Greater Wilmington and Public Attitude—4."

*Chapter 13*

1. *Delaware USA,* Delaware Chamber of Commerce (1969).
2. *Evening Journal,* Apr. 21, 1971.
3. *Congressional Quarterly Almanac,* 1966, p. 1433.
4. *Political Contributions of $500 or more,* Herbert E. Alexander and Caroline Jones, eds. (Princeton, NJ: Citizens' Research Foundation, 1968; 1969).
5. *Evening Journal,* Apr. 21, 1971.
6. *Evening Journal,* Mar. 22, 1971.
7. *Taxes* (Mar., 1966), p. 143.
8. *Evening Journal,* Oct. 16, 1967.
9. *Morning News,* Oct. 14, 1967.
10. *Evening Journal,* Mar. 22, 1971.
11. *Morning News,* June 23, 1970.
12. *Citizens' Research Foundation 1968 Listing,* p. v.
13. *A Side-by-side Comparison, Present Constitution—Proposed Constitution* (Constitution Revision Commission, Feb., 1970), pp. 2–4.
14. John Kenneth Galbraith, *The New Industrial State* (New American Library, 1968), p. 316.
15. "Law for Sale: A Study of the Delaware Corporation Law of 1967," 117 *University of Pennsylvania Law Review* 861, 877 (1969).
16. Ernest L. Folk, "Some Reflections of a Corporation Law Draftsman" 42 *Connecticut Bar Journal* 409, 411–412 (1968).
17. "Law for Sale," p. 870.
18. Ibid., p. 890
19. Ibid., p. 869.
20. Ibid., p. 870.
21. *Morning News,* Apr. 17, 1962.
22. *This Is DuPont,* #28 (1965), pp. 10–11.
23. Interview with Charles E. Welch, Aug. 25, 1970.
24. *Evening Journal,* Feb. 21, 1966.
25. Delaware Water and Air Resources Commission, Air Pollution Control Division, "Proposed Regulations Governing the Control of Air Pollution," mimeographed hearings, Oct. 5, 1967 (Dover, Del.: Wesley A. Coote, Official Court Reporter), pp. 166–72.
26. Ibid., p. 168.
27. *Evening Journal,* Oct. 21, 1970.
28. *Morning News,* Apr. 14, 1971.
29. *Evening Journal,* July 2, 1971.

30. "DuPont III: The Power and the Glory," *Fortune* (Jan., 1935), pp. 134, 137.
31. *Evening Journal,* June 7, 1967.
32. *Evening Journal,* July 31, 1961.
33. *Morning News,* Feb. 18, 1969.
34. *New York Times,* June 29, 1972, pp. 1, 72.

*Chapter 14*

1. "Poverty in 1959 and 1969 by State and OEO Region," *Technical Note 1* (OEO, Jan. 3, 1971). The 1970 Census shows different statistics on the incidence of poverty—60,000 total persons or 10.9% of the state's population. However, census figures may be unreliable because poor people often do not answer census questionnaires. Therefore, we have employed the figures in the special OEO report, which was oriented specifically toward counting low-income persons in the Delaware population.
2. Governor's Task Force on Reorganization, *Final Report on Cabinet Departments* (1970), p. 5.
3. J. William Fulbright, *Arrogance of Power* (Random House, 1966), pp. 53–56.
4. *Evening Journal,* June 29, 1971.
5. *Evening Journal,* Sept. 29, 1971.
6. *Morning News,* July 16, 1971.
7. *New York Times, Business Section,* June 27, 1971, p. 13. (NYT's source: Tax Foundation, Inc.)
8. *Government Finances in 1968–69,* Table 24, US Census Bureau, 1970.
9. *Public Choice in the Delaware Economy* (U. of Delaware, 1969), p. 6.
10. *Report of the Governor's Revenue Study Committee* (1965), p. 79.
11. *Evening Journal,* Sept. 2, 1969.
12. *1967 Census of Governments, State Report #8, Delaware,* p. 8.
13. "State and Local Government Finances in 1942 and 1957," *State and Local Government Study #43,* US Dept. of Commerce, p. 16.
14. *Congressional Quarterly,* July 9, 1971, p. 1489.
15. Ibid.
16. Marvin Brams, *Delaware Inheritance and Estate Taxes* (U. of Delaware, 1969), p. 11.
17. *Public Choice,* p. 118.
18. Ibid., p. 118.
19. Ibid., p. 19.
20. *Delaware, USA* (Delaware Chamber of Commerce, 1969), p. 10.
21. Ibid., p. 76.
22. Marvin Brams, *The Delaware Corporate Franchise Tax* (U. of Delaware, 1969), p. 5.
23. *Report of the Committee to Investigate Delaware State Finances* (1969), p. 8.
24. Brams, p. 37.

25. *Public Choice,* p. 1.
26. *Comprehensive Manpower Study,* 1970, pp. 68–9.
27. John O. Hidinger, *Transit Planning for the Greater Wilmington Area,* p. 31.
28. Ibid., p. 31.
29. Ibid., p. 1.
30. Paul Dolan, *Government and Administration in Delaware* (Crowell, 1956), p. 221.
31. *Evening Journal,* Sept. 18, 1970.
32. *Final Report, Wilmington Medical Study* (Sociometrics, 1971), p. 9.
33. Ibid., p. 8.
34. Ibid., pp. 40–41.
35. *Evening Journal,* Nov. 30, 1970.
36. Ibid.
37. Based on census analysis in *Neighborhood Environmental Analysis* (published by New Castle County, 1968).
38. *OEO Technical Note 1,* Table 2.
39. *Evening Journal,* June 26, 1970.
40. *Evening Journal,* Mar. 26, 1971.
41. Ibid.
42. Florence C. Johnson, "How Workmen's Compensation Laws Changed during 1969," *Monthly Labor Review* (US Bureau of Labor Statistics, Jan., 1970), p. 57.
43. *Evening Journal,* Oct. 29, 1970.
44. Howard James, *Children in Trouble: A National Scandal* (Christian Science Monitor Press, 1969), p. 129.
45. Ibid., p. 128.
46. Ibid., p. 104.
47. Ibid., p. 134.
48. *Evening Journal,* Sept. 23, 1971.
49. Ibid.
50. *Morning News,* June 1, 1971.
51. *State* v. *Cannon,* 190 A.2d 514 (1963).
52. *Morning News,* Jan. 10, 1970.
53. *Morning News,* Sept. 3, 1971.
54. *Morning News,* Sept. 4, 1971.
55. *Evening Journal,* Sept. 4, 1971.
56. *Evening Journal,* Sept. 9, 1971.
57. *Rankings of the States, 1970,* Research Report 1970-R1 (Research Division, National Education Association), p. 46.
58. *Statistical Abstract of the US,* 91st ed. (US Bureau of the Census, 1970) Fig. VII, p. 100.
59. *Evening Journal,* June 8, 1971.
60. *Morning News,* Sept. 8, 1971.
61. Ibid.
62. Statistical Section, *Annual Reports* for 1967–8 and 1968–9, Delaware Dept. of Public Instruction.
63. *Evening Journal,* Oct. 22, 1970.
64. Speech at Governor's Conference on Business and Industry, Wilmington, 1966, p. 5.

65. *Wilmington* (DuPont, 1968).
66. Carnegie Commission on Education, *The Capitol and the Campus: State Responsibility for Post-secondary Education* (McGraw-Hill, 1971), p. 3.
67. Ibid., p. 47.
68. Ibid., pp. 41, 126.
69. *Chronicle of Higher Education,* Mar. 29, 1971.
70. Answer from DuPont Company, dated Aug. 10, 1971, to interrogatory from Delaware Study Group.
71. *Heterodoxical Voice,* Newark, Del., May, 1968.
72. Ibid.

# Appendices

# APPENDIX 1

## Nonprofit Groups with DuPont Executives or Family Members as Directors

*Community Renewal*
Block Blight
Downtown Wilmington, Inc.
Greater Wilmington Development Council
Greater Wilmington Housing Corporation
Penjerdel
Urban Coalition
Wilmington Business Opportunity and Economic Development Corporation

*Social Services*
Boys' Club of Wilmington
Children's Bureau of Delaware
Correctional Council of Delaware
Family Services of Northern Delaware
Girls' Club of Wilmington
Opportunity Center
United Fund and Council of Delaware
YMCA of Wilmington and New Castle County

*Medical Programs*
Blue Cross–Blue Shield of Delaware
Delaware Curative Workshop
Delaware League for Planned Parenthood, Inc.
Delaware Institute of Medical Education and Research
Delaware Mental Health Foundation
Delaware Red Cross
Health Planning Council
Methodist Town House
Peninsula United Methodist Homes and Hospitals, Inc.
Wilmington Medical Center

*Recreational, Cultural, and Historical Groups*
Kingswood Community Center
Mount Cuba Astronomical Observatory, Inc.
Old Brandywine Village
The Playhouse
Recreation, Promotion, and Service

Wilcastle Center
Wilmington Drama League
Wilmington Fine Arts Society
Wilmington Institute Free Library
Wilmington Music School
Wilmington Opera Society

*Environment-Related*
Brandywine Valley Association
Brandywine Valley Conservancy
Delaware Nature Center
Ducks Unlimited
Evergreen Foundation, Inc.
Forward Lands, Inc.
Red Clay Reservation, Inc.
Tri-county Conservancy of the Brandywine, Inc.

*Education*
Delaware School Auxiliary Association
Friends School
St. Andrew's School
Tatnall School
Tower Hill School
University of Delaware
University of Delaware Library Associates
Wesley College

*Horse Racing*
Delaware Park, Inc.
Delaware Racing Association
Delaware Steeplechase and Race Association
Delaware Turf Club

*Other, General*
Delaware Safety Council
Delaware State Chamber of Commerce
Jewish Federation of Delaware

*Private Foundations*
Aeolian Foundation
Averill-Ross Foundation, Inc.
The Baymere Foundation
Borkee-Hagley Foundation
Bradford Foundation
Bredin Foundation
The Carpenter Foundation, Inc.
Charitable Research Foundation, Inc.
Chichester du Pont Foundation, Inc.

The Christiana Foundation
Clifton Center, Inc.
Copeland Andelot Foundation, Inc.
Crestlea Foundation, Inc.
Crystal Trust
The Dean Foundation, Inc.
Delaware Park, Inc.
Ederic Foundation, Inc.
Eleutherian Mills–Hagley Foundation, Inc.
Good Samaritan, Inc.
Holpont Foundation
International Training Organization, Inc.
The Lalor Foundation
The Lesesne Foundation
Longwood Foundation
Nemours Foundation
Orange Street Foundation
Rencourt Foundation, Inc.
Rock Spring Foundation, Inc.
Ross Foundation, Inc.
Sharp Foundation
Student Exchange Foundation
Theano Foundation
Unidel Foundation
Valmy Foundation
Water Research Foundation, Inc.
Welfare Foundation, Inc.
The Wemyss Foundation
Weymouth Foundation, Inc.
Henry Francis du Pont Winterthur Museum, Inc.
Woodstock Foundation, Inc.

## APPENDIX 2

### Agreement Signed by DuPont White-collar Workers

Social Security No.

EMPLOYEE AGREEMENT

THIS AGREEMENT, entered into this day of , 19 , between E. I. DU PONT DE NEMOURS AND COMPANY, a corporation of Delaware (hereinafter called "Employer"), and
(hereinafter called "Employee").

WITNESSETH:

WHEREAS, in its business, Employer has developed and uses commercially valuable technical and nontechnical information and, to guard the legitimate interests of Employer, it is necessary for Employer to protect certain of the information either by patents or by holding it secret or confidential; and

WHEREAS, the aforesaid information is vital to the success of Employer's business, and Employee through his activities may become acquainted therewith, and may contribute thereto either through inventions, discoveries, improvements or otherwise;

NOW, THEREFORE, in consideration of and as part of the terms of employment of Employee by Employer, at a wage or salary and for such length of time as the employment shall continue, it is agreed as follows:

1. Unless Employee shall first secure Employer's written consent, Employee shall not disclose or use at any time either during or subsequent to said employment, any secret or confidential information of Employer of which Employee becomes informed during said employment, whether or not developed by Employee, except as required in Employee's duties to Employer.

2. Employee shall disclose promptly to Employer or its nominee any and all inventions, discoveries and improvements conceived or made by Employee during the period of employment and related to the business or activities of Employer, and assigns and agrees to assign all his interest therein to Employer or its nominee; whenever requested to do so by Employer, Employee shall execute any and all applications, assignments or other instruments which Employer shall deem necessary to

apply for and obtain Letters Patent of the United States or any foreign country or to protect otherwise Employer's interests therein. These obligations shall continue beyond the termination of employment with respect to inventions, discoveries and improvements conceived or made by Employee during the period of employment, and shall be binding upon Employee's assigns, executors, administrators and other legal representatives.

3. Upon termination of said employment, Employee shall promptly deliver to Employer all drawings, blueprints, manuals, letters, notes, notebooks, reports, and all other materials of a secret or confidential nature relating to Employer's business and which are in the possession or under the control of Employee.

IN WITNESS WHEREOF, the parties have signed this agreement in duplicate as of the date written above.

E. I. DU PONT DE NEMOURS AND COMPANY

By ______________________________

______________________________ Dept.

Witness:

______________________ ______________________________ (Seal)

EMPLOYEE

# APPENDIX 3

## Statistics of Taxable Delaware Estates, July 1, 1968–June 30, 1969

| *Class (Net Estate)* | *Number of Estates* | *Gross Estates* | *Total Deductions* | *Net Estates* | *Total Inheritance Tax* |
|---|---|---|---|---|---|
| $ 1– 5,000 | 76 | $ 357,548.52 | $ 120,612.33 | $ 236,936.19 | $ 3,887.17 |
| 5,000– 10,000 | 101 | 1,193,518.15 | 437,148.76 | 756,369.39 | 9,662.99 |
| 10,000– 25,000 | 298 | 5,963,574.13 | 816,449.21 | 5,147,124.92 | 49,154.97 |
| 25,000– 50,000 | 297 | 11,476,259.09 | 1,275,646.36 | 10,200,612.73 | 100,856.68 |
| 50,000– 100,000 | 193 | 13,973,835.51 | 1,494,319.58 | 12,479,515.93 | 177,473.67 |
| 100,000– 250,000 | 157 | 22,165,494.64 | 1,624,886.25 | 20,540,608.39 | 429,645.07 |
| 250,000– 500,000 | 36 | 10,848,258.58 | 540,026.59 | 10,308,231.99 | 274,759.50 |
| 500,000–1,000,000 | 14 | 9,853,470.33 | 920,352.76 | 8,933,117.57 | 299,311.42 |
| 1,000,000–5,000,000 | 9 | 17,455,978.92 | 419,766.06 | 17,036,212.86 | 837,281.39 |
| Over–5,000,000 | 3 | 29,815,250.33 | 1,570,397.55 | 28,244,852.78 | 1,096,462.25 |
| Totals | 1,184 | $123,103,188.20 | $9,219,605.45 | $113,883,582.75 | $3,278,195.11 |
| Total estate tax | 20 | | | | $2,719,721.22 |
| Total inheritance and estate taxes | | | | | $5,998,216.33 |

Based on net assessments.

# APPENDIX 4

## Number of States Having Higher and Lower Death Taxes than Delaware on Selected Size Estates Left One-half to Each of Two Adult Children, 1960

| *Net Estate after Deductions,* But before Specific Exemptions* ($) | *More than Delaware Tax* | *Delaware Tax* ($) | *Same as Delaware Tax* | *Less than Delaware Tax* |
|---|---|---|---|---|
| 25,000 | 21 | 190 | . . . | 28 |
| 50,000 | 30 | 440 | . . . | 19 |
| 100,000 | 32 | 1,340 | . . . | 17 |
| 200,000 | 27 | 4,340 | . . . | 22 |
| 400,000 | 23 | 12,340 | . . . | 26 |
| 600,000 | 22 | 20,340 | . . . | 27 |
| 800,000 | 26 | 28,340 | . . . | 23 |
| 1,000,000 | 27 | 36,340 | . . . | 22 |
| 2,500,000 | 21 | 138,800 | 27 | 1 |
| 5,000,000 | 12 | 391,600 | 35 | 2 |

* Before marital deduction and deduction of federal estate tax in states which allow this deduction.

SOURCE: Advisory Commission on Intergovernmental Relations, *Coordination of State and Federal Inheritance, Estate and Gift Taxes* (January, 1961), pp. 118–19.

# APPENDIX 5

## Directors of DuPont Foundations*

*Averell-Ross Foundation, Inc.*
- C. F. Benzel, Sr., president
- Francis I. du Pont II, vice president
- C. F. Benzel, Jr.
- R. V. King
- William Winder Laird

*The Baymere Foundation*
- William H. du Pont
- Miren du Pont
- Harold Gray

*Borkee-Hagley Foundation*
- H. H. Silliman, president
- Robert B. Flint, vice president, treasurer
- H. H. Silliman, Jr., vice president
- Mariana du Pont Silliman, secretary
- Doris S. Stockly
- Eleanor S. Maroney
- Mariana S. Richards
- William L. Hennessy
- Robert M. Silliman
- George A. Sandbach

*Bradford Foundation*
- M. du Pont Smith, president
- Edward B. du Pont, vice president
- E. Newbold Smith, secretary, treasurer

*Bredin Foundation*
- J. Bruce Bredin, president
- Irenee du Pont, Jr., vice president
- Alfred E. Bissell, vice president
- George B. Pearson, secretary
- Robert B. Flint, treasurer

*The Carpenter Foundation, Inc.*
- Benton B. Wilde, president
- R. R. M. Carpenter, Jr., vice president
- J. Avery Draper, vice president
- William K. Carpenter
- Renee C. Draper

* Information is latest available.

*Charitable Research Foundation, Inc.*
Ernest N. May, president
Grace E. Bacon, vice president
Walter L. Michele, vice president
Joseph W. Pochonis, vice president
Alyce R. Shaw, secretary, treasurer

*Chichester du Pont Foundation, Inc.*
Alice du Pont Mills, president
A. Felix du Pont, Jr., treasurer
Richard C. du Pont, Jr., vice president
Marka T. du Pont, vice president
Allaire C. du Pont
Katherine du Pont Gahagan
James P. Mills

*The Christiana Foundation*
C. Lalor Burdick, president
Elizabeth M. Grasselli, vice president
Jane R. Worth
Sally R. Edmonds, assistant treasurer
Joan S. Edmonds, assistant treasurer
George P. Edmonds, assistant treasurer, secretary
J. Sellers Bancroft

*Clifton Center, Inc.*
Walter S. Carpenter, Jr., president
Walter S. Carpenter III
Edmond N. Carpenter II, vice president

*Copeland Andelot Foundation, Inc.*
William S. Potter, president
Alfred E. Bissell
Lammot du Pont Copeland, Jr.
Henry B. du Pont
R. P. Genereaux
Hugh R. Sharp, Jr.

*Crestlea Foundation, Inc.*
Stewart E. Poole, president
Henry B. du Pont III, vice president
Edward B. du Pont

*Crystal Trust*
Irenee du Pont, Jr.
Margaretta du Pont Greenewalt, advisory trustee
Sophie du Pont May, advisory trustee

*The Dean Foundation, Inc.*
J. Simpson Dean, president
J. Simpson Dean, Jr., vice president
David M. Hillegas, Jr., secretary, treasurer

*Delaware Park, Inc.*

William S. Potter, president
Alfred E. Bissell, vice president
Lewis S. Munson, Jr., treasurer
L. E. Grimes, secretary
George P. Edmonds
Jean du Pont McConnell
Donald P. Ross

*Ederic Foundation, Inc.*

Reynolds du Pont, president
Edith du Pont Pearson
Philip B. Weymouth, Jr.
Rodney M. Layton, secretary
George Winchester

*Eleutherian Mills–Hagley Foundation, Inc.*

Emile R. du Pont, president
Lammot du Pont Copeland
Eleuthere I. du Pont
S. Hallock du Pont
Nicholas R. du Pont
Philip J. Kimball
W. W. Laird
Walter M. Whitehall
Henry B. du Pont III

*Good Samaritan, Inc.*

Walter S. Carpenter, Jr., president
Rt. Rev. Henry Knox Sherrill, vice president
Walter S. Carpenter III, secretary, treasurer

*Holpont Foundation*

Pierre S. du Pont, president
Robert H. Richards, secretary
J. Avery Draper

*The Lalor Foundation*

Charles Lee Reese, Jr., president
Alfred E. Bissell, vice president
J. Sellers Bancroft, treasurer
C. Lalor Burdick, secretary
A. R. Shands, Jr.

*The Lesesne Foundation*

Delaware Trust Company
Patricia du Pont, advisor
Rodney M. Layton, advisor
Arthur de T. Valk, Jr., advisor
Robert L. Wookford, advisor

*Longwood Foundation* ( *as of October 1, 1970*)

- Lammot du Pont Copeland
- Pierre S. du Pont
- Edward B. du Pont
- H. Rodney Sharp III
- Henry H. Silliman, Jr.
- Irenee du Pont May
- Henry B. Robertson

*Nemours Foundation*

- Jessie Ball du Pont (died, 1970)
- Edward Ball
- Alfred du Pont Dent
- Jake C. Berlin
- William Thorton
- William B. Mills
- Tom S. Coldway, representative of the Florida National Bank of Jacksonville

*Oberod Foundation*

- Harry W. Lunger, president
- Jane du Pont Lunger, vice president
- Richard I. G. Jones, secretary, and treasurer
- Philip D. Lunger
- Ann L. Jones
- H. David Lunger
- R. Brett Lunger
- Mary Jane Lunger

*Red Clay Reservation, Inc.*

- Henry B. du Pont, president (died, 1970)
- Lammot du Pont Copeland, vice president
- Edward Beacom, secretary–treasurer

*Rencourt Foundation, Inc.*

- Eugene E. du Pont, president (died, 1966)
- C. Porter Schutt, vice president
- George T. Weymouth, vice president
- W. G. Reynolds, secretary
- Walter S. Carpenter III, treasurer

*Rock Spring Foundation, Inc.*

- Renee C. Draper, president
- J. Avery Draper, vice president
- George Winchester, secretary

*Ross Foundation, Inc.*

- Donald P. Ross
- Wilhelmina du Pont Ross
- Donald P. Ross, Jr.

Robert H. Bolling, Jr.

*Sharp Foundation*

Jesse Loven
Bayard Sharp
Hugh R. Sharp, Jr.

*Theano Foundation*

Bank of Delaware
Mrs. E. Paul du Pont, advisor

*Unidel Foundation, Inc.*

George Burton Pearson, Jr.
Alfred E. Bissell
Henry M. Canby
Walter S. Carpenter, Jr.
Edwin D. Steel

*Walfare Foundation, Inc.*

Henry B. du Pont, president
J. Simpson Dean, vice president
Edward B. du Pont
J. Simpson Dean, Jr.
Henry B. Robertson

*The Wemyss Foundation*

William M. Stirling, president
W. W. Laird
William Poole

*Weymouth Foundation, Inc.*

Andrew G. P. Hobbs
Patricia W. Hobbs
Edmund N. Carpenter II
Walter E. Timm
Eugene E. Weymouth
Ann M. Weymouth
George A. Weymouth
Deo du Pont Weymouth
George T. Weymouth
Betty S. Weymouth

*Henry Francis du Pont Winterthur Museum, Inc.*

Lammot du Pont Copeland, president
Alfred C. Harrison, vice president
William S. Potter, secretary
Alfred E. Bissell, treasurer
Julian P. Boyd
J. Bruce Bredin
Mrs. Lammot du Pont Copeland
Edmond du Pont
Henry B. du Pont

George P. Edmonds
Crawford H. Greenewalt
Mrs. Alfred C. Harrison
John A. Herdeg
Walter J. Laird, Jr.
Mrs. Rodney M. Layton
Mrs. Edward B. Leizenring, Jr.
Wilmarth S. Lewis
George d'F. Lord
Mrs. George d'F. Lord
Edgar P. Richardson
S. Dillon Ripley II
Mrs. Reginald P. Rose
Edward A. Trabant
Charles Van Ravenswaay
Louis B. Wright

*Woodstock Foundation, Inc.*

Allaire C. du Pont, president
Richard C. du Pont, Jr., treasurer
Norman Baum
Helena A. du Pont

# APPENDIX 6

## Total Assessed Value of Real Property of the DuPont Family, New Castle County, 1970

FAMILY LANDHOLDINGS IN NEW CASTLE COUNTY

| | |
|---|---|
| Brandywine Hundred | 1,286 acres |
| Christiana Hundred | 5,692 |
| Mill Creek Hundred | 3,954 |
| White Clay Creek Hundred | 800 |
| New Castle Hundred | 399 |
| St. Georges Hundred (below canal) | 656 |
| Total | 12,787 acres |

TOTAL ASSESSMENT FOR FAMILY LANDHOLDINGS IN NEW CASTLE COUNTY

| | |
|---|---|
| Land | $ 4,660,000 |
| Building and improvements | 17,070,000 |
| Total | $21,730,000 |

PERCENTAGE OF LAND OWNED BY FAMILY

| | *Total Acreage* | *DuPont family* | *Acres not in subdivision** | *DuPont family** |
|---|---|---|---|---|
| Brandywine Hundred | 22,016 | 6% | 15,465 | 12% |
| Christiana Hundred | 21,325 | 27% | 17,818 | 32% |
| Mill Creek Hundred | 27,110 | 15% | 24,480 | 16% |
| White Clay Creek Hundred | 15,840 | 5% | 12,759 | 6% |

* The percent of undeveloped land owned by the DuPont family in each hundred was much higher in 1970 than in 1960 because of the tremendous growth of subdivisions since 1960. However, no figures for the number of acres developed since 1960 are available; therefore, the only reliable estimates had to be based on the 1960 figures.

FAMILY LANDHOLDINGS IN CITY OF WILMINGTON

72 parcels, located around Pennsylvania Avenue near city-county boundary

| | |
|---|---|
| land assessment | $ 400,300 |
| building and improvement assessment | 915,300 |
| Total assessment | $1,315,600 |

# APPENDIX 7

## Total Assessed Value of Taxable Real Property of the DuPont Company, Delaware, 1970

NEW CASTLE COUNTY

| *Location* | *Acreage* | *Building Assmt* | *Land Assmt* |
|---|---|---|---|
| Brandywine Hundred | 658 | $16,465,000 | $ 497,100 |
| Christiana Hundred | 512 | 9,124,900 | 314,100 |
| Mill Creek Hundred | 754 | 3,813,800 | 96,100 |
| White Clay Creek Hundred | 748 | 26,300 | 69,400 |
| New Castle Hundred | 9 | 275,700 | 11,800 |
| Pencader Hundred | 1,260 | 1,745,900 | 167,300 |
| | 3,941 | 31,451,600 | 1,155,800 |

CITY OF WILMINGTON

| | | |
|---|---|---|
| Total land assessment | $ 4,404,897 | 139 acres + 7 downtown blocks |
| Total building assessment | 14,551,593 | |
| Total assessment in city | $18,956,450 | |

SUSSEX COUNTY

| | |
|---|---|
| Seaford nylon plant | |
| Land assessment (727 acres) | $ 326,730 |
| Building assessment | 7,021,115 |
| Total assessment in Sussex | $7,347,845 |

TOTAL TAXABLE REAL PROPERTY OWNED BY THE COMPANY IN DELAWARE, INCLUDING WILMINGTON

| | | |
|---|---|---|
| Total acres | 4,808 | |
| Land assessment | | $ 5,823,627 |
| Building assessment | | 52,824,308 |

# APPENDIX 8

## Selected Taxable Real Property of the DuPont Family, New Castle County, 1970

| *Owner & Location* | *Size & Use (acres)* | *Total Land Assessment ($)* | *Assessment per Acre ($)* | *Total Improvements Assessment ($)* |
|---|---|---|---|---|
| BRANDYWINE HUNDRED | | | | |
| J. Ball du P. | 240.4† | 101,000 | 420 | . . . |
| " | 41.44* | 87,000 | 2,099 | 644,600 |
| Pierre S. du P. III | 19.25* | 20,000 | 1,039 | 263,300 |
| " | 49.00† | 5,400 | 110 | . . . |
| " | 78.07* | 27,300 | 350 | 56,400 |
| Wm. du P., Jr | 18.46* | 15,500 | 840 | 172,300 |
| " | 17.37* | 5,500 | 317 | 8,000 |
| (Hall, Inc., for the heirs of Wm. du P., Jr.) | 238.48* | 200,300 | 840 | 129,700 |
| " | 3.5* | 7,400 | 2,114 | 35,900 |
| CHRISTIANA HUNDRED | | | | |
| J. Bruce Bredin | 12.54* | 3,100 | 247 | 10,600 |
| " | 3.68* | 900 | 245 | 19,700 |
| L. du P. Copeland, Sr. | 31.17* | 3,300 | 106 | 17,800 |
| " | 1.66* | 5,000 | 304 | 42,700 |
| " | 50.75* | 14,900 | 29 | 1,000 |
| " | 107.83* | 25,100 | 233 | 26,800 |

* Improved.
† Unimproved

## Selected Taxable DuPont Family Real Property, *continued*

| *Owner & Location* | *Size & Use (acres)* | *Total Land Assessment ($)* | *Assessment per Acre ($)* | *Total Improvements Assessment ($)* |
|---|---|---|---|---|
| L. du P. Copeland, Jr. | 10.5* | 29,300 | 2,795 | 197,000 |
| " | 5.41† | 1,100 | 203 | . . . |
| A. du P. Dent | 29.16* | 13,000 | 446 | 69,900 |
| " | 50.27† | 16,400 | 326 | . . . |
| Alexis I. du P. | 8.68* | 4,900 | 565 | 29,200 |
| Anne T. du P. | 3.87* | 18,500 | 4,782 | 118,600 |
| Edward B. du P. | 7.70* | 8,100 | 1,052 | 133,400 |
| Elizabeth E. du P. | 60.89* | 25,600 | 420 | 61,409 |
| " | 10.00* | 7,000 | 700 | . . . |
| Irenee du P., Jr. | 89.99* | 56,700 | 630 | 44,400 |
| " | 154.00* | 43,100 | 280 | 14,600 |
| " | 30.00* | 21,000 | 700 | 398,600 |
| " | 240.41* | 143,000 | 595 | 80,300 |
| Reynolds du P. | 8.50* | 2,500 | 294 | 26,700 |
| " | 15.00* | 10,200 | 680 | 113,600 |
| " | 14.85† | 3,100 | 209 | . . . |
| " | 3.41† | 2,700 | 790 | . . . |
| " | 10.09* | 3,900 | 386 | 18,800 |
| S. Hallock du P. | 10.00* | 12,300 | 1,230 | 158,800 |
| " | 2.28* | 4,000 | 1,754 | . . . |
| " | 12.54† | 10,500 | 837 | . . . |

| | | | | |
|---|---|---|---|---|
| " | 7.96† | 7,500 | 942 | . . . |
| " | 4.19† | 5,000 | 1,192 | . . . |
| " | 6.00† | 5,000 | 833 | . . . |
| " | 3.27† | 5,700 | 1,742 | . . . |
| " | 24.06* | 21,000 | 873 | 22,100 |
| " | 4.00* | 5,600 | 1,400 | 6,900 |
| Dorcas Farquhar | 8.4* | 7,600 | 905 | 19,000 |
| C. H. Greenewalt | 20.00* | 14,000 | 700 | 145,600 |
| " | 53.50* | 9,100 | 170 | 6,200 |
| " | 3.00† | 200 | 67 | . . . |
| " | 79.91* | 11,800 | 148 | 18,300 |
| " | 72.60* | 10,200 | 141 | 12,800 |
| " | 18.00* | 5,000 | 278 | 6,000 |
| " | 20.60* | 5,000 | 243 | 15,200 |
| " | 138.25* | 38,700 | 280 | 28,400 |
| Ernest N. May | 61.50* | 25,800 | 420 | 128,200 |
| H. H. Silliman, Jr. | 10.22* | 8,600 | 842 | 104,700 |
| R. R. M. Carpenter, Jr. | 21.31* | 20,900 | 981 | 145,800 |
| W. S. Carpenter III | 47.30* | 24,200 | 512 | 74,900 |
| MILL CREEK HUNDRED | | | | |
| L. du P. Copeland | 20.00* | 2,100 | 105 | 94,800 |
| " | 20.46* | 2,100 | 103 | 500 |
| " | 40.00* | 2,500 | 63 | 900 |
| R. N. Downs III | 153.00* | 11,600 | 758 | 15,100 |
| " | 15.00† | 500 | 33 | . . . |

## Selected Taxable DuPont Family Real Property, *continued*

| *Owner & Location* | *Size & Use (acres)* | *Total Land Assessment ($)* | *Assessment per Acre ($)* | *Total Improvements Assessment ($)* |
|---|---|---|---|---|
| R. N. Downs III | 55.20* | 4,100 | 74 | 3,500 |
| " | 12.00† | 400 | 33 | . . . |
| Henry B. du Pont | 94.63* | 7,000 | 74 | 14,900 |
| " | 54.00* | 1,900 | 35 | 27,300 |
| " | 8.00† | 600 | 75 | . . . |
| " | 62.45* | 6,000 | 96 | 12,700 |
| " | 25.00† | 1,600 | 64 | . . . |
| " | 35.00* | 24,500 | 700 | 184,800 |
| " | 60.00† | 4,200 | 70 | . . . |
| S. Hallock du Pont | 18.27* | 1,700 | 93 | 4,400 |
| " | 16.3† | 600 | 37 | . . . |
| WHITE CLAY CREEK, NEW CASTLE, & ST. GEORGES HUNDREDS | | | | |
| C. Doug Buck, Jr. | 239.97* | 33,100 | 138 | 28,500 |
| " | 33.39† | 3,500 | 105 | . . . |
| Emily T. du Pont | 14.51* | 2,300 | 159 | 3,900 |
| " | 7.00† | 300 | 43 | . . . |
| Richard C. du Pont, Jr. | 170.5* | 12,300 | 72 | 2,300 |
| " | 136.51† | 9,800 | 72 | . . . |

## APPENDIX 9

### Selected Non–DuPont Family Residential Properties, New Castle County, 1970

| *Location* | *Size (sq ft)* | *Total Land Assessment ($)* | *Assessment per Acre ($)* |
|---|---|---|---|
| BRANDYWINE HUNDRED | | | |
| Bellevue Manor, Greenfield Pl | 20,928 | 2,300 | 4,809 |
| Woodsdale Rd | 20,800 | 2,500 | 5,227 |
| Bellevue Rd | 12,760 | 1,400 | 4,800 |
| Lindmere, River Rd | 14,875 | 1,100 | 3,223 |
| Riverside Gardens, River Rd | 15,575 | 1,100 | 3,049 |
| Blue Rock Rd | 15,414 | 2,300 | 6,490 |
| Blue Rock Rd | 7,500 | 900 | 5,227 |
| Hillcrest, Wier Ave | 9,414 | 900 | 4,154 |
| Alapocus | 17,579 | 3,500 | 8,672 |
| Alapocus | 11,620 | 2,300 | 8,620 |
| Augustine Hills | 9,000 | 1,200 | 5,808 |
| Woodbrook | 23,482 | 3,000 | 5,565 |
| Sharpley | 11,200 | 1,900 | 7,389 |
| CHRISTIANA HUNDRED | | | |
| Owl's Nest, Owl's Nest Rd | 107,810 | 4,600 | 1,860 |
| Haystack Rd | 92,799 | 6,700 | 3,145 |
| Haystack Lane | 37,020 | 5,600 | 6,599 |
| Old Kennett & Centerville Rd | 91,098 | 5,500 | 2,631 |
| Greenville Manor | 38,870 | 3,500 | 3,920 |
| Greenville Dvlpt, Brook Valley Rd | 22,502 | 2,400 | 4,646 |
| entire 53 acres of Hillside Farms Development | 2,308,680 | 134,900 | 2,545 |
| Centerville, Kennett Pike | 131,813 | 5,300 | 1,751 |
| Ivy Hill, Snuff Mill Rd | 35,235 | 2,000 | 2,470 |
| Snuff Mill Rd | 50,700 | 2,000 | 1,716 |
| The Meadows, Twaddell Mill Rd | 155,856 | 6,600 | 1,816 |
| Thissell Lane | 156,672 | 5,600 | 1,555 |
| Center Hill, Center Hill Rd | 43,200 | 4,000 | 4,033 |
| Center Hill Rd | 45,600 | 2,900 | 2,770 |
| Westover Hills, Stuart Rd | 16,470 | 3,000 | 7,928 |
| Westover Rd | 170,380 | 9,100 | 5,632 |
| Brandon Lane | 17,120 | 3,900 | 9,918 |
| Faulkland Heights, Newell Drive | 6,807 | 600 | 3,840 |
| Tybrook, Faulkland Rd | 10,320 | 900 | 3,799 |

# APPENDIX 10

## Total Taxable Real Property of the DuPont Company in Delaware, Excluding Wilmington, 1970

| *Location & Name* | *Size (acres)* | *Total Land Assmt ($)* | *Assmt per Acre ($)* | *Total Improvements Assmt ($)* |
|---|---|---|---|---|
| BRANDYWINE HUNDRED | | | | |
| Edgemoor plant | 117 | $151,900 | $1,298 | $ 2,500,300 |
| Experimental Station | 45 | 31,455 | 699 | |
| + | | | | |
| Country club golf course | 342 | 233,926 | 684 | 13,711,400 |
| Paint test facility, Naamans Rd & Concord Pike | 20 | 5,100 | 255 | 14,000 |
| Silverside Rd | 26 | 3,700 | 142 | . . . |
| Germay Industrial Park | 2.3 | 8,700 | 3,348 | 39,300 |
| CHRISTIANA HUNDRED | | | | |
| Newport plant | 117 | 58,900 | 503 | 1,799,800 |
| Newport development lab | 6 | 11,200 | 1,867 | 424,100 |
| Wilmington area engineering construction facilities | 9 | 3,400 | 378 | 59,300 |
| Chestnut Run lab | 165 | 83,000 | 503 | 5,425,100 |
| Centre Rd lab | 68 | 22,900 | 377 | 1,043,400 |
| Former Du P. air field | 128 | 134,700 | 1,052 | 373,200 |
| MILL CREEK HUNDRED | | | | |
| Louviers engineering lab, including golf course | 754 | 96,100 | 127 | 3,813,800 |
| WHITE CLAY CREEK HUNDRED | | | | |
| White Clay Creek reservoir site | 748 | 69,400 | 93 | 26,300 |
| PENCADER HUNDRED | | | | |
| Haskell and Stine labs | 266 | 44,000 | 165 | 779,100 |
| Glasgow plant | 975 | 96,100 | 99 | 747,900 |
| Pencader plant | 19 | 27,200 | 1,431 | 218,900 |
| Eden Park, New Castle Rd | 9 | 11,800 | 1,311 | 275,700 |
| SUSSEX COUNTY | | | | |
| Seaford nylon plant | 727 | 326,730 | 450 | 7,021,115 |

# APPENDIX 11

## Assessment Ratio of Selected Property, New Castle County, 1970

| *Property and Location* | *Assessed Value at Sale (land and buildings) $* | *Sales Price $* | *Assess-ment Ratio* | *Date of Sale* |
|---|---|---|---|---|
| Residential Property | | | | |
| BRANDYWINE HUNDRED | | | | |
| Sharpley | 18,600 | 49,900 | .37 | 1970 |
| Woodbrook | 23,500 | 60,000 | .39 | 1970 |
| Tavistock | 28,200 | 55,800 | .50 | 1970 |
| CHRISTIANA HUNDRED | | | | |
| Haystack Lane property sold by A. du P. Valk to W. H. du P. | 45,300 | 155,000 | .29 | 1970 |
| North side of Haystack Lane | 4,800* | 25,000 | .19 | 1970 |
| 51 acres on Haystack Lane | 64,100 | 640,000 | .10 | 1970 |
| 14.8 acres (sold by W. H. du P. to A. E. Danforth) | 63,500 | 227,500 | .28 | 1970 |
| Old Kennett Rd property (sold by R. S. du P.) | 12,100 | 35,000 | .35 | 1970 |
| 8.5 acres (sold by Russell Peterson to Reynolds du P.) | 29,200* | 130,000 | .22 | 1969 |
| Fox Chase, Old Kennet Rd, bought by W. V. Roth | 28,800 | 157,500 | .18 | 1970 |
| Industrial and Commercial Property | | | | |
| BRANDYWINE HUNDRED | | | | |
| 3 acres adjacent to Edgemoor plant, bought by DuP Co. | 3,900* | 100,900 | .04 | 1969 |
| CHRISTIANA HUNDRED | | | | |
| 35.6 acres sold by D. B. Farquhar to Columbia Gas Systems | 32,400* | 1,037,000 | .03 | — |

* Land only.

Assessment Ratio of Selected Property,
New Castle County, 1970, *continued*

| *Property and Location* | *Assessed Value at Sale (land and buildings) $* | *Sales Price $* | *Assess-ment Ratio* | *Date of Sale* |
|---|---|---|---|---|
| WHITE CLAY CREEK HUNDRED | | | | |
| 47.5 acres bought by DuP. Co. as part of reservoir site | 4,407* | 136,780 | .03 | 1965 |
| 54 acres near reservoir site sold by DuP. Co. to state of Delaware | 5,010* | 376,000 | .01 | 1970 |

# APPENDIX 12

## Fair Market Value and Assessment Ratio for Taxable Real Property of Henry B. Du Pont, New Castle County, 1970

| *Location & Size (acres)* | *Assessment** | *Fair Market Value* | *Assess-ment Ratio* |
|---|---|---|---|
| CHRISTIANA HUNDRED | | | |
| Mullin Tract, 89.4 | 37,800 | 534,000 | .07 |
| Brandywine Tract, 31 | 22,000 | 257,000 | .09 |
| Ashland Tract, 357.5† | 285,300 | 2,725,000 | .10 |
| MILL CREEK HUNDRED | | | |
| Trimble Tract, 14.3 | 6,000 | 93,000 | .06 |
| Armstrong Tract, 54.6 | 20,300 | 328,000 | .06 |
| NEW CASTLE HUNDRED | | | |
| Branwyn Tract, 323.9 | 37,600 | 915,000 | .04 |

* Land, buildings, and improvements.
† Lies partly in Mill Creek Hundred.

# APPENDIX 13

## Fair Market Value and Assessment Ratio for Selected Taxable Real Property, Wilmington, 1970

| *Location* | *Total Assessed Value** | *Total Fair Market Value ($)* | *Assmt Ratio* | *Date of Sale* |
|---|---|---|---|---|
| DUPONT FAMILY PROPERTY | | | | |
| 3001 Penn. Ave | 54,700† | 323,400† | .17 | 1968‡ |
| NEAR DUPONT FAMILY PROPERTY | | | | |
| Matson Run Pkwy | 19,502 | 32,000 | .60 | 1970 |
| Bancroft Pkwy | 10,955 | 17,900 | .60 | 1970 |
| 2013 Penn. Ave. | 39,417 | 100,000 | .39 | 1970 |
| Gilpin Ave | 10,542 | 20,000 | .52 | 1970 |
| Tower Hill site | 248,400 | 1,000,000 | .25 | 1970 |
| IN DOWNTOWN AREA | | | | |
| 845 N Madison | 3,871 | 2,000 | 1.10 | 1970 |
| 703 Market | 102,025 | 100,000 | 1.02 | 1970 |
| 829 Market | 161,930 | 110,000 | 1.47 | 1970 |
| NEAR DUPONT CO. PROPERTY | | | | |
| 100 W 10 St | 151,653† | 621,000† | .24 | 1956 |
| 1201 Market | 48,790 | 180,000 | .27 | 1970 |
| 1206 Market | 16,926 | 60,000 | .28 | 1970 |
| 300 Delaware Ave | 360,433† | 868,000† | .42 | 1967 |
| 1007 N Tatnall§ | 256,255† | 1,926,000† | .13 | 1965 |
| ACROSS BRANDYWINE RIVER | | | | |
| 2318 Market | 10,619 | 13,650 | .77 | 1970 |
| 2810 Market | 8,568 | 13,300 | .64 | 1970 |

* At time of sale.
† Land only.
‡ Bequeathed to Marmot Foundation.
§ Site of new Brandywine Bldg.

# APPENDIX 14

## Total Taxable Real Property of the DuPont Company, Wilmington, 1970

| *Address* | *Size* | *Land Assmt ($)* | *Land Assmt Sq Ft ($)* | *Improvement, Bldg Assmt ($)* | *Use (if known)* |
|---|---|---|---|---|---|
| 1007 Market St | 100,404 sq ft | 1,799,900 | 17.93 | 6,157,600 | DuPont Bldg. |
| 1227 Market St | 1,219 sq ft | 7,100 | 5.32 | . . . | . . . |
| 1301 Market St | 18,524 sq ft | 35,000 | 1.89 | 1,300 | parking |
| 1303 Market St | 34,560 sq ft | 41,300 | 1.20 | 6,000 | parking |
| 1311 Market St | 9,800 sq ft | 22,100 | 2.26 | 1,700 | parking |
| 1315 Market St | 12,075 sq ft | 19,300 | 1.60 | 5,800 | parking |
| 1007 Orange St | 29,000 sq ft | 376,500 | 12.98 | 2,658,600 | Nemours Bldg. |
| 1134 Orange St | 17,444 sq ft | 87,900 | 5.04 | 3,400 | . . . |
| 1201 Orange St | 6,400 sq ft | 14,100 | 2.20 | 800 | . . . |
| 1320, 1330 Orange | 3,520 sq ft | 2,400 | .68 | . . . | . . . |
| 1338, 1340, 1342, 1346 Orange | about 1,100 sq ft ea | 3,700 | .36 | 12,100 | four houses |
| 1007 Tatnall St (lots 1–17) | 55,955 sq ft | 389,500 | 6.96 | . . . | site of new office bldg. |
| 1101 West St | 8,800 sq ft | 68,800 | 7.82 | 182,700 | office bldg. |
| 1111 West St | 1,800 sq ft | 1,900 | 1.06 | 200 | parking |
| 1113 West St | 1,800 sq ft | 1,200 | .67 | . . . | parking |
| 1100 Wash. St | 7,000 sq ft | 69,200 | 9.89 | 51,300 | office |
| 1102-A Wash. St | 2,500 sq ft | 12,300 | 4.92 | . . . | parking |
| 1104 Wash St | 4,088 sq ft | 16,100 | 3.94 | . . . | parking |
| Wash. St betn W 11 & 12 | 8,109 sq ft | 21,200 | 2.61 | 3,000 | parking |

Total Taxable Real Property of the DuPont Company, Wilmington, 1970, *continued*

| *Address* | *Size* | *Land Assmt ($)* | *Land Assmt Sq Ft ($)* | *Improvement, Bldg Assmt ($)* | *Use (if known)* |
|---|---|---|---|---|---|
| 221 & 223 W 10 | 25,400 sq ft | 281,200 | 11.07 | 159,300 | . . . |
| W 11 btn Market & Orange | 10,550 sq ft | 149,300 | 14.15 | 3,800 | gas station |
| 111 W 11 St | 75,180 sq ft | 448,400 | 5.96 | 458,500 | garage |
| 301 W 11 St | 4,125 sq ft | 25,200 | 6.11 | 8,500 | apartment bldg. |
| 303 W 11 St | 3,500 sq ft | 21,400 | 6.11 | 8,600 | house |
| 305 W 11 St | 2,500 sq ft | 17,500 | 7.00 | . . . | . . . |
| W 11, btn Orange & Tatnall | 34,200 sq ft | 250,500 | 7.33 | 3,274,000 | Nemours Bldg. |
| 11 W 12 St | 3,640 sq ft | 10,000 | 2.75 | . . . | . . . |
| 12 W 14 St | 1,200 sq ft | 1,000 | .83 | . . . | . . . |
| 10 W 14 St | 750 sq ft | 1,000 | 1.33 | . . . | . . . |
| West Side of Walnut | 43,056 sq ft | 31,100 | .72 | 9,900 | . . . |
| Maryland Ave btn South & Foundry | 255,878 sq ft | 51,500 | .20 | 693,000 | . . . |
| 1001 Christiana Ave | 22.694 acres | 48,200 | .05 | 690,000 | . . . |
| 1500 Eastlawn Ave | 54,125 sq ft | 6,700 | .13 | 99,800 | warehouse |
| Greenhill Ave cor W 3 | 31,726 sq ft | 13,400 | .42 | 56,900 | shop |
| E Beech St, btn Maryland Ave & RR | 47,570 sq ft | 5,000 | .11 | . . . | . . . |
| E Beech btn Md and RR | 53,200 sq ft | 2,900 | .05 | . . . | . . . |
| Cherry Island Marsh | 108.652 acres | 63,800 | .01 | 3,900 | dump |

# APPENDIX 15

## Selected Non–Dupont Company Taxable Real Property, Wilmington, 1970

| *Address* | *Size (sq ft)* | *Land Assmt ($)* | *Land Assmt/ Sq Ft ($)* | *Improvement Assmt ($)* | *Owner (if known)* |
|---|---|---|---|---|---|
| *Downtown* | | | | | |
| 825 N Market | 1,140 | 38,220 | 33.53 | 11,767 | 825 Market St Corp |
| 900 N Market | 39,906 | 894,222 | 22.41 | 5,840,744 | Shapdale, Inc. |
| 901 N Market | 11,817 | 391,272 | 33.11 | 1,358,728 | 901 Market St Corp |
| 919 N Market | 14,625 | 464,868 | 31.79 | 3,058,167 | Kinlocketal trustees |
| Rodney Square | 58,000 | 1,312,850 | 22.63 | 44,800 | City of Wilmington |
| 1201 N Market | 5,160 | 24,206 | 4.69 | 2,730 | Colonial Parking |
| 1207 N Market | 2,580 | 11,998 | 4.65 | 9,856 | Colonial Parking |
| 1209 N Market | 2,200 | 10,199 | 4.63 | 8,708 | Colonial Parking |
| 805 Orange St | 7,056 | 26,628 | 3.77 | 43,330 | News-Journal |
| 831 N Orange St | 25,760 | 138,747 | 5.39 | 978,705 | News-Journal |
| 839 N Orange St | 1,800 | 17,899 | 9.94 | 34,846 | News-Journal |
| 1200 Orange St | 38,700 | 95,515 | 2.47 | 2,681 | Wlgtn Pkg Auth |
| 901 N Tatnall | 30,525 | 201,761 | 6.61 | 1,539,804 | Diamond State Tel & Tel |
| 911 N Tatnall | 3,840 | 25,970 | 6.76 | 50,785 | Smith trustees |
| 908 N West St | 5,145 | 15,904 | 3.09 | 99,554 | Diamond State Tel & Tel |
| 1015 N West St | 1,785 | 12,621 | 7.07 | 3,374 | Willard Wilson |
| 1102 N West St | 9,025 | 19,551 | 2.17 | 606,921 | Goldsborough |
| 1115 N West St | 36,864 | 106,512 | 2.89 | 958,433 | Wlgtn Pkg Auth |
| 300 Delaware Ave | 36,600 | 393,330 | 10.75 | 4,780,503 | Bank of Delaware |
| 100 W 10 St | 17,900 | 331,933 | 18.54 | 2,920,358 | 100 W 10 St Corp |
| 215 W 11 St | 6,320 | 56,679 | 8.97 | 10,640 | Sun Oil Corp |

# Index